From Empires to NGOs in the West African Sahel

This book looks beyond the familiar history of former empires and new nation-states to consider newly transnational communities of solidarity and aid, social science and activism. Shortly after independence from France in 1960, the people living along the Sahel – a long thin stretch of land bordering the Sahara – became the subjects of human rights campaigns and humanitarian interventions. Just when its states were strongest and most ambitious, the postcolonial West African Sahel became fertile terrain for the production of novel forms of governmental rationality realized through NGOs. The roots of this "nongovernmentality" lay partly in Europe and North America, but it flowered, paradoxically, in the Sahel. This book is unique in that it questions not only how West African states exercised their new sovereignty but also how and why NGOs, ranging from CARE and Amnesty International to Black internationalists, began to assume elements of it during a period in which it was so highly valued.

Gregory Mann is Professor in the history department at Columbia University, specializing in the history of francophone West Africa. Mann's articles have appeared in the *American Historical Review*, *Comparative Studies in Society and History*, the *Journal of African History*, and *Politique Africaine*.

African Studies

The African Studies series, founded in 1968, publishes research monographs by emerging and senior scholars that feature innovative analyses in the fields of history, political science, anthropology, economics, and environmental studies. The series also produces mature, paradigm-shifting syntheses that seek to reinterpret and revitalize the scholarly literature in these fields.

Editorial Board

David Anderson, *University of Warwick*
Catherine Boone, *London School of Economics*
Carolyn Brown, *Rutgers University*
Christopher Clapham, *University of Cambridge*
Michael Gomez, *New York University*
Nancy J. Jacobs, *Brown University*
Richard Roberts, *Stanford University*
David Robinson, *Michigan State University*
Leonardo A. Villalón, *University of Florida*

A list of books in this series will be found at the end of this volume.

From Empires to NGOs in the West African Sahel

The Road to Nongovernmentality

GREGORY MANN
Columbia University

CAMBRIDGE
UNIVERSITY PRESS

32 Avenue of the Americas, New York, NY 10013-2473, USA

Cambridge University Press is part of the University of Cambridge.

It furthers the University's mission by disseminating knowledge in the pursuit of education, learning, and research at the highest international levels of excellence.

www.cambridge.org
Information on this title: www.cambridge.org/9781107016545

© Gregory Mann 2015

This publication is in copyright. Subject to statutory exception and to the provisions of relevant collective licensing agreements, no reproduction of any part may take place without the written permission of Cambridge University Press.

First published 2015

Printed in Great Britain by Clays Ltd, St Ives plc

A catalog record for this publication is available from the British Library.

Library of Congress Cataloging in Publication Data
Mann, Gregory, 1971–
From empires to NGOs in the West African Sahel : the road to nongovernmentality / Gregory Mann.
    pages   cm. – (African studies)
Includes bibliographical references and index.
ISBN 978-1-107-01654-5 (hbk)
1. Sahel – History. 2. Sahel – Politics and government. 3. Sahel – Social conditions. 4. Sahel – Economic conditions. 5. Non-governmental organizations – Sahel. I. Title.
    DT532.6.M36   2015
    966.03'2–dc23   2014021443

ISBN 978-1-107-01654-5 Hardback
ISBN 978-1-107-60252-6 Paperback

Cambridge University Press has no responsibility for the persistence or accuracy of URLs for external or third-party Internet Web sites referred to in this publication and does not guarantee that any content on such Web sites is, or will remain, accurate or appropriate.

Contents

List of Maps and Figures	*page* viii
Acknowledgments	ix
Note on Terminology	xv
Introduction	1

Part I

1.	Knowing the Postcolony	15
2.	A New Republic	42

Part II

	Introduction to Part II: Sahelian Migrations and State Thought	89
3.	"French" Muslims in Sudan	93
4.	Well-Known Strangers: How West Africans Became Foreigners in Postimperial France	120

Part III

	Introduction to Part III: Saving the Sahel	165
5.	Governing Famine	170
6.	Human Rights and Saharan Prisons	209
	Conclusion	243

Works Cited	249
Index	275

Maps and Figures

MAPS

1. The Sahel   *page* xii
2. Mali   xiii
3. Sudan   96

FIGURES

1. A bus slides down the road   166
2. Tin Aïcha: Village Pilote   191
3. Tin Aïcha 4×4   192

Acknowledgments

Books, like corpses, enter and leave the world in the hands of others. This book first began to enter the world more than a decade ago, and many hands brought it into being, often unwittingly. The debts that I, its author, have accumulated during that time are innumerable and impossible to discharge, but I want to acknowledge the largest and most pressing here.

In New York City, I have the absurd good fortune, at once personal and intellectual, to work alongside Fred Cooper and Mamadou Diouf, both of whom are generous senior colleagues pursuing questions not too far from my own. I continue to learn many lessons from them, as I do from the indomitable Luise White. I regret that this book cannot engage more fully with their own recently published or forthcoming work. I have also benefited greatly from the collegiality of Souleymane Bachir Diagne, Evan Haefeli, Mark Mazower, Sam Moyn, Emmanuelle Saada, and Rhiannon Stephens. Cabeiri Robinson, David Marriott, Nick Guyatt, and Nicole Coleman made my time at the Stanford Humanities Center productive and meaningful. Richard Roberts and Sean Hanretta proved to be exceedingly generous colleagues during my time in Palo Alto, but also before and after. Richard helped to find this book a home. In Paris, Danielle Haase-Duboc, Mihaela Bacou, and Brunhilde Biebuyck at Reid Hall gave me all the support anyone could ask for. Emmanuelle Sibeud opened many doors for me, and early conversations with her, Jean-Philippe Dedieu, Brian Larkin, and Julie Livingston proved precious. Sara Berry, whose guidance meant so much to my first book, contributed to this one as well, offering late in the process of rewriting an occasion for dialogue and exchange at Johns Hopkins University. There and elsewhere, the reflections of Leo Villalón proved invaluable, as did those of many other colleagues.

In different ways, Eric Allina, Dahlia el-Tayeb Gubara, Amir Idris, Ryan Skinner, Etienne Smith, Ben Talton, and Marcia Wright nudged this project forward. So too did many of the students from Columbia, NYU, and the Université de Bamako with whom I had the privilege to work.

Nothing would have been possible in Niamey without Seyni Moumouni, and I thank him, Kimba Idrissa, and the staff of the IRSH sincerely. In Bamako, Modibo Diallo proved endlessly generous with his time, enthusiasm, and insight. From Khartoum, Pandora O'Mahony-Adams kindly tracked down and dispatched valuable documents. Back in New York, Laurel Ackerson and Jake Obeng-Bediako proved to be very helpful research assistants. Fabrice Melka in Paris and Alyadjidi Almouctar (Alia) Baby, Timothée Saye, and Abdoulaye Traoré in Bamako were exceptionally professional and accommodating. So too were archivists in each of the many repositories on which this book relies, particularly in the Manuscripts and Archives Division of the New York Public Library.

Emily Burrill hosted Oumou and me in Chapel Hill. We thank her, Eric, and Tiéba of Carrboro, and we are grateful, too, for the warm hospitality of Bruce and Sima and of Daouda and Marie-Christine. Some generous spirits – such as that of Laura Lee Downs, Patrick Weil, Amadou Seydou Traoré, Jean Schmitz, and Christophe Daum – can only be humbly acknowledged, with the hope one day to be able to emulate them.

Much of what takes published form here was first essayed in other venues. I benefited greatly from critiques launched at the Université de Bamako, the Ecole des Hautes Etudes en Sciences Sociales, Sciences Po Paris and Sciences Po Bordeaux, Paris VIII and Paris I, Stanford, the University of Florida, the University of Michigan, the University of Toronto, the Freiburg Institute for Advanced Studies, and various other conferences and workshops. The text was also much improved by the astute comments of the Press's anonymous readers.

This book, nearly completed, took a different turn when Mali unravelled in 2012–13. I rethought and rewrote much of it in the long grind of that crisis, during which many excellent scholars of Mali proved to be exemplary citizens as well. I was proud to be in conversation with Isaie Dougnon, Daouda Gary-Tounkara, Bruce Hall, Baz Lecocq, Johanna Siméant, Bruce Whitehouse, Ingrid Monson, and many others during that time. Baz, Brandon County, Bruce Hall, Jean-Hervé Jézéquel, and Bruce Whitehouse shared valuable documents and ideas with me, and Baz in particular put up with a lot of crap. I have been walking beside and learning from him and Isaie for more than fifteen years. I hope the road will be a long one.

Ousmane Traore remains an exemplary *diatigi*. I owe a great deal to the family of the late Moussa Sidibe, as well as to my own parents and my sisters. No blessing is greater than this one: Oumou has been my companion on much of this road, on which *a ba togoma* has joined us. I offer this book with humility to them, and to the memory of our own Ousmane.

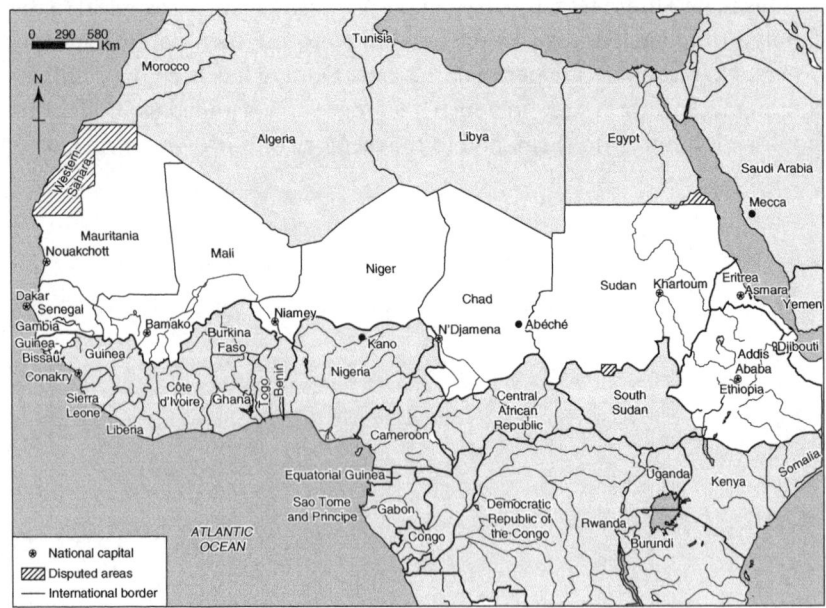

MAP 1 The Sahel

MAP 2 Mali

Note on Terminology

This book involves two Sudans and one Soudan. In order to avoid confusion between the region of the Sudan – from the Arabic phrase "*bilad al-sudan*," referring to Africa south of the Sahara – and the colony and later nation-state of Sudan – that is, the Nilotic Sudan – I have systematically avoided the use of the definite article in reference to the political entity. However, when it is used in quotations, I have kept it, as the meaning is clear from the context. As much as possible, I have avoided reference to the region.

I have kept the French spelling "Soudan" to refer to the colony of Soudan Français, which briefly became the Territory of Soudan and then the Soudanese Republic before becoming the Republic of Mali. I have also kept the adjectives derived from it (thus "Soudanese" for "*Soudanais*").

I use the term "Mande" to refer to the related languages and culture that claim the Mali Empire, founded in the thirteenth century, as part of their heritage. I use the term Mandekan ("the language of the Mande") to indicate the closely related languages of Bambara (or Bamanankan) and Malinké.

For stylistic purposes, I have in certain passages adopted the common West African practice of referring to heads of state by their given names rather than their family names (thus Moussa Traore is Moussa, etc.). I trust that the reference is clear in context.

In the case of a female public figure known by her spouse's family name as well as by her own, I have followed local practice and that of my sources by placing the spouse's family name before the individual's given name. Thus Modibo Keita's senior wife is Mme. Keita Mariam Travélé, but Aoua Keita remains Aoua Keita.

The use of the accented "é" in transcribing family names in the region is inconsistent. I have generally avoided its use unless authors employ it in writing their own names. Thus the name of former Malian head of state Moussa Traore goes unadorned, in contrast to that of author and publisher Amadou Seydou Traoré, who in this instance gets the last word.

Introduction

Frantz Fanon was growing angry. It was 1960, and he was deep in Mali, a vast country, "fervent and brutal," a place where there was "no need of great speeches." The country had just gained independence from France weeks before, and its new president, Modibo Keita, "ever militant," had assured him of his support. Everything was set. Fanon and his colleagues, Algerian revolutionaries seeking to open a southern front for the Front de Libération Nationale (FLN), had already avoided prying French eyes in Bamako and dodged what they took to be a kidnapping attempt in Monrovia. They were headed east and north, to Gao, Aguelhoc, Tessalit. So how to account for the roadblock, the intransigence?

At Mopti, a snag. On the way out of town: a *gendarmes'* roadblock, and the sentries demand our passports. Difficult discussion because, in spite of the document from the Minister of the Interior [Madeira Keita], the *gendarmes* want to know our identities. Finally the commanding officer arrives, and I'm obliged to introduce myself. But it seems we're faced with a man who's after intelligence. He wants to know the nature of our mission and the roles of my companions.[1]

In the end, Fanon and his comrades get out of it. "Promising absolute secrecy," the officer lets the militants go, but that's not the end of their troubles. "The road from Mopti to Douentza is a joke," Fanon tells us.[2] Decades later, when I traveled it on a small but sturdy motorcycle, that joke wasn't funny anymore. But along that same road, some forms of political power were visible to the naked eye, just as in Fanon's roadblock

---

[1] Fanon (1964), 209. This and all other translations are my own, unless otherwise indicated.
[2] Fanon (1964), 210.

experience.[3] What struck me then, and stays with me still, was the immobility of the state, represented by the somnolent gendarmes manning scattered checkpoints, and the humming power of international nongovernmental organizations (NGOs), whose white Toyota Land Cruisers shot like arrows the length of the country. Neither Fanon nor the two Keitas could have imagined such a future, but they'd seen something like it in the past.[4] From the saddle of the motorbike, the easy conclusion was that the state was weak, the NGOs strong. That was wrong.

In 1960, people living in the West African Sahel became citizens of newly independent states. At the same time, many of those living along that long, thin band of arable land limning the Sahara found themselves foreigners in states to which they had long ties. In less than a generation, Sahelians would become the subjects of human rights campaigns and humanitarian interventions. *From Empires to NGOs* looks beyond the familiar political formations that came into being at the end of colonial rule – new nation-states and ex-empires – to consider newly transnational communities of solidarity and aid, social science and activism. In the two decades immediately after independence, precisely when its states were strongest and most ambitious, the postcolonial West African Sahel became a fertile terrain for the production of new forms of governmental rationality realized through NGOs. I term this new phenomeon "nongovernmentality," and argue that although its roots may lie partly in Europe and North America, it flowered, paradoxically, in the Sahel.[5] In this book, my question is not simply how African states exercised their new sovereignties,

---

[3] National highways in the Sahel can be particularly dense with memory and meaning; see Beck (2013); Klaeger (2013); Masquelier (2002).

[4] Modibo and Madeira were not of the same family.

[5] Of course, the term invokes Michel Foucault's governmentality. It is worth recalling his definition of that term, while recognizing that it was not particularly stable. For Foucault, the term identifies a form of power that takes a population, rather than individuals, as its object, political economy "as its major form of knowledge," and security forces as its "primary instrument"; (2007), 87–134, see esp. 108. With the term "nongovernmentality," I mean to invoke the assimilation of forms of governmental rationality by what are commonly referred to as nongovernmental (i.e., nonstate) organizations. I mean something different than do Michael Feher and Stephen Jackson. Feher refers to nongovernmental politics, "as that in which the governed as such are involved" [sic]; (2007), 13. His definition seems remarkably expansive as even totalitarian systems involve their subjects, but nothing akin to NGOs or civil society flourishes within them. As for Jackson, the predicate of his "nongovernmentality" is an atrophied state, particularly Zaire in the 1980s; (2005). The Sahelian case was different – nongovernmentality emerged earlier, and states were stronger – but I want to move away from a zero-sum analytics in which NGO strength is a function of state weakness. I note, too, that the politics I discuss in this book is largely secular. Only in the early 1990s did Islamic civil society associations begin to emerge. On

but how and why NGOs began to assume functions of it in a period when it was so highly valued.[6]

From Empires to NGOs attempts to break out of the colonial and postcolonial frame in which much of contemporary African history is situated. It does so by encompassing the decades of postwar economic growth punctuated by imperial reform (1946–60), African independence (after 1960), and coups d'état (notably in Mali in 1968 and in Niger in 1974).[7] No less significantly, it does so by looking east–west, along some of the many vectors tying the Sahel together as a coherent space, in addition to north–south, within the frame of the former European empires.[8] The gambit is simple: the complexity of postcolonial political memberships might best be analyzed on the margins and on the move. Thus, looking outward from Mali, I examine Sahelian political formations from oblique angles – such as from Khartoum to Paris – and at moments of rapid transition – such as independence. Doing so captures the elaboration of new forms of political rationality by governments and NGOs, and it poses the analytical challenge of reconciling the zone's deep historicity with the vision of the Sahel as a novel dystopic site that has predominated since the 1970s.

THE SAHEL

Originally referring to "the shore" of the Sahara (Arabic, *sahil*) in recent decades, the term "Sahel" has become almost synonymous with crisis. In the context of the region's recent turmoil, government officials from Algeria, the powerful northern neighbor, played on this idea in dubbing the zone "a terribly vast, terribly empty space."[9] Only a few weeks later, former presidents Jacques Chirac of France and Abdou Diouf of Senegal used the French newspaper *le Monde* as a tribune to call for "a new Marshall Plan" for the Sahel.[10] Did they know that some forty years earlier, during the drought and famine of the early 1970s, presidents

---

these, see notably Soares (2005a) and Schulz (2012); on Christian congregations, see broadly Cooper (2006); Piot (2010); Larkin and Myers in Akyeampong, ed. (2006).

[6] On the contingent, unfixed, yet durable quality of sovereignty and the attempts of ex-colonies and new nation-states to generate it, see Howland and White, eds., (2009).

[7] Here I take a cue from Ellis (2002) and Cooper (2002). Such a periodization contrasts with that adopted in some histories of humanitarianism, which sees the period from the end of World War Two to the end of the Cold War as one; Barnett (2011), Fassin (2011), but see de Waal (1998).

[8] Other approaches to the Sahel as a cultural and intellectual unit include Tidjani Alou (2010) and Wise (2001), to name only two.

[9] "l'Algérie defend 'l'intégrité territoriale du Mali,'" *le Monde* April 6, 2012.

[10] Diouf and Chirac, "Urgence à Tombouctou," *le Monde* July 13, 2012.

Hamani Diori of Niger and Sangoulé Lamizana of Upper Volta (now Burkina Faso) had pounded podiums at international conferences, using the same analogy to make the same call?[11] It was then that the term "Sahel" first became part of the lexicon of governments and international NGOs. Versions of the word had long been present in the region's everyday languages, but from the 1970s, the term "Sahel" would evoke poverty for the world at large.[12] Decades later, much the same truths prevailed. Even as Salafist fighters destroyed the tombs of Sufis in Timbuktu, a famine loomed, and Chirac and Diouf lamented the fact that "the security crisis [was] overshadowing a dramatic food crisis," while a population bomb was ticking.[13] Such was their vision of the Sahel, battered between crises, a place where, analytically, you could pick your poison. Tellingly, the very idea of a Marshall Plan implied outside intervention. This was a job for the international community, from the former imperial states of Europe (i.e., "countries traditionally engaged in Africa") to "newly emergent powers." It was a job for strong states, and a question of government. Implicit, too, in their language was a widespread idea, one unremarkable in 2012, hardly thinkable in 1912, and scarcely nascent in 1962: the Sahel was an object of governance within the framework of a shared humanity. The tombs that the Salafists had destroyed were, after all, UNESCO world heritage sites, a fact of which the men wielding the pickaxes were well aware.[14]

---

[11] Amb. Fr. Niger to MAE, DAAM, *Synthèses périodiques*, #11, June 4-17, 1973; #12, June 18 to July 1, 1973, FPU 783; T. Johnson, "6 African Nations End 14-day Talks," *New York Times* Sept. 13, 1973.

[12] Bonnecase (2011). *Contra* Bonnecase and Alpha Gado Boureima, variants of the term "Sahel" derived from the same Arabic root give "*saheli*" in Bamanankan and "*saahal*" in Fulfuulde. Rather than suggesting that it was externally imposed (Bonnecase 2011; Alpha Gado 1993) or misunderstood (Lydon 2009), diverse uses and meanings of the term suggest that it was deeply grounded. No less interesting is the usage of a comparable term – Sudan – that is not synonymous with Sahel, referring as it does to the sub-Saharan region, with its roots in the venerable phrase, "*bilad al-Sudan*," or, "the land of the Blacks." The term Sudan was prevalent in internal and external discourse in the nineteenth and early twentieth century, however, it has faded almost entirely, except of course to designate the Republic of Sudan, even as "Sahel" has become more commonly used.

[13] Both the food crisis and the security crisis – but more important, the frames of understanding either and the modes of engaging with them – are the products of particular historical processes. They will wax and wane; the famine of 2012 never happened partly because of lessons learned since the 1970s. For a critical and historically informed appraisal of the balance between government imperatives and NGO activites in Sahelian food emergencies, see Crombé and Jézéquel (2007).

[14] YouTube clip, Ansar Dine at Timbuktu, http://www.youtube.com/watch?v=-TBSD2VpAzE, last viewed December 11, 2013.

While the Sahel is an apt place to study tattered but resilient sovereignties and the emergence of nongovernmental politics, that history cannot be disentangled from the rise of neoliberalism in Africa. Still, the last decades of the region's colonial history and the first of its independence would constitute an odd moment in which to ground a study of neoliberalism. Indeed, to do so would be profoundly ahistorical. As an economic doctrine, neoliberalism's moment came only in the late 1970s. The World Bank's "Berg report," often taken to announce its arrival in Africa, was released in 1981.[15] In the years following, as much of the world "stumbled" toward implementing economic programs based on neoliberal doctrine, many heavily indebted African states would be shoved in that direction.[16] That history is beyond the horizons of this book, which offers a prehistory of neoliberal Africa, a sketch of the gap between state and government, one that later wedges – not all of them "neoliberal" – would widen. Here I ask how at particular moments certain characteristics of government itself began to be defined as beyond the prerogatives of the state.[17] My questions are propelled by those of others who have explored the deepening shadows along the border between the private and the public in contemporary Africa since the era of multiparty political contestation began in the 1990s.[18] My answers, however, are not. The chapters that follow demonstrate that. They ask, for instance, who gave meaning to the citizenships, European and African, roughly sketched out at independence? Migrants, rebels, policemen, and bare-knuckled diplomats. Not jurists and legislators. Who opened up the civic space for humanitarian action and human rights-oriented

---

[15] Harvey (2007); Harrison (2010); see also Ferguson (2006), 78, 84, 87. Senegal had already received loans conditioned on structural adjustment, starting in 1979; Harrison (2010), 38.

[16] Harvey (2007), 13; see also Konings (2011). For a competing view, see Van de Walle (2001). Mali may have been one of the most "adjusted" of the Sahelian countries, having had the most state monopolies before reform and none after, as did the Gambia; Naudet (1999), 80.

[17] I trace this phenomenon to a different and earlier moment than does, e.g., Charles Piot, whose study of Togo emphasizes the effects of the end of the Cold War for a variety of reasons that do not obtain in the Sahel; (2010), esp. 5.

[18] Some of the richest work on this theme advances the idea of private indirect government, which captures well the permeable boundaries between private and public, legal and illegal, and between gestures of authority and acts of accumulation; Hibou (1999; paraphrasing pg. 6), Diouf (1999), Mbembe (2001), Roitman (2005). Janet Roitman argues that although representations of state power through taxation and economic regulation shifted considerably in the era of multiparty democracy, such changes were indicative of the evolution rather than the demise of state sovereignty; (2005), 22, 200.

interventions that would later swell with local and international NGOs? Those who prized African sovereignty the most; people on the Left, not the Right.[19] And who first tried to prevent West Africans from migrating abroad? New states in the Sahel, notably Mali, but also Sudan. Not France.[20] Most importantly, these inquiries into human rights activism and humanitarian intervention demonstrate that it was not in the period of neoliberal reform during the late Cold War and after, but rather precisely in the wake of independence, when African sovereignty was mostly highly prized, that some of those who had worked to establish that sovereignty began to mortgage it.

From 1960, Sahelian governments secured their independence in different ways, but within a decade, all would be loosely labeled neocolonial regimes. I argue to the contrary that, in parts of the Sahel at least, independence was real, if awkwardly acquired and unevenly exercised. At that time, it was expressed most concretely by asserting autonomy from France in three key sectors reserved for Paris in the 1958 constitution of the French Fifth Republic: diplomacy, defense, and monetary policy. In rejecting French tutelage, Mali went further than any of its neighbors apart from Guinea. Within weeks of acceding to independence, the country had asserted its control over its diplomatic relations, notably with the FLN, as Fanon's visit demonstrates. A few weeks later, the country requested the departure of French forces from its military bases. By July 1962, the ruling Union Soudanaise-Rassemblement Démocratique Africaine (US-RDA) had created a new currency for the new nation. The Malian franc was designed to be "a declaration of political and economic war" against France, President Modibo Keita declared in a closed meeting of the Party's central committee.[21] So by what measure was Mali neocolonial?

Labeling Sahelian states neoliberal is no more useful in analyzing the present than dismissing them as neocolonial was in the past, and it may be no more accurate. By the same token, the effects of neoliberal programs on African sovereignty can neither be ignored nor assumed; they must be demonstrated. They can be paradoxical Neoliberal narrowing of state prerogatives may strengthen the state's ability to fulfill its most essential functions – reinforcing, for example, the customs

---

[19] This argument contrasts with the premises of a broader literature on NGOs in Africa; for a review, see Hearn (2007).

[20] Although the British empire also claimed vast tracts of the Sahel, my attention is focused on the formerly French territories and, consequently, on their imperial government.

[21] *Procès-Verbal* [hereafter, P-V], BPN, August 7, 1962, BPNCMLN 77.

service in Ghana.[22] Historical analyses of Africa's "past in the present" suggest that this should be no surprise. After all, if many of Africa's states act as "gatekeepers" with the limited ambition of controlling linkages between foreign capital and domestic economies,[23] one would expect customs and border control to play a vital role in anchoring their future. On the other hand, the gatekeeper metaphor is of greater help in understanding the flow of commodities and capital (at least in the formal sphere) than it is in accounting for the volume and the economic significance of international migration in much of sub-Saharan Africa, which is a theme of this book. By and large, Sahelian states, with their long loose borders, have failed to control either, and their own policies and those of their neighbors have made smuggling of goods and people ever more lucrative. Farther north in the Sahara, where I do not linger at length, there are indeed "gates," – in the form of taxes levied by armed groups – but states do not keep them.[24]

As a zone of intense mobility and uneven sovereignties, the Sahel offers rich potential for studying evolving political affinities and novel forms of postcolonial politics, as expressed through humanitarianism and human rights. From the Sahel, one sees clearly the emergence of the "politics of the governed," or what Partha Chatterjee calls the politics of "most of the world," awkwardly straddling state and civil society, loosely rooted in the thin but vital soil of the latter.[25] Still, the core of my project is not the Sahel as a locale. Rather, it is the Sahel as an object of governance, investigation, and intervention. It is the "political Sahel," not the geographic one.[26] In the twentieth century, the West African Sahel stretched from Senegal to the Sudanese provinces of Darfur and Kordofan and beyond. From the late nineteenth century, the zone had fallen under French and British rule.

---

[22] Chalfin (2010). Departing from different empirical examples, which nonetheless included the privatization of customs, Hibou arrived at a similar argument; Hibou (1999), esp. 6–7. See also Roitman (2005), esp. 22; Mbembe (2001), ch. 2.
[23] Cooper (2002).
[24] Scheele (2012); on the Lake Chad basin, Roitman (2005).
[25] Chatterjee (2004), 3–4. One can see similar processes at work in South Africa and Cameroon, where the soil is much thicker; Robins (2008); Konings (2011).
[26] Giri (1983), 12. By way of example, nine states comprise the *Comité inter-états de lutte contre la sécheresse au Sahel* (CILSS), created in 1976. They include Senegal, Mali, Niger, Nigeria, Burkina Faso, The Gambia, Chad, and Cape Verde. This is clearly the "political Sahel," inasmuch as Cape Verde is an archipelago and not a classically "Sahelian" country. The first three of these countries, Mali in particular, are at the center of my project.

However, migratory, religious, and kinship networks continued to link parts of the Sahel across imperial boundaries, and successive waves of pastoralists and pilgrims from West Africa settled in Sudan in the first half of the twentieth century. After independence, circa 1960, African nation-states restricted movement across their borders, but ties of migration, activism, and intellectual life bound most of the countries of the Sahel to their neighbors and to postimperial France. Such transimperial and transnational filaments constitute the axes along which my analysis proceeds.

A ROADMAP

Rather than taking the West African Sahel as a place from which to ask the familiar question, "What is the state?" this book asks, "What is government?" I attempt to think through that question – idiosyncratically, perhaps irregularly – in relation to the Sahel. I do so in an opportunistic fashion. Rather than proposing a broad synthesis, the argument coalesces around particular events, or moments when something happens and common sense is both disrupted and re-created. The book is structured around three pairs of chapters, the pairs arranged chronologically: the creation of a society and a public during the period of anticolonial politics; the elaboration of citizenship and belonging by migrants, in the context of decolonization; the rise of humanitarianism and human rights activism as idioms of political engagement in the 1970s. In all but one chapter, that on humanitarian relief, Madeira Keita looms large. The steady presence of the man whose signature Fanon waved at the roadblock compels us to ask how, in the wake of an era in which independence was so highly prized, it was pawned and devalued in the decades to come.

Our story begins out of place, in Conakry, Guinea. There, in the 1940s, a nascent anticolonial politics began to intertwine with emerging forms of social scientific inquiry. That episode itself was brief, beginning, in my telling, when two young men met on a gangplank at the harbor, interrupted when they parted a few months later in a dark and dreary airport. In that postwar moment of imperial reform, Madeira Keita, a West African research assistant and anticolonial leader, and Georges Balandier, a French social scientist, began to elaborate new and particular forms of politics and knowledge, the effects of which would last longer than their relationship. Chapter 1 asserts that the party-state that Keita helped to found in postcolonial Mali understood the object of government to be not only the economy, but society itself. Once in power, the party would identify social forces as the primary constraint on economic growth; its first task was to counter them. It set out to govern aggressively, taking society as its site of intervention, but would fail to nurture any sense of a public or a common good beyond an aggrieved nationalism. Although an idea of the social became domesticated or naturalized, this was a society with precious little place for the "civil," a concept which, along with "the market," would become one of the legitimate arenas of neoliberal politics in future decades.[27] The generative tension between social science and political activism that Keita and Balandier represented is a theme that runs throughout the remainder of the book, as does Keita's own presence.

If Chapter 1 argues that the object of government was society, Chapter 2 asks what forces composed that society and the emergent citizenry with which it overlapped. The years from 1946 through 1960 represent a particularly open political moment across French West Africa. They were marked by the end of the *indigénat* (or "Native" status and the coercive regime that defined it), gradual mass enfranchisement, notably of women, and the emergence of party politics, which was often fiercely contested. In Mali, as the anticolonial US-RDA took power, its leaders dismantled the chieftaincy, which had long been a pillar of colonial rule. Such minor revolutions built up, as if brick by brick, the necessary conditions for a form of egalitarian citizenship. That open moment of postwar political reform both culminated and closed down with independence as the party invested the state.[28] As a key actor in those events, Madeira Keita would play an outsized role in establishing new practices of government in Mali and beyond.

The pair of chapters that follow explore what new citizenships meant, at home and abroad, at the moment when they would have seemed to matter most, as empires dissolved and Sahelian states struggled to establish their independence. In these chapters, I understand the state as an unfinished project, as an entity coming into being, and I argue that migrants, bureaucrats, and diplomats created new forms of political belonging through a haphazard set of practices. Thus, the second pair of chapters centers on African movement and attempts to control it. It accounts for poles of attraction distinct from the colonial metropoles and informed by logics other than exclusively imperial ones. As a pair, these chapters juxtapose West African migration to Sudan, which is little studied, with that toward

---

[27] Hibou (1999). Ironically, the remnants of the party would work to re-create something like civil society years later, while in exile; see ch. 6.
[28] I borrow the language of opening and closing from Cooper (2005; 2008). On the party-state, see Zolberg (1966).

France, much better known. This combination is an unusual one, and not only because of the sharp divide that exists between those who study immigration to the rich countries of the world and those who study "South–South" migrations. Pairing these two phenomena requires moving along two distinct axes: one, West–East across the Sahel, is the subject of Chapter 3; the other, South–North between Africa and France, is the subject of Chapter 4. Pairing them also requires moving between an analysis grounded in the long-term historical trends of a region – one that prizes the depth and resonance of a particular past partly for its own sake – to a truncated history of European empires, their dissolution, and the rise of new postcolonial states. The two chapters complement each other: one phenomenon characterized by its historicity; the other manifesting a contemporary governmental rationality. One is *hajj*, the other, loosely speaking, *hijra*.

By placing in the same frame two such divergent phenomena as pilgrimage across the Sahel and labor migration to France, this pair of chapters offers a new vision of postimperial formations, of the links and disconnections that existed within, across, and after imperial rule, and of the possibilities and failures of new forms of politics and political belonging. In the Sahel, it was this combination of historicity and governmentality, these crises of membership, moments of conflict and exchange, and networks of affinity – as well as the forms of political discourse they generated and the governmental practices on which they relied – that ultimately composed and gave meaning to the nebulous condition dubbed "postcolonial." That condition would continue to evolve in the 1970s as the political idioms in which it was anchored, notably those of sovereignty and citizenship, almost simultaneously gained greater bite in the context of immigration control and lost some of their purchase to an emergent politics predicated on the existence of a shared, nonpolitical, humanity. Thus the next pair of chapters turn to humanitarianism, development, and human rights activism.

"Governing Famine," the fifth chapter, studies the constellations of political authority, international activism, and postcolonial affinity that emerged from the Sahelian drought and famine of 1973–74 and the humanitarian interventions the crisis provoked. This chapter moves between multiple African nation-states, the populations they claimed, and the world of nongovernmental organizations to analyze the famine as an episode in international history and as a formative moment in the shape of the new Sahel. Rather than exploring the causes of the famine, I address the causes of its relief, asking how external empathy translated into action, what effects it had, and why it took the form it did. The chapter focuses on mobilization against the famine by nongovernmental organizations of divergent goals and ambitions, ranging from an African-French network of Leftist scholars and activists known as AFASPA to CARE, the major American NGO, and the African-American organizations RAINS and Africare. I argue that even before West African states adopted the Sahel as a governmental frame of reference in creating a "Sahelian" interstate committee, the practice of relief was changing the meaning of government by prying open a new political space of imported initiatives, controlled distribution, and constrained sovereignty. CARE and other NGOs, a growing number of them African, would continue to expand that space, notably in the 1980s and in the post-Cold War period of democratic transitions across the continent.[29]

Following this historical examination of nongovernmental humanitarianism at work, "Human Rights and Saharan Prisons" (Chapter 6) asks, is the domestication of human rights one of Africa's triumphs? Or is the conquest of Africa a triumph for human rights? It looks for answers in the international human rights campaigns in support of members of the US-RDA government imprisoned after a 1968 coup, the junta's own rivals, and other political activists and dissidents who would join them in the years to follow. This chapter contrasts the activism of Amnesty International to that of AFASPA, with which Amnesty collaborated, and asks how postcolonial solidarities were generated and sustained in the Sahara and the Sahel. I argue that the avowedly apolitical human rights activism represented by Amnesty International in the 1970s had a viral effect: it spread steadily and eventually threatened to void feeble hosts in West African civil society of their particular form of politics. That process unraveled over long years after the release of the last of the US-RDA prisoners, Madeira Keita, in the late 1970s. Having survived a decade of imprisonment in the southern Sahara, Keita made his way home to Bamako. He soon left to recover his strength in Conakry. That coastal city, far from the Sahel, is where our sinuous history of nongovernmentality begins, decades earlier, out of place.

---

[29] Hearn (2007); Raghavan (1992). For a robust critique of both the expanding role of NGOs in South African politics and the literature it has generated, see Robins (2008), 22–24. For historical perspective, see Michael (2004), Igoe and Kelsall (2005), and Jennings (2008). On humanitarianism as such, a provocative but often historically shallow anthropological literature has recently emerged in which African history and politics are more often the scenery than the subject. Compelling examples include Fassin (2011) and Agier (2011).

PART I

I

Knowing the Postcolony

The Republic of Mali became an independent nation in 1960 with the break-up of the Mali Federation and the socialist option of September 22nd. And again in 1961, with the expulsion of French troops from military bases on its territory. And again in 1962, with the creation of the Malian franc. These at least were the perceptions of the ruling party, the Union Soudanaise-Rassemblement Démocratique Africain (US-RDA). But when did Mali become a society? This chapter asks how party leaders understood what they sought to govern and what the effects of that understanding were. It asks what it meant in Bamako in the 1960s for the US-RDA leadership to perceive of Mali as a society and to attempt to govern it as such.[1]

One place to begin to think about these questions is on a quay in Conakry, in the neighboring territory of Guinea, where two young men met in 1946.[2] One, waiting dockside, was Mamadou Madeira Keita, a low-level civil servant and archivist. Years later, when he was a political prisoner in the Malian Sahara, some would argue (with a good deal of exaggeration) that he was "the first francophone African ethnographer."[3] The other, descending the gangplank, was the Frenchman Keita had come to meet. Georges Balandier was unknown then, but his name is familiar now.[4] Conakry was his second African port of call. The work with which

---

[1] These questions are partly provoked by a reading of Mitchell (2002) and Latour (2005).
[2] Balandier (1966), 228.
[3] Guiart (1976), 153.
[4] On Balandier and his influence, a sample of work representative of different decades and approaches might include Adler and Balandier, eds., (1986); Maffesoli and Rivière, eds., (1985); Meillassoux (1981), preface; Moore (1994), 99–104; Copans (2001a; 2001b); Saada (2002b); Balandier, Steinmetz and Sapiro (2010).

he would make his name remained literally over the horizon, in Brazzaville. Yet the encounter between Keita and Balandier was foundational for both men. For the young Frenchman, Guinea, like postwar French Africa, was more than a laboratory. It was a workshop;[5] he was one of its creations. Conakry, and Guinea at large, was also the crucible in which a powerful anticolonial politics would be forged by Madeira Keita and his allies. In this particular corner of West Africa, that politics and an emergent, engaged social science conditioned each other, like the two strands of a double helix, each a necessary yet ultimately contingent element of the other's structure. Those links did not last long. In fact, they proved nearly as ephemeral as the conjuncture that enabled them. Still, they were not without effect. Diverging from a well-established literature on the connections between the social sciences – notably anthropology – and European colonial rule,[6] here I privilege the political, arguing that anticolonial activism both effected and was affected by a shift more profoundly epistemological than methodological in the practice of the social sciences (more precisely, sociology and ethnography) in West Africa.[7] One forgotten moment when the two began to come together was on that quay.

THE ANTICOLONIALIST

The young archivist who awaited Balandier on the quay in Conakry was an exceptional figure, one of the architects of a new form of radical anticolonial politics in francophone West Africa that is now largely obscured. Mamadou Madeira Keita was an agent of the West African social science research institute (Institut Français de l'Afrique Noire; IFAN). He was also a founding figure of both the interterritorial, anticolonial political party known as the Rassemblement Démocratique Africaine (RDA) and of its Guinean chapter. Born in Kourounikoto in the Soudanese (later Malian) *cercle* of Kita around 1917 and educated at

---

[5] I draw the workshop analogy from Schumaker (2001). The distinction between Africa as a site for the working out of scientific models developed elsewhere and as a site of scientific production in, of, and for itself merits further reflection; see Bernault (2001); Cooper (2005); Mbembe (2001); and Tilley (2011).

[6] Recent interventions into that discussion include Tilley (2011) and Sibeud (2011).

[7] This finding complements that of Schumaker (2001) and echoes to some degree that of el Shakry (2007), in which the focus extends to human geography and demography, in addition to anthropology. My approach differs from that of Jean-Hervé Jézéquel, who focuses on the "social history of agents and institutions of research"; see Jézéquel (2011), esp. 53.

French West Africa's highest institution of learning, the *Ecole Normale de Gorée* (later the *Ecole William Ponty*), Keita had trained as a librarian and archivist in the office of the governor general in Dakar and in Conakry before the Second World War. Mobilized from October 1938 to October 1940, he served in Dakar and left the ranks of the colonial military (the *tirailleurs Sénégalais*) as a staff sergeant (*sergent-chef*). Keita then worked as an archivist and librarian for the government of Guinea in Conakry and Kouroussa. In 1944, he established the IFAN center in Guinea, a center that grew out of the archive, and which Balandier would be sent to take over. He would remain there, periodically serving as interim director, until 1950.[8]

While at IFAN-Conakry in April 1946, Madeira Keita stepped into a pivotal role in the city's emerging Communist Study Group (*Groupe d'études communistes*, GEC), which had been animated by French Communists until Keita, Sékou Touré, and a few other West Africans became involved.[9] Six months later, he would write to Théodore Monod, IFAN's director in Dakar, asking for a leave of absence to represent Guinea at the conference in Bamako at which the RDA would be created on October 22nd. Monod granted his request on the condition that he arrive back in Conakry on October 24th in time to greet the new director, Balandier, who would arrive shortly thereafter.[10] This must have been a rushed trip, and it meant that when Keita met Balandier, he had only just returned hours earlier. In the same days and weeks that he worked with Balandier, he was also working with Touré (who had also been in Bamako), Ray Autra, and others to found the Guinean branch of the RDA, the party that would evolve into the Parti Démocratique de la Guinée (PDG).[11] Within months of returning from Bamako, Keita was holding meetings at Conakry's Rialto cinema to establish the RDA's

---

[8] *Notice de Renseignement Concernant Madeira Keita*, 1960, ANM NIII 1C1542; "Activités du Centre IFAN," *Etudes Guinéennes* 7 (1951); Autra [Traoré] (1964): 5–35; see 14–16.

[9] Suret-Canale (1994), 57–9. Letter of Madeira Keita to Jean Suret-Canale, April 17, 1987, Fonds Suret-Canale, ADSSD 229J65.

[10] Mamadou Madeira Keita, aide technique de l'IFAN, to M. le Directeur de l'IFAN, Dakar, Oct. 3, 1946, #164 IFAN/G, and note in margin signed "Monod." IFAN-Guinea A1/17, Collection IFAN-Dakar.

[11] "Ray Autra" is a moniker based on reversing the syllables of Traore's family name in the French slang style known as *verlane*. As he appeared in archival records and signed his own publications as Ray Autra, I use that name here. Autra will play an important supporting role in our narrative. Touré would become Guinea's first president at independence in 1958, ruling autocratically through the PDG until his death in 1984.

Guinean chapter.[12] Keita quickly folded one of the colony's fledgling political parties, the Parti Progressiste Africain de Guinée, into the interterritorial initiative, and in years to come he and Touré would struggle to integrate the other, ethnically or regionally based parties. Police reports echoed the press in referring to Keita as the Guinean RDA's chief organizer (*"responsable"*), and he would be elected its first secretary-general.[13] His wife, the schoolteacher Mme. Keita Nankoria Kourouma, was a leader and cofounder of the women's wing of the movement in Guinea, and their house served as a meeting ground for anticolonial activists.[14] Madeira Keita's importance in anticolonial politics is less often underestimated than overlooked entirely by historians hypnotized by Touré,[15] yet a 1948 report from the head of security in Guinea makes his importance clear:

Very intelligent, subtle, and an ardent partisan of the Communist doctrine, Madeira is indisputably the soul and the brains of the group (i.e., the RDA), and it seems certain that, if he were transferred to another territory in the Federation..., the RDA could not easily find in Guinea a leader and a coordinator who would be his equal.[16]

---

[12] Announcement, *la Guinée Française*, 3014, March 6, 1947.
[13] *Renseignement, Conakry, Destinataire: Haut-Commissaire de la République, Gouverneur Général de l'AOF (Direction des Affaires Politiques et Administratives)*, March 10 1947, ANS 17G573; Madeira Keita, Secretary-General, "la Vie de la Section," *Phare de Guinée*, 1, 1, Sept. 27, 1947. The RDA in Guinea would become the PDG in 1950, although it is frequently referred to as the RDA through Guinea's independence in 1958; *Rapport politique, Guinée 1950*, ANS 17G573; Morgenthau (1964), 234.
[14] On the women's movement, see Schmidt (2005), ch. 5; Pauthier (2007). An image of Madame Madeira Keita's *carte d'electeur* can be found in S. Keita (1978), vol. 1, n.p.; her status as a teacher apparently gave her the right to vote several years before other West African women obtained it. Mme Keita was a leader of the RDA women's wing in Guinea and Mali, which sent her as a delegate to many international meetings and conferences through the mid-1960s. According to one of her sons, the demands of her family eventually took precedence over her international activism; int., Papa Madeira Keita, Bamako, June 21, 2008.
[15] E. Schmidt's work is symptomatic, according Keita a minor role, occluded by that of Sékou Touré, and failing to recognize the interterritorial basis of French West African politics. Schmidt's focus on "the masses" and Sékou Touré tends to obscure the collective leadership of the PDG-RDA and the role of leaders other than Touré; see Schmidt (2005, 2007b). Schmidt's *Cold War and Decolonization in Guinea, 1946–58* recognizes Keita's role more systematically, but sends him offstage after his 1952 transfer to Dahomey, which merely marked the end of his Guinean sojourn; (2007a), 38, 64. It is no surprise that work published in Conakry while Touré was in power also diminishes Keita's role: Camara (1973); S. Keita (1978).
[16] Pierre Ottavy, Chef de Service de la Sûreté de la Guinée Française, to M. l'Inspecteur Général de la Sûreté en AOF, Nov. 5, 1948, #1176/PS, ANS 17G573.

In years to come, Touré would become that man, and more. But in 1948, his alliance with Keita seems to have been based on a loose division of tasks. Keita, the intellectual, led the party – albeit in close collaboration with others – served as its spokesperson, and would later edit one of its short-lived newspapers, *Coup de Bambou* (1950–51).[17] Touré was the secretary-general of the Guinean chapter of the powerful, French Communist trade union, the *Confédération Général du Travail* (CGT), and in 1948 he exchanged a position in the Guinean postal service, in which he had led early postwar strikes, for one as an accountant in the federation-wide colonial civil service.[18] Touré's strong allies in the labor movement in West Africa and Europe helped to protect him to some degree from persecution by the colonial administration, but on the other hand his status as a civil servant – one long held by Keita – made him vulnerable to punitive transfers from one territory to another. This balance was a delicate one, and it tipped in June 1950, when Touré led a general strike in Conakry over the minimum wage.[19] He sought a leave of absence from the civil service, which the administration refused, assigning him instead to Niger. Touré in turn refused to go, and after a voyage to Warsaw that raised his international profile, he was dismissed from the civil service early in 1951. He left almost immediately for a long sojourn in France, returned to contest unsuccessfully a seat in the territorial assembly, and finally came out of the political wilderness in July 1952 when he succeeded Keita as secretary general of the Guinean RDA, and 1953, when he won both a seat in the assembly and a territory-wide increase in the minimum wage, following a 67-day strike.[20]

In the wake of the 1950 general strike, Keita too was on the ropes. Guinea's governor had already banned meetings of the RDA. In August, after years of harassment from the colonial administration – this at least was mutual – Keita was suspended from his duties and his salary cut off after he refused a transfer out of Guinea.[21] In November, a court fined Keita 100,000 francs for libel in a case brought by Irencé Montout, a

---

[17] The phrase "stroke of bamboo" refers to the fatal sunstroke the French believed might befall those who went without a pith helmet; Bianchini (2011), 32–33. The newspaper redefined it as a fatal blow to colonialism; *Coup de Bambou*, 1, April 5, 1950.
[18] Lewin (2009), 76, 157.
[19] Lewin (2009), 159–60; Cooper (1996), 280.
[20] Lewin (2009), 143–44, 160–63, 185; Cooper (1996), 310.
[21] *Notice de Renseignement...*, 1960, ANM NIII 1C1542; *Premier Congrès Territorial du PDG (Section Guinéen du RDA), Rapport Général d'Activité 1947–1950, Présenté au Nom du Comité Directeur par Mamadou Madeira Keita, Secretaire-Général*, ANS 17G573; Lewin (2009), 160 n308.

colonial administrator from the Antilles, against *Coup de Bambou*.[22] A six-month suspended sentence hung over his head after that case, and other judgments had already gone against him, leaving him with heavy fines to pay and the prospect of multiple months' imprisonment.[23] Ironically, the article that provoked Montout's lawsuit may have been written by Touré, under the pseudonym Erdéa (phonetically, RDA).[24] Whoever the author was, Keita was the defendant. He was silenced, and *Coup de Bambou* swept from the table. This was check, but not yet checkmate.

That year, politics was souring all around. Keita found himself on the wrong side of a battle to maintain the parliamentary alliance between the French Communist Party (PCF) and the RDA. Led by the Ivoirian Félix Houphouët-Boigny, the RDA had decided to break with the PCF altogether. Keita disagreed strongly, but his dedication to party discipline would eventually oblige him to accept a maneuver designed to make the party less threatening to the colonial state and more effective in its metropolitan legislative coalition.[25] Touré had been persuaded to follow the new party line, and over the next few years would work to keep his CGT and his RDA activities distinct.[26] For Keita, this compromise must have been especially galling. Unlike Touré or Houphouët-Boigny, he never enjoyed parliamentary immunity or the relative protection from the colonial administration that presence in France or a high profile in the labor movement could provide.[27] He was more vulnerable than his peers, and suffered accordingly. Nonetheless, Keita would maintain his position as secretary general of the Guinean RDA affiliate (now renamed the PDG) until 1952, when he was reintegrated into the ranks of the civil service and transferred to Dahomey.[28] His transfer was meant to neutralize him politically and to

---

[22] *Semaine Politique et Sociale en Guinée*, Nov. 13-20, 1950, ANS 17G573.

[23] "En Correctionelle," *la Voix de la Guinée*, 29, Aug. 10-17, 1950; 32, Aug. 24–Sept. 7, 1950; also, Lewin (2009), 142–43.

[24] The article in question appears to have been Erdéa, "Montout, Colonialist Nègre,' *Coup de Bambou*, 6, April 14, 1950. Lewin states that Touré signed articles under that name; (2009), 142–43.

[25] After the PDG broke its ties with the French Communist Party on the orders of the interterritorial RDA and of Félix Houphouët-Boigny in 1950, Keita would contest Touré's accommodationist alliance with Houphouët-Boigny; *Note sur la Position Politique Actuelle de Madeira Keita*, n.d. (Dec. 13, 1951), ANS 17G573. The maneuvering behind this disaffiliation is detailed most recently in Schmidt (2007a), ch. 2.

[26] Cooper (1996), 311, 412–13.

[27] Morgenthau notes that "in French law, trade unionists had special legal protection"; (1964), 227.

[28] On his position within the PDG, see Territoire du Niger, *Renseignements a/s Copie Document PDG*, July 3, 1952, #530/C/355/PS, ANS 17G573. On the transfer to

decapitate the PDG, just as Guinea's security chief had proposed four years earlier.

For a short time it would seem to have worked, but Keita's political career was far from over. In 1956, he was reassigned to Bamako, where he quickly rose in the ranks of the US-RDA. By then, Sékou Touré had long filled the void opened by his departure from Conakry. From Bamako, Keita reported to his colleagues on the political situation in Guinea, where opposition to the RDA remained strong and electoral violence was common. Keita argued that much of the violence was ginned up by the colonial administration and that the stakes in Guinea were particularly high.[29] This proved prescient. In 1958, Guinea would be the only territory to refuse to join the French Community under the constitution of the Fifth Republic. By rejecting that constitution in a referendum, the country would gain immediate independence. Within months, Keita would be leading the negotiations for Soudan's own exit from the French empire.

Overlooking the politics of Keita and his allies contributes to the misapprehension that francophone Africa was "always" neocolonial, and it occludes the region's tradition of political radicalism. What it meant to be anticolonial changed over time. In the 1940s, it meant contesting the dual authority of French administrators and canton chiefs in the countryside, demanding equal pay for equal work in the formal sector, and struggling to give content to the promise of colonial citizenship held out by the Fourth Republic and its French Union. By 1960, it meant seeking distance from France on an international stage. Concretely, it was expressed through support for the Algerian revolution and nonalignment, attempts to establish multiterritorial political units such as the Mali Federation or the Ghana–Guinea–Mali union, the expulsion of French military bases, and the creation of national currencies. Abolition of the chieftaincy represented an important fourth element. In different ways, Mali and Guinea pursued each of those objectives, but at its heart this was a transterritorial politics, just as the RDA was a transterritorial party.

Dahomey, see *Notes Africaines* 57 (1953), 32. Riven by regionalism and skeptical of federation (the raison d'être of the RDA), Dahomey lacked a strong RDA affiliate party; Morgenthau (1964), 315–16. I have found no trace of political activities on Keita's part while in Dahomey; this question requires further research.

[29] Madeira Keita, "ancien secrétaire général du PDG, pour le Bureau Politique de l'Union Soudanaise," *Etude sur les évenements de Conakry*, Nov. 1956, attached to Direction des Services de Police, Territoire du Soudan Français, "Renseignements...," no. 239/CL/SU, Nov. 27, 1956, ANM NII 1E1244.

THE SOCIOLOGIST'S ASSISTANT

In 1948 such events were years in the future. Nonetheless, recognizing Keita's political commitments and establishing the weight of his influence are necessary steps in understanding the context in which Balandier would produce his canonical diagnosis of "the colonial situation."[30] Keita's career as a militant and party leader was intertwined with his work as a researcher and archivist. Other leading RDA militants also worked for IFAN, but Keita would become the most politically powerful of them.[31] His exposure to the social sciences colored the ways in which Keita thought about two of the key social issues – youth and urbanization – that would animate postcolonial politics, and it informed his vision of a closely related problem that would provoke great controversy in Mali, namely the reform of marriage and marriage payments.[32] In short, illuminating the political commitments Keita brought to the intellectual project in which he was engaged reveals a complex shared lineage of particular, historically situated forms of anticolonial politics and social science.

It is hard to imagine that Keita's years with IFAN had no effect on his approach to political problems. The nature of that effect cannot be

---

[30] First published in 1951, "*La Situation Coloniale: Approche Théorique*" is the rare academic article to spark (and to merit) sustained engagement on the fiftieth anniversary of its publication and in the years since; Balandier (1951). On the article's canonical status, see Copans (2001a; 2001b); Smouts (2007); and Saada (2002b), which includes Balandier (2002); Conklin (2002). See also Cooper (2005), Chapter 2.

[31] Other Soudanese active in both the RDA and IFAN were Mamby Sidibe and Dominique Traore. Sidibe established IFAN in Niamey in 1944 and Traore became "head of the ethnography laboratory" in Bamako; Jézéquel (2007), 161. Sidibe was an early, leading member of the RDA in Niger and Soudan and the doyen of Soudan's Territorial Assembly, an important point in West African politics; *Assemblée Territorial, Soudan Français – Procès-Verbaux, Session Ordinaire*, March–April 1953. He was also a proponent of reforming the chieftaincy by marginalizing the powerful canton chiefs and submitting the village chiefs to elections; this policy was in keeping with US-RDA's drive toward the gradual abolition of the chieftaincy (see Chapter 2). See Mamby Sidibé, "Soudan: Justice ou Bon Plaisir?" *Afrique Nouvelle* (Dakar), 7, Jan. 17, 1952; Snyder (1965), 11–13, 40–41. Belonging to an older generation, Traore's political career was more limited. However, at the founding RDA congress in 1946, he served as president of the Commission on Social Issues, for which Madeira Keita served as secretary; Lisette (1983), 36–41. Another important figure in the early RDA, the Dahomeyan S.A. Adande, worked for IFAN in Dakar. He became Minister of Justice in independent Dahomey (later Benin); Adedze, (2003), 39.

[32] The best work on youth and urbanization in this period remains Meillassoux (1968). Marriage reform under the US-RDA was immensely important politically; see Burrill (in press). Here mention should be made of two of Keita's early publications: "La Famille et le Marriage chez lez Tyapi," *Etudes Guinéennes* 2 (1947), 63–66; "Aperçu Sommaire sur les Raisons de la Polygamie chez les Malinké," *Etudes Guinéennes* 4 (1950), 49–55.

assumed; the traditionalist intellectual Amadou Hampaté Bâ, then the sole African to hold the same rank at IFAN, was closely allied with an officer in French military intelligence, Commandant Marcel Cardaire, who in his scientific endeavors, was in turn a protégé of the influential ethnographer Marcel Griaule.[33] Together, Bâ and Cardaire sought to protect what they saw as a distinctly African Sufi tradition from West African, Egyptian, and Saudi reformers. Keita, on the other hand, participated in studies of emerging urban societies undertaken from a theoretical perspective attentive to relations of power and committed to engaging with the dynamism of the objects of study. He was involved with one of the most innovative of the social science research agendas then at work in francophone Africa, one that tried to take the measure of contemporary African social life as it was lived, while recognizing that political struggle loomed large within it.

In IFAN-Conakry, that innovative agenda was in its infancy. Nonetheless, it is worth lingering there, while considering the research center as a kind of workshop in which the spheres of social science and politics (understood narrowly in terms of activism, and broadly as an ethics) were not entirely distinct.[34] In the last years of the Second World War, just before he began to build the Guinean RDA, Keita worked to establish the new IFAN center in Conakry and to organize the colony's archives. On a peninsula jutting from Guinea's coast into the Atlantic, Keita labored alongside Ray Autra in a recently abandoned leprosarium that lay at the end of the road dividing the city's European and African cemeteries. In another part of the former leprosarium, which served as an antechamber to the burial ground, the bodies of Africans would linger before burial, the cemetery reserved for them being so crowded that still decomposing corpses often had to be to be displaced to make room for new ones.[35] Here, in the intermittent absence of a European director, Keita remained a librarian-archivist "responsible for day-to-day

---

[33] Only one African in French West Africa held a higher rank than Bâ and Keita. On IFAN's hierarchy, see *Décision Constatant les Passages d'Echelon des Fonctionnaires du Cadre Superieur de l'IFAN*, April 17, 1958, ANM NIII 2G1317. On Cardaire, Bâ, and the counterreform movement, see Brenner (2001, 2000). Bâ would go on to direct Mali's Institut des Sciences Humaines, which succeeded IFAN-Soudan, before serving as ambassador to Cote d'Ivoire and dedicating himself to his literary career.

[34] Here my interpretation of IFAN-Conakry diverges sharply from those of Benoît de l'Estoile and Agbenyega Adedze, who see the IFAN organization as a whole as an instrument centralized in Dakar to practice a social science designed to further colonial rule; see de l'Estoile (2005); Adedze (2003).

[35] Moving the African cemetery to a more accommodating site was one of the RDA's first successful initiatives; Autra (1964), 14 n18; Balandier (1948a), 401.

administration and financial management."³⁶ Mere days after returning to Conakry from the founding Congress of the RDA in Bamako in October 1946, he went to the port to welcome the center's new director, who was arriving from Dakar.³⁷ Relations that Balandier would later describe as "affectionate, friendly" and "not very hierarchical" began there, in a situation that could hardly have been more colonial, as the Frenchman assumed the leadership of IFAN-Conakry. For Balandier, Conakry would represent a transformative episode in his political awakening. When he left Guinea in August 1947, Keita was "the only person who came to see [him] off ... standing helpless in the rain ... in that primitive and sinister Conakry airport."³⁸ After his departure, it would appear that Keita once again took over the day-to-day running of the Institute under the supervision of Jean Poujade, a jurist presiding over the city's court.³⁹

As the publications emerging from this place, and more broadly this moment, make clear, in the brief period that Balandier and Keita worked together, IFAN-Conakry had begun to incubate a critical, politically engaged social science. At the time, the IFAN centers of the different French African colonies were establishing their own journals; in Conakry Balandier launched *Etudes Guinéennes*, asserting in an editorial foreword, "We have to go beyond the stage of picturesque relations and colonial novels. There is more here than those childish surroundings. There are men who are neither as simple – you know the classic assimilation of the Black man to a child – nor as strange – when the observer relied on superficial impressions – as it was customary to say. In this domain," he wrote, "everything remains to be done (*nous avons tout à faire*)" in order to understand what Guinea had been historically and to attempt "a thorough and objective analysis" of what it was

---

[36] *Notes Africaines* 37 (Jan. 1948). Keita appears to have been acting director of the institute from its founding early in 1944 until the arrival of Raymond Schnell, a botanist, in November of that year. Schnell served as director for one year. A three-month interval separated his departure and the arrival of his replacement, Jean Joire, who served from February to July 1946. In November 1946, Balandier arrived. He left in August. Keita appears to have served as acting director during each moment of transition until Balandier's arrival, even if he did not hold that title. The best account of IFAN-Guinea in these years is Autra (1964). See also IFAN-Guinea A1/17, Collection IFAN-Dakar. I thank Dr. Jean-Hervé Jézéquel for sharing his photographs of this collection with me.

[37] Mamadou Madeira Keita to M. le Directeur de l'IFAN-Dakar (Théodore Monod), Nov. 15, 1946, IFAN-Guinea A1/17, Collection IFAN-Dakar.

[38] Balandier (1966), 230; Balandier, Steinmetz, and Sapiro (2010), 53.

[39] "Activités du Centre (2' semestre 1947)," *Etudes Guinéennes* 2 (1947), 77; "CentrIFAN 'Guinée,'" *Notes Africaines* 37 (1948), 12, 16.

becoming.[40] In the pages that followed, both men wrote on issues that would continue to capture their interest in the years to come. Balandier, in an article on "*Ethnologie et Psychologie*" in the very first number of the new journal, would embark on an exploration of the relationship between the two fields of inquiry that would also animate "*la Situation Coloniale.*"[41] In it, he rejected the ethnographic impulse to offer totalizing portraits of "pure" or traditional collectivities and insisted instead on the study of "societies *as they are now.*"[42] Based on concrete examples, such studies would need to focus on individuals, not groups. That is where psychology came in, as a necessary tool for ethnographers committed to analyzing in a rigorous and concrete fashion life as it was lived by individual people.

Madeira Keita's article in the same number illustrated just how difficult that task would be, even as it seemed to ignore Balandier's advice. Qualified by an editorial footnote – surely Balandier's – specifying that Keita drew his own examples from "the Malinké of the regions of Kouroussa and Kankan," "*le Noir et le secret*" suggested a paradox between the rapidity with which news traveled in rural Africa and the high value African societies placed on discretion, secrecy, and "esotericism." In it, Keita noted that faced with "metropolitan and even native researchers ... informants are reticent ... they lead the interviewer astray. They are perfectly aware that 'paper' is very indiscreet."[43] He went on to

---

[40] Balandier, "les Etudes Guinéennes," *Etudes Guinéennes* 1 (1947), 5–6; Balandier (1977), 64. Adedze misapprehends this journal and its stance, assuming like de l'Estoile that its financing and institutional structure entirely predicated its politics. He fails to note the evolution of *Etudes Guinéennes* after the departure of Balandier and Keita, when it became much weaker; Adedze (2003), 342.

[41] The pairing was a crucial element of the original argument. The perspective behind it can be seen in "*le Noir est un Homme.*" It juxtaposes rather sharply with a contemporary concern to reassert the historicity of diverse "colonial situations," both in their particularity and in their broadly comparative dimensions, including across the *longue durée*. In other words, in a strand of work conversant with avowedly postcolonial work but skeptical of both its novelty and the ambition of some of its claims, historical reasoning is now assigned a task similar to that once given to psychology. See Bayart (2011); Burbank and Cooper (2008); Cooper (2005); Schaub (2008); and Stora (2007). As Emmanuelle Sibeud has observed, the pre-eminent role accorded to history, rather than to literature, distinguishes a predominantly francophone conversation around postcolonial scholarship from a predominantly Anglophone one; Sibeud (2007); Smouts (2007). The volume edited by Patrick Weil and Stéphane Dufoix represents a significant and relatively early intervention in this regard; Weil and Dufoix, eds. (2005).

[42] Balandier, "Ethnologie et Psychologie," *Etudes Guinéennes* 1 (1947), 47–54. Emphasis in the original.

[43] Madeira Keita, "Le Noir et le Secret," *Etudes Guinéennes* 1 (1947), 69–78; see 77.

note that a *griot* (traditionalist) had told him as much when his questions on the history of the Mali empire (13–16 c.) had gone too far: "We cannot give you the information that you want. You will write it down for the schools, and we will lose a source of income."[44] No native informant, Keita had gone beyond transcription and translation to lay bare the material conditions in which knowledge was produced and exchanged.

Given his political activities at the time, it is perhaps understandable that in the pages of *Etudes Guinéennes*, Keita was as discreet as his informants. Nonetheless, in a review dominated by European authors, he would publish two other articles. They are notable less for the richness of their exposition – very brief pieces were the norm at the time – than for their author and their subject matter. The first, "*la Famille et le mariage chez les Tyapi*," comments favorably on marriage practices among a very small ethnic group that favored "the liberty of the individual, and especially of women," emphasized a bride's consent, and kept marriage payments modest.[45] The article, however, would seem to have been drawn from the archive, rather than the field. Based, as a footnote to the title explains, on an administrator's 1910 response to a questionnaire from the *Société anti-esclavagiste de la France*, this short piece is evidence of Balandier's policy of publishing the rich material on Guinea that could be found in the colony's archives, which Keita managed.[46] In the second article, on his own ethnic group, the Malinké, Keita broached the questions of polygyny, bride-wealth, and levirate marriage. With a mild critique of previous ethnographic work on the question, which poorly understood the economic motives of polygyny and tended to regard the widow in a levirate marriage as "movable goods" (*un bien mobilier*), Keita suggested that economic and political forces had begun to change these family structures in fundamental ways. Levirate marriage was on the way out, the family itself had lost its cohesion, and women of all social classes were waging a "patient, stubborn" campaign against polygyny. That campaign, he wagered presciently, would prove to be a long one.[47]

---

[44] Keita, "le Noir," 78. Part of Keita's duties at IFAN included transcribing the discourse of griots; "Activités du Centre (1' semestre 1948)," *Etudes Guinéennes* 3 (1949), 84.

[45] Keita, "la Famille," 66.

[46] Indeed, two other articles in the same number were the work of a colonial administrator, A. Delacour, who had written them in 1910. Keita and Balandier had drawn them from the archives, and Balandier had made minor adjustments to "Sociétés Secrètes." See Delacour, "La Propriété et ses Modes de Transmission chez les Coniagui et les Bassari," *Etudes Guinéennes* 2 (1947, 53–56; and "Sociétés Secrètes chez les Tenda," *Etudes Guinéennes* 2 (1947), 37–52.

[47] Keita, "Aperçu Sommaire."

Knowing the Postcolony

These were observations made without real method. Still, they testified to a particular way of seeing the world – as had Keita's first published work in 1938[48] – and their subject matter would prove more than pertinent to Keita's political and administrative career. In the absence of direct evidence, one can only wonder if he found the time to revisit his notes on secrecy when, a few short years later, he became Minister of Information for the République Soudanaise. By the same token, if it seems unlikely that his mind turned toward the pages of *Etudes Guinéennes* when the US-RDA debated its new marriage code a decade later, he would have been one of the few people in the room to have thought systematically about the issue from both within and beyond a social scientific frame of analysis still then moving beyond the frames of ethnicity and custom.

Another journal was just beginning to appear at the same time. *Présence Africaine* is rather better known than *Etudes Guinéennes*, but Balandier had a role in the creation of both.[49] Both he and Keita would publish in its pages, although the latter's contribution would appear only in 1960.[50] In addition to holding a place on the editorial committee of the new review, Balandier published a set of quite distinct articles in its first numbers. "*Femmes possédées et leurs chants*" would have been at home in *Etudes Guinéennes*, were it not for its setting in the Lébu villages between Dakar and Rufisque where Balandier had conducted his first research on the continent. However, "*l'Or de la Guinée Française*," "*Erreurs noires*," and "*le Noir est un homme*" reveal another side of Balandier's emerging perspective.[51] They both echo and go beyond what Balandier had published in *Etudes Guinéenes*; not for the last time, his work published in France re-assembled and refined his work published in Africa. "*Erreurs noires*" and "*le Noir est un homme*" argue for what might now be termed a critical antiracialism, and the latter article, which appeared in the first number of *Présence Africaine*, resonates strongly with Balandier's editorial foreword to the first number of *Etudes Guinéennes*. "*Erreurs noires*" is

---

[48] Madeira Keita, "Tombouctou: notes de voyage (septembre-octobre 1937)," *Bulletin d'Information et de Renseignments du GGAOF*, 192, May 9, 1938, 142–44.

[49] As indeed did Guinean anticolonialism. After Balandier's departure from the editorial board of *Présence Africaine*, Ray Autra joined the board beginning with the new series in 1955. Autra would become *Directeur adjoint* of IFAN-Conakry, and in 1965, director of the renamed *Institut National de Recherches et de Documentation*. He would relaunch *Etudes Guinéennes* as *Recherches Africaines* in 1960; Autra (1964). In 1961, he was imprisoned by Sékou Touré. On his release, he returned to the institute before being named ambassador to Algeria.

[50] Madeira Keita (1960).

[51] Here my reading differs from that of Hassan (1999).

even more striking, as Balandier states bluntly the anticolonialists' antagonism toward the canton chiefs yet dissimulates the identity of his interlocutor, who is clearly Keita. Keita accuses the chiefs of "collaboration," and Balandier ponders this word, still a powerful one in the wake of the war, coming to it as an existentialist. "On whom do scorn and the blow of the whip fall," the article asks? "On the slave (*nègre*), on the Jew, on you who accept it."[52] Even if Keita's name was obscured, the links between a specific anticolonial politics and the intellectual world of the new journal could not have been more evident.

Following Balandier's own injunctive, let us continue to privilege the concrete. A brief empirical article, "*l'Or de la Guinée Française*" offers a tantalizing hint of the links between fieldwork and political activism.[53] A study of "artisanal" gold-mining around Siguiri – the region bordering those Keita studied in "*Aperçu sommaire ...*" and "*le Noir et le secret*" – "*l'Or*" is the product of fieldwork possibly conducted with Madeira Keita, including translations of several terms from Malinké into French.[54] In the article, Balandier reports visiting a site along the road to Bamako where as many as 10,000 people were at work; he notes that other sites supported populations twice as large.[55] These were not industrial sites; they were smallholdings worked by hand. The limited role industrial technology and capital played in the process of mining, as well as the diminished presence of political institutions, rendered the mines a productive yet inchoate space, one in which "the ethnic community ... breaks apart in favor of the cosmopolitan society that is established at the placer mine. This becomes, for a good half of the year, the real living [social] unit, to the detriment of the village. It demonstrates, in its political and ritual aspects, flexibility and eclecticism."[56] In short, social life was regenerated beyond the confines of the village, in innovative and improvised sites that resembled cities less than camps.

While for Balandier the mines were dynamic sites to be analyzed scientifically, Keita and his comrades sought to mobilize Siguiri politically. In

---

[52] Keita is identified elsewhere by name, but here by his initials; Balandier (1948a), 400, 403–04.
[53] Balandier would return to this theme and this research in *Ambiguous Africa*; (1966), 65–75.
[54] It is also possible that this fieldwork was conducted with Ray Autra or another Malinké-speaking IFAN research assistant. However, Autra does not figure prominently in Balandier's memoirs. To the contrary, Keita does, and the publications of Keita and Balandier suggest very strongly that they conducted their research in the same places and times, as do Keita's other activities.
[55] Balandier (1948b), 523.
[56] Balandier (1948b), 547.

other words, what Balandier saw – a new, nonethnically bound community coming into being – the RDA sought to realize as a political party organized around a common cause, rather than ethnic or regional affinities. Keita's own traces in Siguiri are unclear, but the sequence is suggestive. In the first number of *Etudes Guinéennes* in 1947, Keita reported that Balandier had undertaken fieldwork there; this was clearly the trip from which the *Présence Africaine* article was drawn.[57] A year later, in *Phare de Guinée*, an RDA newspaper that both Touré and Keita helped to edit, one of the party's allies, the ethnic and regionalist Union du Mandé, published an editorial opposing plans by the colonial administration to establish a cooperative structure in the gold mines.[58] The administration's move was portrayed as a naked attempt to stabilize the mines and control the market in gold while keeping prices artificially low. Itinerant miners would thereby be pushed out of a market that they had created and away from sites that they had opened up. Meanwhile, implied the article, African gold traders and middlemen would be cut out of the formal sector and forced into smuggling. Better to invest in modern methods of production and regulate conditions of labor than to regulate the market itself, it was argued.[59] The Union's intervention had echoes in Paris, where Guinea's Mamba Sano and other RDA representatives proposed legislation liberalizing the West African gold market.[60] In doing so, the party hoped to secure the patronage of Dioula traders and the support of the Union du Mandé. In the end, it would lose the latter.

In any case, the article is not Keita's. His traces can be found elsewhere. Keita and his long-time ally Dr. Koniba Pléah, who was stationed in Siguiri, established an RDA section in the town in November, 1948, thereby bringing competition between the Union du Mandé and the RDA into the open.[61] Originally from Soudan, Pléah had only arrived in

---

[57] M. K. (sic; Madeira Keita), "Notes," *Etudes Guinéennes* 1, 1 (1947). The mines were then producing a small fraction of what they had before the war; "Siguiri: Reprise de l'Activité des Mines d'Or," *la Guinée Française*, 2094, Feb. 11, 1947; Balandier (1948b), 539.

[58] Union du Mandé, "A Propos de la Coopérative de l'Orpaillage," *La Phare de Guinée*, 7, Feb. 1948 (article dated Jan. 2, 1948). Keita had briefly succeeded in incorporating this regionalist party, of which Sékou Touré had been an early member, into the Guinean RDA; *Renseignements, Origine: Conakry*, July 13, 1947, ANS 17G573; letter of Madeira Keita to Jean Suret-Canale, April 17, 1987, Fonds Suret-Canale, ADSSD 229J65; Lewin (2009), 95–96. The party would soon join an anti-RDA coalition; *Voix de la Guinée*, 1, Aug. 7, 1949; *Coup de Bambou*, 5, April 12, 1950.

[59] Here Balandier would have disagreed. Capital-intensive, industrial mining had never proven profitable in the area; Balandier (1948b), 542, 545.

[60] Lisette (1983), 175.

[61] In a letter, Pléah characterized the Union du Mandé as a regionalist party holding contradictory positions; Pléah to Doudou Guèye, Oct. 12, 1948, BPN 136d528.

Guinea the year before. He had quickly fallen into the orbit of Keita, his "*koro*" or "elder brother," lodging with him in Conakry and "accompanying him in Communism."[62] Posted to Siguiri by the colonial medical service in June 1948, he would only last six months there, having incurred the enmity of both the colonial administrator, a strong Gaullist with whom Keita had clashed, and of the Union du Mandé.[63] By the time he was transferred elsewhere, Pléah's organizational work had already been done, but the biggest political question remained the mines: Who had the right to work them, who set the prices, and to whom did the subsoil belong? With Pléah gone, and the alliance between the RDA and the Union du Mandé broken – but before the RDA split with the PCF – the administration would give the Union what it sought: a free market in gold and assurance that the mineral wealth of the Siguiri region would constitute a *"reserve indigène"* closed to European mining companies.[64]

From the mines around Siguiri, questions emerge. Was the kind of political work Keita engaged in merely incidental to the work of social scientific research? Did this climate of anticolonial activism and political maneuvering influence Balandier's study of Guinea's gold fields, or his later diagnosis of the "Colonial Situation"? Did anticolonial politics and engaged social science go hand in hand, or did they simply happen to run on parallel tracks? In any case, even before Siguiri, the paths of Keita and Balandier had already diverged. Keita would soon endure persecution, repression, and unemployment. Having in his telling been hustled out of Guinea in August 1947, Balandier had been reassigned to French Equatorial Africa, a posting considered one of the least desirable in the empire.[65]

THE "COLONIAL SITUATION" IN WEST AND CENTRAL AFRICA

There, in the Fang villages of northern Gabon, Balandier encountered a crisis of social reproduction that he attributed to what he would term "the colonial situation."[66] In 1950, that argument moved from embryonic form

---

[62] Pléah to Doudou Guèye, Oct. 12, 1948; Pléah to S.-G. du Symepharsa (sic; Professional Trade Union of African Doctors, Pharmacists, and Midwives of Guinea), March 7, 1949, BPN 136d528.

[63] *Renseignements, Origine Kankan, a/s Activités du Médecin Africain Koniba Pléah, en Service à Siguri*, Dec. 19, 1948, ANS 17G573; Pléah to S.G. du Symepharsa, March 7, 1949, BPN 136d528.

[64] *Voix de la Guinée*, 24, July 6-13, 1950; 27, July 27–Aug. 3, 1950; 31, Aug. 24–31, 1950.

[65] Balandier, Steinmetz, and Sapiro (2010), 53.

[66] On Balandier's work in Gabon see Mann (2013a), 109–14.

in the *Bulletin* of the Institut d'Etudes Centrafricains in Brazzaville to an article on "Aspects de l'évolution sociale chez les Fang du Gabon" in *Cahiers Internationaux de Sociologie*. The next year it would achieve its mature expression in the same pages as "*la Situation coloniale.*" In that canonical article, Balandier would argue that contemporary Africa represented a particular situation in which colonized society – African societies – and colonial society – that for which empire was a condition of its existence and reproduction – formed an ensemble or system that had to be studied in its concrete manifestations and as a totality ("*en tant que totalité ... [ou] un complexe*").[67] Anthropology had failed to capture the dynamism of colonized societies because it was caught between theorists in search of purity and applied anthropologists slavishly devoted to empiricism.[68] Sociology was the best instrument for such a study, he argued. "Dynamist" and "engaged," it represented a discipline suited to a "new Africa."[69] His preference for sociology harmonized with that of a nascent African intelligentsia which rejected with increasing vehemence the traditionalist, even "folkloric," ethnographic approach that seemed to them – and to him – to characterize the discipline of anthropology.[70]

---

[67] It has been argued that Balandier adopted the concept of the "situation" from Max Gluckman while being informed by the sociology of Marcel Mauss; Naepels (2010); Cooper (2005), 35–36. See Gluckman, *Analysis of a Social Situation in Modern Zululand*, which was originally published in *Bantu Studies* 14, 1 (March 1940) and 14, 2 (June 1940), and in *African Studies* 1, 4 (Dec. 1942) and later republished in book form (1958). However, Balandier's sources for the phrase and the concept were multiple, and Gluckman may not have been the most important among them; Copans (2001b). In both the eponymous article and in a forerunner to it published in the same journal one year earlier, Balandier cites the psychologist Octave Mannoni as his source for the phrase "*la situation coloniale,*" while tracing it back to Louis Wirth; (1951), 46; (1950a), see 77. Indeed, one section of Mannoni's *Psychologie de la Colonisation* is entitled "*la Situation Coloniale et le Racisme*"; (1950), 108–120, see also 10–11. Balandier was originally less hostile to Mannoni's project than some readings of "*la Situation Coloniale*" suggest. In a review of the book, he proclaimed it "brilliant" if deeply flawed and lacking specificity and methodological rigor, and it inspired a second article by him as well; see his review (1950b) and (1952). Finally, the concept of the "situation" played an important role in the existentialist philosophy of Jean-Paul Sartre, who published the first of a series of collected writings under the title *Situations* with Gallimard in 1947. Sartre's influence on Balandier's writing is apparent in the young social scientist's first articles in *Présence Africaine*, for which both men sat on the editorial board. Balandier discusses the existentialist influence in (2002).

[68] Balandier (1951), 45–6, 76. For astounding evidence of this impasse, see Godelier (2005), 252.

[69] Balandier (1955; 2nd ed., 1985), ix. See also Balandier (1955a); Balandier (1965); Copans (2010), 88–9.

[70] Copans (2010). Ironically, Balandier made precisely this point in a note on a 1949 conference of Africanists in Ibadan, Nigeria ... one to which the delegation from French Equatorial Africa (AEF), included no Africans; Balandier (1950c), 80. For a defense of the ethnographic approach by one of Balandier's primary targets, see Griaule (1948).

Those insights – the political lessons learned mostly in Guinea, the scientific ones in Gabon – would animate Balandier's work in the years to come, including his 1955 *Sociologie des Brazzavilles noires* (note the plural). There, Balandier would insist that the city and the rural areas were interdependent, a relationship in which the role of the colonial state could not be discounted.[71] Among francophone social scientists Balandier's work was innovative in that he significantly modified the long-prevalent thesis that Africans experienced urbanization as a form of "uprootedness" (*déracinement*) in which their static or primitive societies were transformed.[72] He recognized that the future of the city in Africa was neither colonial nor "White," and he never ignored the intensity or rapidity of the transformation that mid-twentieth century African societies were experiencing.

SOCIALIST GOVERNMENT AND "SOCIOLOGY"

Keita and Balandier would not experience that transformation together. While Balandier observed it, Keita would attempt to master it. In 1956, in the wake of the *loi cadre* (framework law) that established territorial autonomy by dissolving the federal government in Dakar, Keita returned from his political exile in Dahomey to his home territory of Soudan Français. There he worked as an archivist and served as interim director of the IFAN center.[73] As that colony became an internally governed territory, and then a Republic within the French Community, he rose in the ranks of government as well as within the US-RDA.[74] Keita's roots in Guinea's early anticolonial politics, Conakry's GEC, and the

---

[71] Balandier (1955), 32–45.
[72] For a rich and relevant attempt to think through such social developments, see Meillassoux (1968). Meillassoux was a student and something of an acolyte of Balandier. He was also attentive to Madeira Keita's status as an anticolonial social scientist who had become a powerful minister. Meillassoux pays homage to Keita in the book's preface, but in his fieldnotes rues the suspicion he encountered from Keita in his role as Minister of the Interior; Fonds Meillassoux, B7.2, B7.3. Keita's attitude may have been conditioned by the fact that before training under Balandier, Meillassoux had worked as a translator in the United States. Indeed, *Urbanization of an African Community*, his major study of Bamako in the 1960s, was written in English and still awaits publication in French.
[73] *Notes Africaines*, 72 (1956); *Rapport Annuel de l'IFAN, 1956*, ANS 2G56–6; *Rapport Annuel de l'IFAN, 1957*, ANS 2G57–20.
[74] At independence, Keita would become Minister of Defense and Security, later serving as Minister of Information, of Labor and of Justice. *Notice de Renseignement*..., ANM NIII 1C1542; Imperato and Imperato (2008), 169; *Livre d'Or de la République du Mali* (1963); and int., Papa Madeira Keita, Bamako, June 21, 2008.

transterritorial RDA meant that his presence in Soudan strengthened the hand of the US-RDA's more militant wing – figures such as Aoua Keita, Seydou Badian Kouyaté, and Mamadou Gologo – against the more moderate party leader Mamadou Konaté and his allies, such as Jean-Marie Kone. In fact, Madeira Keita almost certainly served to "stiffen" the politics of the US-RDA in the wake of Konaté's sudden death from hepatitis in 1956. In May 1957, he was named Minister of the Interior of the Territory of Soudan. It was his signature as minister – not that of head of government and US-RDA Secretary General Modibo Keita – that authorized the strongest single move against the colonial system made before independence, namely the dismantling of the chieftaincy and the gradual dismissal of the *chefs de canton* beginning late in 1957.[75] He would remain in government through independence in 1960, acting as a leader of the delegation that negotiated the Mali Federation's emergence within the French Community and as a key figure in establishing the Republic of Mali in the wake of the Federation's collapse in August. That same year, the editors of *Présence Africaine* claimed that he was "as popular in Guinea as Sékou Touré himself" even though he had left the country nearly a decade earlier.[76]

In Mali, Madeira Keita was more powerful than popular.[77] Under the socialist government of Modibo Keita from 1960 to 1968, he occupied various ministerial posts, changing one portfolio for another, but never leaving government. Madeira Keita's political influence would wax and wane, but his ministerial positions served as a barometer or bellwether of "radical" influence within the politburo, or *Bureau Politique Nationale* (BPN).[78] A well-informed French ambassador considered him both the most pro-Soviet and the most "xenophobic," meaning anti-Western, of the Malian leadership.[79] Keita consistently held hard-line positions; for instance, in the wake of a high-profile treason case in 1962, he argued that, were it up to him, death sentences handed down by Popular Tribunals

---

[75] See Chapter 2.

[76] Editorial footnote to Keita (1960), 3.

[77] For instance, Keita lived in a protected villa on the edge of Bamako, in what is now Korofina Nord, rather than in a popular neighborhood; Campmas (1976), 470; author's fieldnotes, June 21, 2008. Villas in that neighborhood were the subject of popular criticism; *Synthèse des Procès-Verbaux d'Assemblées Générales tenues les 11 et 12 Sept 1967 dans les comités de Bamako I par les délégués du CNDR*, BPN 50d138.

[78] Ambassador France to S. E. M. Couve de Murville, Ministère des Affaires Etrangères (MAE, France), Sept. 18, 1962, #258, 2522, MAE.

[79] Pierre Pelen, Ambassador of France to Mali to MAE, DAAM, April 28, 1965, #70, 2522, MAE.

would be carried out expeditiously.[80] Although he lost that particular battle, the CIA recognized him as a leader of the "younger militants" within the Party and one of the most powerful voices in the BPN, which was the heart of government under the US-RDA.[81] Within what had become a single-party state,[82] Keita served as a member of the party's ruling bodies, the BPN and the *Comité National pour la Défense de la Révolution* (CNDR) that superseded it from August 22, 1967, until the coup d'état of November 19, 1968.

Keita's politics had influenced Balandier greatly at a key moment in his "intellectual conversion."[83] Did the type of analyses of African social life generated by Balandier and his peers influence Keita's vision of the societies he would play such an important role in governing? I argue that they did, but the line is not a taut one. After independence, social scientific knowledge was both produced and consumed in West African capitals including Conakry and Bamako. However, Guinea and Mali never developed social scientific traditions that were as simultaneously "nationalist" and programmatic as was the case in Nasser's Egypt, for example;[84] nor did positivism carry the same weight in what were both scientific and political interventions. Although social science, broadly construed, was valued as a necessary tool of ambitious independent governments, its use was above all rhetorical.[85]

Echoes of the type of social scientific discourse and analyses that emerged from the work Balandier and Keita conducted together can be found in the governing rhetoric of the US-RDA and in the party's theoretical debates on the structure of Malian society. Those echoes emerge in the archives of the US-RDA's BPN and its militia, the Milice Populaire. An engaged sociology not dissimilar from that of *Brazzavilles noires* (1955), *Sociologie Actuelle de l'Afrique Noire* (1955), or *Afrique ambiguë* (1957) can be seen in analyses of

---

[80] *Procès-Verbaux des reunions du BPN, 1962*, BPNCMLN 77. The introduction of the Malian franc had provoked demonstrations in Bamako for which three prominent opponents of the US-RDA – Fily Dabo Sissoko, Hamadoun Dicko, and Kassoum Toure – were held responsible. They would later die in custody; see Chapter 6.

[81] CIA, *Ghana and Mali as exemplars of African Radicalism*, National Intelligence Estimate, July 11, 1962. NSF, Box No. 8, Folder 60, LBJ Presidential Library. See also Mazov, who draws on similar sources; (2010), 155, 218–19. This perception was shared inside the US-RDA; Campmas (1976)

[82] Keita (1960).

[83] The phrase is from M. A. de Suremain, although she places that conversion in Dakar, which Balandier visited before Conakry; de Suremain (2004), 654–55.

[84] This in spite of the urging of Autra (1964). For Egypt, see el Shakry (2007), 218.

[85] Copans (2010).

Knowing the Postcolony

urban disorder generated within the US-RDA and particularly in Keita's Ministry of the Interior. For example, if a long synthetic CNDR/BPN report of 1967 on youth prepared under Keita's ministry had the ring of the familiar, this may well be because key points of its analysis had been heard before. The CNDR/BPN report, part of a discussion in which Keita clearly played an important role, made implicit reference to a vision of the African city that Balandier had developed 10 years earlier:

Leaving to the sociologist the problem of going further into the question [of the link between capitalist modernity and the degradation of morals], one can nevertheless bear in mind the fact that our societies are moving from the stage of closed populations to populations open to the outside world.[86]

In this new phase, the report went on, Mali encountered Western capitalism in decline, and its youth moved quickly from a *"situation innocente"* to a moral crisis. For sociologists, this might be mere food for thought. For an ambitious postcolonial government anxious to maximize rural production, the situation demanded action.

Controlling the youth in Bamako – fighting tea drinking, sexual exuberance, and "moral decline" – had become a predominant concern of the US-RDA by 1967. Young people had access to too much money and freedom of movement, the authority of fathers was weakening, families were in crisis, and sexual liberty abounded. Statistics showed that cases of pregnancy in schools threatened to double in 1967, and rather than being limited to schools, the rise in pregnancy out of wedlock could be seen in the villages as well.[87] These issues directly affected members of the highest ranks of government.[88] Whether in Bamako or in smaller towns, the urban scene remained the key battleground for the preservation of morals as, in the eyes of the US-RDA, exposure to the idle leisure of tea drinking in informal salons (*grinw*) and to dance societies focused on Western music and fashion corrupted youth absolutely.[89] That corruption, particularly in

---

[86] *Rapport de Synthèse sur le problème de la moralité et la licence chez la jeunesse*, 1967, BPN 110d420. The identity of the author of this report is unclear. However, there is good reason to think that Madeira Keita was behind it. In July 1966, the BPN had charged him and Youth Commissioner Gabou Diawara with conducting a study on *"le militant vigilant et responsible [et] la dégradation des moeurs."* P-V, CNDR, July 18, 1966, #5/CNDR, BPN 230d835.

[87] *Rapport de Synthèse*..., BPN 110d420.

[88] Modibo Keita to BPN, various government ministers, May 6, 1967, #161/PG/CSB, BPN 135d527.

[89] See Meillassoux (1968); Rillon (2010); US-RDA, Section de San, Bureau Executif des Jeunes, 4' Conference de Section, *Rapport d'Activités et d'orientation*, May 29, 1967, BPN 103d390.

terms of sexual liberty, was then transmitted to the villages via the very youth organizations – with their evening rehearsals, conferences, and competitions – on which the party relied.[90] Intervention in urban contexts called for urban techniques: more surveillance of cinemas, dances, and parties (*bals* and "*parties-surprise*"), action against hotels and brothels, and control over the circulation of automobiles, which could be used for illicit encounters. The CNDR's counteroffensive to the moral crisis of the nation's youth also had a discursive element. To combat the hedonist philosophy of *yéyéism*, interpreted here as sexual liberty and personal autonomy, the US-RDA leadership sought to promote alternative messages through the same venues by which intelligence was gathered.[91] These problems seemed to call for policing and propaganda, but the analysis applied to them was self-consciously sociological in nature. Governing cadres disdained ethnography as a colonial means of analysis that had sustained the power of Muslim religious leaders, canton chiefs, and elder men, but sociology appeared to be a particularly valid means of analysis of a new society.

As an applied science, sociology shared with African socialism the great theoretical challenge of the absence of classes as such. The US-RDA had long insisted on this point, in spite of strong pressure from Soviet Premier Nikita Khrushchev himself to hew closer to Soviet orthodoxy.[92] At the party's second seminar, held in September 1962, both Madeira Keita and Seydou Badian Kouyaté lectured militants on the need for a socialism "adapted to our realities." They envisioned a Malian socialism that would be built up from the villages and out from the party, one which recognized that Mali's social hierarchies existed independently of control over the means of production.[93] When Kouyaté gave a presentation in Paris based on a book promoting these ideas, he was subject to a blistering critique by the *Association des Etudiants Maliens* (AEM), and notably by the young Ibrahima Ly. Only one student, Victor Sy, rose to defend Kouyaté's position, arguing that "although he is not a Marxist-Leninist,

---

[90] The same phenomenon obtained in Guinea, in which participation in youth organizations was mandatory and more extensive, as was party membership; see Straker (2009). In Mali, the party struggled to subordinate various associations of young people to its own youth wing; Meillassoux (1968).

[91] P-V, CNDR, Jan. 23, 1967, #7/CNDR, BPN 230d835.

[92] Mazov (2010), 9, 221–23.

[93] U.S.-RDA (1962). As Kouyaté would point out, unlike imperial Russia or China, Mali did not have a class of landless peasants, or indeed of small-scale, rural landlords; (1965), 15, 143–44.

I reach out my hand to him ... The essential point is not the class struggle [but that Kouyaté] is advocating socialism." For his peers, however, Kouyaté's socialism substituted a romantic vision of village life for a realistic assessment of the need for class consciousness among urban workers allied with the poor peasantry. They compared, him, damningly, to Tanzania's Julius Nyerere and Senegal's Léopold Sedar Senghor.[94]

Years later, as the party moved into the phase of the "Active Revolution" after 1966, the song remained the same. In 1967, in one of his rare public speeches, Madeira Keita openly rejected the possibility that "social classes" with distinct relationships to modes of production existed in Africa. By arguing that "class conflict" represented a lesser threat to Africa than did neocolonialism, Keita exposed himself to the criticism of students more doctrinaire than he.[95] To the language of class he continued to prefer that of "*couches sociales*," or social strata, a term that Modibo Keita also promoted,[96] and that Balandier employed in his own contemporary discussion of the inadequacies of class as an analytical tool in the African context. Balandier argued that the new African nations were generating innovative social structures to which the analytic categories of sociology would be forced to adapt. In Africa, he noted, "the nation, the state, and modern economies ... are *under construction*"; the only true social class coming into being was defined by its access to political power, not its economic role.[97] Madeira Keita concurred, but he and his comrades had drawn a bolder conclusion: because class distinctions were not acute,

---

[94] *Les Dirigeants Africains face à leur peuple, Ouvrage de Seydou Badian Kouyaté, Conférence du 7 Mars 1965*, and *Compte-Rendu sur la Conférence du 7 Mars 1965 de la FEANF...*, March 12, 1965, #363/AV, vu et transmis par l'ambassadeur Ya Doumbia; BPN 72d211. Ly was a former president of the FEANF, a hard-Left students' organization with which the AEM was affiliated. Under military rule in the 1970s, both Ly and Sy would be imprisoned for their politics; see Chapter 6.

[95] Ambassador Pelen to MAE, DAAM, April 8, 1967, #27. *A/s Conférence de M. Madeira Keita sur l'idéologie et la formation idéologique des cadres*, 2522, MAE.

[96] Modibo Keita spoke of "*couches sociales*" in a conference at Bamako's Ecole Normale d'Administration (ENA) on June 11, 1966. Questions addressed to him on that occasion were skeptical but less overtly hostile than those addressed to Madeira Keita in 1967 and 1968. See Ambassador Pelen to MAE, DAAM, June 18, 1966, #59, 2522, MAE; and Ambassador Pelen to MAE, DAAM, June 14, 1966, #569/573, 2522, MAE. See also Ambassador Pelen to MAE, May 8, 1968, #58/DAM, pg. 3, fn. 1, Bamako 57 CADN. Modibo Keita also used the term in closed CNDR meetings; see, e.g., P-V, CNDR, July 4, 1967, #8/CNDR, BPN 230d835.

[97] Balandier (1965), 133, 141, original emphasis; see also Mercier (1965). The latter part of this argument was pursued in regard to Mali in Amselle (1978, 1985). It had become an important theoretical question. See, e.g., the work of Senegalese sociologist and leader of the Parti Africain de l'Indépendance (PAI) Majhemout Diop; Diop (1971).

countries such as Mali and Guinea could best be governed by single parties like the US-RDA, which encompassed difference within their ranks.[98] Thus, led by its cadres, a party like the US-RDA could realize the social revolution an absent proletariat could not assure. In Guinea, the same intellectual maneuver – insisting on the absence of classes – had helped to subordinate the once powerful labor movement to Sékou Touré's PDG.[99] As the "theoretician" of the US-RDA regime,[100] Madeira Keita seemed to draw on sociology to define an African socialism in which the party cadre, and not the worker, was pre-eminent.

Was anyone listening? In May 1968, over a year after his last public speech, Madeira Keita delivered another on "*la Révolution et son contenu au Mali*," at the Ecole Normale Supérieure in Badalabougou (Bamako). There, Keita found himself confronted by forceful arguments from skeptical students who rejected the government's vision of the Active Revolution, Keita's justification for the creation of the Malian franc and its 1967 devaluation, and his analysis of Malian society. If his language here had sharpened over the last year – he adopted the vocabulary of class – so had that of his audience. Keita was obviously not the only government minister to be interpolated by angry students around the world in that rebellious spring of 1968, but Bamako was not Paris, or even Dakar. In this case, Keita took several dozen questions in a marathon seven-hour meeting. In the judgment of the French ambassador, "The questions asked erred in the lack of political maturity of those who asked them. Others demonstrated indisputable treachery, if not absolute insolence, and M. Madeira Keita was obliged to react strongly to it."[101] In the wake of this embarrassing episode, the CNDR went on the offensive, castigating on Radio Mali and in the daily *l'Essor* those it called the "parrots of Marxism."[102] The National Youth Committee demanded a purge of institutions of "counter-revolutionary intellectuals," while the increasingly powerful

---

[98] Keita (1960).
[99] Cooper (1996), ch. 11.
[100] Ambassador Pelen to MAE, May 8, 1968, #58/DAM, Bamako 57, CADN. Kouyaté might once have held claim to this distinction, but his voice had never been as influential as that of Madeira Keita.
[101] Ambassador Pelen to MAE, May 8, 1968, #58/DAM, Bamako 57, CADN.
[102] Ambassador Pelen to MAE, Tel., chiffrement, May 14, 1968, #405/409, Bamako 57, CADN. "La Conférence du camarade Mamadou Madeira Keita, membre du CNDR, Ministre du Justice et du Travail," *l'Essor*, May 7, 1968, #5371; see also *l'Essor*, May 9, 1968, #5373; May 14, 1968, #5376. In this period Radio Mali and *l'Essor* maintained a hard "Leftist" editorial line; Campmas (1976), 426–27.

militia had two of Madeira Keita's Badalabougou critics hauled in for questioning.[103] There in the transcripts of the interrogation of one of them, the luckless student Djigui Diabate, emerges the question of sociology.[104]

Ironically, the very act of hauling in Diabate spoke to a particular vision of society. Although Radio Mali branded him a "parrot," Diabate was also a griot, and by custom he would have been accorded a broad liberty of expression. Keita and the militia would have none of it, because in their view such traditions relied on unacceptable social hierarchies.[105] All this remained unspoken during Diabate's interrogation, in which class rather than caste became the bone of contention. Although the questions themselves are absent from most of the transcript, Diabate's answers make it clear that he was sparring verbally with adversaries who were easily confused. What was the role of the intellectuals in the Revolution, they apparently asked him? And what was the role of the other social classes? "I'm not a sociologist," he replied, "and I can't offer a complete analysis of social classes, this is beyond my abilities."[106] Diabate's modesty was not necessarily misplaced; he had failed to pass his baccalaureate exam. Why then was he talking about sociology with militiamen? What Diabate expressed as essentially a question of intellectual competence – whether he had the training to propose a more rigorous analysis of Malian society and politics than Keita offered, a point on which he wisely deferred – his interrogators rephrased as the arid intellectualism of a "totally rootless element" who kept the company of a Frenchwoman. The anti-intellectualism of the militia comes as no surprise, and the record of the interrogation comes to no conclusion. Yet the confrontation at Badalabougou and the interrogations that followed demonstrated both the regime's intolerance and the inability of its "theoretician" to control the party's message before a crowd of intellectuals who spoke the same analytical language.[107] Why was that language "sociology"? And what did Djigui Diabate and the militiamen mean by it?

---

[103] Commission Nationale de la Jeunesse, *Rapport de Presentation*, n.d. (1967), BPN 50d138. On the militia, see Mann (2003).
[104] Milice Populaire, Secrétariat Permanent de Bamako, *Note ... sur l'Audition de Djigui Diabate et Yamadou Diallo*, June 3, 1968, BPN 146d568.
[105] Compare the robust practice of internal dissent portrayed in Keita (1960), 11.
[106] *Note ... sur l'Audition de Djigui Diabate ...*, BPN 146d568.
[107] Ambassador Pelen to MAE, May 8, 1968, #58/DAM, Bamako 57, CADN.

SOCIOLOGY AS TALISMAN

Although sociology was taught at Bamako's Ecole Normale in the 1960s – and although the debate over "classes" versus "strata" was a charged one – it would have been an incidental element in the curriculum of the school for party cadres that was launched in 1967.[108] At Mali's new Institut des Sciences Humaines, efforts to create a sociology section had run aground against bureaucratic inertia, in spite of the argument that the initiative would have allowed the government to "link theoretical research to ... social and economic planning."[109] The term "sociology" was not being invoked rigorously by the CNDR, by Djigui Diabate, or by anyone else.[110] Instead sociology served a kind of talismanic function.[111] Yet whether sociology's function was analytic or talismanic mattered little, and it could be both at once. Like other newly independent African governments, and perhaps more directly, the US-RDA looked to sociology, among other disciplines, to provide the tools of analysis for a society experiencing rapid urban and demographic change. It did so partly because the discipline tended to frame its own analyses in terms of changing relations of production rather than of fixed systems of thought grounded in ethnicity, custom, or religion, but it was not ensnared in the concept of class struggle. Most important, it emphasized the possibility of a transformative future, a possibility in which governing cadres were deeply invested.

In 1960, that future seemed imminent, and once-progressive work such as "The Colonial Situation" no longer captured it. Years after George Balandier and Madeira Keita had met at the foot of the gangplank in Conakry, the link between the two men had long waned through force of

[108] *Programme de l'ENS, toutes sections*, 1964, ANM NIII 1G2697; *Rapport de la Commission de Politique Général sur l'ouverture et le fonctionnement de l'école superieure des cadres du parti*, n.d. (1967) and *Rapport de la Commission de Politique Général du CNDR sur le fonctionnement de l'école superieure des cadres du parti*, n.d. (1967), BPN 50d138.

[109] Maurice Godelier, *Proposition pour un programme de developpement de l'Institut des Sciences Humaines du Mali (1964–1968)*, Jan. 1965, BPNCMLN 56.

[110] Copans suggests this rhetorical practice was widespread; (2010), 77.

[111] Its rhetorical power is perhaps best illustrated in the forgotten title given by his publisher, François Maspero, to one of Frantz Fanon's canonical texts. In its 1966 version and in the integral 1968 version which includes Fanon's original preface, *l'An V de la Révolution Algérienne* was presented as the subtitle to *Sociologie d'une Révolution*; Fanon (1968). This is the text published in English as *A Dying Colonialism* or in the original 1965 edition, *Studies in a Dying Colonialism*. The first French edition was published in 1959. Maspero invoked sociology, however loosely and "misleadingly" as the science appropriate to the study of revolution; Macey (2000), 398.

circumstance. The RDA and the PCF had also long parted ways. Nonetheless, lessons first learned in Guinea continued to resonate. Intellectual labor of the kind that Balandier and Keita engaged in generated tools for thinking through phenomena that a newly independent government would define as imminently political, thereby confronting itself with a daunting set of tasks. Convinced that – in the absence of classes – internal impediments to Mali's modernization were grounded in its social structure, the US-RDA set out to stake a bold claim for what government would do: it would reorder society itself. The party would govern aggressively and brook no dissent. In 1968, when Keita and Balandier last saw each other, this strategy had nearly run its course as the party succumbed to cynicism and the use of coercion to pursue ever more implausible economic objectives. At that time, Madeira was a powerful government minister on yet another official trip to Paris. It would be one of his last. In November, a coup led by aggrieved junior officers overthrew the US-RDA government and the military hierarchy with it. Along with Modibo Keita and many other colleagues, Madeira was imprisoned, and he and Balandier lost touch entirely.[112] The coup of 1968 derailed the US-RDA's socialist experiment, but could not reverse all of the party's achievements. Under the party's guidance Mali, like its neighboring territories, had left the fold of the empire for the ranks of "the Third World" constituted as a nation, considered a society – albeit one in which very little space was carved out for civic life or "civil society" distinct from state and party – and called a republic.[113] It is to the last of these characteristics that we now turn.

---

[112] Balandier (1997), 260. Balandier suggests that Keita died in prison, while in fact he lived another twenty years after his release; Balandier, Steinmetz and Sapiro (2010), 53. On Keita's imprisonment see Chapter 6.

[113] The phrase "the Third World" was also tied to Balandier. He had not invented it, but had promoted it, thereby providing at least part of the intellectual scaffolding for constructing a new world of independent nation-states and dismantling empires. Balandier, ed., (1956); Balandier, Steinmetz and Sapiro (2010), 57.

2

A New Republic

Long before its socialist experiment had come to an abrupt end, Mali, like its neighbors, had been dubbed a republic twice over: in 1958, still within the French Community, as Soudan and in 1960 as Mali. Setting the new republic in its West African and French imperial context, this chapter measures its emergence via two transformations that came largely from without – the end of the *indigénat* and the enfranchisement of women (first as mothers, later as female citizens, but always as women) – and one that came from within, the abolition of the canton chiefs and the sketching out of an unfinished blueprint for rural democracy. Those transformations gave meaning to the idea of a republic of citizens in the postcolonial Sahel, an idea whose potential remains unrealized and whose value the catastrophe of 2012–13 has only accentuated. Like so many others, that story begins with an ending.

WHAT WAS THE INDIGÉNAT?

The question of the republic begins where the *indigénat* ends. Structuring political life until its abolition in 1946, the *indigénat* was not particular to the territories of the Sahel. Rather, it represented the obscure core of the French colonial state. Throughout the first decades of the twentieth century, an ever-expanding and contracting spectrum of political statuses, exemptions, and privileged categories developed around the *indigénat* in both meanings of that term: the regime of sanctions and the status of the native (*indigène*). This spectrum is potentially more revealing and surely no less significant than one of its poles taken alone, namely the narrow category of colonial citizens on which a rich

A New Republic 43

literature exists.[1] Indeed, until the creation of an imperial citizenship within the French Union in 1946, susceptibility to or exemption from the *indigénat* represented both marker and motive for the proliferation of political statuses in French colonial Africa.

A regime of exception based on rule by decree, enacted in often arbitrary and sometimes spectacular punishments, and concerned primarily with asserting administrative power, the *indigénat* was established in Algeria before its use spread across the empire of the Third Republic. It was built into the legal system of the new federation of French West Africa (AOF).[2] Thus, courts operating under "customary" and colonial law evolved side by side with a *tertium quid*, an unspoken and roughly sketched domain of "non-law" virtually from the moment of their creation. Crimes – such as murder, theft, and the like – fell under the purview of colonial tribunals on which local notables sat, presided over by French *commandants*. Offenses, on the other hand, however loosely defined, were met with arbitrary albeit limited sanctions at the discretion of local *commandants*. Thus, in spite of a complex system of courts and colonial justice (an oxymoron one should not allow to become naturalized), the *indigénat* provided legal cover, however scant, for colonial coercion until after the Second World War. In 1946, the *indigénat* finally fell to a long-running process of reform that had been at work within the colonial administration and the Ministry of Colonies for more than two decades before being pushed along by General Charles de Gaulle, head of the provisional government of the French Republic, beginning in Brazzaville in 1944.[3] A parliamentary assault led by newly elected African representatives such

---

[1] On the AOF, see notably Diouf (2000); Shereikis (2001); Coquery-Vidrovitch (2001); Conklin (1997); Johnson (1971); Crowder (1967). See also Saada (2002a). Asiwaju made a similar point, directing his argument against studies of assimilation and association; (1979), esp. 40.

[2] On the development of colonial legal structures in the AOF, see Roberts (2005), chs. 2–3.

[3] Ch. De Gaulle, Decree 46-D137 (illeg.) of Dec. 22, 1945, printed in *Journal Officiel de la République Française*, Dec. 26, 1945, promulgated in the AOF on Dec. 29, 1945, printed in *Journal Officiel de l'AOF*, 42, 2201, Jan. 5, 1946, and Télégramme Arrivée Gouverneur Général de l'AOF (GGAOF), from Paris [Ministry of] Colonies, signed M. Moutet, Feb. 28, 1946, #215/CIRC AP/1; telegram, Haut Commissaire de l'AOF Cournarie to Governors, AOF, and to the Circonscription of Dakar, March 8, 1946, ANS 17G168. The *indigénat* had been abolished in Algeria in 1927; Saada (2002a), 368. Asiwaju overreaches the evidence in attributing its demise in West Africa to local resistance, especially violence and emigration; (1979), 69–70. I would argue that it was abolished not because it was ineffective, but because it was too effective at underpinning a certain kind of empire, one that postwar conditions rendered impracticable. By the same token, its abolition represented not a step toward eventual independence, but rather greater incorporation into the republican political system, which was then undergoing profound change. On these points,

as Lamine Guèye, Félix Houphouët-Boigny, and their allies delivered the coup de grâce. Along with the very status of colonial subject (a phrase also captured by the term "*indigénat*"), it was abolished throughout an empire that was even then being formally reconstituted as the French Union, in which former subjects would hold an ambiguous citizenship.

For decades, the *indigénat* had enshrined administrative power and ensured that colonial administrators, particularly *commandants*, could inflict swift and severe punishments for any challenge, real or perceived, to their personal authority and that of the colonial state. It was perhaps the most important element of the administrative toolkit. When, as recounted by a prominent historian, men and women spent long nights along the marshes of the inland delta of the Niger slapping the water with their hands in order to quiet the frogs that troubled an administrator's sleep, the *indigénat* was at work.[4] In 1932, when an African auxiliary (*garde-cercle*) stuffed recalcitrant taxpayers into a small dwelling in which ten of them would suffocate and die, it was the *indigénat* that originally provided legal justification for his actions.[5] And in the same year, when a man died of a cerebral hemorrhage after a week in detention, the only charge against him – the cause of his imprisonment – was a "bad attitude towards paying his taxes," an offense punishable under the *indigénat*.[6]

The *indigénat* defined the very status of "native" on which colonial rule relied, and as a "code," it listed offenses that "by definition only 'natives' could commit."[7] In short, the *indigénat* was ultimately both a set of sanctions and a colonial state of being.[8] The term "*indigénat*" itself is often translated as "the Native Code," a phrase that suggests a false parallel to "Native" or "customary" law in the British colonies. "Customary" law worked to enable British rule by establishing and protecting the authority of African chiefs or elders. The *indigénat* did no such thing, not, at any rate, after a period of experimentation in which it empowered *chefs de canton*.

---

see generally Arendt (1994 [1948]), esp. ch. 8; more specifically, see Cooper (2005), ch. 7; Cooper (2014), ch. 2.

[4] Int., Bakari Kamian, Bamako, July 11, 2002.

[5] Accounts of the tragedy can be found in ANS 15G38, ANM 2D105FR, and ANM 2D27FR. This appears to have been a technique repeated elsewhere, sometimes with the addition of hot peppers thrown on coals in a confined space to create a noxious and suffocating gas. For similar examples, see Brunschwig (1983), 143; Saul and Royer (2001), 100; and Bâ (1994), 174–79.

[6] *Registre d'écrous*, San, 1932, ANM 2M309FRd17. Note this man was not charged with failing to pay his taxes, but simply failing to do so with good will. In the pages that follow, I consider the Soudanese *cercle* of San as exemplary of dynamics at work elsewhere.

[7] Saada (2002a), 368.

[8] On the latter sense of *indigène* and *indigénat*, see Mbembe (2001).

A New Republic

That moment ended in 1912. Thereafter, the *indigénat* served to protect administrative authority. Just as "customary" law was not necessarily customary, this "Native Code" was neither "native" in origin nor truly a code.[9] It never relied on the fiction of custom and was not intended to buttress the power of chiefs. Instead, it propped up bureaucracy and rule by decree in much of colonial West Africa. Its indeterminate nature – neither law nor its opposite – served to realize the dual and contradictory imperatives of assuring an expansive and rapid field of "action," so cherished by *commandants* and their champions,[10] and extending the control of the colonial administration, from the ministry in Paris to governors-general and governors in colonial capitals, over its own agents in the field. And it did so amid the appearance of reform and of the gradual extension of the rule of law.

Reform did not run counter to the logic of the *indigénat*. Rather, it was integral to it.[11] The narrative of reform, driven and chronicled by governors and administrators until the *indigénat*'s demise, would suggest that the administration grew increasingly rational and liberal as it approached a horizon beyond which it would be grounded exclusively in law rather than in administrative authority. Yet we would do well to incorporate that language of reform as a fundamental element of the object of study, the *indigénat*, rather than as its antidote or, less dramatically, as evidence of its amelioration. Colonial administrators used the ongoing process of reform, or the extension and amelioration of legal systems, as rhetorical cover for their continued reliance on the type of violence they themselves associated with colonial conquest.[12] That alibi was made increasingly necessary by metropolitan critics of the colonial regime, by anticolonial African radicals and activists (often writing from France, where the *indigénat* did not apply), by the increasing managerial and bureaucratic approach to governance adopted at the colonial capitals, and by the growing attention paid to an administration that could never quite realize the claim that the empire

---

[9] Although the *indigénat* was not technically a code, it is often described as such, and I have retained the term for felicity of usage and to diminish repetition. Colonial jurists often distinguished it from a code by referring to it as a "*régime*"; Merle (2002), 79. On the irregular practices of colonial judgment and punishment that existed before the *indigénat* was elaborated in the AOF, see Roberts (2005), esp. 60–61. On codification, see also Wilder (2005), 106–11; Jézéquel (2006); and Comité d'études historiques et scientifiques de l'AOF (1939).

[10] Delavignette (1950).

[11] Compare Foucault's argument on prison and reform; Foucault (1977), esp. 82.

[12] *Fraternité* rejected that argument; see "Supprimons la Justice Indigène," *l'AOF*, March 8, 1946, reprinted from *Fraternité*, Jan. 30, 1946, clipping in ANS 17G168.

represented a boon rather than a burden for the metropolitan state. In short, law itself was neither a culprit nor an agent of colonial rule.[13] It was at once a tool – its utility is evident – and an alibi.

Practicing the *Indigénat*

If the *indigénat* enabled sanctions on the margins of a bureaucratic state, it did so by concentrating power in the hands of its most essential actors, the *commandants*. As the ultimate "kings of the bush," those officers bore many of the characteristics of sovereigns. *Commandants* had the power to accuse, condemn, and sanction in an instant with little oversight, and in the local courts they sat in judgment over charges they had brought, thereby serving as both judge and prosecutor.[14] For these men, in the approving words of an administrator in Guinea, the *indigénat* served as "a procedure of intimidation."[15] Whether in the *chef lieu de cercle* or while engaged in "the art of going on tour"[16] in the bush with an escort of *gardes*, *commandants* – with few exceptions – greatly prized the power the *indigénat* gave them to exact swift and immediate sanctions. Indeed, the speed with which it enabled them to mete out punishment remained one of their key and most common arguments in favor of the *indigénat*.[17] They placed great emphasis on the fact that those they punished could be imprisoned on the same day, without appeal or reference to an administrative superior; such efficiency made their power appear unconditional.

Yet although the keeping of records on offenses and punishments was mandated within the administration,[18] in the interwar years its "men on the spot" frequently rejected what they saw as the extension of centralized bureaucratic power and an encroachment on their own personal authority. Many of them resisted both their own subordination within the hierarchy of the colonial administration and the draw of what Robert Delavignette termed the "colonial society," European and bourgeois, that lured them away from "the colony" they sought to master.[19] At stake, in either case,

---

[13] For law as a culprit, see Mamdani (2001); for arguments in which law would seem to be an agent, Merle (2002); Saada (2002a).
[14] In criminal courts, they could impose the death penalty, subject to review by the governor.
[15] Quoted in Young (1994), 155; see also Cohen (1971), 120.
[16] Delavignette (1950); see also Simonis (2005).
[17] Such rhetoric appeared as early as 1912; Manière (2007), 209.
[18] Cohen (1971), 68; Buell (1928) I, 1016.
[19] On the distinction between the colony and colonial society, see Delavignette (1950), ch. 2; Balandier (1951).

was the transformation of a much-prized form of personal power into its own rationalized and bureaucratic shadow. As Isabelle Merle suggested, much of the effort at "reform" of the *indigénat* was, therefore, devoted to attempting to control *commandants* and other colonial agents.[20] Yet because decisions repealed by governors and governors-general more often than not dealt with faits accomplis, reversals of the decisions of *commandants* did little for those who had already been jailed for their offenses and released; they represented instead attempts to assert central control that were effectively doomed to fail.

Given the intensity of the struggle for bureaucratic control that reform of the *indigénat* represented, it is no surprise that in practice, the gamut of offenses sanctioned under it tended to expand continuously, even as it contracted formally. For what were people punished? More than half of all recorded punishments under the *indigénat* in the mid-1930s were related to taxation and labor requisition,[21] yet these were not the sole offenses leading to the exercise of the *indigénat*. Peasants could be jailed or sanctioned for neglecting any number of orders, included planting too few peanuts, failing to cultivate ricin, growing too much pepper and selling it to African traders, emptying reserve granaries, and so on. Still, the contradictions of the *indigénat* elude ready analysis. Under the Vichy regime, administrators in Dakar explicitly forbade the use of the sanctions recognized by the *indigénat* to punish those who refused to produce nonedible crops destined solely for export.[22] That the principal tool used to sanction colonial coercion could not be employed to force export-oriented production at a time of war and economic crisis is astounding. Even in times of acute crisis, the *indigénat* was exercised to protect neither extraction nor custom, but rather the power of *commandants*.[23]

Collective punishments, too, underscored the exceptional nature of coercion in the colonial state. They were common in the AOF, but illegal under French law, which is built on the principle of individual sanction.[24] Collective punishments were meted out for evading taxes, interfering with recruitment, or refusing the orders of the administrators, *chefs de canton*,

---

[20] Merle (2002); also Cohen (1971), 68; Saada (2002a).
[21] DAPA, Rougier, *Note sur l'indigénat en AOF*, Nov. 5, 1936, ANS 17G84; see also, Asiwaju (1979), 60–1.
[22] DAPA to *Directeur des Services Economiques*, GGAOF, Dakar, Feb. 20, 1942, #430 AP/1, ANS 17G168.
[23] *Punitions Disciplinaires*, San, 1941–44, ANM 2M170FR.
[24] Merle (2002), esp. 85. Examples are numerous, including *Peines disciplinaires*, San, 2' trimestre, 1921, ANM 2M239FR; *Peines disciplinaires*, San, 1943, ANM 2M170FR.

or *gardes-cercle*.²⁵ In the 1940s, planting the wrong strand of cotton, or even hoeing a cotton field poorly, could result in sanctions inflicted on a collectivity rather than any individual.²⁶ Such collective punishments relied on a central proposition: that the *commandant* (or his agent) faced populations or collectivities with some uniform legal or juridical status. There could be no *indigénat* without *indigènes*, or more precisely, without colonial subjects. Yet the phenomenon of reform undermined that central proposition by introducing exemptions for individuals and for social categories.

Category Errors

Given the amount of power it invested in them, it is no surprise that *commandants* opposed with near unanimity efforts to reform the *indigénat* by extending exemptions from it, whether to particular individuals or to entire social categories of colonial subjects, such as women. Not only was the *indigénat* as a set of sanctions central to the day-to-day operations of colonial rule but also, more abstractly, it marked the boundary between the statuses of subject and citizen that provided its logic. Exemptions risked blurring the stark divisions between categories of people that lay at the core of the colonial system, and they would also eventually produce a heterogeneous spectrum of people occupying distinct juridical categories, even if these may have been recognized in theory more often than in practice.²⁷ How were *commandants* to distinguish between those whom they could punish summarily and those who could claim some legal protection? How were they to impose collective punishments on groups of people with distinct statuses? Their self-interested pragmatism aside, the aspirations of Africans with subject status, and notably *évolués*, caused the issue of exemptions to surface again and again, whether pushed by dissidents and reformers in Dahomey, Paris, or Dakar.²⁸

---

[25] *Punitions disciplinaires*, 1941–44, ANM 2M170FR.
[26] In 1941, seven people paid 45 frs. a piece for that offense; *Punitions disciplinaires*, 1942, ANM 2M170FR. On the deep connection between cotton cultivation and state power, see Roberts (1995).
[27] On colonial difference, see Chatterjee (1993), 10, 16–24.
[28] On Dahomey, see Buell (1928) I, 1017, and "Quelques révendications dahoméennes," *les Continents*, 1, 8, Sept. 1, 1924. See also DAPA AOF, note for GGAOF re. *Voeux exprimés par les populations du Dahomey à la mission parlementaire*, Dec. 28, 1937, #3106/AP/1, ANS 17G97. Manière provides some context for this contention (2007).

A New Republic

In the words of the Minister of Colonies, such individual exemptions represented "a kind of ... promotion to a superior social state,"[29] one usually offered, at least in principle, in exchange for service to the empire. Yet what did such a promotion entail? Neither citizenship nor anything like it, but rather the privilege – for oneself and one's immediate family – of being subject to "*la répression judiciaire*" rather than "*administrative.*"[30] The same offenses identified in the *indigénat*, those that "only a native could commit," obtained, but the certificate of exemption obliged a *commandant* to bring his complaints before the tribunal over which, of course, he presided. By 1936, African employees of the administration, licensed merchants, school graduates, and war veterans could claim such political privilege. Former soldiers had figured among the very first to be exempted, in January, 1918,[31] and their collective exemption had sparked serious disagreement between different levels of the administration, as *commandants* in rural *cercles* howled that a too-liberal central administration had effectively disempowered them. The law exempting veterans from the sanctions of the *indigénat* gradually came to be disregarded in practice,[32] and was reaffirmed in 1924, when the "circle of exemption" was widened.[33] Following veterans' exemption from the *indigénat*, the relationship between "native status" and categories or individuals would grow increasingly complex.

In a series of decrees issued from 1929 to 1936 that applied at various times to the different territories of the AOF, West African women and children younger than 16 were excluded from the *indigénat*'s sanctions – a fact that has left little trace in the historiographic record.[34] Women across the AOF only became immune from the summary sanctions associated with the *indigénat* (*peines de simple police*) in December, 1936, having at different times been exempted from corporal punishment, imprisonment, and finally fines.[35] Yet their exemption was never absolute (and indeed

---

[29] Minister of Colonies, ministerial circular of November 20, 1924, quoted in Buell (1928) I, 1018.

[30] DAPA, Rougier, *Note sur l'indigénat en AOF*, Nov. 5, 1936, ANS 17G84.

[31] They thereby attained a status that colonial agents including *chefs de canton* had only earned the previous year 1917; Conklin (1997), 310–11.

[32] CdC Koutiala, *Rapport Politique, 4' trim.*, 1921, ANM 1E23FR.

[33] Buell (1928) I, 1017; Asiwaju (1979), 53.

[34] The date of this reform is noted as 1924 in Conklin (1997), 310–11; cf. Buell (1928) I, 1017; as 1934 in Cohen (1971), 119; and as 1935 in some archival documents, e.g., DAPA, HCAOF, 3 May 1941, #1197/AP/2, ANS 17G97. The process culminated in 1936; see GGAOF to Minister of Colonies, Dec. 18, 1936, #1929, ANS 17G97; and DAPA, Rougier, *Note sur l'indigénat en AOF*, Nov. 5, 1936, ANS 17G84.

[35] DAPA, Rougier, *Note sur l'indigénat en AOF*, Nov. 5, 1936, ANS 17G84.

applied only to the punishments, not the offenses themselves). Within a few years, Dakar responded to the demands of lower-level administrators by suggesting that for any action involving public hygiene, the production and consumption of food, or the authority of an administrator's convocation, women would once again face the threat of administrative sanctions.[36] The following year saw another "derogation from the exemption" of women; they could now be fined for refusing to accept French currency, particularly bills.[37]

The waxing and waning of such exemptions caused confusion among administrators themselves, not least because many decrees were quite narrowly applicable to particular locales. In a flurry of paperwork, *commandants* and governors sought greater clarity: where could women be imprisoned, and where could they only be fined? In which subdivisions of which particular *cercles* of Niger did the *indigénat* continue to apply, and to whom?[38] Did the *indigénat* apply to colonial subjects in Dakar? Even the local administration mistakenly believed that it did not – and the metaphor of conquest could hardly be used to justify the policing of a colonial capital with an enfranchised population – but in fact the *indigénat* did apply. It had simply never been put to use there. Rather than either enforcing or abolishing it, the city's administrator suggested that there was some political advantage in maintaining its indeterminate status.[39]

As the granting of exemptions became more common, the logic of the *indigénat* became more convoluted, and the inadequacies and inconsistencies of the entire system increasingly apparent. Other groups tried and failed to seek recognition of their collective claims to special status. African Christians, for instance, demanded exemption, based on the logic that as Christians they were no longer "native." If their civil status (*statut personnel*) in family law cases was no longer "customary" but "Christian," and if they were no longer subject to the judgments of chiefs, they argued, then their relationship with the administration should also change.[40] In spite of such skirmishes around categories of exemption, historians have more

---

[36] DAPA, HCAOF, May 3, 1941, #1197/AP/2, ANS 17G97.
[37] DAPA, *[Rapport] en Commission Permanente du Conseil de Gouvernement*, no date (document stamped Nov. 2, 1942); GGAOF, T.L. Circulaire to Governors, Nov. 10, 1942, #998, ANS 17G168.
[38] See *Extrait du Rapport d'Inspection Coste du 1 février 1938*, ANS 17G97.
[39] Administrateur en Chef des Colonies, Administrateur de la Circonscription de Dakar et Dépendances to GGAOF (DAPA), Jan. 14, 1937, #107 AG, ANS 17G97.
[40] Governor General Brévié, *"les missions chrétiennes et la Société indigène,"* circular, Feb. 6, 1933, #37 AP/2, ANS 17G73.

A New Republic

often focused their attention on the relationship between individuals and the *indigénat* – or more accurately its inverse, citizenship.

Only a very small elite ever attained French citizenship, as opposed to acquiring it through birth in one of the Four Senegalese Communes as those known as the *originaires* had done. Most of those who did obtain it otherwise had requested citizenship in exchange for some particular service they may have rendered to the colonial state.[41] The colonial administration shared their logic. The revision of 1924 allowed for the possibility that exceptional or "worthy" individuals of *indigène* status might be granted an exemption from "disciplinary punishments," but such exemptions were slow in coming. A decade later, the rhythm of exemptions would increase, reaching a tempo of 400 to 500 individuals (and by extension their families) per year from 1934 to 1938.[42] In a colonial federation of some 15 million – and bearing in mind that some 4 million continued to live under the unreformed code of 1887 – Dakar's Director of Political Affairs was rather optimistic in arguing that at such a rate, "a significant part of the population" would soon be exempt.[43] In fact, in the West African colonies of the "empire of law," to be subject to law was an exceptional achievement.

Ending the *Indigénat*

Like those whose status it described, the *indigénat* was always subject to evolution.[44] In 1924, a major revision to the regime diminished the severity of punishments that could be exacted, but it notably excluded the areas of the AOF that were considered to be still in a "semi-barbarous state": these comprised almost the entire federation and certainly the vast majority of

---

[41] Coquery-Vidrovitch (2001).
[42] DAPA, Conseil de Gouvernement to GGAOF, Nov. 25, 1938, ANS 17G168.
[43] DAPA, Rougier, *Note sur l'indigénat en AOF*, Nov. 5, 1936, ANS 17G84. For instance, in San in 1935, no one enjoyed this type of exemption. In 1936, however, the *commandant* proposed exempting five men of particular use to the colonial administration; two were *chefs de quartier* in San, and three were scions of the towns' ruling families. As far as the records indicate, for the next ten years, until the abolition of the *indigénat*, those men were the only individuals to be so recognized in a *cercle* of some 148,000 people. See E. Levasseur, *Commandant de cercle* (CdC) of San to Governor, Soudan Français (GSF), April 20, 1935, #127; and *Etat nominatif des indigènes du cercle proposés en vue de bénéficier des dispositions de l'article 5 du décret du 15 Novembre 1924 sur l'indigénat* (n.d., 1936), ANM 2M170FR.
[44] For instance, Manière counted 94 texts regulating the *indigénat* in Dahomey from 1887 to 1946; Manière, (2007), 13, fn 19.

its population.[45] The same revision began to exempt categories of people. From 1936 to 1938 the Popular Front scrutinized the *indigénat* once again, although a move to reconsider the code was already underway and had provoked the handful of exemptions discussed above. It is unclear whether the short-lived Popular Front regime had a great effect on the exercise of the *indigénat*, at least not on the ground.[46] Fundamental change in the relationship between law and bureaucracy would be a long time coming.

While West African prisons were packed, in Paris and Dakar further change was on the horizon. In the last years of the Third Republic, administrators had sought to refine a colonial practice that would become more repressive before coming to an end. The Popular Front's Governor General in Dakar, Marcel de Coppet, moved to reform the *indigénat* gradually, and in consultation with his subordinates across the AOF, by changing the status of particular territories of the AOF and by accelerating the extension of individual exemptions. After the fall of the Popular Front, the Second World War reopened the question of whether categories of people would be exempted. A decree of April 19, 1939 would assign ex-*tirailleurs* (soldiers) to French criminal courts, which could exclusively apply the French penal code and metropolitan regulations. Some veterans applauded the 1939 decree;[47] however, *commandants* were hardly enthusiastic.[48] By 1941, ex-*tirailleurs*' unique legal status had once again been withdrawn, enabling the heightened repression of the Vichy and Free French years.[49] The idea that ex-*tirailleurs* and others who had served France should have some kind of particular legal status remained an important one throughout the war. At the imperial conference at Brazzaville in January and February 1944, General Charles de Gaulle spoke of creating a new category of privileged colonial demi-citizens who

---

[45] Exempt from the reforms were the colonies of Upper Volta, Mauritania, and Niger, most of the Soudan, Guinea, and Dahomey, and all but ten *cercles* of the Côte d'Ivoire. In other words, Senegal was the only colony to experience reform across the entirety of the territory; Buell (1928) I, 1019, fn 60.

[46] Brot (1999). In San, the number of people imprisoned (that is, those held at the end of the year, not the total number incarcerated over its course) doubled under a reform-minded CdC in the years of the Popular Front; ANM 2M106FR.

[47] "Les Anciens combattants noirs d'AOF manifestent leur attachement à la France," *Journal de Rouen*, May 1, 1939, CAOM Agefom 389 13/b.

[48] R. Cazenave, CdC San, *Rapport Annuel sur la fonctionnement de la justice indigène, 1939*, 29 Jan. 1940, ANM 2M106FR. See also *Rapport Annuel ...*, Dec. 31, 1940, ANM 2M106FR; Mann (2006), 111–16.

[49] *Rapport Annuel sur la fonctionnement de la justice indigène, 1941*, Jan. 16, 1942, ANM 2M106FR.

would enjoy a political status somewhere between that of the subject and that of the citizen. Although no immediate action was taken, two years later and in the aftermath of the war, the variety of forms of political belonging in the French empire had expanded dramatically. A new electorate included veterans and members of certain other select categories;[50] its ranks would expand considerably over the next decade. The exemptions of individuals or of social categories would rapidly become moot as African representatives to the new Constituent Assembly acted quickly against the *indigénat* and assured its abolition in 1946. Under the Fourth Republic, former colonial subjects saw that status abolished. All were now citizens, although the constitution left open the question of how they might exercise that citizenship.[51]

If in 1946, France was offering a new bargain to its former subjects, and African politicians in Paris were working to sweeten its terms, *commandants* in West Africa were far from being uniformly supportive of the new regime. Reforms enacted in the months before the complete abolition of the *indigénat* were simply ignored by local administrators, who continued to detain people and inflict heavy fines in spite of ministerial orders to the contrary.[52] In San, the *commandant*'s *adjoint* (the deputy or "*petit commandant*") undertook a tour to the *cercle*'s rural markets to explain the new political arrangement and its meaning, but he did not make explicit one of the most significant changes, the abolition of the *indigénat*. Neither, of course, did he point out that two of the key provisions of the new system – the abolition of the *indigénat* and of forced labor – were not granted by France, but won by African parliamentarians.[53]

Such a subterfuge was not available to the feared Governor Edmond Louveau two years later. When he toured the towns of southern Mali to explain the new constitution of the Fourth Republic and the French Union, he was accompanied by the two key leaders of the anticolonial RDA party, Mamadou Konaté of Soudan Français and Félix Houphouët-Boigny of the Côte d'Ivoire. Gathering crowds of up to 3,000 people in early-morning

---

[50] These included functionaries, religious leaders, those literate in French or Arabic, and members of the Chambers of Commerce; Thompson and Adloff (1957), 58.
[51] Cooper (2014), ch. 2.
[52] de Benoist (1982), 52–3.
[53] Adjoint Mader, *Rapport de tournée*, Oct. 21, 1946, ANM 1E38FR. The law abolishing the *indigénat* is known as the first *Loi Lamine Guèye*. It was adopted on May 7, 1946; de Benoist (1982), 52. The law abolishing forced labor, adopted on April 11, 1946, was known as the *Loi Houphouët-Boigny*; on its political impact, see Cooper (2000). On the context of Mader's tour, see Mann (2006), 119–21.

open-air marketplaces, Louveau used blunt language to illustrate the roles of the parliamentarians, who made law, and the role of the administration, which applied it. The contortions of his speech reveal the confusion of authority engendered by its multiplication under the new constitution, the absence of a shared understanding about what law meant, and most of all, the profound transformation in political power caused by the abolition of the *indigénat*:

> I'm going to explain to you how the French constitution works. ... What I am saying ... is not politics. The administration is not political. We are here to apply the law and the law is the same for everyone: all French citizens, they [Konaté and Houphouët-Boigny] and I alike, are equal before the law; whatever their political party or their skin color, all French citizens are equal before the law. It's the law that creates custom; it's the law that commands everyone. The law is made in Paris, in meetings of all the deputies from here and from the metropole. ... Everyone is submitted to it. ... If the law is broken, people are brought before the courts. The judge does not take orders from the deputies or from the governor, he judges according to the law and according to his own judgment. ...
>
> In sum, the deputies ... make the custom, which is the law, and then only the government has the power to apply it, and the only representative of the government here is the administrator. The Chamber of Deputies is like the Council of Notables, and the administrator is like the chef de canton.
>
> Do you understand?[54]

Apparently the answer to Louveau's question was "No." What Louveau and his adjoint hoped to get across in their windy speeches, people in Soudan interpreted with thousands of individual acts of rural rebellion, demonstrating that the balance of power among the new political parties, the administration, the chieftaincy, and the judiciary was not at all clear.[55] Troubled administrators, particularly those of the "old school," then set out to prove that they remained in command, and that imperial reform did not necessarily mean a change in everyday practice in the colonies.

Formulated in Paris and Dakar, the abolition of labor requisitions and the end of the *indigénat* did not have immediate effect in Soudan. The gap broadened between colonial practice and imperial theory, seen here in the form of a spectrum of political statuses whose continuing expansion had been reversed. Abolition meant a new uniformity in political status within and between West African communities. But it did not mean the end of

---

[54] *Rapports de tournée du Gouverneur Louveau, Tournée Sud et sud-est*, Nov. 1948, ANM 1E94FR. This particular speech was delivered in Dioila, Feb. 20, 1948 [sic dates]. The text is presented as being "the literal translation from the shorthand."

[55] See, e.g., Adjoint Mader, *Rapport du Tournée ...*, Oct. 21, 1946, ANM 1E38FR; CdC San, *Rapport sur la justice ...*, Feb. 28, 1948, ANM 2M106FR.

coercion, arbitrary exactions, or the advent of an empire of law. Rather, many administrators saw the abolition of the *indigénat* as an abdication of authority. It introduced a distinction between administrative and judiciary authority, which, they argued, "the African has not understood.... Seeing that the power to sanction no longer belongs to the man who had the power to command, he has concluded that authority itself is weakened. Thus the expression *fanga bana*, "'authority no longer exists,' [in which] ... the power to command is associated with the power to punish."[56]

The shift from the period of a virtually premodern sovereignty in colonial rule – in which power emanated from a central figure, the *commandant*, rather than from the law – came to a close with the end of the *indigénat*. From that moment the *gardes* also witnessed a decline in their coercive power. Interpreters, who in many *cercles* maintained the prison registries that would allow them to control the duration of a subject's detention, lost power as well.[57] The next generation of administrators would have to find other ways to pursue their administrative and political objectives. They encountered a new scenario, a shift to a system in which a government of wide aspirations generated an entire matrix of rules, decrees, and regulations. No longer could the *commandant*, in the words of a long-time colonial clerk, simply reach for his long-form notebook, sign a slip of paper to be torn from it, and send anyone ("a civil servant or anyone else!") to prison for a fortnight, after which the unlucky prisoner might be told, "this was a warning."[58]

It is sorely tempting to connect the practices of rule enabled by the *indigénat* and the kind of arbitrary police powers exercised by *commandants* and *gardes-cercle* to the type of authoritarianism and small-scale government violence that has afflicted too many African states since independence.[59] Indeed it is hard not to see traces of colonial governance, particularly a predilection for emphasizing authority over law, in the newly independent regimes of the 1960s and 1970s and their successors. The *indigénat* gave legal standing to the local despotisms of colonial *commandants* and created a culture of *commandement* – and fear – that continued to inflect postcolonial African political culture and relations

---

[56] Rocca Serra, CdC San, *Rapport sur la justice, année 1947*, Feb. 28, 1948, ANM 2M106FR.
[57] E.g., Cercle de Sikasso, *Rapport Annuel sur la justice indigène, année 1941*, ANM 2M170FR.
[58] Int., Amadou Théra, San, July 2, 1998; ibid., August 1, 1998.
[59] Mamdani (1996); Mbembe (2001), ch. 1, esp. 25, 31–32.

between citizens and agents of the new states.[60] But the differences are important. Colonial violence enforced a certain kind of exclusion, that of the "native" who would remain a subject. Postcolonial violence and coercion, on the other hand, were frequently (and paradoxically) designed to force participation in a new political community, one that at least in theory was based on the emerging principles of citizenship and equality.

The true significance of the *indigénat* can be fully captured neither by the everyday "intimidation" it enabled (as vital as that is for understanding the history of colonial rule) nor by the development of a set of reforms and an evolving set of political memberships around it, even if it engendered a complex multiplicity of political statuses with which postcolonial governments would grapple. The *indigénat* produced an enduring fusion between being governed and being administered. Like a black hole, the power of the *indigénat* – its gravitational pull – ordered what surrounded it. Its collapse made a republic possible, and made talk of it meaningful. Among other reforms, its collapse also enabled the uneven integration of metropolitan and colonial political life, a life in which former "*indigènes*" who were not quite citizens – including women and other subjects of chiefs – could take part as an empire of subjects became what Frederick Cooper has termed an "empire of citizens," still structured by categories of exclusion and inclusion.[61]

THE MOTHERS' VOTE

Among those categories was that of women, and it is a revealing one. Exempted early on from the *indigénat* yet excluded from the institutional manifestations of political life, in the early 1950s women came to occupy an exceptional and somewhat contradictory place in politics as voters enfranchised by their role as mothers. In Soudan as in the rest of francophone sub-Saharan Africa, paths to suffrage passed through membership in distinct social-political categories, most of which were defined in relation to the colonial state: veterans, graduates, civil servants, and licensed merchants, among others. In such a list, "mothers of two children" – or three, or four – is a striking exception. How did motherhood and suffrage come to be linked? And why two children rather than three, four, or one? The enfranchisement of mothers of two (or more) children who were living or who had died in the service of France ("*vivants ou*

---

[60] See Ly (1997 [1982]).
[61] Cooper (2014).

morts pour la France") became law in May 1951, some five years before universal suffrage in West Africa. It did so in a fashion that suggested that the categories of the *état providence*, or the social welfare state, provided a way to mark difference within what, under the Fourth Republic, had become an empire grounded in a shared citizenship. This is nearly right, but not quite: for bureaucrats, mothers' exemption from taxes enabled their suffrage, because they existed as a separate census category. The new dispensation also underscored one of the curiosities of West African decolonization in general: enfranchisement was a swinging door, both an entrance and an exit.

Some seven years after women in France won the vote, a law governing the election of representatives from the overseas territories enfranchised mothers of two children in French possessions south of the Sahara. In the French National Assembly, much of the debate on that law hinged on the question of whether a single or a double college was more appropriate in Africa, as well as on the number of deputies each territory could send to Paris. Blocked on both these questions, African parliamentarians and their allies sought to expand the number of voters in the second college. From the scrum around the electoral law – in which the Assembly of the French Union, the National Assembly, and the Conseil d'état were at odds – the suffrage of mothers emerged. In the end, the peculiar characteristic of their suffrage was conditioned first and foremost by the short deadline before the next elections – three weeks! – and the lack of a viable civil registry (*état-civil*) in the territories. Here the debate quickly shifted from principles to practicalities. Soon, the question became how to give the vote to women, not why to do so. The "why" was lost in a general, if loose, sense of agreement that universal suffrage would be the distant endpoint of a gradual process of reform. When Senghor, serving as secretary (*rapporteur*) for a parliamentary committee, argued that "a limited franchise is an unjust franchise," no one challenged him on this statement of principle.[62] The point of contention was elsewhere, around the question of the single college; it was not who could vote, but for what. While voices as strong as those of Senghor and Sissoko argued strongly for the single college,[63] others held out for protecting European commercial interests by maintaining two distinct electoral colleges.

African parliamentarians would lose that argument, but around mothers agreement coalesced, albeit gradually. Unlike the single college, that

---

[62] *Débats de l'Assemblée Nationale (France), 1ᵉ Legislature (Volume 51), Sessions de 1951*, V, session of April 24, 1951, 3840.
[63] *Débats*, V, session of April 24, 1951, 3905.

debate seemed to be low-stakes, and victory appeared possible. Rather than "why mothers?" or "why women?" the debate quickly turned to the question, "mothers of how many children?" Senghor's original proposal had mentioned three. Those who sought the broadest expansion of the electorate proposed two, and the Minister of Overseas France, François Mitterand, agreed in principle to four. Nobody proposed one, or none. Mitterand's position, contested by others in the Assembly, was that mothers of four children were specifically counted in the census because they were exempt from the head tax.[64] Representing Chad, Gabrielle Lisette would have none of it. A colonial administrator himself, Lisette, who was RDA, argued that all mothers figured in the census roles. He may have been overstating his case, but he called on an unnamed colleague who was a *chef de canton* (possibly Sissoko) to confirm his assertion. Lisette argued that the enfranchisement of mothers was entirely possible, and that mothers of four children could be put on the voter rolls "tomorrow," if that was what the legislature decided.[65] Ultimately, it did. The amendment voted on the afternoon of May 22nd enabled mothers of two children "*vivants ou morts pour la France*" to vote in legislative elections to be held only a few weeks later.

All things considered, the move was a strange one. The enfranchisement of West African women is out of sync both with the metropolitan and the colonial narrative of female suffrage. It is even out of sync with what transpired in the Four Communes of Senegal. There, after mobilizing in protest at being deprived of a right extended to French women elsewhere, women *originaires* began to vote as soon as their metropolitan peers did.[66] Women in the rest of French West Africa did not become voters as women; they became voters as mothers first, and as women years later.[67] In other words, they became voters at least partly because of the particular form of suffering (and implicitly, wisdom) that their legislative champions took motherhood to represent.[68] This is quite the opposite of the theories of republican universalism that served to impede women's suffrage on the grounds of their "particularity," or by which a woman was "too marked

---

[64] *Débats de l'Assemblée Nationale (France), 1' Legislature (Volume 51), Sessions de 1951*, VII, session of May 22, 1951, 5734.
[65] *Débats*, VII, session of May 22, 1951, 5736.
[66] Marie-Andrée du Sacré Coeur (1954), 478; Cooper (2009), 97–98; Cooper (2014), ch. 1.
[67] A very small number of women may have been enfranchised from 1945 due to their educational or professional status.
[68] *Débats*, VII, session of May 22, 1951, 5736.

A New Republic 59

by ... her sex" to be a "true abstract individual."[69] It also escapes the frame of the "family vote" debate that raged in France during the Third Republic, even if the arguments were similar and the clashes familiar.[70] The family vote was quintessentially patriarchal: it was intended to secure the power and privilege of fathers and husbands over that of single men. Women's vote was not a family vote; it was a mother's vote. Like many legislative achievements, a coalition made it possible. Feminists, Communists, and parliamentary representatives of the African territories allied on this question. Another force was not present in West Africa. Absent the vote of settlers and the careful balance by which the European franchise was protected in Algeria, West African mothers obtained the right to vote several years before their Algerian Muslim counterparts.[71] Of course, settler colonies were hardly fertile territory for democratic politics. Nonetheless, the sequence of suffrage bears reflection. France had held elections for centuries, and its subjects and citizens had struggled over suffrage throughout that time.[72] In Algeria, the first parliaments with Muslim representation were decades old. In most of French West Africa, parliamentary participation – in the French Union, the national assembly, and territorial assemblies – preceded the suffrage of mothers by a mere five years.

Was their participation more than symbolic? That is, once enfranchised, did mothers actually vote? And if they did, did their votes have any effect? Were they as divided as those of men, or did women voters represent a bloc? Were their votes lost to fraud? The few scholars who have taken note of the mothers' vote have suggested that it had little effect, arguing that most women did not take advantage of it.[73] However, the evidence is inconclusive. Women's participation varied widely by locale, and in some places it may have been crucial. In the years immediately following the passage of the law, the US-RDA sought to target the new categories of voters and crafted its electoral strategies with them in mind. In 1958, the party named Aoua Keita to its central committee, and put her forward as a

---

[69] Rosanvallon (2001), 522–23.
[70] Downs (2013); Pollard (1998), 15–16. Francine Lefebvre, an advocate for the mothers' vote in the National Assembly, argued that although senators had been able to block any move toward women's suffrage in France for decades, she would fight their efforts to do so in the overseas territories; *Débats*, VII, session of May 22, 1951, 5735.
[71] Muslim women in Algeria first voted in November 1958; Droz (2008), 30.
[72] Rosanvallon (2001).
[73] Morgenthau (1964), Thompson and Adloff (1957), 59–60; Coquery-Vidrovitch (2010), 287.

candidate to the territorial assembly the following year. Whether and how competing parties might have seized on the same opportunities is less clear: the PSP generally fought to maintain a narrow franchise. Still, women activists proudly showed their party colors, dressing all in blue (PSP) or white (US-RDA) under towering headwraps. In Bamako, women engaged in pitched street battles fought along party lines,[74] and when Aoua Keita campaigned in one village near Koutiala, women chased her out of town.[75] In the rough and tumble politics of the 1950s, women appear at least as often as street fighters as they do as voters, and Keita's candidacy was unique.[76]

The first effect of the reform was some small degree of chaos. Coming as it did just weeks before the legislative elections of June 1951, this was hardly surprising. In Senegal, administrators were confronted with the need to revise electoral lists almost ad hoc in order to include two new categories: mothers of two children who were living or who had died in the service of France, and "heads of family or of household" eligible for taxation. The former category was clear, if difficult to count precisely, while the second turned out to be much less precise than had been anticipated. Heads of family and heads of household represented two distinct categories. The second could be thought to include most adult men. In the "traditional milieu," the first was much narrower, as extended families generally lived in a single compound made up of several distinct households clustered around an elder male who, among other things, settled the tax burden of his younger male relatives. In most territories, administrators argued, only city dwellers who had lost touch with their roots (*déracinés*) lived in independent households. Therefore, if only heads of family were taken as electors, this would ease the administrative burden of expanding suffrage. However, it would have the unintended effect of enfranchising many women – mothers of two children – whose husbands could not vote, particularly *en brousse*.[77] The passage of two new laws enfranchising heads of household in 1952 would correct this "regrettable anomaly," but the fact remains that women had secured a significant place

---

[74] See, e.g., *Verité*, 515, Dec. 19, 1956; Diallo (2005), 184. On the political activities of educated women in this period, see Barthélémey (2010), 266–71.
[75] Keita (1975), 390.
[76] Keita would serve as a deputy throughout the First Republic. After 1964, another female deputy, Namissa Touré, joined her in the National Assembly; Barthélémey (2010), 274.
[77] [D]APA, Senegal, *Rapport sur le déroulement des operations électorales du 17 juin 1951*, St Louis, [date illegible; after 21 juin] June 1951, #249, stamped "secret," ANM NIII 7D2515.

A New Republic 61

in the formal political sphere.[78] Even before the 1952 revisions (that is, when most women could vote and many men could not) the number of registered voters had shot up across the AOF, increasing sixfold in the Soudan.[79]

Even by the narrowest definition of the household, the new influx of electors would mean that polling stations would have to accommodate far more voters than they were designed to do. The administration recognized this problem immediately, accepting it as the inconvenience it was, but US-RDA militants complained bitterly that "thousands" of people were prevented from voting.[80] Many of them were mothers of two children, who in some places represented 20 percent of the newly constituted electorate. Where they registered, the majority of them voted.[81] In any race with slim margins, if mothers preferred one candidate to another their votes might determine the outcome. In Gao, where Aoua Keita and her allies had been at work establishing the US-RDA, the party had great success in the June 1951 elections, particularly with people dismissed as "new voters lacking political experience who had been won over by demagogic promises."[82] Still, the place to look for the effects of the new law is not only in the elections that immediately followed its passage, but in the campaigns in years to come, particularly in the five years before the *loi cadre* brought universal suffrage. This was an important period in which the US-RDA would slowly build its majority. The interterritorial RDA had broken with the French Communist Party in 1950, and at the end of 1952, the colonial administration began to adopt a less antagonistic posture toward the US-RDA.[83] The party was better able to campaign, particularly in the countryside, even if the political opposition remained fierce. During that time, voters were not idle. By Tony Chafer's count, there were six major election

---

[78] Marie-Andrée du Sacré Coeur (1954), 484.
[79] Thompson and Adloff (1957), 59; de Benoist (1982), 537, 544. Thompson and Adloff note that the number of voters increased a mere 22% in Dahomey, and around 1% in Cote d'Ivoire, before the Ivoirian lists were corrected; ibid.
[80] [D]APA, Senegal, *Rapport sur le déroulement...*, ANM NIII 7D2515; Moussa Doucouré, Sec. Pol. US-RDA, Comité Directeur de l'US-RDA to GSF, Sept. 1, 1951, #134/CD, ANM NII 7D1217.
[81] Marie-Andrée du Sacré Coeur (1954), 484.
[82] Gao, *Revue des événements, 1' trim. 1952*, March 27, 1952, ANM 1E17FR. The following year, the party still won the elections in the second college, but lost ground to the PSP; *Revue des événements, 2' trim. 1952*, June 26, 1952, ANM 1E17FR. Danioko's view on US-RDA "success" is more mitigated; (1984), 186.
[83] GSF Etcheber, Circular to "Administrateurs du Soudan," Dec. 31, 1952, #502, reproduced as appendix 22 of Danioko (1984).

campaigns in AOF between 1951 and 1956.[84] They established the rhythm of political life. The US-RDA was keenly aware of the fact that many women were registering to vote in them, and that women played a key role in party activities, notably in urban districts such as Bamako's Bagadadji.[85] In 1955 a delegate from the BPN, Makane Macoumba, told a committee of women in Bamako that "they would determine the results of the upcoming elections."[86] This was the classic claim of a stump speech, but it would never be more true. By the end of the next year, with the passage of the *loi cadre*, universal suffrage in a single college was the law of the land. The mothers' vote had become an historical anomaly, but one that continued to resonate. In 1958 labor leader Mme. Sow Aissata Coulibaly urged her fellow women workers to vote "No" in the referendum on the Fifth Republic, declaring "History will never say that I deliberately chose slavery for myself, my husband, and my children. ... I will vote no as a worker, no as a woman, and no as a mother."[87] This was powerful rhetoric. Coulibaly knew what she meant, and the mention of motherhood was more than incidental. Hers was a dissident, minority position, but under the new rules, the US-RDA would dominate the electoral scene, establishing a political hegemony that by 1960 looked to be unbreakable.

END OF THE CHIEFTAINCY

Meeting with Tanzanian President Julius Nyerere, members of his government, and the BPN of the US-RDA in 1965, Modibo Keita declared that two things had secured the party's grip on political hegemony: the "Africanization" of the civil service and the elimination of the chieftaincy.[88] Both look now to be minor, even inevitable, tactical victories in a longer struggle for political independence, by which they are overshadowed. In fact, they were the necessary preconditions for securing that independence in the highly particular form that it took. Without them, Mali would in all likelihood never have developed its own currency or pushed the French military from its bases on national territory. Moreover, the major political battles of the 1940s and 1950s were not about national independence, and none of the Soudanese parties was truly a "nationalist"

---

[84] Chafer (2002), 147.
[85] P-V, BPN, 3 April 1954 and n.d. (Feb. 1955), BPNCMLN 74.
[86] Reunion des presidentes, associations feminines, March 19, 1955, BPNCMLN 74.
[87] Quoted in Traoré (2008), 328.
[88] BPN, April 16, 1965, BPNCMLN 83.

A New Republic 63

party, at least until 1958. The issue that divided them more than any other was that of the chieftaincy; the power, comportment, and composition of the administration ran a close second. The PSP was widely considered a *faamaton*, a party of chiefs, and with good reason.[89] The US-RDA, on the other hand, was at its core a party of civil servants and teachers, precisely the people who would rise in status should the administration be "Africanized."[90] They intended to govern aggressively, and dismissing the chiefs would enable them to do so. The combination of Africanization and the end of the chieftaincy not only confirmed the ascendancy of the US-RDA, it established a particular notion of what government was and could do in independent Mali. After all, the question, "What is government?" begs the question, "Who governs?"

The question had been posed before, by the colonial administration itself, and the answer provided was striking. In the period between the passage of the *loi cadre* – which established territorial autonomy by dissolving the AOF – and the creation of the République Soudanaise two years later, the question of how to devolve power and responsibility confronted the territorial government just as it would soon confront the postcolonial state.[91] In a meeting of the Soudan's *commandants* in the presence of their governor and of the territory's new ministers, one answer was provided.[92] The responsibilities of the territory would be distinguished from those of the central state (France), and new governing councils would allow "populations" greater participation in the management of their own affairs. The first initiative would require the creation of two parallel bureaucracies, each of which could second civil servants to the other. Less important than the mechanics was the fact that this would create a whole new set of openings waiting to be filled by "local elites," in a process dubbed "Africanization."[93] The second initiative, the councils,

---

[89] In the Soudan's assemblies from 1947–52, all of the RDA deputies were "commoners," and several of the PSP deputies were chiefs; Morgenthau (1964), Appendix VIII, 404. Two of the three main factions within the PSP, including the dominant one led by Fily Dabo Sissoko, sought to maintain close ties with the chiefs and to nominate the party's candidates from among their ranks; GSF to HCGGAOF, Dec. 19, 1952, #701/APAS, ANM NI 3D1194. Both Sissoko and Hamadoun Dicko, one of his greatest rivals within the party, were from chiefly families; see Sidibe (2007), Pelckmans (2011).

[90] Morgenthau (1964).

[91] The language of devolution is Cooper's; (1996), part IV.

[92] I.A.A. Gabriau, comments to Conférence des CdCs du Soudan, et al., May 29, 1957, ANM NI 1D1177.

[93] Former ambassador to Mali (1960–64), Fernand Wibaux would later argue that Africanization was one of the goals of the *loi cadre*, which was intended to offer Africans an apprenticeship in government; (1992), 460–61. On Wibaux's long career,

would require "decentralization." A further step in the "democratic apprenticeship" of the AOF, councils administering rural communities (*"collectivités rurales"*) could hardly avoid trespassing on the prerogatives of *chefs de canton*. Even so the precise role of the chiefs went unstated, and no one uttered the word "chieftaincy" aloud. Still, the message had to be clear: the chiefs' days were numbered.

In short, the reforms Keita highlighted in his meeting with Nyerere had been foreshadowed but never realized by the colonial administration. Keita went well beyond what the *commandants* had envisioned. Take Africanization. After the *loi cadre*, which created new openings for the African civil servants who constituted the RDA's base, Keita and his comrades sought systematically to push French administrators out and to replace them with Soudanese. Their efforts at Africanization went a good deal further than those of some of their neighbors, particularly Niger, Chad, and Mauritania. In those territories, French schooling was much less available than it was in Soudan, and as a result few trained cadres were available to step into administrative positions. French expatriates effectively administered Niger for over a decade after independence.[94] The Malian case could not have been more different: by 1961, all of the *commandants de cercle* were Malians.[95] The same was true of the officer corps. Although certain key technical posts remained in the hands of Frenchmen (and later of expatriates of other nations), they were comparatively few in number, and those positions were less politically sensitive than those Frenchmen held in other territories, despite the fact that the

during which this once-socialist diplomat became Foccart's "right-hand man," see Bat (2012), 609–10.

[94] During its brief tenure in the territorial government in Niger, through September 1958, the Sawaba party had been frustrated in its attempts to promote African administrators and indeed to exercise its own perogatives under the tutelage of the French governor; Van Walraven (2013), 111–12. On Chad, see Nolutshungu (1996); Thompson and Adloff (1981).

[95] In 1959, Modibo Keita proudly announced that 20 of the territory's 21 *commandants* were African; Fédération du Mali, République Soudanaise, *Session Budgétaire de l'Assemblée Législative*, Nov. 17, 1959. The same was true of "all the heads of subdivisions or adminstrative posts, police commissioners and the *adjoint* to the Chief of Security"; Danioko (1984), 215–16. The vast irrigation project known as the Office du Niger was one important exception to this general trend. The "Africanization" of the *cercle* of Bamako was completed in July 1960, when Oumar Ly became its first African *commandant*; MIM D7/42. The exception, until July 1961, may have been the *commandant* of Ségou, Félix Jouanelle, a Frenchman who had married into a local family and who may have taken Malian nationality; Simonis (1993), 605. Other Frenchmen who served in the Malian government or directed state-owned companies took Malian nationality and would be threatened with the loss of their French citizenship; SGCAAM, Note à l'attention du M. le Président de la République, April 9, 1964, FPR 239.

A New Republic 65

French population in Mali increased after independence.[96] Africanization proved to be a game of sharp elbows, but an even deeper transformation was the abolition of the chieftaincy. There the stakes were even higher.

The abolition of the position of canton chief and the dismantling of the cantons themselves between 1958 and 1960 represented the culmination of a decade of political war waged by US-RDA militants and their opponents in the countryside as well as in the towns. Well aware that a republic governed by chiefs was a republic in name only, the Party sought to subordinate them to the administration, but quickly learned that this was likely to be impossible. Two contradictory structures – a centralized bureaucratic administration with modernizing aspirations and a hereditary chieftaincy condemned as "archaic and anti-democratic"[97] – could not work together smoothly. Years of struggling with both the structural complexities of the chieftaincy and individual opponents who were themselves chiefs pushed the US-RDA to dismantle an institution that had been an essential cog in the colonial system. The fact that they did so is in some ways less surprising than the fact that their neighbors, barring Guinea, did not. Rather, RDA governments in Niger and Upper Volta redefined the role of chiefs while leaving them in office.[98]

Tinkering with the chieftaincy was nothing new. The French themselves had been at it for years, alternately empowering and disempowering their African auxiliaries, attempting to establish a balance of power between administrative subalterns and men considered local royalty. Decades of colonial rule demonstrated no shortage of political experiments. These ranged from naming low-born men to posts they never otherwise would have held to manifesting strict attention to tradition or to attempting to frame and confine the authority of troubled chiefs by buttressing them with appointed councils (*conseils de notables*). None of these measures offered a way out of the conundrum posed by the practice of subordinating chiefs to

---

[96] C-G de France à Bamako to MAE, Direction du Personnel et de l'Administration Générale, Dec. 28, 1968, MAE 2536; cf. Simonis (1993), 607–08.
[97] Modibo Keita, Fédération du Mali, République Soudanaise, *Session Budgétaire de l'Assemblée Législative*, Nov. 17, 1959.
[98] It is commonly argued that only Guinea abolished the chieftaincy. See among others Schmidt, (2007a); Suret-Canale (1988a). This is an error. Upper Volta worked to diminish the power of the chiefs in the years immediately before and after independence; Skinner (1989), 204–05. In Niger, the Sawaba-led government dismissed several chiefs in 1958, but the French governor quickly reinstated them; van Walraven (2013), 139–40, 202–03. Later, Hamani Diori's government sought to win chiefs' support while diminishing their authority, and Niger would leave the canton intact; Idrissa (2001a); PPN (1961).

administrators while attempting to preserve their local authority. And none was as extreme as those the RDA would adopt after years of deliberation, beginning with Madeira Keita's propositions in the immediate postwar years.

In Conakry, in the first few months after the establishment of the interterritorial RDA, Keita had questioned the chiefs' legitimacy in the starkest terms, condemning them as "collaborators." The term pricked the emerging anticolonial conscience of his interlocutor, Georges Balandier, a former *résistant*.[99] In spite of the fact that Keita had an "uncle" who was a *chef de canton*, his views would not soften over the years.[100] In a 1949 report on the chieftaincy to the second congress of the RDA, meeting in Abidjan, Keita argued that kings and chiefs had once ruled legitimately. No longer. The colonial administration had corrupted the institution by appointing "former interpreters, *tirailleurs*, militiamen, and houseboys (*domestiques*) ... With these new mannequins, the chieftaincy lost all its sense. The chief was no longer the best soldier [or] the wise guide beloved by his subjects (*administrés*). He had become a mistrusted person, always worried, always under threat of being dismissed."[101] This passage might be read as a defense of tradition, but Keita did not propose a return to the *status quo ante*. Rather he urged that the transformation of the chieftaincy be made total, with chiefs being elected "at every level." The next year, at the first territorial meeting of the Guinean RDA – the last that Keita would lead – a motion called for "the democratization of the chieftaincy, with free elections of chiefs, [who should be] sufficiently paid, assisted by elected councils, and protected from arbitrary administrative acts."[102] This position would evolve over time, and RDA activists would insist on distinguishing between canton chiefs and village chiefs. In 1952, RDA elder Mamby Sidibe would argue for the election of the latter by heads of family (*chefs de famille*); in 1956, Paul Traore Sibiry argued for electing the village chiefs and abolishing the position of the canton chief

---

[99] Balandier (1948b) 403–04; see chapter 1.
[100] Madeira Keita to "Cher Monsieur," Théodore Monod, requesting leave to attend the conference creating the RDA, Oct. 3, 1946; IFAN-Guinea A1/17, Collection IFAN-Dakar.
[101] Madeira Keita, *Rapport sur le problème des chefs africains*, presented to the Second Congress of the RDA, Jan. 1949, Abidjan; Danioko (1984), appendix 33.
[102] Mamadou Madeira Keita, Secretary-General, *Rapport Général d'Activité 1947–1950*, presented on behalf of the Executive Committee to the First Territorial Congress of the PDG (Section Guinéen du RDA), ANS 17G573.

altogether.[103] That was the road the US-RDA would take, but it would prove to be a long one.

The stakes could hardly have been higher. When colonial *commandants* summoned their *chefs de canton* to warn them that they would all be fired if the US-RDA were to win elections, they were proven right, albeit only in the long run and not in the way they had meant it.[104] Once the US-RDA came to power in a context of territorial autonomy and universal suffrage, the canton chiefs did lose their jobs. Little surprise, then, that the political contest in Soudan as among its neighbors was intense. From the first territorial elections in 1946 through the elections of 1957, when the US-RDA won a majority, the political process had been fraught with violence.[105] Even on the eve of the party's victories, its deputies received death threats, and canton chiefs in many parts of the territory campaigned actively against US-RDA candidates.[106] In Yanfolila, the chief stated flatly that he would never accept an RDA civil servant in his village. Even collecting the wild bush fruits that blossom in the rainy season was forbidden to people who favored the party.[107] In the grazing lands of Diré, an African veterinarian refused to vaccinate the livestock of RDA supporters, leaving only the herd of the sole PSP party member protected against disease.[108] Minor insults and indignities cascaded, sometimes giving way to major injuries. Aoua Keita famously recounts being verbally abused by a veteran in the *cercle* of Koutiala who told her that he had several wives to "scratch his back" every night and no lessons to learn from a woman who did not know her place. In some southern villages during the same campaign of 1959, "the powder spoke," and at least one man died.[109] Every election left blood on the floor, often literally.

This poisonous politics was the product of a long-running political war in which the stakes only grew higher and higher. The war had been fought

---

[103] Mamby Sidibe, "Soudan : Justice ou bon plaisir?" and related articles in *l'Afrique Noire*, 7, Jan. 17, 1952; Paul Traore Sibiry, "Décapitons le canton," and related articles arguing divergent positions in *Afrique Nouvelle*, 483, Nov. 6, 1956.
[104] Danioko (1984), 188.
[105] On 1946-47, see Danioko (1984), 188; for later events, see, e.g., Telegram from Niafunké to "Deputé Modibo," n.d. (April 1957) and GSF to CdC Niafunké, April 9, 1957, ANM NI 3D1194; Réunion extraordinaire du BP, Nov. 24, 1957, BPNCMLN 83.
[106] Barema Boucoum to GSF, Feb. 11, 1957, Mamadou Fadiala Keita to CdC Macina, March 28, 1957, CdC Macina to GSF, March 28, 1957; all in ANM NI 3D1194.
[107] BPN, P-V, Dec. 13, 1957, BPNCMLN 83.
[108] *Rapport de tournée effectuée par le Conseiller Territorial Ba Ahmadou*, Diré, Feb. 27, 1958, BPNCMLN 83.
[109] Keita (1975), 388–91.

mostly in the countryside, where the chiefs could hardly fail to see the storm coming as imperial reforms and expanded suffrage brought the US-RDA to power. In late November 1956, in the wake of the *loi cadre*, chiefs from all over the AOF had met in Dakar to establish a union that would protect their interests. By that point, the logic of the labor movement had come full circle: the men who had incarnated the idea of a stable, precapitalist rural order on which the administration could build were now engaged in a form of collective action that defined them as civil servants and underscored their material reliance on the state. "The chiefs refuse to play the role of scapegoats for the administration and targets for the political parties," read a phrase in their resolution, one that became a headline in *Afrique Nouvelle*.[110] Still, the very act of creating a union made their opponents' argument for them. In a pointed article in the same newspaper a few months earlier, Saifoulaye Diallo, Sékou Touré's lieutenant in the PDG, had asked whether the chieftaincy was "traditional or administrative?"[111] By creating the union, the chiefs admitted that it was both, but that was unsatisfactory.

The core of the chief's grievance was that political reforms such as the extension of imperial citizenship had sapped their authority and rendered their task of keeping order and collecting taxes in the countryside virtually impossible.[112] Their status had been unclear since the immediate postwar years, and that lack of clarity was ever more troubling.[113] As the chiefs pointed out when they met in Dakar, no mention of the chieftaincy itself can be found in the constitution of 1946. It was equally absent from the new *loi cadre*, where one might have expected to find it.[114] What they wanted, above all, was a text defining their position, with its rights, duties, and privileges. What, they asked, was the role of a chief in a new Africa? That question provokes others, which they did not pose. One was old: What was the basis of chiefs' claim to power – the weight of the colonial state or of tradition itself? Another was new, and more troubling: Could a fellow citizen be expected to relate to a chief as a subject might have done? In theory, citizens were

---

[110] Almamy Koressi and Mamadou Hady Ly, "Les chefs refusent d'être 'les boucs emissaires de l'Administration et la cible des partis,'" *Afrique Nouvelle*, 488, Dec. 11, 1956.
[111] Diallo, "La Chefferie Administrative ou Traditionelle?" *Afrique Nouvelle*, 460, May 29, 1956.
[112] See Keita Ouremba, "Démocratisons la chefferie," *Afrique Nouvelle*, 483, Nov. 6, 1956.
[113] Dimier demonstrates the depth and significance of this problem within the French administration and even the Conseil d'état; (2003), 103–05.
[114] Koressi and Ly, "Les chefs refusent ...," *Afrique Nouvelle*, 488, Dec. 11, 1956.

A New Republic

equal; chiefs and subjects clearly were not. Could a new citizenry and an evolving chieftaincy coexist?

Although the chiefs met in the federal capital of Dakar, the political war over the chieftaincy would largely be waged in Guinea and Soudan. There, support for a dramatic reform of the chieftaincy seemed to be strongest, and the new union would choose its leaders, President Almamy Koressi and Secretary General Mamadi Kourouma, from those two territories.[115] An association of chiefs existed in both Guinea and Dahomey, and early in 1957, the new union would come to the Soudan.[116] The US-RDA saw the union as an invention of the colonial administration.[117] Its emergence highlighted the dual nature of the problem of the chieftaincy, political and administrative. There was no avoiding the fact that across the AOF, the conflict between the chiefs and "the parties" (really one party, the RDA) was at its root political. Yet the solution to the dilemma as a whole lay in recognizing that it was equally an administrative one and tackling it as such. Doing so made a new set of tactics available to Keita and his comrades, who were recently empowered by the combination of their victories at the polls and the effects of the *loi cadre*. Having lost elections when they mattered less, the US-RDA had the good fortune to win them when they mattered more. By 1957, when the party secured its majority, control over the territorial assembly meant not only control over its budget, but also the ability to form a government. This was a golden opportunity, and the party's leaders, notably Idrissa Diarra, tried to assure that its militants would have the good sense to profit from the lessons they had learned during their long years in the opposition.[118] On the other side of the aisle, Fily Dabo Sissoko expressed his confidence in the fact that "France" would never abolish the chieftaincy.[119] However, in the new political scenario, it was no longer up to "France."

---

[115] "Les Chefs de l'AOF décident de se grouper en syndicat," *Afrique Nouvelle*, 487, Dec. 4, 1956.

[116] Madeira Keita, *Etude sur les evenements de Guinée*, prepared for BPN US-RDA, Nov. 1956, forwarded as "Renseignements (très confidentiel) ...," Territoire du Soudan Français, Direction des Services de Police, Nov. 27, 1956, #239/illeg., ANM NII 1E1244; Danioko (1984), 209.

[117] Idrissa Diarra, *Circulaire à toutes les sous-sections de l'US*, n.d. (Feb-March 1957), ANM NI 3D1194.

[118] Idrissa Diarra, *Circulaire...*, n.d. (Feb-March 1957), ANM NI 3D1194.

[119] *Verité*, 523, March 13, 1957; this may be the same speech in which Sissoko reportedly said that his seat in the assembly would never be soiled by the presence of a *bilali* (slave or person of slave ancestry); "Bon rétardataire," *l'Essor*, 2443, March 4, 1957; also cited in Danioko (1984), 109.

The first new tactic was a simple one. Once in government, the US-RDA simply refused to appoint new chiefs when sitting ones died. As Minister of the Interior, Madeira Keita orchestrated an evolving practice that essentially condemned the canton chiefs to fade away by neglecting to make new appointments. Arguing for this approach in a meeting of the Bureau at the home of the late Mamadou Konaté one night in July 1957, Makane Macoumba captured this idea with the phrase "suppression by extinction."[120] Although a clear policy had yet to emerge from debates within party circles, by that time a gradual move toward abolition was afoot. At the end of 1957, Madeira Keita made clear to the *commandants* – a group subordinate to him but not yet 'Africanized' – that he intended to slow down the nomination of new canton chiefs while their status was being debated. On the other hand, he wrote, the nominations of new village chiefs – following, for instance, death or resignation of their predecessors – would be handled expeditiously. In the new dispensation, village chiefs would be vital. Moreover, all new chiefs were to be elected by "committees on custom," a surprisingly moderate proposal that would soon be swept away in favor of a public vote.[121]

The second tactic was more aggressive. After sharp internal debate, the BPN decided only a few months later that no mistake or infraction on the part of the canton chiefs would be tolerated. Given any excuse, the government would simply fire them and leave their posts vacant.[122] This dynamic was already at work. On the advice of the *commandant de cercle* of Timbuktu, Keita had dismissed the chief of the canton of Rhergo for insulting and threatening a member of the territorial council, Abdoulaye Nock. Although the ex-chief complained that he had been provoked by Nock's griots and even tried to sue to get his job back, Keita's decision was firm.[123] Stripping Mahamane Bawani of his post achieved three things at once: it weakened the PSP, which was strong in that particular canton; it affirmed the authority of councilors and of the Minister of the Interior; and it marked an early blow in what would become a rapid and steady

[120] BPN, P-V, July 30, 1957, BPNCMLN 83.
[121] See Minister of the Interior, Soudan Français, Circular to *commandants de cercle*, Dec. 18, 1957, # 292/DI/2; Minister of the Interior, Soudan Français, Circular to all *cercles* and *subdivisions*, Dec. 31, 1957, # 198/DI, both in ANM NI ID2940.
[122] BPN, P-V, Feb. 17, 1958, BPNCMLN 83. Compare *Verité*, which accused the US-RDA government of appointing chiefs as it saw fit; *Verité*, 828, May 31, 1958. The real threat to the chieftaincy as an institution was not only that chiefs were dismissed – the colonial administration had done the same – but that posts were left vacant.
[123] Min. Interieur décision #44442/DIL [sic notes], Dec. 20, 1957; CdC Timbuktu to Chef du Territoire, Oct. 31, 1957, #77c, MIM 56.

A New Republic

drumbeat of dismissals that carried on through 1958 in places such as Sikasso and Douentza, and in 1959 in Nioro, Bandiagara, and elsewhere.[124] Keita held firm in not naming new chiefs, in spite of what must have been strong pressure to do so. In May 1958, he refused to replace a canton chief he had dismissed with an RDA stalwart who had "suffered" for the party. Rather than rewarding loyalty and past service, as the colonial state would have done, Keita held the line, insisting that the *chef de subdivision*, a civil servant, should "administer [the former canton] himself."[125] The vise of the new administration continued to tighten around the chiefs, and a new rule mandated that towns and cities with elected municipal governments (*communes de plein et de moyen exercice*) no longer fell under the authority of canton chiefs.[126] Although at the outset this looked like a dual system of government – democratic in town, authoritarian in the villages – in fact the writing was on the wall for all of the canton chiefs.

They would not go quietly. Arguing that they had been unfairly treated, several former chiefs adopted Bawani's tactic and sued the territory's government, targeting Madeira Keita in particular in his role as Minister of the Interior.[127] Others were less confrontational, although not more subtle. Having been battered and bruised, at least rhetorically, in the electoral campaigns of 1957, some chiefs refused to carry out their most essential duty vis-à-vis the administration, collecting taxes. They either let the taxes sit with the village chiefs who had collected them or they told the central administration that it was simply impossible to collect taxes when their authority had been undermined.[128] In some places, the dismissal of the chief was a popular measure; in others, less so. In the *cercle* of Kayes, one canton organized a festival to celebrate the dismissal of their chief: 41 bulls and 141 sheep were to be slaughtered for the event, to which the US-RDA leadership was invited.[129] Not everyone was pleased with such

---

[124] ANM 2E147FR, dossier 1; ANM 2E118FR.
[125] Meeting of Bureau Politique and Sécretaires Généraux of *quartiers*, May 2, 1958, BPNCMLN 83.
[126] Arrêté territorial #461 D. I.-3, *JOSF*, April 10, 1958. At the same time, the number of such *communes* increased substantially as many smaller towns were elevated to this higher status. Ernst has this *arrêté* do more than it does, attributing it with abolishing the chieftaincy; (1976), 93.
[127] MIM 56; see in particular the case of Moussa Sanogo of Kapolondougou (Sikasso).
[128] Min. Interieur Madeira Keita, Circular to CdCs and Chefs de Subdivision, Dec. 19, 1957, ANM NI 1D2940.
[129] *Recueil périodique des principaux renseignements reçus par le bureau d'études de l'AOF*, #13, Nov. 23 to 30, 1958, SHAT 10T148.

radical change. In Macina and Bandiagara, people sought to hold on to their chiefs, and in the former a petition circulated to that effect.[130] In the *cercle* of Bamako, two of the smaller cantons sent delegations to the *commandant* asking that their chiefs be maintained in office and that their collective identity as cantons be maintained.[131] Much more was at stake than the positions of individual chiefs, their families, and their retainers. As in the contemporary process of decentralization, entire villages risked the loss of social status, economic opportunity, and access to state investment in infrastructure if chiefs from other communities were selected to replace those who departed, or if, as would come to pass, the cantons were dissolved.[132]

Administrators, too, were not unanimously in favor of the new dispensation, and the attitude some of them adopted earned a sharp rebuke from the party newspaper, *l'Essor*.[133] Some *commandants* quietly contested the legitimacy of the new territorial government by suggesting to the chiefs that Bamako's reform was merely a storm that would blow over. Others foresaw an administrative nightmare, a vision they expressed directly to the Minister of the Interior. As the *commandant* of Bandiagara noted, the canton chiefs represented an important step in the hierarchical ladder, and without them as intermediaries, one civil servant might be confronted with scores, even hundreds, of villages to administer. There was no sense, he wrote, in extending the purview of government while at the same time reducing its capacity.[134] Yet in the end, the strongest argument against the chiefs – for those who needed persuading – was arguably the most anodyne one. Simply put, chiefs cost more than civil servants did, and their management was less efficient.

Reflecting on the situation he stepped into on coming to power as the Minister of the Interior in 1957, Keita noted that the territory of Soudan

---

[130] BE/AOF 130–31, Dec. 15 [1958], SHAT 10T702; *Recueil périodique* ..., #16, Dec. 15 to 30 1958, SHAT 10T148.
[131] Administrateur en chef Blondiaux, Bamako to Chef de Subdivision Central de Bamako, n.d. (Oct. 3, 1958), #214/CF, MIM, Correspondances et Divers, 1958–60 (unnumbered box, hereafter MIM 1958–60).
[132] Madeira Keita, Circular, Dec. 18, 1957, #292, NI 1D2940. Scholarship on decentralization since the 1990s (some of it very good) tends to overlook entirely the historical depth of the problem, while locating its institutional imperatives in international organizations; see, e.g., Fay, Koné, and Quiminal (2006); cf. Dimier (2003). Diawara offers a history of decentralization, but does not address this period; (2011). On the ramifications of African states' uneven extension of authority, see Boone (2003) and Herbst (2000).
[133] "A/s de la suppression ... ," *l'Essor*, 2960, Dec. 24, 1958.
[134] CdC Bandiagara to Min. Interieur, Dec. 23, 1958, #721, MIM 1958–60.

A New Republic 73

had been quite simply "under-administered."[135] In a process he termed "decentralization," he had then set out to create as many as 500 new administrative posts, to transform subdivisions into free-standing *cercles*, and to break large *cercles* such as Bamako into smaller units.[136] It would be much cheaper to operate administrative posts in these new districts, in which village chiefs and civil servants would work together, he reasoned, than it would be to sustain the canton chiefs, who cost the territory at least a million francs per year.[137] At the end of 1958, a congress of the US-RDA resolved to eliminate all of the canton chieftaincies,[138] and Territorial Vice-President Jean-Marie Koné announced that each individual village would establish a council to select its future chiefs.[139] The party's declaration and Koné's initiative were both a bit premature. In fact, it took another eighteen months to carry through with the process of stripping the canton chiefs of their functions and attributing their responsibilities to administrators or village chiefs. By June 1960, Madeira Keita could announce to the *conference des cadres* of the US-RDA that all of the canton chiefs had been dismissed, with the exception of those in the vast and thinly populated Saharan zones where the chiefs of nomadic tribes had been maintained. As for village councils, this initiative was partly derailed.

Originally intended as an experiment in rural direct democracy, the village councils represented a key element in a new architecture of

---

[135] "l'Organisation administratif de la République Soudanaise," *l'Essor*, 3401, June 4, 1960.
[136] The term "decentralization" appears in Min. Interieur Madeira Keita to CdC Koutiala, Dec. 4, 1957, #281/DI; see also correspondance between Madeira Keita and *commandants* of Koutiala and Bamako, MIM 1958–60.
[137] The territory's budget for 1959 indicates a little over 1,000,000 was allotted for "chieftaincies" in that year; Tableau annexe I à la loi no. 59–15 du 22 Mai 1959, Budget de la République Soudanaise, *JORS*, June 15, 1959, 501. See also *Primes de Rendement–chefs de cantons, du tribu et assimilés*, Min. Interieur Soudan, Decision #38/DI2, March 31, 1958, ANM NI 1D2940. Bamako's *commandant* believed the figure to be ten million; CdC Bamako to Min. Interieur March 18, 1958, #54, C.F., MIM 1958–60.
[138] "Resolution de Politique Générale, 5' Congrès, Août 1958," reproduced in Campmas (1978), 225. When implemented, this decision met with resistance from many administrators charged with carrying it out; "Les Chefferies de canton déclarées vacantes en quasi-totalité," *l'Essor*, 2956, Dec. 19, 1958.
[139] J.-M. Koné, Président du Conseil de Gouvernement à Président d'Assemblée Territoriale, Nov. 1958 (n.d., stamped "arrivé le 12 Nov. 1958, #744"), ANM NI 1E1907. In this interregnum, the person holding Koné's position was effectively charged with the day-to-day running of the territory, under the supervision of the *Chef de territoire*, formerly the governor.

authority in rural Mali.[140] In this new dispensation, the village – or among nomads, the fraction – would be the "real base of democratic organization in our state."[141] The new arrangement was resolutely republican; the accretion of affiliations that had defined some cantons in ethnic rather than geographic terms was to be ignored.[142] In the new village councils, everyone would live under the same local authority. But the key to the new arrangement was the assertion that the village was the basic administrative unit in Mali, and that "every citizen belongs to a village." This was true neither in the Sahara nor in the south; both nomads and a growing number of city dwellers belonged to no particular village. Moreover, in the published text no mention was made of nomads at all; it was only in the version printed in *l'Essor* that fractions were equated to villages.[143]

Other important reforms did not survive; "democracy" dilated, opening and closing. The most important attribute of the new village councils would have been its ability to elect the village chief. Very quickly, however, that power was lost; the local administrator would name the chief, in consultation with the council. In the opinion of Madeira Keita, this would allow the administrator to avoid installing an incompetent, inefficient, or unpopular chief. French intelligence saw this as an aggressive bid by the new government to secure its power, but of course this was no more power than the colonial state had long exercised.[144] Other transformations were no less important, and they generated questions that echoed the debate over suffrage. Who would sit on the village council: heads of families (*dutigiw*), or heads of households (*gwatigiw*)? In most of Mali's villages, the first option would preserve the power of the gerontocracy, whereas the latter would allow the participation of younger married men living under the authority and in the compounds of their fathers or grandfathers.[145] In either case, this would have been exclusively male suffrage.

---

[140] This architecture would be paralleled by cooperatively run structures for production and distribution; the latter in particular would fail. See Diarra (1964), Diarrah (1986), and van Beusekom (2008).

[141] Madeira Keita, "Les Reformes de structure dans la République Soudanaise," *l'Essor*, 3398, June 1, 1960; Modibo Keita, speech of Oct. 1, 1961 in Keita (1965), esp. 79–80.

[142] See, e.g, the cantons of the *cercle* of Nioro, which included "Kaarta-Soninke, Peulhs Rangabes, Foulbeskaartankes, Ouassoulonkes," and so on; Min. de l'Interieur, Féd. du Mali, Rép. Soudanaise, Décision #741/DI-2, Dec. 31, 1959, ANM 2E147FR.

[143] Ordonnance #43 D. I. portant organisation des villages au Soudan et créant des conseils de villages, JORS, numéro spécial, April 1, 1959, XXXV–XXXVIII. Compare Madeira Keita, "Les Reformes de la Structure . . . ."; U.S.-R.D.A. (1962), 31.

[144] *Recueil périodique* . . . #31, May 21 to 27, 1959, SHAT 10T151.

[145] That is to say, elder males within the patriline. The PSP opposed consulting heads of household ("*goatigiuis*" [sic., *gwatigiw*]); *Verité*, 584, July 19, 1957.

A New Republic

In the end, the councilors themselves were elected and empowered to nominate a chief whose appointment the administration would confirm or deny. Could women cast votes in the elections to the village council? In one draft, they could not; in another, final, one, they could. Could women serve as councilors? In early versions, they could; later, their role was limited to that of electors.[146] The victory, then, was a partial one, and the "universal suffrage" that obtained in national elections had been set aside at the village level. The tide went out on other democratic initiatives as well. In the context of the Mali Federation, Madeira Keita had spoken confidently about installing regional assemblies across Soudan to parallel structures that existed in Senegal.[147] This project collapsed, abandoned in the original trauma of the break-up of the Federation.

When the new government pursued these policies of decentralization, democratization, and abolition of the chieftaincy across the territory, it did so unevenly. Still, what appeared from a Saharan perspective to be a policy of "indecisiveness and makeshift pragmatism, cloaked in socialist rhetoric" was actually the reflection of a strategy developed over many years and with much debate.[148] The goal was never truly in doubt. Yet the Saharan region serves as a test case, demonstrating that the Party pushed harder where it felt strongest, but did so taking into account both the character of the chief and his relations with the administrators on the ground. The dismantling of the cantons and the dismissal of their chiefs affected other regions of Mali before the Sahara, which was effectively considered another country both by its inhabitants and by many of those who sought to govern it.[149] That perception neither began nor ended with the US-RDA government, but the party's years in power confirmed it de facto while denying it de jure. On the one hand, the US-RDA attempted to maintain a parallel between the way it governed nomads in the North and the rest of country – thus by analogy, and for instance, if village councils were to be elected elsewhere, "fraction" councils would be elected in the North. On the other hand, the Party approached the problem of tinkering with structures of authority gingerly, perhaps bearing in mind the

---

[146] *Recueil périodique* ... #32, May 28 to June 3, 1959, SHAT 10T151; Sall (1989), 29, quoting law on GPRSM, #60–9, June 9, 1960; Cf. J.-M. Koné, *Projet d'arrêté organisant les cercles* ... n.d. (Nov. 1958), and *arrêté* signed Madeira Keita, n.d. (Nov. 1958), ANM NI 1E1907.

[147] Madeira Keita, "Les Reformes de la Structure ... ."

[148] Lecocq (2010), 146. In fact, many within the US-RDA had hoped for a more rapid process of reform; BPNCMLN 83.

[149] Lecocq (2010).

admonition of one of the last French Saharan officers, Captain Bretaudeau, that even after decades of colonial rule, "outside of tribal authority, there is only anarchy in nomad country."[150] In the Sahara, the chieftaincy was diminished, not discarded. To the contrary: the responsibilities of *chefs de fraction* increased.[151] Following the death of Attaher ag Illi, the government left the position of the *amenokal* (leader) of the Kel Adagh officially vacant in the crucial years immediately before the Tuareg rebellion of 1963–64. When the Kel Adagh chose Attaher's son Zeyd as his successor, the administration insisted on naming another potential heir, Intalla, the new *amenokal*, but "only unofficially."[152] Such policies were surely maladroit, even "incoherent," and they helped push Zeyd into rebellion. But in the Sahara, governing via chiefs was at once ideologically unacceptable and politically necessary. In the wake of the rebellion in the Adagh, some chiefs served as mediators, and they were restored to their functions in 1965.[153] Only in the context of the Active Revolution in 1967 would the Party officially abolish the chieftaincy in the North. That policy would not outlive the regime itself.[154]

By attacking the chieftaincy and dissolving the cantons, the new government had gone some way toward creating a republic founded on equality among citizens during the short period in which the Soudanese Republic formed part of the French Community. That was no small achievement. Perhaps more importantly in the long term, the territorial government had opened up a new political space that the party would strain, and fail, to fill. That move was imperfect in telling and fatal ways. The US-RDA's long-simmering project of establishing a democracy in the rural areas in which the vast majority of the population lived contrasts sharply with its intolerance of dissent, its suppression of minority parties, and the extreme sanctions to which it submitted its opponents. Among the first supporters of the old aristocracy to suffer the consequences of that contradiction was Moussa Diarra, a former member of the PSP and a descendant of the Ngolossi Diarra of Ségou, a family that had resisted the invasion of el

---

[150] Captain Bretaudeau, Subdivision de Menaka, n.d., MIM D7/20.
[151] On the first point, see Boilley (2012 [1999]), 355–56; on the second, Lecocq (2010), 145.
[152] Lecocq (2010), 146–49. Also, Boilley (2012 [1999]), 317.
[153] Lecocq (2010), 149.
[154] Arrêté #1197, D. 1–2, Dec. 29, 1967, cited by Danioko (1984), ch. 7. Under Moussa Traore, the *amenokal*'s status would again be "elevated," and Intalla would eventually serve as the deputy from Kidal; Boilley (2012 [1999]), 364. He was also a leading figure in the UDPM party from the time of its creation in the late 1970s. On the chieftaincy in the Sahara post-independence, see notably Klute (1999).

hajj Umar Tal a century earlier. Within the Soudanese Republic, Diarra tried to establish a regional political party, the *Union Démocratique Ségovienne* (UDS). One thing led to another, and the tinder of local politics soon ignited. A police commissioner was killed; the government razed a village in retribution and packed Diarra off to prison.[155] Others would soon endure similar repression: Fily Dabo Sissoko, Hamadoun Dicko, and Muhammad Mahmud Ould al-Shaykh, the so-called "*qadi* of Timbuktu," among others.[156] Its authority contested at home and abroad, the new government had taken the gloves off even before independence.

NOBILITY OR SELF-DETERMINATION?

Madeira Keita's sweeping statement dismissing the last of the canton chiefs preceded by only nineteen days the Mali Federation's solemn declaration of independence on June 20, 1960. Unlike Keita's condemnation of the chiefs, that first version of "independence" would soon look tepid and incomplete. In negotiating the status of the Mali Federation within the French Community, Keita and his colleagues had insisted on the autonomy of the Malian army and rejected the possibility of mutual defense. However, the same accords entailed the continued presence of French military bases on Malian federal territory in places as far apart as Dakar and Tessalit.[157] With such imperial privileges intact, what had looked like independence in June was thought to be something else altogether by September. By then the Mali Federation – an untenable marriage between Senegal and Soudan – had collapsed, and the Soudanese Republic had been pushed toward another version of independence. In his speech to an "extraordinary" congress of the US-RDA on September 22, 1960, the day taken to mark the birth of the Republic of Mali, Secretary General Modibo Keita would claim that the collapse of the Mali Federation had assured, even completed, the independence of Senegal and of other African states. In his recounting, the Republic of Mali itself had also been liberated

---

[155] Among the best sources on the repression of the UDS are Simonis (1995); Danioko (1984), 228n61; Dallier, Amb Fr to MAE, DAM, Jan. 27, 1969, #8 DAM, CADN 63. Moussa Diarra was the father of Cheikh Modibo Diarra, Mali's interim Prime Minister during the political crisis of 2012.
[156] On Sissoko and Dicko, see Chapter 6. On Ould al-Shaykh, see Lecocq (2010), 52-58 and Hall (2011b), 299-306, 314.
[157] "La conférence des cadres de l'Union Soudanaise-RDA," *l'Essor*, 3396, May 30, 1960. See also *l'Essor (Hebdo.)*, April 8, 1960.

and was now free to pursue "a true socialism [oriented] uniquely in relation to the interests of the most disadvantaged sectors [*couches*] of society." Idrissa Diarra hammered the same themes. In his own speech, Diarra insisted that the demise of the Federation freed the Republic to pursue its own path. Following the line of analysis dear to the Soudanese – by which Senegal needed Soudan's riches[158] – Diarra argued that without Senegal applying the brakes, Soudan could choose socialism.[159] This "option," as it became known, represented the real rupture of September 22nd, and for years, the date would be celebrated as the anniversary of the "socialist option," rather than of independence as such.

The socialist option represented the party's second dramatic choice in two years, and its commemoration demonstrates that the bright horizon of "independence" was actually a blurry boundary. The first choice had been made in 1958, when the US-RDA advocated agreeing to the proposed constitution of the French Fifth Republic, which created a Community of states exercising internal autonomy while reserving the domains of diplomacy, security, and monetary policy for Paris. The question would be posed in a referendum, in which 98% of voters would accept the new bargain. Although in hindsight the conclusion might seem to have been foregone, the moment was charged and dense with events. In Bamako just before the September vote, Senator and PSP Political Secretary Mamadou Mbodge was murdered in the street in what had begun as a minor scuffle between party militants. While Madeira Keita – as Minister of the Interior and acting president – called for calm, PSP party leader Fily Dabo Sissoko claimed that Mbodge was only the first of a series of targets already identified by the RDA.[160] Within a week, the RDA would lose someone too, although not to violence. The death of Ouezzin Coulibaly stripped Upper Volta of its leader, the party of one of its leading lights, and Houphouët-Boigny of a close lieutenant. The funeral drew a strong delegation from among the US-RDA leadership. They would return home,

---

[158] See, for instance, fiche marked "*Eléments du dossier soudanais recueillis auprès d'un membre de la Délégation malienne,*" Sept. 1, 1960, stamped "secret" and "seen by the General," FPR230.

[159] "Rapport sur la situation politique par le President Modibo Keita" and "Discours d'ouverture prononcé par le Secrétaire Politique Idrissa Diarra," *Congrès Extraordinaire de l'US-RDA les 22 et 23 Septembre 1960*, CADN Bamako 55.

[160] Danioko (1984), 215–16, 227 n60; "Un incident fortuit finit par tragedie," *l'Essor*, 2865, Sept. 3, 1958; Sissoko, "In memoriam: à Mamadou Mbodje," *Verité*, 905, Sept. 10, 1958; Sory Konake, "2 Sept., journée de deuil," *Verité*, 915, Sept. 22, 1958.

hold an extraordinary meeting, and emerge to advocate for a "yes" vote accepting the constitution.[161] Guinea's PDG, on the other hand, abstained from attending, and Sékou Touré shirked both his obligation to Coulibaly and his widow and a final meeting with the RDA leadership before the climactic vote. Guinea's voters would go on to vote "No," making Guinea the sole territory to reject the constitution and the first to accede formally to independence, in October.[162]

While Guinea refused to enter the Community, the Soudan went farther in. A month after Guinea's precipitous exit from the French empire, Soudan became the first territory in sub-Saharan Africa to exercise the option provided by the new constitution to become a member state within the Community.[163] On the face of it, this contrast is puzzling as the history of anticolonial activism in the two countries was deeply entwined, and they would become close if wary allies in the 1960s. But in 1958, the Soudan's leaders, as were others elsewhere, were working toward the elaboration of some kind of multiterritorial grouping. The US-RDA had intended its "Yes" vote to preserve the possibility of moving toward a collective unified independence.[164] It reduced the question to independence now – in haste, uncertainty, and isolation – or later, in unity. In contrast, and although their motivations differed, Sékou Touré, Soudanese labor activist Mme. Sow Aissata Coulibaly, and Sissoko's faction within the PSP had each sought to frame the vote as a choice between slavery and freedom.[165] As we have seen, Sow said so explicitly, and the PSP's newspaper *Verité* implied as much by identifying a "No" vote as a vote for nobility (*horonya*), a term that it used as synonymous with "independence" or

---

[161] Aoua Keita narrates forcefully the intertwined drama of politics and mourning; (1975), ch. 8.
[162] Two recent works demonstrate that the positions taken by Touré and the PDG were in the words of Abdoulaye Diallo "ambiguous and tardy"; Diallo (2008), 268; Schmidt (2005). Diallo argues that students and teachers pushed the political leadership to support the "No" position; Schmidt and Pauthier (2007) underscore the role of women.
[163] Senegal and Mauritania did the same immediately afterward; *Afrique Nouvelle*, Nov. 28, 1958, #590.
[164] In a September 1959 party congress, Modibo Keita would further justify the "Yes" vote as necessary in light of the incomplete "Africanization" of the administration, the determined resistance of the PSP (which would have opposed whatever position the Party took), and most importantly, the fact that the remnants of the colonial administration – "having created the mystique of the Black [Soudanese] and the White [Saharans]" – would have ginned up a conflict that would have cost the Soudan its Northern half; Campmas (1978), 141.
[165] Touré in particular grounded his rhetoric in the past by referring to his putative ancestor Samori Touré, the anticolonial empire builder captured 60 years to the day before the vote would be held.

"liberation."[166] In the same pages, however, one could read dissenting views. Under the headline "The Soudan's 'Yes' is more Noble," Hamadoun Dicko made the RDA's argument even as he criticized the party's tactics. A "Yes" vote left the door open for federation with other territories, he wrote, and only unity within the Soudan and beyond could secure the territory's independence.[167] Yet Soudan was far from being unified. In a debate before a youth conference with Majhemout Diop, the Senegalese leader of the minority Parti African de l'Indépendance (PAI), Madeira Keita not only failed to persuade his audience to accept the RDA's choice, he was shouted down.[168] In the wake of such sharp debate, Dicko, Keita, and the US-RDA would prevail, but that result likely owed more to party discipline and to the support of the administration than to any other factors.

And then there was the other referendum, the dog that did not bark. Before entering the Community by voting "Yes," the political leadership of the Mali Federation had assured itself of a way out. Senghor was, after all, one of the French empire's constitutional architects. He knew enough to build in a safety exit, one that he had demanded through unofficial channels late in the day.[169] It existed in two forms. The territories that made up Mali could leave the Community either through a process negotiated by the elected leadership of France, the former territories, and their new Federation or via a second referendum in which the question of whether to stay or go would once again be put to the electorate. In 1959, Madeira Keita, Idrissa Diarra, and Valdiodio N'Diaye of Senegal pushed hard for the second option, as did the PAI and the powerful union UGTAN.[170]

---

[166] For PSP language, see in particular "Chant Malingué," Verité, 918, Sept. 25, 1958. This song uses the Mandekan term "*horoya*" or "*horonya*" rather than "*yéréta*" to refer to independence. While the latter suggests self-determination, the former means "nobility," as opposed to slave descent. The song valorizes a return to the past and to tradition, in which social hierarchies distinguishing servile or noble descent played an important role. It is also worth pointing out that in the Mande episteme – that which claims roots in the thirteenth century Mali empire – refusal is noble.

[167] Hamadoun Dicko, "Le Oui du Soudan a plus de noblesse," Verité, 922, Oct. 2, 1958; and "Bâtir notre Soudan," Verité, 925, Oct. 6, 1958.

[168] Diallo (2005), 177–78; Direction des Services de Police de Soudan, Bamako, Synthèse mensuelle des renseignements, Aug. 4, 1958, CADN Bamako 1. On the PAI in Mali, see Touré and Bamba (2002), ch. 2. Ironically, Madeira Keita was defending a position that was not his own.

[169] Senghor, audio interview, 1986, Afrique, une Histoire Sonore: 1, le Temps des indépendances (RFI, 2001).

[170] P. Lami, Haussaire Dakar to SEGEPROCOM, Paris, Sept. 24, 1959, #00234 (Secret), FPR230.

More moderate voices saw the referendum as an absolute last resort. In July, this debate came to a boil at a congress of the newly formed Parti de la Fédération Africaine (PFA), which brought together the US-RDA and Senegal's new coalition, the Union Progressiste Sénégalaise (UPS). Fearful of its home crowd and eager to calm the European population of Bamako, the US-RDA – or its moderate wing – had preferred to hold the meeting in Dakar, where Senghor, Mamadou Dia, and their partisans would be able to temper support for a referendum.[171] There, Dia told the Soudanese that if they chose to go to a vote, Senegal would not follow them. Rather, Senegal would choose the Community over the Federation.[172] In a closed meeting, Diarra branded his Senegalese counterparts who advocated negotiation cowards, but Modibo Keita shared their reluctance to invoke the option of the referendum. After giving tempers time to cool, Dia, Senghor, and Modibo Keita prevailed; they would push for a negotiated "transfer of power ... by *friendly* means ... without haste but without delay."[173] This, of course, merely put off a looming conflict. A document circulating in the office of Jacques Foccart, then Secretary General for the Community, argued that a referendum had to be avoided at almost any cost, as it would result in Soudan's rupture with France, producing "an enemy implantation in the heart of our Sahara."[174] Irrespective of the outcome in Senegal, which seemed harder to predict, another referendum would produce "at least a Guinean scenario (*processus*) and at most an Algerian one," the note warned darkly. The transfer of powers, on the other hand, might convince the Malians that a reformed Community would offer "not something less than independence, but independence itself." This would require the transformation of the Community from an "institutional" to a "contractual" one, composed solely of "independent states united by freely agreed-upon links." Whether such a Community was possible remained to be seen.

While Foccart worked to orchestrate a meeting between General de Gaulle and the leadership of the Mali Federation, Senghor was staving off

---

[171] Modibo Keita attempted to address the concerns of Bamako's Europeans in an event at the Soudan Club, which had long been an elite and segregated gathering place. His speech marked the first time Africans were allowed to enter the Club as guests; *Note sur la situation au Soudan*, July 20, 1959, FPR230, dossier 2.

[172] Note on Congrès constitutif du PFA, n.d. (July 1959), dossier "PFA/Mali," FPR230.

[173] Lami, to SEGEPROCOM [Foccart], Sept. 24, 1959, #00234 (Secret), FPR230. Original emphasis.

[174] *Note sur l'Orientation de la Communauté*, Nov. 19, 1959, FPR239. It is unclear who penned this note, and whether its view was the dominant one within the Secrétariat Général. See also Bat (2012), 115.

critics of his party's gradualist politics by arguing that "a Nation does not emerge from spontaneous generation, and an independence can not be improvised. It must be prepared; it must be organized."[175] He might have added, "It must be debated." He, Dia, and Modibo Keita struggled to agree on what they wanted of de Gaulle. After multiple drafts of correspondence and at least two months of back and forth, they would define their common goal as "independence within the framework of a multinational confederation with France."[176] They asked that everything be put on the table: new accords on cooperation, a renewed discussion of common institutions such as the Senate and high courts, and, most controversially, a re-examination of the issue of a common citizenship in the Community.[177] Of the latter, Modibo Keita wanted no part. Dia, in contrast, saw it as advantageous to Senegal, where the *originaires* had known French citizenship for generations.[178] Defense accords and military bases, too, would prove to be thorny issues.[179] Where would French troops be stationed? What role would they play in time of war, or in maintaining public order?[180] With such questions very much in mind, France and Mali sat down in January 1960 to negotiate the Federation's place in the Community, only fifteen months after the dramatic vote of 1958. Although Senghor presided over the Malians, his deputy was Madeira Keita, who led the tightly disciplined Soudanese delegation. By

[175] Senghor, Fédération du Mali, République Soudanaise, *Session Budgétaire de l'Assemblée Législative*, Nov. 17, 1959.
[176] See exchange of letters between the Federation, as represented by Senghor, Dia, and Modibo Keita, and Gen. De Gaulle, particularly multiple drafts of letter of Nov. 26, 1959, in FPR233 and FPR239. In addition to the final text sent to De Gaulle, Foccart's office possessed drafts internal to the Mali Federation.
[177] The French government was well aware that negotiations with Senegal and Mali would set a precedent for all the other sub-Saharan territories; Bat (2012), 113–18. On the complexities surrounding citizenship in particular, see Cooper (2014).
[178] Paris instructed its representatives in Dakar to act to ensure that Dia would prevail. S. G. Presidence de la Communauté to Haussaire, Dakar, Secret, coded, Dec. 18, 1959; *Note à l'attention de M. le Président de la Communauté* [on citizenship], n.d. (March 1960?), FPR239.
[179] *Note sur l'Orientation de la Communauté*, Nov. 19, 1959. Negotiators for the Federation would accept bases only in Dakar, St. Louis, and Tessalit (in the Soudanese Sahara). They refused to allow them in the Soudanese towns of Bamako, Kayes, Gao, and Koulikoro; Note pour M. le Président de la Communauté [on military issues], n.d. (March 1960?), FPR239.
[180] The question was more than theoretical. Touring eastern Soudan with Madeira Keita, Bakary Djibo, the leader of Niger's dissident Sawaba party, warned that the presence of French troops had played a role in his removal from office in 1958; Haut Commissariat auprès de la République Soudanaise to Presicom Paris, Nov. 20, 1959, no. 00760, FPR230. On Djibo and Sawaba, see van Walraven (2013) and Djibo (1992).

that time, the Soudanese "had 'eaten lion' and [become] intransigent."[181] Having compromised on the "Yes" vote, many of them hoped to go further, faster, now. They would have to wait, but not very long.

As it happened, in both Senegal and Soudan, independence would be improvised after all. The Mali Federation broke apart in acrimony and confusion in August 1960.[182] Each in its own way, the two republics that emerged from it would sacrifice the value of unity to the imperative of autonomy. The Federation's collapse should not have been a surprise. Reduced to two unevenly matched members by the early exits of Dahomey and Upper Volta, its design had long been unstable. Soudan's population was larger and more rural than that of Senegal, and its experience of colonial rule had been shorter and more brutal than in much of the neighboring territory. The leaders of the Federation competed as often as they cooperated, and the threat of divorce hung in the air. The consequences of the break-up are more important than its immediate causes, which lay in the tensions surrounding an interstate conference (scheduled for August 20th) and the election by the federal assembly of a head of state for the Federation (scheduled for one week later). In the latter contest, each side accused the other of seeking to install its own candidate. Yet among the Soudanese, many were in favor of electing Lamine Guèye, the doyen of Senegal's representatives, the parliamentary hero of 1946, and – as one correspondent put it in a letter to de Gaulle – "the elephant who had cleared the forest path."[183] Once Senghor's patron, Guèye was now his rival, a fact that left both Dia and Senghor suspicious of Soudanese intentions. On the 16th, Senghor summoned Claude Hettier de Boislambert, France's representative in Dakar, to tell him that neither the conference nor the election would be held and that "Mali, in its federal form, is dead (*a vécu*)." Senghor needed to know what action French forces might take if either the Soudanese or the Senegalese attempted a coup against the other; he was more than satisfied when Hettier de Boislambert

---

[181] Excerpt of an unofficial letter without identification, apparently from a Frenchman in Soudan and addressed to Jacques Foccart, n.d. (Nov. 1959), FPR233, dossier 2.

[182] The most recent re-interpretation of the Federation's collapse can be found in Cooper (2014), 398-413.

[183] El-hadj Cheikh Ba Baidy, Chef du Bureau à la régie fédérale du Mali, réprésentant à Thiès du grand marabout Serigne Cheikh Amadou M'Backe de Touba to De Gaulle, Feb. 25, 1960, FPR233, dossier 2. On Soudanese support for Guèye, see *Note a/s éléments du dossier Soudanais recueillis auprès d'un membre de la délégation malienne*, Sept. 1, 1960, stamped "secret" and "seen by the General," FPR230. Houphuet-Boigny also believed that Guèye would have been elected president as Modibo Keita wished; Reprexfrance, Abidjan, to Communauté Paris, Aug. 25, 1960, #3319-3327, FPR230.

declared neutrality.[184] For days the two sides feinted and circled like wary wrestlers, swatting and measuring. Grappling for control of the security services, Modibo Keita lost his poise when he attempted to dismiss Dia, the Minister of Defense.[185] Over-extended, Soudan was thrown, and Keita and his comrades arrested.[186] The Soudanese cried foul, simultaneously appealing to De Gaulle as a referee and accusing his representatives of rigging the match. But Dia and Senghor had the home field advantage.

The Senegalese sealed their ex-partners into a train, destination Bamako. They claimed as their prize independence – from Mali, not from France – and closer ties to the former metropole. At a rally along the Soudanese side of the rail line that connected the two territories, Modibo Keita told a crowd that France had split the Federation because he wanted to create an African currency.[187] Still hoping that De Gaulle would refuse to condone Senegal's departure by recognizing its independence, Keita hinted that if he did, the Soudan would recognize the FLN's provisional government of Algeria, the GPRA, and insist that Soudanese serving there be repatriated.[188] That raised the stakes again. In the summer of 1960, the most immediate crisis for France was not in Mali, but in Algeria. There the break-up of the Federation might serve France well – as Senghor had been at pains to make clear – because Senegal would support, or at least would abstain from condemning, French positions in the UN General Assembly.[189] Yet such a minor diplomatic advantage would at best offset Soudanese support for the GPRA. Worse, should the Soudanese call on the United Nations, Guinea, or the Soviet Union in an attempt to save the Federation – as Patrice Lumumba had just done in the Congo – the situation might spiral out of control, bringing an "end to the French presence in West Africa," as one analyst warned.[190] The Congolese

---

[184] Hettier de Boislambert, Note a l'attention du PM, Aug. 16, 1960. He would have a similar conversation with Modibo Keita a few days later, by which time the rupture had broken into the open; Hautrep Dakar to Communauté Paris, Aug. 20, 1960, #10220, FPR230.

[185] *Note a/s éléments du dossier...*, FPR230.

[186] *Note a/s éléments du dossier...*, FPR230.

[187] Wibaux, Bamako to Communauté Paris, Aug. 22, 1960, FPR230. When Jacques Foccart visited as an emissary of General DeGaulle, Keita told him he did not intend to create a new currency; Consul Gén. Bamako to Communauté Paris, Sept. 22, 1960. #3800–3801, FPR239.

[188] Wibaux, Bamako to Communauté Paris, Aug. 22, 1960; *Note: Militaires d'origine malienne en service en Algérie*, Aug. 29, 1960, FPR230.

[189] Hettier de Boislambert, Note a l'attention du PM, Aug. 16, 1960, FPR230.

[190] *Note sur la situation politique dans la Fédération du Mali*, Aug. 18, 1960, DAG.1, FPR230.

comparison was ominous precisely because it was relevant. French officials were not at all sure that Senegal's secession was legal, and the nearest precedent (only two months old) was the breakaway Congolese province of Katanga. There the United Nations and the Cold War superpowers had charged headlong into an emerging crisis over which Brussels (never mind Léopoldville) had lost control. Because its leaders had agreed to the constitution they now rejected, the legal basis for Senegal's secession was considered even weaker than that of Katanga. French diplomats did not want to have to defend it, but the Senegalese would not be made to wait.[191] Eager to contain the conflict, France sponsored Senegal's admission to the United Nations only to see the same patronizing courtesy rejected by the Republic of Mali a few months later.[192]

By that point, late in 1960, the US-RDA had announced its "socialist option" and decided that Soudan would henceforth be known as Mali. The term "independence" had a new resonance best captured in the Bambara term "*yéréta*," which suggested self-determination, and which the US-RDA and the PAI had long preferred to the "*horonya*" of the PSP, a party Madeira Keita abolished by administrative fiat. As it came to pass, Mali's self-determination was really that of the US-RDA, now liberated from both a complex federal architecture and a troublesome political opposition. The specific technical meaning of "*indépendance*" – within the French language texts, among the negotiators – was naturally more precise and less readily secured. The two terms would only truly be reconciled in July 1962, when the new Republic of Mali abandoned the French-backed CFA and created the Malian franc. By then, Mali had already expelled the French army from its territory. In the context of the Algerian war, the departure of the last French forces, particularly from air bases, was more than symbolic in its effects.[193] For over fifty years, until the crisis of 2013, it distinguished Mali from its francophone and Sahelian neighbors, where French bases remained, and it helped to make Mali a key diplomatic player in Africa and in the Third World. As for the great

---

[191] *Note sur la situation politique* ..., Aug. 18, 1960, DAG.1; Communauté Paris to Fransulat Bamako, Communiqué à Hautrep Dakar, Sept. 9, 1960; P.M., Secrétaire d'Etat aux relations avec les états de la Communauté to Reprex Abidjan, Sept. 4, 1960, FPR230.

[192] Présidence de la Communauté, Note à l'attention de M. le Prés. de la Communauté, Dec. 21, 1960; Tel. Chiffré, départ. Présidence de la Communauté, SG to Fransulat Bamako, Oct. 1, 1960. #2008–2015, FPR239; see also Doumbia (2010).

[193] The Saharan bases figured in the FLN's efforts to open a southern front, which motivated Fanon's visit to Mali in the vignette with which this book begins. On the creation of the Malian army, see Mann (2003).

misadventure of the Malian franc, it marked both a real will to break from France and a step too far. The franc was a luxury that neither Mali nor the US-RDA could afford. Instead, it weakened the national economy (largely due to speculation and smuggling) and turned some of the party's oldest allies, Dioula merchants, into enemies.[194] Yet creating it was a powerfully symbolic act. Already, in 1960, the Federation had pushed hard for the right to create its own currency, but failed to prevail in negotiations with a French delegation acutely aware of what was at stake.[195] Two years later, the new Malian franc allowed Political Secretary Idrissa Diarra to mark the second anniversary of the "option" of September 22, 1960 by claiming a tripartite achievement: "the complete substitution of the colonial state by a Malian state, the total evacuation of the French military bases, and the establishment (*émission*) of our national money."[196] This was a strikingly consensual and rather normative idea of what independence meant, and it belies the thesis that the Sahelian states were all, uniformly, and always open to external proxy government. Mali, like Guinea, met all three criteria; none of its Sahelian neighbors did. This understanding of the nature of Mali's sovereignty, shared by figures as distant as Jacques Foccart and Idrissa Diarra, left open two enduring questions. The first was whether the new single-party government had the means to match its ambitions. Shorn of chiefs and dissident cadres, could its administration be as effective as the party was aggressive? The second was the thorny question of political belonging. That question is best explored where it overlaps with the third, and the stickiest, of the three elements that had anchored sovereignty in the 1958 constitution, diplomacy – not the high caliber diplomacy of the United Nations, but the small bore skirmishing of bureaucrats, diplomats, and migrants for control over mobility in foreign lands. In the vast, lightly governed spaces of the Sahel, such control was devilishly hard to secure, and cherished all the more.

---

[194] Amin (1973), 133, 227–36. Relations between the party and the merchants had been souring for some time; Amselle (1977), 262–66; BPN meeting of March 30 and April 3, 1954, BPNCMLN 74. The fate of Kassoum Toure, who died in custody alongside Sissoko and Dicko, provides the most striking example of how badly they had deteriorated.
[195] FPR233, dossier 2.
[196] *Allocution prononcée par Idrissa Diarra le 22 Sept. 1962*, typescript in author's possession.

PART II

INTRODUCTION TO PART II

SAHELIAN MIGRATIONS AND STATE THOUGHT

In a classic essay on "Immigration and State Thought" Abdelmalak Sayad argued that the way one thinks about immigration is a product of state thought – that is, "thought that reflects the structure of the state" – and that "thinking about immigration means thinking about the state [for] ... it is 'the state that is thinking about itself when it thinks about immigration.'" Sayad added that, "It is in the very nature of the state to discriminate, and, in order to do so, to [distinguish] between the 'nationals' it recognizes as such and in which it therefore recognizes itself ... and 'others' with whom it deals only in 'material' or instrumental terms."[1] Sayad was a sociologist, not an historian. Empire was the precondition, not the subject, of his studies of Algerian migration to France, and his vision of the state was a normative one. Yet taking off from Sayad's insight, the pair of chapters that follow examine the recomposition of forms of political identity in turbulent times, such as at the dissolution of empires and the establishment of African independence. They understand the state as an unfinished project, as an entity coming into being. Here we profit from what Sayad termed immigration's "secret virtue": it offers "an introduction, and perhaps the best introduction of all, to the sociology of the state."[2]

First, let's experiment, for a moment, in thinking like a state. In 2001, the Government of Mali reported that a mere 3.7% of the country's migrants were in Europe, in spite of the fact that it was these migrants

---

[1] Sayad (2004), 278–79; see also Bourdieu (1993).
[2] Sayad (2004), 279. Spire offers a rich example of such a sociology (2008); see also Dedieu (2012).

who garnered by far the most attention from journalists, governments, NGOs, and scholars. On the contrary, some 91% of Mali's migrants were in Africa itself, where their presence drew much less attention.[3] Whereas in a 2001 census of Malians abroad, the Malian government counted 21,964 Malian migrants in France, Spain, and Portugal combined, the same census counted 100,000 Malian migrants in Sudan alone. It estimated that some 200,000 Malians lived in Egypt and Sudan taken together, whereas it estimated that some 100,000 lived in France. To recap, the number of migrants *counted* in Sudan was equal to the number of migrants *estimated* by the Government of Mali to be in France. The method of this census is opaque, and it begs a number of questions. Does "Malian" refer to citizenship, self-identification, or country of origin? Did embassies in Paris and Khartoum count migrants in the same way? What was at stake for each "migrant" in being counted as "Malian" in France, in Sudan, or elsewhere? What kinds of histories do numbers in this census reveal or conceal, not only about how fungible such political identities are, but also about where they come from and how they are secured?

The juxtaposition of migration to these two states, France and Sudan, is an unusual one, and not only because of the sharp divide that exists between those who study immigration to the rich countries of the world and those who study "South–South" migrations. Pairing these two phenomena requires moving along two distinct axes: one, West–East across the Sahel, is the subject of Chapter 3; the other, South–North between Africa and France, is the subject of Chapter 4. Pairing them also requires shifting from a region not defined by a state to an imperial frame and moving between an analysis grounded in the long-term historical trends of a region – one that prizes the depth and resonance of a particular past partly for its own sake – to a truncated history of European empires, their dissolution, and the rise of new postcolonial states. The gambit of these two chapters is simple: this unexpected juxtaposition exploits immigration's "secret virtue," not to pursue a sociology of the state, but to bring out the contrast between the novelty

---

[3] Délégation Générale des Maliens de l'Exterieur, Ministère des Affaires Etrangères et des Maliens de l'Exterieur, *Repartition des Maliens de l'Exterieur par Juridictions (Estimations 2001)*. Note that this census was conducted before the outbreak of the Ivoirian Civil War in 2002, the conflict in Darfur in 2003, and the independence of South Sudan in 2011. The first two conflicts politicized West African or Sahelian identity, and the Ivoirian events in particular compelled many people of Sahelian birth or ancestry to leave the Cote d'Ivoire. Bearing those factors in mind, the fact that the census is out of date is something of a virtue, because it gives some sense of scale to the phenomena of intra-African migration before those conflicts. I would like to thank Bruce Whitehouse for sharing this census with me.

of late imperial and postcolonial governmental practices and the historical depth of Sudanic Africa.

By taking the contraction of empire, rather than its establishment, as a point of entry into the history of Sahelian migrations, the following two chapters reveal the extraordinary fluidity of terms of political membership at a moment of transition within long-running African historical developments that preceded and survived modern empires. For the Sahel, the late 1950s and early 1960s represented both a period of decolonization, state formation, and imperial dissolution *and* a crisis of individual and collective political membership; moreover, for much of the Sahel, this period saw the most vigorous pursuit of state formation in the twentieth century. The decomposition of empire posed large questions about boundaries, states, and a new international system, but it also posed smaller questions about the limits of political communities. In the wake of expansive if ill-defined notions of citizenship and nationality developed under the French Fourth and Fifth Republics[4] – and in the aftermath of Sudanese independence – migrants found themselves squeezed by new states' dual imperatives of creating compatriots (or citizens) and creating foreigners. The former project – that of making colonial subjects into imperial citizens – had been the strategy of imperial France over two decades of decline. The independent states, by which I mean both the former imperial power and the new postcolonial states, sought to create foreigners as well as citizens; they intended to exclude as well as to include.[5]

The next two chapters seek to understand the development of postcolonial "state thought" and its limits by focusing on travel papers and the passport – the cornerstone of contemporary states' understanding of migration control – and on attempts to impose a regime of bureaucratic governance on the frontiers of old empires and new nation-states.[6] In

---

[4] See the work of Cooper (2005, 2014), Weil (2002), and Shepard (2006).
[5] Herbst argues that this challenge is central to African governance; (2000), 228.
[6] Passports have a history of their own. In a study grounded in Europe, John Torpey saw the passport as structuring sovereignty, as limiting and defining rights, and as allowing states to control entry into their territories, which was a new capacity of European states in the eighteenth and nineteenth centuries; (2000). Radhika Viyas Mongia argued that the "passport not only is a technology *reflecting* certain understandings of race, nation/nationality, and state, but was also central to *organizing* and *securing* the modern definitions of these categories"; (2007), 196, emphasis in the original. On this point, Adam McKeown agrees with Mongia, arguing that such documents do not define political identities, they create them; (2009). In other words, as a technology of state control, the passport worked to establish, rather than to bound, political formations that have become naturalized. That project had its origins in the nineteenth century, and it was Mediterranean as well as European or imperial; Clancy-Smith (2011), 328, see also 215–19.

Sudan in the late 1950s and early 1960s, and in France a little later, passports and travel papers became tools of aggressive inclusion. The governmental practices that emerged around them destabilized the apparently straightforward emergence of nation-states from empires, even as they became necessary components of pilgrims' and migrants' interactions with Sahelian states, their neighbors, and France. They also obscured the racial distinctions that had lurked behind the extension and recognition of nationality elsewhere in the imperial world:[7] for instance, French diplomats actively sought to assert and secure the "French" identity of non-French speaking West Africans in foreign lands, and they did so precisely by extending papers. These were nationals in whom, for a brief moment at least, the French state recognized itself, while Sudan and Mali recognized something very different. Under the "suns of independence" (B., *yérétatilew*) in the postcolonial Sahel, travel papers marked the horizons, but not yet the limits, of evolving political communities.

---

[7] See also Mongia (2007).

3

"French" Muslims in Sudan

The West African presence in the Nilotic Sudan is old, deep, and dynamic, and the West–East Sahelian axis long predates the arrival of European empires. But if they did not generate that axis of migration, the presence of those empires was the precondition for its transformation. In the twentieth century, pilgrimage routes, the phenomenon of the pilgrimage itself, and colonial awareness of it concealed new forms of migration from the West. In this period, when one looks at pilgrims, one should see migrants. Such a perspective requires adjusting our vision in two ways. First, social scientists have produced excellent studies of the phenomenon of the overland pilgrimage and pilgrim communities in Sudan and in Chad. But whether these are framed as studies of migration as such or emphasize instead the religious and phenomenological aspects of the *hajj*, they do not draw out themes of state practices and logics or of postcolonial politics.[1] Rather, they naturalize the frame of government itself. Second, the political entities by which pilgrims and migrants were identified – and by which they on occasion identified themselves – underwent rapid changes during their long, and sometimes endless pilgrimages, rendering their own political affiliations obscure, or at least multiple. For long years, that did not matter at all. Then suddenly, for a few years in the mid-1950s, it mattered a great deal.

---

[1] For instance, Bawa Yamba's invaluable *Permanent Pilgrims* (1995) is essentially a phenomenological study of the enduring liminality and paradoxically settled transience of Hausa in Sudan; in reading it for traces of governmentality, one must approach it from an oblique angle. Like that of Bawa Yamba, al-Naqar's studies are superlative (1969b), (1972). Rich studies of pilgrims as migrants include notably that of Birks (1978). See also Delmet (1994), Duffield (1981), Hino (1986), and Works (1976). For a partial history of the pilgrimage from Senegal, see Mbacké (2004).

PILGRIMS, FOREIGNERS, AND IMPERIAL SHADOWS

Although by mid-century pilgrims would be identified by nationality, older forms of identification remained at work. These migrants were not "Malians," "Nigeriens," or "Nigerians"; they were Muslims, Takarir or Fellata. In previous centuries, merchants, pastoralists, and pilgrims to Mecca had constituted the West–East flow of migrants; among the latter group, many took years or even decades to make the pilgrimage, settling for long periods of time and often setting down permanent roots.[2] From the early eighteenth century, scholars with origins in the Futa Toro and Hausaland had served as prominent counselors in Fur courts.[3] In a context in which the question of who got there first would often determine access to land, water, and grazing rights – and which was marked so dramatically by the tumultuous years of the Mahdiyya (1881–98) – it is no surprise that a separate term exists for the pioneers of the eastward migration. That term, "*muwallid*," originally referred to those, mostly Fulani and Beriberi, who had been "born in" Sudan of foreign parents; "born in" is the common meaning of the term.[4] Some sources date the *muwallid* communities of the Western Sudan to the seventeenth century, others to the nineteenth.[5] The date by which they had arrived is probably less important than the fact that they had been present in Sudan before the era of Muhammad Ahmad, the Mahdi (1844–85), who would find at least one of his key lieutenants among them.[6] Other so-called "Westerners," including notably a veteran of Uthman dan Fodio's early nineteenth century jihad establishing the Sokoto caliphate of Northern Nigeria, would rally to the Mahdi's

---

[2] Among other sources, see d'Escayrac de Lauture (1853), 450–51 and ibid. (1855–56a). Gustav Nachtigal records substantial East–West trade in the 1870s; Nachtigal (1971 [1879–89]), 202, 354. He himself reached Wadai, just west of Darfur in a caravan coming from Bornu that included Shinqiti, Hausa, and "Fellata" pilgrims; 23, 39.

[3] Nachtigal (1971 [1879–89]), 283.

[4] Writing on the Hadrami diaspora in the Indian Ocean, Ho equates the term with "Creole"; (2006), 68, 224. In this case, following his lead would obscure the particular weight the term would come to have as a politico-administrative category.

[5] On the *muwallid*, see Duffield (1983), 15–16, and *infra*; Bawa Yamba (1995), 4–5, quoting Balamoan (1976); al-Naqar (1972). On the Islamization of Darfur via "holy men from the West," see O'Fahey (2008), 224–27. Note that this historical process by which Muslim scholars and pilgrims from West Africa introduced Islam in part of the Sudan is an important corrective to the idea that West African Islam is a derivative version of a purer "Arab" Islam coming from the East.

[6] Biobaku and al-Hajj (1966); Mamdani (2007), 138, 141.

successor, the Khalifa Abdullahi b. Muhammad (r. 1885–98), whose grandfather "appears to have been Fulani."[7] These ties went in both directions: in roughly the same period, *shaykhs* from Darfur and Kordofan frequented the court of one of Sokoto's commercial entrepôts, Zaria.[8] By then, Sokoto was a vast, well-established state with one of the largest plantation economies in the world and a renowned intelligentsia. It is no surprise that Darfur and Kordofan would be pulled partly into its orbit (please see Map 3).

Already, from the late 1830s if not before, another Western import, the Tijani Sufi order (*tariqa*), had begun to take root in Darfur under the guidance of a *shaykh* from Shinqit (Mauritania).[9] He would establish a lodge (*zawiya*) in the region in the 1870s. The *tariqa* would wilt under the regime of the Mahdi only to be revived by the *hijra* fleeing British rule in the West. In the relatively brief period between the collapse of the Mahdiyya in 1898 and the British conquest of 1916 – a period in which Ali Dinar re-established an effective if diminished administration in Darfur – a *shaykh* from Macina (Mali) would bring new life to what would become an important Tijani community. Along the way, the Tijaniyya would become "the dominant order in Darfur."[10] Later, via the branch of the *tariqa* centered on the Senegalese *shaykh* Ibrahim Niasse (1900–75), its shoots would become intertwined with those of Sokoto.[11] Thus, in spite of the complex and ambivalent stance of the Sokoto leadership toward the *hajj* and those who undertook it, and its hostility toward still vibrant Mahdist ideas in the twentieth century,

---

[7] O'Fahey (2008), 14. O'Fahey (2008: 281 n. 24) notes that "there is a specifically Darfurian Fulani dimension to the Mahdiyya that invites further research."

[8] Staudinger (1990, vol. 1), 245. In Sokoto in the 1820s, Hugh Clapperton had met "Fellata" pilgrims from the regions of Futa Toro, Timbuktu, and Jenne en route to Mecca. Their planned routes would take them through Darfur and Kordofan; Clapperton (2005), 299, 300, 324.

[9] Seeseman (2000a), 395. Al-Karnasi states that the Tijaniyya first appeared in Darfur in the 1810s, and more of its adepts arrived after the defeat of the Umarian empire (in today's Mali) in the 1860s; (1987), 386–87.

[10] O'Fahey (2008), 124.

[11] O'Fahey (2008), 124, 295; Seeseman (2000a, 2000b). As many other West African Muslims would do, Niasse gave the name "medina" – the common Arabic noun for a town – to a settlement he founded in Senegal. In contrast, his adepts across West Africa and in Sudan named their own settlements Kosi, after the small village where Niasse received his divine message and which "in the parlance of [his] followers ... has become synonymous with mystical knowledge"; Seeseman (2011), 6, 63, 147. On the naming of new settlements to inscribe a particular Muslim geography, see Robinson (1985) and Babou (2005).

MAP 3 Sudan

the bond between Sudan's western provinces, Hausaland, and the Western Sahel would remain multiple, braided, and Muslim.[12] These are some of the shadows, both of the distant empire of Sokoto and of the Tijaniyya.[13]

[12] On ambivalence and internal debate among Sokoto's leadership toward the *hajj*, see Umar (2006); al-Naqar (1969b), 166–83. Scholars of the Maliki school of law, dominant in West Africa, had long voiced ambivalence or even opposition to undertaking the pilgrimage from West Africa, seeking to elevate other meritorious acts in its place. Muhammad Bello, caliph of Sokoto and son of Uthman dan Fodio, wrote memorably that when the devil saw someone studying the Qur'an, he would tempt him to perform the *hajj* instead. The believer would set the Holy Book aside and set out, yet Mecca was far away and the voyage difficult. Finally, the believer would accomplish neither study of the Qur'an nor the pilgrimage. The devil would have won; al-Naqar (1969b), 341–42.

[13] A point of clarification: the *Tijaniyya* in the Western Sudan – particularly in parts of contemporary Mali, Guinea, Senegal – did not assume the functions of political organization that other *turuq* did in places such as Mauritania and Libya. The Umarian jihad in particular never produced a stable form of sovereign political power.

Colonial conquest would first strengthen and later profoundly transform that bond, and it would deepen the shadows. The fall of the Sokoto caliphate to British—and more importantly, Christian—invaders in 1903 spurred a wave of settlers to undertake a *hijra* to Darfur while it was still under Muslim rule. Over the next two decades, the consolidation of British rule in Sudan, weak as it often was, would generate the infrastructure – from rails to irrigation schemes – that attracted or enabled future generations of migrants to settle still farther east.[14] If few pilgrims desired or could afford to take the train, many simply followed the rails on foot. They settled along the rail lines that would eventually lead from Darfur to Kassala, near the Ethiopian border, and beyond;[15] in the Blue Nile province; in the Nuba mountains; on the irrigated land of the Gezira project, which opened in 1924; and around the "mechanised crop production schemes of the Gedaref."[16] Although pilgrims came from across the Sahel, as far west as Senegal, territories nearer to Sudan sent more migrants, just as one might expect. Tens, possibly hundreds of thousands of labor migrants came from Chad, and many pilgrims from Niger and Nigeria, but also from Upper Volta and all along the Niger River. After the Second World War, as independently organized caravans began to make the overland *hajj* by truck, the number of West African pilgrims increased exponentially.[17] In the next few decades, travel by air would supplement, but not replace, the overland routes. The flood of pilgrims had many causes other than technology, infrastructure, and the lure of well-watered land. The center of gravity of Muslim practices was shifting in those same years, from the esoteric to the exoteric, from recognizing authority grounded in closed hierarchies and genealogies to those grounded in experience and the external manifestations of piety.[18] Thus, the *hajj*. As more pilgrims went, others followed. Extrapolating from a late colonial census that is widely

---

[14] Bawa Yamba in particular notes the importance of infrastructure, arguing that it helped to "sustain" the migrations; (1995), 63.
[15] The rails reached el Obeid in 1909, and Nyala in Darfur 50 years later; Birks (1978), 18; O'Fahey (2008), 301. Although the colonial state ultimately built the railroads, both a railroad to el Fasher and a telegraph line between el Fasher and el Obeid had been planned by the Khedive of Egypt in the 1870s; Ensor (1881), v–vi, 114. The railroad would have enabled easier access to the excellent gum arabic of Kordofan, and to the less significant yet valuable trade in ostrich feathers; d'Escayrac de Lauture (1853), 569–72.
[16] Hassoun (1952); Birks (1978), 64–5. Birks provides a map based on the 1955–1956 census. By "West Africans," Birks means "those born of parents in or from West Africa," which he defines as the area west of the Chari river, which runs between Chad and northern Cameroon; (1978), xii, 62.
[17] Mann and Lecocq (2007), 372–76; Lecocq (2012).
[18] Soares (2005b); Hanretta (2009).

considered a benchmark, a geographer writing in the 1970s calculated Sudan's West African population as "well over a million."[19]

This was a major demographic transition. Given the importance of infrastructure, empire, and secular as well as spiritual temporalities to it, one could even call it modern. Yet non-European empires continued to cast their own shadows. In spite of the superficial homogeneity of the "Westerners" – they were all Muslims; many spoke Hausa or Fulfulde; the large majority had origins in Northern Nigeria or Niger – distinctions remained within that broad category. The British government would accentuate these. For instance, in 1930 it created a new district (provisionally termed a *"dar"*) in the Blue Nile province expressly for Mai Wurno, the anti-Mahdist son of Sokoto's Mohammed Attahiru I, who had made the 1903 *hijra* after his father's death. The move testified to the numerical importance of migrants from Sokoto as a potential labor force, including on future irrigation schemes. Yet Mai Wurno was given jurisdiction neither over migrants from Sokoto elsewhere in Sudan nor over the *muwallid*, those descendants of previous generations of migrants, or any other "indigenous population."[20] Thus one empire adopted traces of another to set the frame in which political power would be exercised.

Although the *muwallid* may have been considered autochthones, at least by the administration, Mai Wurno and his subjects could be referred to by the more general and imprecise terms "Fellata" or, less commonly, "Takarir" (and their variants). The former term appears as a family name or moniker, including among well-known Tijani *shaykhs*,[21] but it also refers broadly to those migrants who came to labor in Sudan. Thus in the decades following the transition from slave to migrant labor, Sudanese land-holders apparently analyzed the changing times in a simple dictum: "Allah took away our slaves but sent us the Fellata."[22] "Takrur" (plural

---

[19] Birks (1978), xii, 62, 134. Although not without flaws (Birks 1978: 62), the 1956 census falls fortuitously within the period of greatest interest for my larger study. Some years later the anthropologist Bawa Yamba reported estimates of the number of West Africans in Sudan as ranging from between 900,000 and 3 million; Bawa Yamba (1995), 6. It is not clear where the larger number comes from, and it likely includes Chadians. Balamoan claims that at the time of independence, over half of Sudan's population may have been of foreign, predominantly West African, origin; (1981), 4–5; see also editor's foreword, pg. xiii. This seems highly unlikely, and Balamoan was not a demographer.

[20] Duffield (1981) 43; also Hassoun (1952), 62, 74–5.

[21] E.g., Seeseman (2000b), 113.

[22] Wingate (1909), pg. 55, cited in McLoughlin (1962), 363; see also Daly (2007), 124. Some of Bawa Yamba's interlocutors perceived the term "Fellata" as pejorative, although as applied to himself, a visiting anthropologist engaged in fieldwork, he did not find it to be so; (1995), 5, 206–07, n 4. See also Duffield (1981), *infra*.

Takarir) resonated differently, although in a fashion harder to define. As a term that had, for a millenium, referred loosely to the Senegal river valley and by extension to the Western Sahara and the Sahel, "Takrur" seems to have had several different senses in mid-twentieth century Sudan, just as it had for centuries previously in the Western Sahel.[23] A hundred years earlier, Pierre Henri Stanislas d'Escayrac de Lauture, a French geographer writing from Cairo, understood it to indicate that a pilgrim came from the West, as far away as Jenne. Those whom he had met in the northern Sudanese town of Dongola had traveled alone, on foot, and without money, in order to discourage thieves. Thus pilgrims were numerous but caravans were few.[24] For him the term "Belad-et-Takrour" (or "*bilad al-takrur*") meant the land of the converted; the Fellata were only a subset, categorized in a fashion typical of late nineteenth-century Europe as "less black in skin tone and more intelligent than the other [Takarir]."[25] Following the mass migration into Sudan, the term "Takarir" could refer broadly to all those from West Africa in Sudan, and not only those who had come after the first wave; the term "Fellata" did much the same work.[26] In other circumstances, "Takarir" meant more precisely Hausa, as opposed to Fulani, settlers. Alternately, it could refer only to first-wave immigrants whose presence was seen as legitimate because they were pilgrims on the way to or from Mecca, rather than refugees from the British conquest of Sokoto or indeed labor migrants (such as those from Chad) coming to work on the railroads or irrigation schemes or to settle newly watered land.[27] Finally, in Saudi Arabia itself, the term was used in the most general sense and in an unflattering fashion by which, according to Issa Ongoiba, who made the pilgrimage overland from Mali in the 1940s, "In Mecca ... if you've got some money, the Arabs no longer call you Takrur ... [but] a black Arab."[28]

---

[23] Al-Naqar examines the orgins of the term and its "Middle Eastern" use; (1969a). El Hamel does the same for the Western Sahel; (2002), ch. 6.

[24] D'Escayrac de Lauture (1853), 568.

[25] D'Escayrac de Lauture (1853), 449; ibid. (1855–56a), 11, 60. See also (1855–56b).

[26] Bawa Yamba (1995), 148.

[27] Duffield (1981), 1.

[28] Radio broadcast of interview with al-hajj Issa Ongoïba, Radio Dambe (Bamako), Feb. 8, 2003, obtained by Dr. Baz Lecocq and translated by Gomba Coulibaly. Writing on Eritrea, Grisman offered a racialized etymology of "Takruri" as "from afar" or "sullied!" (sic); (1955), 42. Terms derived from Takrur remain in use in contemporary Sudan and Saudi Arabia, although the general term "Fellata" is more widely used to refer to "people from the West," especially settled pilgrim communities; personal communication, Dahlia el-Tayeb Gubara, January 14, 2008. According to al-Naqar, that term has its roots in Kanuri, in which it refers to the Fulani; (1969a), 365. To avoid giving the impression that West

Such etymologies do not figure in the state logic that constructs a census like the one Sudan undertook in 1955–56. They were themselves historical artifacts from a past the new state did not care to share, or even to recognize. For Sudan on the threshold of independence, the Fellata or Takarir were officially "Westerners (of doubtful nationality)" or "Foreigners of West African Origin: a) with Sudanese status [or] b) with Non-Sudanese status."[29] Little matter that for London and Paris the Takarir were British subjects or French nationals. In Sudan's western provinces in particular, the colonial presence itself had been brief and starkly minimal. In spite of the fact that the shadows cast by the European empires deepened paradoxically in their twilight years, they did not obliterate those of the Mahdiyya, the Sokoto caliphate, or the Tijaniyya. Indeed, a serious look at "the colonial period" in western Sudan, and especially in Darfur, quickly reveals that it is hardly more than a thin seam between two tumultuous moments of imperial collapse: that of the Muslim empires of the nineteenth century and that of the European empires of the twentieth. At independence that seam would be papered over, both in census categories to which historic links were irrelevant and in the fitful extension of a regime of governmental rationality – and the documents that went with it – over an internally dynamic and relatively *longue durée* process.

The "Problem of Papers"

An altogether different "world on paper" had long been key to the activities of West African pilgrims who financed their travels by trading, especially in the production of amulets, which was "by far the most common trade they plied."[30] In the period of independence, adult pilgrims began to carry passports with the names of children of the same sex as their bearer inscribed in them alongside an identity photo. As a Hausa pilgrim from

---

African origins were systematically denigrated in the *hijaz*, it is worth mentioning another term with a distinct valence, *Shinqit* (thus *Bilad Shinqit*, etc.), referring to the caravan town of that name in Northern Mauritania, whose scholars and scholarship were highly respected; on Shinqit, see Lydon (2009), 6–7, 11, 82–84.

[29] Barbour (1966), 118. The first category, those of "doubtful nationality" numbered 63,388; the second (a) 14,912; (b) 106,413. The total given for the two categories taken together was 182,613, or 74.2% of the "Persons from Abroad" in Sudan. This represented a mere 2.5% of the national population.

[30] Al-Naqar (1972), 113. See also Bawa Yamba (1995); O'Fahey (2008), 227–28; and Ongoïba interview, Radio Dambe (Bamako), Feb. 8, 2003. I take the phrase "world on paper" from Hawkins (2002), although his analysis does not address this world in particular. Contrast Ghislaine Lydon's "paper economy of faith"; (2009), 3, 277.

Nigeria who made the voyage east in around 1960 told Bawa Yamba, "at the border [between Abéché, Chad and el Geneina, Sudan] they examined our passports. They looked at the picture of Aysha, my deceased daughter who shared a passport with my wife. The official looked at the photograph and asked, 'where is Aysha?' I said, 'she died in Kassoli [Chad].' And he put a cross on her photograph." Pilgrim passports were frequently scarred with these "little red crosses in ink on the faces of ... loved ones," lending support to Bawa Yamba's evocative observation that "the Sudanese villages of these pilgrims are, in effect, liminal stations strung between home and Mecca, along a route emotionally charted with the graves of the beloved ones they have lost on their way."[31] Indeed, papers were often necessary even to be allowed to bury one's dead. Bawa Yamba recorded from former pilgrims the sad story of one of their servants who died near Fort Lamy (N'Djamena) and whom the French authorities would not allow to be buried because the pilgrims did not have "the right papers." Some distance from Fort Lamy, the *sarkin zongo* (Hausa, chief of the foreigners' quarter) of another town took the corpse, claiming it as that of one of his own people in order to be authorized to bury it the same day.[32] What can these stories about pilgrims' passports and papers – evocative and imprecise as they are – tell us about "organizing and securing the modern definitions of ... categories"[33] such as nation and nationality in a long moment of extreme political flux? About governmentality, membership, and empire? About entangled histories?

For a Malian who began his own pilgrimage in 1944, "It's not like now, [when] in order to go you have to first get the papers. Then, you simply decided and got up to go. Only along the way would you run into difficulties because of the problem of paper."[34] "The problem of papers" would arrive along the way, but it would only become acute on the border between French Chad and British Sudan, or, more frequently, on the Red Sea ports of Suakin, Massawa, or Port Sudan. On the coast, pilgrims needed not only to change their Sudanese pounds into Saudi ryals, they also had to obtain travel documents attesting to their political identity and verifying that they could neither spread nor contract particular contagious diseases. Yet for European empires, attempting to establish the identities or

---

[31] Bawa Yamba (1995), 60, 63, 2.
[32] Bawa Yamba (1995), 55. On the Hausa community in Chad, see Works (1976).
[33] Mongia (2007), 196.
[34] Ongoïba interview, Radio Dambe (Bamako), Feb. 8, 2003. Transcript in author's possession.

political provenances of individual pilgrims had long been a headache best avoided.

In both Sudan and Eritrea, the solution had been found in a laissez-faire policy in which Italian, French, and British administrators took part for decades. Saudi Arabia had begun requiring passports of African pilgrims in 1926,[35] but European empires simply accommodated that demand by coming to an informal arrangement among themselves. Before 1956, all West Africans passed for British subjects, the Nigerian Bureau claimed French West Africans as their own, and the Sudanese government provided travel papers. In short, a French administrator's analysis of Eritrea holds for Sudan as well: "Mixed up with Natives from British West Africa under the generic appellations 'Takruri' ... our people have benefited from an intentionally lax regime."[36]

Such a policy was ill-suited to cope with two postwar phenomena: the fact that from the late 1940s, many more Muslims began to undertake the pilgrimage across the Sahel; and the uneven emergence of new nation-states from European empires. British and French colonial administrators would devote a good deal of energy to tinkering with the establishment of a new migration regime that would respond to these changes. In the 1950s, they held a series of meetings in Dakar, Brazzaville, Khartoum, and Accra to elaborate a system of travel documents for those moving between French and British Africa. The core of their system was a simple "travel certificate" (*carnet de voyage*), adopted because, as a British bureaucrat drily phrased it, "[T]he issue of passports to Africans wishing to journey between ... French and British West Africa and the introduction of a visa system are in present circumstances impracticable."[37] Following the same logic, when the French proposed exchanging a duplicate of the necessary documents, so that each administration would have a full set complete

---

[35] Lecocq (2012), 199.
[36] *Rapport Happé, 2ème partie: Informations sur quelques pays du Mer Rouge: Soudan, Yemen, Aden, Somalie, Ethiopie, Erythrée*, Sept. 15, 1958, MAE, DAM, CADN Khartoum 110; *Affectation à l'ambassade* ... s.d.; and *P-V de la réunion relative au Pèlerinage tenue le 15 et 16 avril tel qu'il a été amendé et approuvé au cours de la réunion qui s'est déroulée au palais le 17 April 1955*, traduction MAE, DAM, CADN Khartoum 155. Italy lost Eritrea in the Second World War. Britain effectively took over the territory from 1941 until 1952. Ethiopia then governed the territory until it became independent in 1993.
[37] Chief Secretary, West African Territorial Secretariat to HCAOF, Sept. 19, 1955, CADN Kano 9. Administrators were especially anxious not to hamper trade between Niger and Nigeria.

with photographs and fingerprints, the British demurred.[38] Those on the *hajj*, at least ostensibly, continued to escape from the more onerous of the governmental requirements. Nigerian pilgrims, for instance, did not pay a repatriation deposit, and the government of that colony created a special "pilgrim" passport for them.[39] These could soon be found on the black market in Maiduguri (Nigeria), where a man named Ali Hassan and his family, all French nationals from Niger, refused to buy them, reporting the counterfeiter to the police instead.[40] Thus we see in the context of the pilgrimage themes that played out for labor migrants to France as well, as the next chapter demonstrates. These include a French governmental desire to develop increasingly precise identity documents; the rapid emergence of a market for forgeries and false papers; and most important, the fact that new nation-states restricted mobility and forced responses from contracting empires.

The Sudanese Frontier

The independence of Sudan in 1956 thoroughly challenged the "laissez-faire" status quo as the new government, in keeping with Saudi demands, sought to create a more stringent system of immigration and border controls.[41] The two states had similar motivations. In spite of a "terrifying" history of public health – or its absence – in the frontier province of Darfur, the imperial governments had only begun to discuss establishing quarantines on its vastlong western border after a smallpox outbreak in 1951.[42] By independence, Sudan had passed a Quarantine Law and was in the

---

[38] *Minutes of a Conference held at Accra on 15th to 17th September 1955 to consider the use of Travel Certificates and the control of Frontier Traffic*, CADN Kano 9.

[39] *Convention franco-brittanique sur la circulation des voyageurs*, Annexe D: "Circulation des voyageurs entre l'AOB, l'AEF, et le Cameroun sous administration française," Brazzaville, July 3 to 5, 1956, CADN Kano 9. Bawa Yamba interviewed a man who still kept his proudly; (1995), 59–60.

[40] Resident, Bornu, Maiduguri Provincial Office to M. le Grand, Consul de France at Kano, 3 April 1959, #IMM/8; and Resident, Yerwa to Commissaire de la Sûreté nationale, Service national de police, Fort-Lamy, n.d., CADN Kano 9. In light of Hassan Ali Hassan's rectitude, the British resident hoped to persuade the French to provide the proper travel documents in Chad to Hassan and the 20 other members of his party. Unpersuaded, a French officer sought in a handwritten note to send them back to Niger.

[41] The administration of Niger emphasized the Saudi origin of these demands. Circular, Min. Interieur p.i., for Chef du Territoire du Niger to tous cercles et subdivisions, Dec. 18, 1958, #77/MI; Bakary Djibo, Min. Interieur for Chef du Territoire du Niger, à tous cercles et subdivisions, Dec. 5, 1957, #105/MI, CADN Kano 9.

[42] Daly (2007), 170–71.

process of bringing its practices into line with international standards.[43] It would soon be running a year-round quarantine camp at Geneina, as well as seasonal transit camps, and it laid on special train service during the *hajj* season, when its borders were open for pilgrims.[44] Yet public health concerns were clearly only part of the picture. Reluctant to be saddled with the cost of supporting or repatriating impecunious pilgrims, Khartoum also began to demand the payment of a substantial deposit upon entry.[45] Those who could not provide it risked finding themselves stuck in Fort Lamy because, as with all such regulations, a domino effect meant that each eastern state's new requirement would soon be reflected in the practices of its western neighbor.[46]

In short, the new state had begun to seek greater control over its territory. As early as 1955, Sudan had attempted to limit the entry of "foreign Africans."[47] Khartoum also declared that it would no longer provide pilgrims with passports allowing them to cross the Red Sea and enter Saudi Arabia.[48] New Sudanese and Saudi demands meant that Sudan's neighboring empires would have to provide national passports for their pilgrims.[49] This was difficult; they had never really done so before, and few of the West Africans who had come to Sudan before 1956 and remained there had any papers at all. Nonetheless, Sudan's intransigence on the issue would only be compounded by the sharp souring of relations with France and Great Britain in the wake of the Suez debacle, provoking a minor sideshow to a major crisis. As new governments sought to control

---

[43] Daly (2007), 192.
[44] *Press Release from Information Division, Ministry of Research and Information, Lagos: Arrangements for 1959 Pilgrimage, April 22, 1959*, No. F. 72 (sic), CADN Kano 11.
[45] Birks (1978), 26. The fact that Nigerian pilgrims were exempted from this requirement considerably boosted the value of Nigerian papers.
[46] Chef du Territoire du Niger à tous cercles et subdivisions, March 7, 1958, #30/MI, CADN Kano 9. The AEF government also required a deposit for repatration, again exempting Nigerians; Délégué Chad to Chefs de region, de districts, et. al., May 4, 1957, #176D, Annexe D. This had the effect of not only multiplying the motives for evasion of state scrutiny – which on Sudan's long and porous western border, was easy enough to do – but also encouraging increasingly complex forms of duplicity, such as the forgeries mentioned above, and the practice of Nigeriens passing for Nigerians. See, e.g., Consulate de France, Kano, Direction Générale des Affaires Politiques to MAE, Paris, April 8, 1955, CADN Kano 11.
[47] MAE to MinFOM, Aff Pol's, 2ème bureau, n.d. (1955), CADN Kano 11.
[48] MAE to MinFOM, Aff Pol's, 2ème bureau, n.d. (1955), CADN Kano 11; see also *P-V de la réunion* ... April 17, 1955, MAE, DAM, CADN Khartoum 110.
[49] Min. Interieur, A. Maiga p.o. Chef du Territoire du Niger, à tous cercles et subdivisions, Dec. 18, 1958, #77/MI, CADN Kano 9.

their own territories and regional dynamics began to prevail over imperial policies, the entire laissez-faire system was in distress.

Further complicating matters, at the time of Sudanese independence, a new framework law, the *loi cadre*, had just "balkanized" francophone Africa. The ex-colonies now had to pay their bills and harmonize their policies as more than a dozen territories rather than as two centralized federations. When the territories became semi-autonomous republics within the French Community, a new set of problems arose: Who would take over the supervision of the pilgrimage, a function in which the French Union had invested considerable effort,[50] at a time of independence or internal autonomy? Who would pay for it? Who would be responsible for those "indigent" pilgrims – mostly Chadians and Nigeriens – expelled from Saudi Arabia or for "French" pilgrims expelled from Egypt?[51]

Already, in 1956, the French ambassador in Khartoum believed, or perhaps feared, that the Government of Sudan would easily give Sudanese nationality, both in order to secure a necessary and cheap labor force and in order to boost its total population, which would in turn strengthen its claim to a larger share of the waters of the Nile and of UN development funds. This meant that from his perspective an entire category of people for whom he struggled to find an apt designation – "*Français Africains*," "*français d'Afrique du Soudan*," or "*nos compatriotes africains*" – faced the threat of being abandoned by France and scooped up by Sudan. Worse, they might become "stateless" (*apatrides*).[52] The embassy could sit by and let this happen, but the ambassador worried that doing so would reflect negatively on France's "African vocation" at a moment when that "vocation" was undergoing a crucial test south of the Sahara as well as in Algeria.

The 1957 Sudanese law on nationality must have surprised the ambassador and his peers. The law limited Sudanese nationality to those who were present in territory that became the state of Sudan since before conquest in 1898 and to their descendants. A modification in the 1970s would expand those terms, but still restricted the status to those who were present before the opening of the Gezira irrigation scheme in 1924.[53] This

---

[50] Mann and Lecocq (2007).
[51] Amb Fr Khartoum to MAE, March 19, 1960, #192/CT; MAE, DGAP, DAL to Amb Fr Khartoum, July 28, 1959, CADN Khartoum 110.
[52] Amb Fr Khartoum to MAE, Aug. 10, 1956, #248 AP/L., MAE, DAM, CADN Khartoum 110.
[53] Duffield (1983); Bawa Yamba (1995), 219 n19. El Sheikh suggests that the year 1924 may have been chosen because it marked the National Revolution, or perhaps because – although a Sudanese nationality as such did not exist – in 1923 Great Britain had

meant that Westerners would not be considered Sudanese by a new regime intent on the Arabization of Sudan.[54] With this law, Sudan became one of very few African countries formerly under British rule to extend citizenship based first and foremost on ancestry (a *jus sanguinis* approach) rather than on place of birth (*jus solis*), thereby missing an opportunity to consolidate its claim over an expansive territory by incorporating all of those present on it.[55] Instead, Khartoum chose to create a category of outsiders. Yet the new lines were not marked only by soil or blood. A policy of "Arabization" could be seen in language requirements as well. If a 1948 "Definition of 'Sudanese' Ordinance" allowed those without nationality who had lived in Sudan for 10 years to become Sudanese if they had "adequate knowledge of Arabic, or other [sic] language in common use in the Sudan,"[56] the 1957 law mentioned *only* Arabic. Those without it would have to have been resident in Sudan for "more than twenty years" before becoming eligible.[57]

Ironically this restrictive text was passed just before the country's first post-independence parliamentary elections, elections in which the Umma party, whom the Fellata strongly supported, won a plurality – albeit without obtaining a majority – and maintained its place in the ruling coalition. Why did a restrictive nationality law, which ought to have disenfranchised part of their constituency, have little apparent impact on the party's fortunes? And why has this more restrictive text consistently been depicted as more permissive than the original?[58] The answer to this paradox might lie in the instructions issued by the Sudanese

empowered Khartoum to issue passports to those subject to its administration; (1975), 93–96. I suspect that the date may have been chosen in relation to the Gezira scheme.

[54] Mamdani (2007), 179–80. Although policies that look like Arabization began under the parliamentary regime, that process took full form under the military regime that came to power in 1958. It was one of the causes of the long-running civil war that pit the North against the South, and eventually Khartoum against much of the rest of the country. De Waal, following Dornboos, prefers the term "becoming Sudanese" to "Arabization"; de Waal (2005), 196. I have preferred the latter here because of the focus on language acquisition. Moreover, although the phrase "becoming Sudanese" well represents the complexity of the issue on all sides, "Arabization" better captures the government policy in particular.

[55] Herbst (2000), 240; el Sheikh (1975). The distinction between the two approaches should not be overdrawn. Elements of both appear in the texts themselves, as Patrick Weil's study of French nationality would lead us to expect; Weil (2002).

[56] "Definition of 'Sudanese' Ordinance," July 15, 1948, as reproduced in Balomoan (1976), 400–02, see 401.

[57] One also had to be "of good character." Sudanese Nationality Act, 1957, as reproduced in Balamoan (1976), 402–07, see 403. See also Bawa Yamba (1995), 219 n19.

[58] Scholars of Sudanese politics have argued mistakenly that the 1957 law was more inclusive than the 1948 ordinance, and that only the later law allowed for naturalization and the

election commission to officials drawing up voter rolls not to "go deep into the niceties of the nationality law [which] is a very difficult and complicated act ... If you are satisfied that it is an obvious case and the person concerned is clearly Sudanese ... register him and let the other party object or appeal."[59] By this standard, fully five of every six people who sought to be included on the Sudanese voter rolls were.[60] Over the course of the next decade, as parliamentary regimes alternated with a military one, the Umma party would maintain a stronghold in Darfur and among the Fellata.[61]

In spite of its immediate and somewhat contradictory political impact, the nationality law would have material as well as symbolic importance. One needed citizenship in order to get a license for trade or "basically any occupation other than small-scale cash-crop production or unskilled manual-laboring."[62] After 1960, Nigeria, the place of origin of many Westerners, established a similar set of requirements: those in Sudan who sought Nigerian citizenship were required both to speak Hausa – which some had lost in favor of Arabic[63] – and to know the names of village chiefs from their home districts in Nigeria. Knowing and recalling the latter was a nearly impossible task for those who had left the country decades earlier, and the requirement "seem[ed] designed to make it impossible for any of the pilgrims to pass the test."[64] Caught between these complementary and restrictive nationality laws, many Hausa and other West Africans in Sudan found themselves effectively stateless and economically disadvantaged.

---

recognition of nationality by descent. None of this is true. They seem not to have referred to the texts themselves; see Bechtold (1976: 158), whom Daly cites (2007: 182).

[59] Election Commission, Directive No. 3, quoted in Gosnell (1958), 410. Precisely the opposite tack seems to have been taken in the 1953 elections; Bechtold (1976), 157; Willis (2007), 491. On Sudanese elections in the 1950s, see Willis and el Battahani (2010), 196–200.

[60] Silberman (1958-59), 362.

[61] Daly (2007), 197; Bechtold (1976), 195. In 2010 census takers aided by the party of incumbent Omar al-Bashir reportedly registered many "newcomers from Chad and Niger" as Sudanese, allowing them to vote. Presumably these new voters were considered sympathetic to the Arab Gathering, which sought to unite Sahelian Arabs, and to Bashir's government. These "newcomers" had settled land from which much of Darfur's population had been displaced. See Crisis Group, *Africa report* # 72 (2010), 1, 10 n85. This is presumably one of the reasons that the Umma party would eventually boycott the election, thereby facilitating Bashir's victory.

[62] Duffield (1983), 59, as quoted in Bawa Yamba (1995), 142–43.

[63] Bawa Yamba (1995), 219 n24. By the same token, Nachtigal had noted a century earlier that many people with roots in Bornu no longer spoke Kanuri; (1971 [1879–89]), 363.

[64] Bawa Yamba (1995), 143.

In contrast with the exclusionary Sudanese and Nigerian approaches, the French state actively sought to claim pilgrims and migrants as French nationals. Its diplomats in Sudan hoped to maintain France's position as an African power and to realize, in however partial a manner, the promise of a new citizenship for former subjects in one of the constituent republics of the French Community. That citizenship was ill defined but, for a brief moment, porous and inclusive. There was no expectation that a French national would speak or understand French, and still less that he or she would have the papers to prove his or her nationality.[65] This was an expansive and assimilating, albeit deeply paternalistic, imperial citizenship, one elaborated for a future that did not come to pass.

Be that as it may, by 1958, the stakes would become even higher than the ambassador's phrase ("our African vocation") had suggested. Questions of passports, diplomatic representation, and organization of the pilgrimage were crucial to the notion of the "French Community" in Africa because, again, along with defense and control over the currency, diplomatic representations figured among the three thoroughly centralized functions that the Community had maintained. Others had all been devolved onto the territories, now dubbed republics, which were former colonies. Yet in Sudan, the French embassy would struggle to establish the relevance of its diplomatic protection to French Africans expelled from Egypt in 1959 and from Saudi Arabia in 1960.[66] Sudan, not wanting to admit them, sent some directly on to Abéché without reference to the French embassy. This begged the question, if other states did not recognize the French claims on African pilgrims, then what were those claims worth? And if the Community was not a collectivity grounded in a shared political identity, what was it?

In 1958, just after the Sudanese law was elaborated, the French *Ministre des Affaires Etrangères* assigned the task of surveying "French nationals" in Sudan to René Gros, an administrator with experience in Chad, knowledge of Arabic, and an interest in labor migration.[67] The results were surprising. Following visits from representatives of the various Chadian

---

[65] By the same token, no competence in French was required of current or former French nationals migrating to France from West Africa before or after independence; see Chapter 4.

[66] Amb Fr Soudan to MAE, DGAP, DAL, June 15, 1959, #334 AL; Amb Fr Soudan to MAE of Soudan, Oct. 14, 1959, #182; Amb Fr Soudan to MAE, DGAP, DAL, Sept. 25, 1959, #533AL; R. Gros, *Mission de Recensement des ressortissants africains français*, March 19, 1960, #35, CADN Khartoum 110.

[67] Gros, *Note préliminaire, Recensement des Ressortissants Africains français au Soudan*, Nov. 1958, CADN Khartoum 155. A similar diplomatic mission to Kumasi and Accra had encountered quite a considerable number of French African migrants, as well as a social

"collectivities" in Khartoum, news of Gros's survey gave rise to an influx of people packing the offices and crowding the verandah of the cultural center to demand French nationality. As Westerners came spontaneously to register themselves, Gros noted that, "It's remarkable that all of those surveyed have been in Sudan for at least 5 years, and some for 15 years or more. That proves that our emigrants (*ressortissants*) do not intend to abandon their original nationality. If some of them have accepted a Sudanese identity card, they have done so by simple opportunism, without feeling in anyway bound by that document."[68]

Although, in Sayad's terms, these Westerners might not have "recognized" themselves in the state that recognized them, Gros quickly found many more "French" Africans in Khartoum than he had expected. His colleagues had anticipated that some 100,000–200,000 people of this status were in Sudan in 1958.[69] They soon realized that this was a serious underestimate; Gros boosted this figure to 300,000 before he even began his survey. The ambassador might have agreed that the preliminary estimates had been too conservative. Whereas a previous study had estimated that there were 3,000–4,000 French Africans in all of Khartoum, after personally visiting one of the city's unplanned settlements (*bidonvilles*) in 1956, he knew there must be many more. Gros found 8,000–10,000 "*Africains français*" in one district alone.[70] Among them numbered many Chadians, Hausa merchants from Niger, and "citizens of the republics of the Community with largely Muslim populations: Mauritania, Senegal and Soudan Français as well as Oubanigans [Central Africans]." Thanks to Gros, wrote the ambassador, "Hausa from Niger in particular – who were traditionally under the protection of the Sudanese and the British, and who passed themselves off as Nigerians – increasingly associate with us, request our [diplomatic] protection, and register at our consulate."[71] In short, it was the pilgrims themselves who were

---

scientific inquiry led by Jean Rouch and Marc Piault. L. de Guignard, Amb Fr Ghana to MAE, DAL, June 24, 1958, #222/AL, ANM NI 1D2940.

[68] Gros, *Note préliminaire* ..., CADN Khartoum 155. Their nationality might have been better described as recently secured.

[69] *Note pour la direction générale du personnel*, Oct. 18, 1958, MAE, DAM, CADN Khartoum 155.

[70] Gros counted 2,000 West African households, and estimated that there were 5 inhabitants per household "which would appear to be a minimum"; Gros, *Note préliminaire* ..., CADN Khartoum 155. The previous study had been conducted by J. Mouradian, who would work in Jacques Foccart's office after 1960, handling among other questions those relating to the pilgrimage; see FPU 3386.

[71] *Affectation à l'ambassade de France à Khartoum de 2 administrateurs...*, s.d., MAE, DAM, CADN Khartoum 155.

recognizing the potential value of changing political statuses and of maintaining a plurality of them in the liminal years at the end of British rule in Sudan and at the beginning of a short sharp transition within the French empire in the Sahel. Yet as the overlapping imperial shadows of Britain, Sokoto, and even Takrur waxed and waned, new nation-states began to throw their own. That history is more somber and more brutal than the shadow metaphor would suggest.

PILGRIMS, SLAVES, AND PASSPORTS

Let's think like another new state. The Republic of Mali's interest in West African pilgrims was intense, even passionate, because of its deep concern in the early years of its existence that the pilgrimage served as both a screen for the development of a resistance movement among Saharans opposed to being ruled from Bamako and as a cover for the pawning or selling of household slaves and vulnerable travelers in Saudi Arabia and neighboring states.[72] From this perspective, the French practice of granting travel documents, or *laissez-passer*, to "Malian" pilgrims was deeply troubling. It facilitated the movement of Tuareg leaders who performed their own *hijra* while bringing with them Bellah – that is, people of servile status or ancestry – particularly women and children.[73] Thus as eagerly as French diplomats had sought to reclaim their nationals or "*ressortissants*" in Sudan in the late 1950s, the Soudanese Republic – the state that became Mali – fought to stake its own claim. Within a year of independence, the gloves would come off entirely. In a letter to the Saudi Director of Security, the Malian commissioner for the pilgrimage, Abdoul Wahab Doucouré, insisted that travel papers offered by the French were "illegal" and that Paris' embassy in Khartoum "had no authority to issue *laissez-passer* to Malian nationals." By providing them, the French government was encouraging "the traffic in slaves."[74]

---

[72] Abdoul Wahab Doucouré, *Rapport sur le pèlerinage, 1961*, BPN 104d398. See also MIM E1/1, and Lecocq (2010), 116–27.

[73] Lecocq usefully defines "Bellah" as "originally a Songhay word for all Tuareg of lower social status or a derogatory term for all Tuareg, [which] quickly gained administrative and political acceptance to denote slaves." In the late twentieth century, some "intellectuals of unfree origins" began to use it as a distinct ethnonym; Lecocq (2005), 48–49. See also N. Keita (2012). Hall prefers to use both "Bellah" and the Tuareg term "Iklan" (2011a, 2011b). The important point is that both terms designate disputed and unstable categories.

[74] The letter is reproduced in Doucouré to Min. Interieur, May 6, 1961, MIM E 1/1. The French colonial administration had been concerned with possible trafficking along

"French" Muslims in Sudan 111

This charge was as spectacular as its history was complex. Understanding Doucouré's accusation requires unraveling a complex historical knot, one composed of two major strands. The first is an emerging Tuareg dissident movement whose key figures, most of them Kel Adagh, sought some form of Saharan autonomy and rejected the Bamako government as – alternately, instrumentally, and sometimes incongruously – pro-Israeli, "fetichist," and too Black.[75] Already simmering in the mid-1950s – before African independence had taken shape but when Saharan autonomy was one of its potential forms – that movement would smolder in the early 1960s and break into open rebellion in 1963, just after the emergence of new nation-states seemed to have foreclosed the possibility of Saharan unity. In the years before the civil war in the desert broke out, the US-RDA government would alternately excoriate its more prominent Tuareg opponents and seek to cajole some of them into returning from self-imposed exile in North Africa and the Arabian Peninsula. Meanwhile, one of the key figures of this movement, Mohamed Ali ag Attaher Insar, himself a former chief (*amenokal*) of the Kel Intessar and one-time PSP candidate for the Territorial Assembly, would pull taut the second strand of our historical knot, that of the slave trade.[76]

In the mid-1950s, the future of the Sahara was a question for Saharans and specialists. France began to carve a "new Saharan colony," to be known as the *Organisation Commune des Régions Sahariennes* (OCRS), out of its existing possessions in West Africa and the Maghreb, and

---

pilgrimage routes as recently as the 1950s; on the Soudan Français, see Hall (2011a), 79–84, and Lecocq (2010), 116–27; for the Red Sea region, *Rapport Happé, 2ᵉ partie: Informations sur quelques pays du Mer Rouge: Soudan, Yemen, Aden, Somalie, Ethiopie, Erythrée*, Sept. 15, 1958, MAE, DAM, CADN Khartoum 110. Doucouré and Keita were attentive to the issue as early as 1958, but African independence would change the stakes entirely; Doucouré to Min. Interieur Keita, July 19, 1958, MIM BO 100.

[75] Lecocq has demonstrated the shared contempt and, in some cases, naked racism that obtained between some Tuareg "nobles" and much of the US-RDA leadership at the time (2005, 2010). For instance, in letters he sent to Mali from Libya in order to mobilize Tuareg opposition to Bamako's rule, Mohamed Ali ag Attaher Insar had expressed his disdain for a government composed of "*nègres*" and "*fetichistes*"; see Doucouré, *Compte-rendu de la mission effectuée en Arabie Saoudite au cours du pèlerinage 1960*, MIM E1/1. On the pro-Israeli charge, Doucouré, *Rapport sur le pèlerinage, 1961*, BPN 104d398. On Israel's diplomatic traction with the US-RDA, see Lecocq (2008); van Beusekom (2008), 18. Internally the US-RDA leadership was more ambivalent about Israeli overtures than was publicly apparent.

[76] On Mohamed Ali's early political career, see Lecocq (2010), 44–45. The BPN was deeply ambivalent about the possibility that Mohamed Ali would return to Mali. When he began to express interest in doing so, the BPN grew suspicious of his motives; see, e.g., P-V, BPN, May 4, 1962, BPNCMLN 77.

established a new ministry to govern it.[77] Soudan's territorial government was firmly opposed to such a move, but France was looking to hedge its bets in the event of Algerian secession.[78] Meanwhile, Tuareg and others tried to decide where best to lay their own. In this complex political scenario, the continued existence of slavery, and an active trade in people, focused the attention of many, from American President Dwight D. Eisenhower to French West African commissioners for the pilgrimage. Unlike the Saharan ministry, slavery made good press. In 1954 *l'Afrique Nouvelle*, a Catholic paper based in Dakar, had run a series of sensational and well-researched articles on the accusations of Awad el Djoud, a Bellah from Goundam, that Mohamed Ali had facilitated his pilgrimage, then once in Saudi Arabia sold him as a slave to Prince Faysal.[79] Having escaped and made his way back to the AOF, Awad had brought a criminal complaint against Mohamed Ali. This was not good news for the French administration. Embarrassing as the sale of one French national by another might have been, the tempest could have been contained within the relatively tiny teapot of an African weekly had *Paris-Match* not picked up a version of the story in 1955. The mass circulation magazine ran a piece that Mohamed Ali would dismiss as scurrilous in conversation with the AOF's commissioner for the pilgrimage, Chef de Bataillon Amadou Fall, in Medina during that year's pilgrimage season. Ali had found Awad a job in Prince Faysal's household because, he told Fall, "I didn't need him, since I had my own blacksmiths and servants (*serviteurs*)."[80] Fall took this as an implicit admission that Mohamed Ali held slaves, but he recognized that the slave trade to Saudi Arabia put the French Union in a delicate position, inasmuch as both victims and perpetrators were its citizens.[81]

---

[77] Lecocq (2010), 48.
[78] "M. Madeira Keita a exposé à Paris le point de vue du Soudan sur le problème du Sahara," *Soudan Matin*, 571, Nov. 20, 1957.
[79] See Hall (2011a), 79–84; Lecocq (2010), 116–27; Miers (2003), 348.
[80] *Rapport de Chef de Bataillon Fall, Commissaire du gouvernement pour le pèlerinage de 1955*, pg. 47, MIM D7/14. On Tuareg social categories, see Lecocq (2005), Keita (2012).
[81] Mali would inherit this problem, albeit in a simplified version, when the citizen-perpetrators would rebel against its government. However, early on the regime made the same choice France had, to set aside the issue of slavery and trafficking in exchange for cooperation on the issue of Saharan autonomy. In 1960, Mali's representative would signal to Mohamed Ali that because his convictions for slave-trading dated from the colonial period – that is, a scant few years earlier – the government would overlook them if he were to return to Mali; Doucouré, *Compte-rendu ... 1960*, MIM E1/1. Such conciliatory measures failed; Mohamed Ali would later supply some of the arms with which the rebellion in 1963 was launched, and he became "one of [its] main political leaders." In 1964, he was expelled from his refuge in Morocco and imprisoned in Mali;

The question of slavery was no less delicate within Saudi Arabia. Under pressure from Eisenhower, again according to Fall, Faysal had closed the slave markets that scandalized the American president, but the Kingdom would refuse to sign the United Nations' Supplementary Slavery Convention of 1956.[82] In 1962, having become Prime Minister, Faysal would ban slavery outright while promising compensation to "deserving" masters.[83] But because Faysal himself had manumitted his own slaves before his decree was announced, the writing was likely on the wall. In that case, if the market for slaves was like any other market, demand would have increased before an anticipated prohibition, as households attempted to secure labor that would soon become scarce.[84]

As the AOF's commissioner for the pilgrimage in 1954 and 1955, and as a Senegalese Muslim, Fall seemed to feel the injustice of slavery and trafficking deeply.[85] Passports, he thought, were the answer: "draconian conditions" should be imposed for obtaining them.[86] If the French government could better identify who was leaving its territory – that is, crossing the Chad–Sudan border – and who sought its travel papers to cross the Red Sea, then it could stop the clandestine export of women and children in particular. This might explain why, a few years later, after young Aysha had died on her voyage east through Chad, a border guard would cross out her portrait on her mother's passport.[87] It also helps to explain why, in 1961, Doucouré accused Paris of abetting the slave trade by delivering passports to Africans who had been French.

Doucouré's position was emancipatory and anticolonial, and he might have expected the Saudis under their new leader Prince Faysal to be at least mildly sympathetic to it, particularly at the height of the Algerian

---

Lecocq (2010), 193–94, 196, 213–14. After his liberation in the late 1970s, he went into exile.

[82] Lecocq argues that the scandal that erupted around Awad might have contributed to a change in Saudi policy; (2010), 117.

[83] Faysal (1963), 162. Faysal would accede to the throne in 1964.

[84] This assumes that slaveholders felt that they would not be stripped of their "property," which probably would have seemed a safe bet. In the event "substantial indemnities" were paid to them; Clarence-Smith (2006), 183; Miers (2003), 350; Awad (1966), 120–23.

[85] Based on 1954 and 1955 reports, the second of which pays much more extensive attention to the question of slavery. For reasons that are unclear, but which may be related, 1955 was Fall's last pilgrimage season. The 1956 report by Boubacar Diallo Telli leaves politics and slavery aside in favor of close attention to the logistics of the official pilgrimage. Note that whereas previous commissioners had been military men, Diallo Telli was a civilian. See MIM D7/12, D7/14, D7/15. Telli would later become a leading figure within the Organization of African Unity, before being imprisoned and killed by Sékou Touré.

[86] *Rapport de Chef de Bataillon Fall ... 1955*, MIM D7/14.

[87] Bawa Yamba (1995), 60; cited above.

revolution, in the wake of the Suez crisis, and in a period when France had no diplomatic representation in Saudi Arabia.[88] But the joint effort of Doucouré and Minister of the Interior Madeira Keita to claim pilgrims, migrants, and Bellah as Malians was an also important attempt to extend a new regime of governmental rationality, inflected with the ideology of independence, along a venerable but dynamic axis. They and their colleagues understood very well that – even more than control over borders – travel papers represented sovereignty, as did control over people's movements.

In 1960, just a few months before independence, a letter sent from Mecca to Gao made the stakes of their endeavor bitterly clear to Soudanese authorities attempting to combat the enslavement and sale of pilgrims. In this letter, a Bellah man begged his "father" to tell the authorities that his "aunt" and her daughter were attempting to sell his mother, his brother, and himself in Mecca. Write to the judicial authorities and tell them that we are "citizens (nobles) [sic] whom it is prohibited to sell," he pleaded. Let them know that "people from the formerly French West African territories" are bringing "nobles" on pilgrimage with them as employees, then attempting to sell them in the *hijaz*.[89] Although Gao's commandant forwarded the letter to Madeira Keita, the paper trail ends there. The effects of the Bellah man's gambit on his immediate fortunes are unknown, but he was not the last Malian to face enslavement. His letter was one of many coming from the *hijaz*. Taken together, they raised fears that Bellah from the Niger Bend – many of whom had fled from or rebelled against their masters in their recent years, and many of whom were loyal to the US-RDA[90] – faced real danger abroad. Under such circumstances, the US-RDA, and the Interior Ministry in particular, took an aggressive stand on the pilgrimage, even as it attempted to cajole Mohamed Ali to end his opposition to Bamako's authority.[91]

---

[88] In this period, the Italian embassy represented the diplomatic interests of France and the Community.

[89] It seems to me likely that at least some of the kinship terms in this letter – father, aunt – are euphemistic, but the letter describes a scenario much like that of Awad. Letter attached to CdC Gao to Min. Interieur, June 15, 1960, #230/cf, MIM E1/1. Hall quotes from another such letter (2011a), 84.

[90] Mauxion (2012); Hall (2011a), 76–79.

[91] Even as Malian authorities were receiving letters from people claiming to have been sold in the *hijaz*, they obtained copies of correspondence demonstrating that Mohamed Ali was attempting to stir up opposition to the imminent independence of the Mali Federation and of Niger. See Mohamed Aly [sic] Lansari, le Gouverneur Général de Tombouctou et les

For several years, the Soudan Français and before it the AOF had offered two kinds of aid to pilgrims: the organization of collective voyages, in which dignitaries and notables were often guests of the government, and assistance to impoverished pilgrims who sought to return home.[92] On the advice of Doucouré, Madeira Keita announced in 1960 that, following that year's pilgrimage season, the Malian government would no longer assure the repatriation of indigents. Given the rapid increase in the number of overland pilgrims, that long-standing policy had come to represent a heavy burden on the territory's budget, and Keita and Doucouré thought that by offering repatriation they were encouraging people who did not have the means to make the pilgrimage to do so. The great danger was that poor and vulnerable pilgrims could fall into exploitation and slavery. In 1960, Doucouré had managed to repatriate 235 indigent pilgrims, but he noted that many more – from Timbuktu, Mopti, and Goundam, but also Bandiagara – were "prevented [from leaving] by their new masters."[93]

Doucouré waged an open struggle in Saudi Arabia with Mohamed Ali, Marouchett ag Moussa, and Sidi Mohamed ag Zoukka, three Tuareg former chiefs whom he sought to have arrested by the Saudi police.[94] In the event, the Saudis agreed to expel some of these men to Sudan, their point of embarkation. They in turn would take the fight to Doucouré, who had developed a host of enemies. In addition to Mohamed Ali, Marouchett, and Sidi Mohamed, they included Bourahane, the *moutawaf* or designated host for the Malian pilgrims, whose monopoly Doucouré had broken, and Mali's "Wahhabis," whom he had antagonized in the 1950s when he had been a key figure in Bamako's counter-reform movement alongside Amadou Hampaté Bâ.[95] In a stream of letters to the government, they accused him of mismanaging the delegation of pilgrims and sought to have him stripped of that function.[96] This tactic seems to have backfired. Al-hajj Umar Tal, great grandson of the nineteenth-century

---

tribus du Touareg dans le Sahara Africain [sic], "les Revendications des pays de Tombouctou arabe [sic]," May 22, 1960, forwarded by Abdoule [sic] Wahab Doucouré to Min. Interieur and Mohamed Aly [sic], writing from Libya, to "Mon frère et ami Abdramane Benzacou," copy received by Min. Interieur, on May 21, 1960, MIM BO 100.

[92] Mann and Lecocq (2007).
[93] Doucouré, *Compte-rendu* ... 1960, MIM E1/1.
[94] Doucouré to Min. Interieur, May 6, 1961. MIM E1/1. My understanding of this episode is substantively informed by discussions with Baz Lecocq, but I remain responsible for the interpretations.
[95] On the counter-reform movement, see Brenner (2000, 2001), Soares (2005b).
[96] Letters attacking and defending the organization of the pilgrimage, and particularly its medical staff, can be found in MIM E1/1. Doucouré himself had reported some problems with the medical mission in his 1961 report. The BPN paid attention to these complaints,

jihadist al hajj Umar Tal al-Futi, helped lead Mali's official delegation from 1962 or 1963 to 1966, and he would defend Doucouré's actions.[97] With the help of such support, Doucouré would survive the campaign against him, which continued.

The stakes were high. Doucouré was convinced that some of the "indigent" pilgrims being repatriated had actually been dealing in slaves, and that they were returning to Mali to seek new victims.[98] The practice of repatriation continued to pose serious problems, and the government worked to shed that burden. Neither berating pilgrims for seeking repatriation nor attempting to discourage new departures seemed to be effective. In a 1961 circular calling for a "vast educational campaign" on the hazards of the pilgrimage, Madeira Keita lamented the fact that the number of pilgrims continued to increase, and he warned that countries such as Nigeria and Sudan that sold passports to pilgrims were motivated solely by greed. That same greed would render "clandestine" pilgrims vulnerable to enslavement in Mecca, where a "Black adolescent" could be sold for as much as 1,500,000 CFA.[99] In response to Keita's circular, administrators in San, a *cercle* that sent a significant number of pilgrims, held a meeting with religious leaders and *hajjis* to encourage others not to go. There Kola Yaya Boucoum, a locally influential and controversial imam who had not made the *hajj* himself, told prospective pilgrims that "should they die, extremists who undertook the journey without sufficient resources will not be forgiven [their sins]."[100] The result of the meeting was mixed – many of the former pilgrims were proud of the suffering they had endured and did not want to discourage others – but at least the

but ultimately supported Doucouré; P-V, BPN, May 29, 1962 and Oct. 4, 1962, BPNCMLN 77.

[97] On the ancestry of Mali's delegate, see al-Naqar (1972), 145. His position on Doucouré is expressed in Tal al-hadji Oumar dit Karamoko Imam, Ouloufoubougou (Bamako) to Min. Interieur, n.d. (1962), MIM E1/1.

[98] Undated, unsigned ms. pages, apparently from Doucouré, 1962, MIM E1/1. This was not an entirely new phenomenon; French administrators had recognized that repatriation might encourage the overland pilgrimage; that they had likely repatriated the same people more than once, although identities were hard to establish; and that they had "repatriated" to West Africa people who were in fact Saudi nationals; *Commission [sur la] politique à l'égard du pélerinage à la Mecque, (1956)*, SHAT 15H83.

[99] Madeira Keita, Minister of the Interior, Circular to all Governors of Regions, CdCs, and Heads of Subdivision, June 26, 1961, #225 MIITCAB, Confidential, MIM E1/1.

[100] P-V, meeting of 5 August 1961, San, forwarded by CdC San to Min. Interieur, Aug. 20, 1961, #68/c, MIM E1/1. On the reform movement in San, in which Boucoum was involved, see Mann (2003). Ambivalence about the pilgrimage was old among West Africa's *ulema*, even beyond the Sokoto context discussed above; see al-Naqar (1969b); Umar (2006).

government's position was clear. In yet another unanticipated irony of independence, the ostensibly virtuous enterprise of the pilgrimage could be qualified as "clandestine" before the same label was attached to Malian migration to France.

As I argued above, the slave trade and the Tuareg dissident movement that later broke into open rebellion were distinct but braided issues from at least the mid-1950s. The history of the Tuareg rebellion and its aftermath has been recounted authoritatively elsewhere.[101] Let's follow for a moment the smaller thread by returning to Abdelmalek Sayad and his theme of recognition. In vulnerable pilgrims and migrants, leading figures in the US-RDA government "recognized" themselves in terms that were more than instrumental. Rather they were deeply affective. Hints of this passion had already appeared in the final report on the *hajj* written by Commissioner Fall, and they would recur in the Malian government's extensive responses to a 1966 United Nations survey on slavery.[102] As for Modibo Keita and Madeira Keita, they seem to have felt the sting in the language of Mohamed Ali, who refused to be governed by *"nègres."*[103] The lines were clear. For them, he was a *négrier* (slave trader) and the epitome of a nomad who claimed origins in the Maghreb, or what they called "White Africa."[104] He believed himself superior and could not be trusted. Whatever his suspicions might have been, Modibo hoped to avoid provoking rebellion, and he sought reconciliation with Mohamed Ali and other Northern dissidents. This may have been a lost cause. Before a Saharan insurgency burst into the open in Mali in 1963, a very different clash over Bamako's authority had already begun in the *hijaz*. There Doucouré, in close liaison with Madeira Keita and helped by Faysal's abolition policy, had brought the fight to Mohamed Ali. When 120 "Malian slaves" sought refuge in the country's new embassies in Jeddah and Cairo in 1962, the arrest of those accused of trying to sell them must have brought a grim satisfaction.[105]

But a problem remained. It was the problem Doucouré had encountered on an airstrip in Jeddah in 1961: the Malian exile Sidi Mohamed ag Zoukka accompanied by 29 women and a couple of men, all of

---

[101] Lecocq (2010), Boilley (1999).
[102] Awad (1966). On Dr. Mohamed Awad, an Egyptian geographer, and the background and results of his report, see Miers (2003), 361–66.
[103] Doucouré, *Compte-rendu* ... 1960, MIM E1/1.
[104] P-V, BPN, Feb. 9, 1962 and Feb. 27, 1962, BPNCMLN 77.
[105] P-V, BPN, Sept. 18, 1962, BPNCMLN 77.

whom Doucouré had good reason to believe had been brought from Mali for sale in the *hijaz*. All had obtained their papers from the French embassy in Khartoum. This was the incident that led him to protest to the Saudis that the French government had "no authority" over people from Mali, and that it was encouraging "the traffic in slaves."[106] The rhetoric was hot, but the evidence was strong.[107] By 1963, two years after Doucouré's encounter with Sidi Mohamed on the airstrip, and just after Faysal's abolition decree, Saudi Arabia would refuse to recognize travel documents issued to African pilgrims by the French government.[108] Also in 1963, France would sign new accords on mobility with Mali, Mauritania, and Senegal (1964), the trio of Sahelian states from which most sub-Saharan migrants came. Posing new constraints on emigration to France, these new diplomatic agreements had been pursued by the African governments rather than by the former metropole. The timing is coincidental, but the historical conjuncture is an important one. On two fronts at once, the new African states could claim to have won this minor skirmish in the battle to establish their sovereignty. In northeast Africa, not only did papers matter, but it mattered that someone claimed slaves as citizens. In short, it mattered to which state they "belonged," and how that belonging was recognized. But the issue of slavery offers only one answer to the question of how and why it mattered as much as it did. Another lies in acknowledging the more mundane aspects of managing the pilgrimage itself as important elements of statecraft not only for Saudi Arabia and the Sahelian states, but also for a postimperial France increasingly invested in informal and symbolic means of expressing its power. Such an acknowledgment

---

[106] Doucouré, *Rapport sur le pèlerinage, 1961*, BPN 104d398; and Doucouré to Min. Interieur, May 6, 1961, MIM E1/1.

[107] That is to say, evidence for the effect of extending French travel papers was strong, but I differ with Doucouré on the cause. If French diplomats facilitated trafficking, there is no evidence that they did so knowingly.

[108] Tél. à l'arrivée, Amb Fr Niamey, Origine: Diplomatie Paris, April 25, 1963, CADN Niamey 16. Although Mali, and perhaps its neighbors, saw this as a victory of sorts, the French were themselves ambivalent. The MAE sought to keep a French hand in the organization of the pilgrimage and asked its embassies to confirm the willingness of their host governments to see their citizens represented by France. On the other hand, Foccart's office was content to cede the expense and the responsibility to African states and to close down consulates such as the one at Asmara rather than "to demonstrate our impotence to our former nationals (*ressortissants*)"; Mouradian, *Regles de séjour des africains étrangers en Ethiopie*, Note à l'attention de M. le S.G., June 25, 1963, FPU 3386.

leaves open the question of whether, in Sayad's terms, France recognized itself in formerly French West African Muslims. To the best of their power, Mali and Sudan refused to allow it to do so. But much the same battle between newly independent states over the objects and subjects of government would play out very differently along another axis, in France itself.

4

Well-Known Strangers: How West Africans Became Foreigners in Postimperial France

In Paris, in March 1965, Robert Delavignette took a bus.[1] A Black woman collected his ticket. When he got off the bus, he found three men, Black men, emptying trashcans. All this provoked, in the mind of this retired colonial administrator, a reflection on the place of Blacks in France. The three men were there as workers, and they came from the independent states south of the Sahara. Like the ticket collector and Delavignette's fellow passengers, they had become "part of Paris." No one was interested in their presence. Passersby did not find it remarkable, but Delavignette did. The ticket collector, he wrote, was from the Antilles or Réunion. She was therefore a French citizen (and she did not have much in common with the trash collectors, other than the color of their skin and the fact that they lived and worked in Paris). As for the trash collectors, they were all citizens of new states that were formerly French colonies. They were thus "foreign nationals" (*ressortissants étrangers*), a phrase with which Delavignette slipped reflexively into administrative language. Were they also foreigners?

During the First World War, Delavignette recalled, Lucie Cousturier, a French painter who welcomed West African soldiers in her home outside Fréjus, considered them (or their grandfathers) "unknowns" (*inconnus*), and she made an enormous effort to get to know them.[2] His bus trip inspired a question for Delavignette: Were the Blacks he had run into just as unknown (for "us") fifty years later? "They do not give [that] impression," he wrote. In any case, the ticket collector could not in any way be considered a foreigner, but the men could. That quality of

---

[1] Delavignette (1965).
[2] Cousturier (1920, 1925).

the well-known stranger represents a point of departure, for the quality of "foreigner" was not natural. It was with decolonization, wrote the French historian Pap Ndiaye, "that French identity reoriented itself around a continent and a [skin] color. Put differently, subjects became strangers (*étrangers*). Colonial visibility [that is, in public life, in the legislature, and so on] gave way to postcolonial invisibility."[3] After 1960, "the Black population ... grew progressively even as it disappeared as a political issue." Ndiaye is not wrong, but his account short-circuits a moment I take to be important: the creation of African citizenship.

We've seen how West Africans came to be considered foreigners in Sudan. But how did such well-known strangers become foreigners in France? Such a question might appear absurd,[4] but we are now accustomed to the existence of independent African states, the collapse of the French empire, the failure of the most ambitious forms of pan-African unity such as the Mali Federation, and, above all, to an inhospitable Europe. However, the postwar years had represented what Frederick Cooper would term an "opening" in which West African migrants benefited from the peculiar political status of citizens of the ill-defined and multi-layered polity sketched out but not defined by the constitution of the Fourth Republic (1946–58).[5] After 1958, they were citizens of the Community. As a result, for the last years of colonial rule and the first of independence, Malians, Senegalese, and Mauritanians – who represented some 90% of sub-Saharan African migrants in France – could legally enter and work in that country with little administrative formality.[6] They had all formerly held French nationality, which their legal presence in France allowed them to maintain at least until 1962, when Mali began to restrict the definition of a still amorphous African citizenship.

As a step in an exploration of what African citizenship and sovereignty came to mean in the immediate wake of independence, this chapter recasts the history of colonial and early postcolonial West African migration to France – and indeed West African citizenships – as an ad hoc and uneven

---

[3] Ndiaye (2008), 390.
[4] Indeed, a whole literature of alienation attests to the idea that West Africans felt themselves to be, and were told that they were, foreigners. Much of this work is canonical within francophone literature and film. See, e.g., the poetry of Léopold Sedar Senghor; C.H. Kane, *l'Aventure ambigüe*; Y. Oulouguem, *Lettres à la France Nègre*; Ousmane Sembène, *le Docker noir* and *la Noire de* .... These themes are explored in D. Thomas (2006).
[5] Cooper (2008; 2014); see also Decottignies and de Biéville (1963), ch. 1.
[6] Note that twenty years later, by 1981, they would represent "less than half of Africans in France (students not included)"; Manchuelle (1997), 217. We must assume that the category of migrant changed in this period as well.

creation of migrants, bureaucrats, politicians, social workers, hosts (B., *diatigiw*), and entrepreneurs through which West Africans became "foreigners" and political and administrative statuses (or the documents that represented them) became a range of abstract yet marketable commodities.[7] In those years, migrants and bureaucrats lent meaning to the rapidly changing forms of membership reflected in juridical and diplomatic exchanges and in the very papers they circulated, examined, or carried in their pockets, whether these were legitimate or borrowed, faked or stolen.

Quite aside from the work they performed on construction sites, on docks, and in kitchens, West African migrants and the traffickers, forgery artists, border guards, and bureaucrats with whom they interacted gave a meaning to French and African citizenships that was dramatically different from what the African political elite intended, French functionaries desired, or historians of decolonization have recognized. The struggle over what had become international migration in the immediate wake of African independence was a struggle for control over the meaning of political membership that followed the end of empire. In short, the intersection between mobility and documentation represented a key terrain for working out what exactly African citizenship and sovereignty would mean.

Nevertheless, my focus in this chapter is deliberately not on West African students, soldiers, and workers.[8] Instead, I highlight a shared ambivalence about West African migration that prevailed in government offices in Paris and in Bamako and in the border posts of Marseille, Le Havre, and Roissy between roughly 1958 and 1974, 1963 being a pivotal year. Drawing on the archives of French ministries – notably the Ministry of the Interior – and of the Malian BPN, this chapter explores the tangled histories of shifting political statuses, evolving administrative and police

---

[7] As we saw, Torpey argues that the creation of passports and the assertion of state monopolies over the control of circulation of people, particularly entry into national territory, were key elements in constructing national sovereignty in Europe in the nineteenth and twentieth centuries; Torpey (2000). I am arguing that migrants themselves actively participated in the construction of new postcolonial citizenships via their adaptive use of passports and travel documents and their practices of evasion. The same is true of postimperial (in this case French) citizenship, but that is not primary area of concern in this chapter; on decolonization as formative of French citizenship see Shepard (2006) and Cooper (2005; 2014).

[8] Cultural and social histories of people of West African origin in France are numerous. Particularly valuable are Dedieu (2012); Guèye (2001, 2006); Manchuelle (1997); Stovall (2001); and Winders (2006). On the diaspora in France more broadly, see Keaton, Sharpley-Whiting, and Stovall, eds. (2012); Ndiaye (2008); Tshimanga, Gondola, and Bloom, eds. (2009).

practices, and expanding circuits of knowledge and strategy around African migration in a crucial period of postcolonial transition. During those years, the practices of bureaucrats and migrants alike changed rapidly and unevenly, while the language in which French government employees discussed the presence of West African migrants changed more slowly. The African states, on the other hand, developed their own policies, of which Mali's was the most clearly hostile toward migrants and expatriates. For newly independent states, breaking away from the colonial economy meant asserting that one's citizens were someone else's strangers. The accretion and generation of multiple forms of political membership empowered the citizens whom fresh and fragile states sought to control, suggesting that the conditions under which new nations would exercise their independence would not be determined solely by the former imperial power, by Cold War rivals, or by the new occupants of governor's mansions transformed into presidential palaces. They would also be determined by people on the move who would shape the contours of new nation-states, both African and French.

TRACKING SUBJECTS

At independence, in the wake of decades of migration control and a shorter period of open borders, Africans were not as "well-known" in France as the title of this chapter might imply. Barring the hundreds of thousands of soldiers brought to fight the world wars or to man garrisons, few West Africans had come to France before the late 1950s, and most who did remained in the port cities of Le Havre and Marseilles, at institutions of higher learning, notably in Paris, or in military camps outside towns such as Fréjus on the Mediterranean coast. Nonetheless, as François Manchuelle and others have demonstrated, modern (voluntary) maritime migration from particular areas of the West African Sahel has a long history.[9] From the mid-nineteenth century, the Senegal River Valley of present-day Mali, Mauritania, and Senegal, including the region of Futa Toro, has been the cradle of a laboring diaspora that has extended to and receded from such points as Kayes, Dakar, Saint Louis, Brazzaville, and Marseille – in other words, across West and Equatorial Africa, and beyond.

After the First World War, those migrants who came to France – a category composed for several decades almost uniquely of men – attracted

---

[9] Manchuelle (1997); Timera (1996).

the attention of the Ministry of the Interior's surveillance agency, known as SLOTFOM,[10] which was dedicated to tracking colonial (later "Overseas") subjects and which would provide future generations of historians with the makings of an "urban ethnography of intersecting immigrant political communities."[11] SLOTFOM agents monitored migrants from the colonies in the 1920s and 1930s, their reports often echoing and amplifying the concerns of their superiors, who viewed colonial subjects in the metropole as simultaneously a social ill and a potentially infectious political danger. However, SLOTFOM's agents recognized that their own numbers and knowledge were inadequate to the task of surveilling the diverse African communities in France; at any rate, the agency devoted most of its resources to the surveillance of Southeast Asians. Less than a handful of agents were dedicated to monitoring the social and political networks of West African students and workers in France, and they had little ability to tabulate, much less control, the circulation of West Africans between France and the AOF. What was clear was that the numbers were relatively small, the migrants were almost all men, and that the majority of them were colonial subjects, rather than citizens.

While metropolitan agencies struggled to surveil migrants who had arrived in France, the colonial state itself sought to restrict their circulation between metropole and imperial space, to channel labor within the empire, and, no less importantly, to curtail movement across imperial boundaries. The administration of the AOF and the Ministry of Colonies shared one primary concern so evident that it hardly needs restating: the evolution of a colonial economy, particularly a labor market, favorable to the interests of European enterprises. As early as 1914, the administration of the AOF was discussing how to limit West African emigration to Europe and to neighboring British colonies such as Gold Coast and Gambia, while encouraging migration from the Sahel to the federation's two primary cash-crop producing colonies, Cote d'Ivoire and Senegal. The advent of the First World War directed administrative energies elsewhere, even as it accentuated the problems of potential conscripts fleeing for British territory and produced

---

[10] From 1916 to 1954, the French Ministry of the Interior operated a *Service de Liaison avec les Originaires des Territoires Français d'Outre-Mer*, known in its early years as the *Service de Contrôle et d'Assistance en France des Indigènes des Colonies*, both rather polite names for a surveillance organization. The name SLOTFOM reflects the political categories of the late 1930s and 1940s (*français d'outre-mer* as opposed to *indigènes*). The difference is instructive: people once referred to as "Natives" were dubbed "overseas Frenchmen." I have used SLOTFOM throughout in order to be consistent with the appelation in the archives.

[11] Wilder (2005), 158.

a small number of African soldiers seeking to remain in France. For the next decade, holding ship captains responsible for the costs of eventual repatriation of illegal emigrants to France was generally considered control enough, and even this sanction was not exercised consistently.

The year 1925, however, witnessed a resurgence of the ambition of controlling West African migration, both within the AOF and beyond; such control would come to be seen as a core function of the colonial state. In that year, the head of the AOF's Department of Political and Administrative Affairs, Ferdinand Rougier, proposed the establishment of a broad set of reforms intended to unify the disparate regulations then in effect in Senegal, Cote d'Ivoire, and other territories of the AOF. Key to his reform were proposals to control African mobility and to establish personal identity cards for African subjects (*indigènes*). Both measures were to be progressive: lieutenant-governors would first control movement from the AOF to neighboring territories, then movement between colonies within the AOF, and finally movement between *cercles*. Rougier's goal was to "to extend this obligation progressively to voyages between one administrative district and another, to changes in residence from one village to another." As for the identity cards, they too would be issued progressively, first to "heads of family, then [to] the rural population, finally to all Natives without exception ... to arrive at a generalized [system of] identification." The cards would note the bearer's familial relations, place of birth, domicile, legal status, thumb prints, and would include a photo "if possible."[12] Given the limited resources available at the time, Rougier's proposal was audacious. The bureaucracy lacked the necessary material or human resources to carry out such a plan. Nonetheless, it was partly enacted. A 1928 decree would require West Africans to have an identity document delivered by the local (*cercle*) administration in order to leave the federation or to travel between the AOF's ports; African noncitizens – the vast majority of the population – were also required to have an "emigration permit" obtained from the lieutenant-governor or his delegate.[13] The practice of demanding permits

---

[12] The original draft of the proposed decree would have forbidden the emigration of married women (absent the husband's assent), nonmarried women (absent the consent of the family head), and men of recruitment age. Rougier, DAPA, Nov. 12, 1925, CARAN 21G77/200mi3044. On the effects of such regulations on women migrants in this period, see Rodet (2009).

[13] Decree of April 24, 1928, Article 1, *JORF*, April 28, 1928, 4834–35. A later policy in Dahomey that restricted local movement was praised as well; DAPA, AOF for Dir. des Finances et de la Comptabilité, June 18, 1936; both in CARAN 21G37/200mi3031.

was abandoned after the Second World War although identity cards remained obligatory; intriguingly, even as presumably equal citizens within the Fourth Republic, Africans bore cards that indicated their "*race*," or ethnicity.[14]

French immigration policy in West Africa therefore rested on a technique – the identity card – and two imperatives. The first was to underscore the singular political status of colonial subjects while protecting the labor supply necessary for the export economy; Dakar had a voice in this discussion. It sought to learn from the immigration policies of the North and South American states and ultimately obtained, via Paris, relevant documents from the Canadian government.[15] Canada had struggled to prevent immigration from South Asia, but opposing migration within a single empire had posed delicate legal problems, as in the face of South Asian protests London was discomfited by Ottawa's inclination to draw juridical distinctions between subjects of the Queen on overtly racial grounds.[16] The peculiar model of what was effectively a self-governing settler state could hardly fit the West African context, but the administration's other concerns were less contingent on particular circumstances. The second imperative of French colonial immigration policy was to address public health concerns both within the empire and across imperial boundaries; here Paris made the decisions. A decree of 1938 mandated that "immigrants coming from Algeria and from the French colonies or protectorates be required to undergo a medical exam and an administrative verification of the fact that they met public health requirements before embarking for France." Without a new booklet "equivalent to a medical passport," they would not be allowed to embark.[17] Via texts such as these, the elements of a policy on migration between West Africa and France had been solidly established in the years immediately before the Second World War. They included public health measures (*contrôles sanitaires*), identity

---

[14] Gary-Tounkara (2008), ch. 5, esp. 175; [Senegal] Arrêté 5241/AP, Oct. 17, 1949 and Arrêté 6202, Dec. 4, 1949, SRAD 1D17.

[15] Dir du Cabinet (du GGAOF) to Min. Dir. des Services Economiques, April 17, 1936, #507c, CARAN 21G77/200mi3044.

[16] Instead, the Canadian government adopted a subterfuge, mandating that only those arriving directly from their country of origin would be admitted to Canada. At the time, no direct link between South Asia and Canada existed; Mongia (2007), 202.

[17] *JORF*, 151, June 29, 1938, 7521, CARAN 21G77/200mi3044. Maladies in question include those covered in the *Convention Sanitaire Internationale* of June 21, 1926, plus others listed in an appendix (absent); apparently, judging from the preamble, these are "*maladies dites sociales*" to which workers coming from the colonies might expose people in the metropole (although the inverse was as likely to be true).

cards that asserted the bearer's identity as a French colonial subject, and the practice of demanding a deposit from migrants to offset the cost of possible repatriation. That neat trio failed to account for two other important forces: imperial reform and migrants' practices of evasion.

The emerging apparatus of migration control faded in importance in the postwar period of economic expansion and enhanced freedom, including liberty of movement, before reappearing in unexpected ways in the first years of African independence. After 1946 "*AOFiens*" were no longer legally "Natives" (*indigènes*), but citizens, a status that remained to be defined. As vague as the meaning of such citizenship was, the abolition of Native status – the *indigénat* – heralded a new period of migration within the AOF and between its various colonies. Most concretely, passes and permits were no longer demanded of migrants, although an identity card was still officially required. Opportunities for work and trade would attract Sahelian migrants to the coastal territories (the Côte d'Ivoire above all) and to France, just as expanded access to higher education would draw greater, although still small, numbers of students to the metropole. Through the mid-1950s, West Africans came to France in a mere trickle; they may have left territories such as Soudan at the rate of a few dozen a month. However, they traveled with relatively little formality, and circumvented even that which existed. A series of "Information Cards concerning French West Africans entering the metropole" (*Fiches de Renseignement concernant un originaire [de l'AOF] se rendant en Metropole*), a form of paperwork then obligatory for travelers, reveals that even in these early years of rather light migration controls, methods of skirting the state's restrictions had already emerged. Sparsely detailed as they are, one finds a pattern in the cards that would later become widespread as the volume of migration increased: the same names are recorded as making round-trips so rapid and frequent that it is impossible that they represent one individual and his voyages.[18] Instead, *papers* made round trips, and the people who used them made one-way voyages. Sailors had long shared their papers with one another, as had laborers and, probably to a lesser extent, soldiers. The same tricks were quickly adapted to air travel, a mode of transportation that nonetheless lent itself to tighter control as the vessels were smaller and the distinctions between passengers and crew sharper. Over a dozen years later, the French immigration services would catch on to the phenomenon while studying passenger

---

[18] Based on cards from March and October 1953, June, July, and August 1954, and May 1955; CARAN 21G174/200mi3099.

manifests, reporting "the departure – within a very few days – of the same voyagers, whose return has not generally been noted. The only plausible explanation is that we are in the presence of an organized traffic that sends useful papers back to be used again."[19]

Although the cards from the 1950s might not reveal who actually made the voyages, they do indicate who secured the papers in the first place. Among recorded passengers, salaried workers predominated, and their numbers included drivers, mechanics, cooks, and personal servants accompanying European employers, as well as sailors looking for work in Marseille or Le Havre.[20] Air France flights between Bamako and Paris carried students, traders (*commerçants*), and much of the Soudanese and Voltaïque political elite (including Mamadou Konaté, Modibo Keita, and Nazi Boni). During particular seasons, the plurality of air passengers were students from Bamako headed to Paris, and many of them were the sons and often the daughters of parliamentarians and politicians.[21] Students were eligible for exemptions from paying a repatriation deposit, and they seem to have used their own papers. Traders, however, did have to offer such a guarantee, and they took the lead in manipulating the immigration system. As Paris began to attract traders and workers, in addition to students, an older circuit of migration changed. African mariners began to put down roots in French ports, notably in Marseille, as the shipping industry abandoned the coal-fueled boats that had consumed so much African labor. Facing an increasingly difficult maritime labor market, those sailors sought work on shore as dockers, bartenders, or restaurant workers, and many would never return to independent West Africa.[22]

Between 1946 and 1960, that is, in the wake of the abolition of the *indigénat* and before independence, West African migrants benefited from the peculiar political status of French nationals holding citizenship

[19] Pref., Dir. SCTIP to Dir. R.G. de la Sûreté Nationale, April 11, 1968, #386, CAC 19850087, Art. 9.
[20] Cards in CARAN 21G174/200mi3099.
[21] The cards suggest that about half of the students leaving Soudan for France were young women like Fatimata Coulibaly, daughter of Mamadou Coulibaly, a US-RDA militant and parliamentarian. The cards would seem to overrepresent dramatically the number of West African women in higher education in France: Is it possible that female students were more likely to return home during vacations than were male students and therefore would have been counted more often? The number of *Soudanaises* with scholarships to study in France in the late 1950s was small. Not more than 10 of 209 scholarships in 1959 went to women; this amounts to less than 5%. *Bordereaux récapitulatif de paiement des bourses du décembre 1959*, ANS FM65; for one particular case, see Diallo (2005), 91. On female students and graduates of West African schools in this period, see Barthélémy (2010).
[22] Bertoncello and Bredeloup (2004).

in a poorly-defined polity.[23] They also benefited from a period of economic growth. Laborers were badly needed. By the late 1950s, in light of the war in Algeria, some employers preferred West African to North African workers, at least politically,[24] and the metropolitan government had little interest in controlling the still-small influx of West African laborers into the economically necessary but politically insignificant and nonunionized fields of casual labor and construction work (in contrast, the Ministries of Labor and of the Interior were very interested in controlling the much larger flows of Portuguese and Spanish agricultural workers, whose presence they regarded as potentially long-term).[25] As for the rapidly evolving but still colonial state in West Africa, it had abandoned the essentially autarkic model that had previously determined its approach to emigration. Indeed, none of the earlier models of migration quite fit the West African case. West African migrants to France were neither foreigners, whose presence fell formally under the purview of the *Office National de l'Immigration* (ONI),[26] nor Algerians, who were after all second-class citizens from a territory still defined as an integral part of France. Nor indeed could the colonial model of restricting migration in order to limit its political consequences – and to prop up a weak colonial labor market – be applied to the semi-autonomous territories whose advent was signaled by the Loi Cadre (1956) and the creation of the Fifth Republic and its French Community (1958). A new model had yet to be established. Ultimately it would fall to the postimperial state of France and the independent African governments to attempt to do so, but the migrants themselves continued to play an important role in giving meaning to inchoate categories of political membership.

---

[23] Decottignies and de Biéville (1963), 15-17. See also Cooper (2014); compare Coquery-Vidrovitch (2001).

[24] Ambivalence about employing unskilled West Africans apparently grew over time; see letter of employer, dated Feb. 13, 1967, CAC 0019770346, Art. 10. This letter was circulated within the administration to prove the point that some employers systematically refused to consider requests for employment from West Africans and Maghrebians. See also Direction Centrale des R.G., *Immigrés Africains en France*, July 15, 1969; and an unsigned *Etude sur l'immigration des travailleurs africains en France*, May 30, 1969, CAC 19940023, Art. 20.

[25] The importance of this point should not be underestimated. Students of African migration to France, and of postcolonial migration generally, often overlook other communities of migrants and flows of migration that fall outside their brief. African migration was of limited significance, in absolute numbers, in comparison to migration from southern Europe.

[26] Note that recruitment was privately managed, and the ONI was involved with only about 1/5 of migrants; Wihtol de Wenden (1994). A 1955 decision by the Conseil d'état had established that the ONI did not have purview over sub-Saharan Africans, thereby affirming the lack of administrative control over their mobility; Ndiaye (2008), 209.

PRODUCING STRANGERS

After 1960, were West Africans French, formerly French, or foreign? What relationship would obtain between individual West Africans, or between migrants as a category, and new states? At the time of independence – as Algerian immigration, which had long been closely watched, fell under increasingly strict surveillance – the status of sub-Saharan Africans remained in flux. In the first years after 1960, migrants from the Western Sahel needed neither a residence permit (*carte de séjour*) nor a work permit (*carte de travail*) in France; a passport was unnecessary, as an identity card would suffice. Attracted by a vibrant labor market, their numbers grew rapidly. In the first months of 1962, some 100 Malians came to France each month.[27] A year later, that number was 500, and scarcely any departures were recorded.[28] By 1969, the *Renseignements Généraux* (R.G., the domestic intelligence agency) reported that some 40,000 "African workers" were in France. The majority lived in and around Paris, and another quarter of them in Marseille. The R.G. calculated that some 40% of them were Malian, 25% Senegalese, and 25% Mauritanian. In addition to the workers, there were as many as 10,000 students, and some 13,000–15,000 West Africans entered or left the country annually.[29] Independent analyses put the numbers much higher, yet the figures they proposed varied widely: some 50,000–60,000 in 1963, 25,000–45,000 in 1964, and 200,000–250,000 in 1969.[30] Many more men than women came to France, an imbalance that only began to shift after 1974.[31] None of these numbers could have been very accurate, either in scale or proportion, especially in light of the circulation of false papers. Yet a statement from a government report at the end of the decade would have resonated even more strongly at its beginning: in a country of millions, West African

---

[27] Min. Interieur (Direction Générale de la Sureté Nationale; Direction de la Réglementation) to MAE, pour le Min., Dir. du Cabinet, Yves Bourges, May 15, 1962, #779, MAE 2541.
[28] MAE, DAM to AMBAFR BKO, Jan. 21, 1963, MAE 2541. Another document cites an average of 700 West African entries into France in the first months of 1963; DAM, Direction des Conventions Administratives et des Affaires Consulaires, to AMBAFR Bamako, Nouakchott, and Dakar, June 29, 1963, MAE 2541.
[29] *Note sur les Immigrés Africains en France*, Direction Centrale des R.G., July 15, 1969, CAC 1994002, Art. 20.
[30] For 1963 and 1969, N'Diaye (1970), 21; for 1964, Delerm (1965), 72 and Delavignette (1965), 69; see also Diarra (1968), 890–91. Figures diverge greatly based on the sources, and are often internally contradictory; see, e.g., Ndiaye (2008), 203.
[31] In 1974, some 14% of West Africans in France were female. That number grew steadily thereafter, under the policy of family reunification. Still, it had reached only 40% in the 1990s; Ndiaye (2008), 203, citing C. Poiret (1997); see also Lambert (2002).

migration "is not cause for concern in a quantiative sense, but ... remains alarming in social terms and in terms of public health: material and psychological misery accompany the housing and living conditions, all of which carries a very high social cost."[32] In short, the numbers themselves did not mean as much as the challenge West Africans posed to a particular form of government, one expressed through concern for the conditions in which daily life was lived.

French policies limiting African immigration came into effect only gradually, remaining relatively permissive through the 1960s. In July 1962 the Préfecture de Police, representing professionals who had long been charged with controlling immigration from all countries, asked that administrative barriers similar to those that applied to foreigners be required of Africans in order to enable greater surveillance and control of them. Sub-Saharan migrants had never been submitted to the same bureaucratic regime as Algerians, not least because they were "colonial" not "territorial" visitors.[33] The very cautious Minister of Foreign Affairs refused the request on the somewhat shaky grounds that "such a measure would run the risk of compromising the situation of French nationals in those countries."[34] Beginning in 1963, new papers were demanded of African migrants, but a passport remained superfluous. The French government signed revised accords or "*Conventions pour la circulation des personnes*" establishing new administrative procedures with Mali (March 8, 1963), Mauritania (July 5, 1963), and Senegal (January 21, 1964).[35] Having been the first of these, the French–Malian accord would serve as a

---

[32] *Etude sur l'immigration des travailleurs africains en France*, May 30, 1969. Unsigned, agency unclear, *Note en copie à M. le Bellec, chargé de mission, secrétariat générale à la présidence de la République*, CAC 19940023, Art. 20. When queried by the DGSN in 1967, the municipal administration of Toulon reported that it had no problems with its small community of some 800 sub-Saharan Africans, but noted a population of some 17,000 Portugese and 8,000 Spaniards. *Note de renseignements*, Toulon, Oct. 9, 1967, CAC 19850087, Art. 9.

[33] For instance, they had never needed a French identity card, and it is not clear that they had indeed been eligible for one.

[34] Spire (2005), 208–09. The same concern had informed discussions in 1960; see Cooper (2009), 113. Many Europeans left Mali after independence and the establishment of the Malian franc; Simonis (1993), vol. II, 607–08. However, the number of expatriate Frenchmen grew some 25% (to 2,546) between 1960 and 1968. Most of the newcomers were either teachers or "*coopérants techniques.*" C.-G. de France à Bamako to MAE, Direction du Personnel et de l'Administration Générale, Dec. 28, 1968, MAE 2536.

[35] Senegal's existing convention had been signed in April 1960 and inherited from the Mali Federation. Administrators within France were confused on this point, on which Senegalese diplomats in France insisted; André Guillabert, H.-R. de la Rép. du Sénégal (in France) to Min. S. d'Etat chargé des relations avec les états de la Communauté,

template for similar accords in years to come.[36] People from these three countries intent on coming to work in France would now need a labor contract (*contrat de travail*) and a medical certificate (*certificat de contrôle médical*).

The alternative was to come to France as a "tourist," armed only with a three-month return ticket and an ID card. This is what the vast majority of migrants began to do. Boats arriving in Bordeaux from West Africa in 1965 discharged hundreds of African "tourists," who the *Direction des Renseignements Généraux* recognized had no intention to leave France after three months, but intended to look for work instead.[37] The fact that this thin form of migration control was a fiction was readily apparent, and the new conventions hardly appeared to present serious hindrances to further movement. Yet the fiction seemed to mean very different things to R.G. agents, who expressed their frustration at taking part in a farce, and to some French employers, who benefited from cheap, albeit generally unskilled, labor. In sum, practices of immigration control could be reduced neither to treaty nor to laws and policies. Rather, those texts left considerable room for maneuver for states and competing agencies within them. Migrants, traffickers, and employers exploited those spaces. Civil servants developed practices of exception that they often attempted, ex post facto, to transform into the policies that – until immigration became an electoral issue in France in the 1970s – generally did the work of law.[38]

The shadowy space between bureaucracy and law was familiar territory to many of those charged with patrolling it. From 1963, after some debate within the agencies concerned with immigration over whose responsibility sub-Saharan, formerly French migrants should rightfully be, responsibility for the control of Africans arriving at the country's borders and for surveillance of those already in France increasingly fell to "specialists" who had served in Algeria or the colonies. Shortly after the first two

Oct. 11, 1960, Paris, FPU 558. The Republic of Mali had decided that the break-up of the Federation nullified such accords. Therefore, Mali and France negotiated and signed a set of new accords on technical, economic, cultural relations in 1962 and 1963; MAE 2531.

[36] As, e.g., in Chad; Amb. France Tchad to MAE, Tchad, April 25, 1969, #1237, CADN Ndjamena 21.

[37] Direction des R.G., lists of West Africans disembarking at Bourdeaux, 1965, CAC 19940023, Art. 20. Congo-Brazzaville was another popular destination for Malian "tourists," "many" of whom in 1963 made requests for visas for Brazzaville via the French diplomatic representation in Bobo-Dioulasso; B. Laussac, Consul de France à Bobo-Dioulasso to M. l'Ambassadeur de France en H.-V. à Ouagadougou, Nov. 25, 1963, MAE 2541. Delavignette suggests that the "tourism" dodge was common knowledge; (1965).

[38] See Spire (2005, 2008); Lewis (2007).

conventions on circulation of migrants were signed, the Minister of the Interior began to make a case for giving responsibility for watching over African migrants to the *Service des Affaires Musulmanes* (SAM), an agency formerly charged with surveillance over North Africans, particularly Algerian Muslims, in France.[39] In December, the Prime Minister charged the SAM with collecting figures on the number of Africans who entered and left France. The SAM was best suited for such a task, in the opinion of his representative, because "only former administrators of Overseas France [could] have the necessary foundational knowledge in this domain."[40] The perceived familiarity that obtained between migrants and bureaucrats was deeply paternalistic: from the point of view of administrators, it was necessary to "know" one's migrant, just as one had "known" one's subject (*administré*), one's Muslim, or one's "Native" (*indigène*). It was far from peculiar to the civil service. For instance, the men in charge of the workers' hostels, or foyers, were often former NCOs in the colonial army, both French and African, and the director of the well-known SOUNDIATA association was a French member of the order of White Fathers who had once worked in Mopti.[41]

This "recognition" was deeply paradoxical. African literature on the migrant experience before 1974 – and indeed after – frequently emphasizes the extreme alienation of new arrivals in a familiar but mythical France.[42] This well-attested phenomenon nonetheless contrasts sharply with the fact that into the 1970s – even as medical certificates and labor contracts stamped by the Labor Ministry became formal requirements for all African workers – French bureaucrats continued to insist that West Africans were not to be considered foreigners. Particular offices within the government were categorical on this point. As a report from a subagency within the Labor Ministry stated in 1971:

---

[39] On the SAM, see Shepard (2006), 165–67.
[40] Exposé de M. Laurent, Administrateur au Service des Affaires Musulmanes du Min. de l'Interieur sur "Opération – Rélais," (n.d., 1964), CAC 0019770346, Art. 10. In addition to creating new posts for civil servants made redundant by decolonization, the Ministry of the Interior pushed surveillance of Algerians and other Africans in France as a substitute for diplomatic action to control immigration. By the same token, former officers from colonial Algeria were assigned to lead the *Service d'Assistance Technique* (SAT); Spire (2005), 208, 203–04.
[41] Hmed (2006); Mamadou Niambele, Directeur INPS, *Rapport de Mission: Immigration des travailleurs maliens en France*, n.d. (December 1963?), ANM, (uncatalogued), pg. 38. Hereafter, INPS, 1963. See also Bonnet (1990).
[42] Thomas (2006); see fn 4 above.

Workers from these eight states (that is, the former states of the AOF and Togo, not including Guinea) *are not considered foreign workers* because they are not required to hold work and residency permits in order to engage in paid labor in France.[43]

Lying behind such discussions was a larger and more important question: Were Africans foreigners (*étrangers*) at all? Early calls for the regulation of African migration saw the need for "a solution no doubt *more flexible* than the legislation on the residency of 'foreigners,'" a phrase that clearly distinguishes between Africans and *étrangers*.[44] On the other hand, as the Director of the Social Service for Immigrant Assistance (*Service Social d'Aide aux Emigrants*) argued in 1965, many immigrants arrived in France "absolutely illiterate and completely ignorant of the French language ... making them inapt for any salaried work whatever." Would it be in their interests, she asked, to create a special employment office for "Black workers" as had been created for refugees?[45] Or, conversely, as a policeman posed the question six years later, would it be in the interests of the workers themselves if their peculiar legal status was abolished and they were submitted to the same legal regime as other migrant workers – that is, to the ONI – which would at least preserve "their dignity and their identity?"[46] In short, in considering the special case of West African workers, representatives of diverse branches of the French state called on concepts drawn from one end of the juridical spectrum – demi-citizens of France, former holders of French nationality – to another, its opposite – refugees without state support of any kind, complete strangers to France – passing by way of the solution that would eventually become commonsensical, the recognition of their status as citizens of independent nation-states. Taken in its entirety, the discourse is jarring for the contradictory premises it encompassed: not only were citizens of West African states not foreigners, their status could be assimilated to that of the stateless. The questions posed were not idle ones. They spoke directly to the forms of government to which West Africans would be subject and with which they would engage. In the previous decades, indeed

---

[43] Sous-direction des mouvements de population (Min. Travail), *Les travailleurs de l'Afrique Noire*, 20 Sept. 1971, CAC 19810201, Art. 2. My emphasis.

[44] *Les Travailleurs d'Afrique Noire en France*, report sent by Dir. Gen. Sûreté Nationale to M. le Préfet, Chef SCTIP, date and number not listed here, but referred to elsewhere as #6266, May 29, 1963, CAC 19940023, Art. 20. Referred to hereafter as *Les Travailleurs d'Afrique Noire en France*, May 1963.

[45] Directrice, SSAE, Réunion du 7 Jan. 1965, Comité national du service social de la main d'oeuvre etrangère, CAC 19810201, Art. 5.

[46] Cabinet de Préfet de Police, Service d'Assistance Technique, March 30, 1971, CAC 19960311, Art. 5.

in the last century of their shared political history, no question had been more immediate. But times had changed. To understand just how much, we must grasp the analytical stick by the other end.

RECOGNIZING CITIZENS

As Abdelmalek Sayad's work insists, migration has two sides.[47] In different ways, newly independent states, and Mali in particular, also had an interest in "disciplining" migration. In fact, it was Mali and not France that first moved to control the movements of its citizens, the "nationals in which it recognized itself," in Sayad's terms.[48] In February 1962 – before the new Afro-French conventions on circulation of migrants were signed – Mali's new nationality law asserted that anyone born on Malian territory had Malian nationality that took precedent over other, earlier forms of political membership.[49] The law was intended both to advance the principle of African unity by making Malian nationality available to Africans with origins in neighboring states, and also to make it more difficult than it had previously been for Malians to reject the new nationality in favor of older ones.

The new nationality law quietly did away with a political status that was an embarrassment to the independent regime. It did so with such subtlety that many people did not realize that they had let a separate political status slip away, or that, according to French law, if they resided in France they could reclaim French nationality and hold it in addition to another nationality; this allowance for multiple nationalities – the *cumul des nationalités* – was *thought* to be exceptional in French jurisprudence.[50] The new law was the first of several US-RDA policies that had the dual aim of unequivocally asserting Malian

---

[47] Sayad (2004).
[48] Sayad (2004), 279.
[49] In fact, the law was rather ambiguous. A Malian could lose his or her nationality by "*l'acquisition volontaire ... ou l'attribution d'office d'une autre nationalité ... ou 'par le comportement du malien cumulant deux nationalités,'*" but the new law made no explicit reference to the French nationality law of July 28, 1960, with which it seemed to be in contradiction; Decottignies et de Biéville (1963), 235. Of course the authors of the law might well have considered that as a sovereign nation, Mali did not need to make reference to the laws of others in crafting its own. The Malian law was notably more aggressive than its Senegalese counterpart, which sought to "open ... nationality to [certain] people from neighboring territories," but did not assert the primacy of Senegalese nationality over others; Cooper (2009), 114. Revisions in the late 1960s made the Senegalese law more restrictive; Zatzépine (1975), 189–97.
[50] Decottignies and de Biéville (1963), 18. Cf. Weil (2002), 256–59.

independence from France and of controlling a population that felt its own economic imperatives. In fact, the nationality law is best understood in relation to two other important moves discussed in Chapter 2: the expulsion of French forces from their military bases on national territory, which was mandated in January 1961 and completed in September; and the establishment of the Malian franc, distinct from the French-backed CFA, in July 1962. Again, this trifecta was meant to define Mali's independence as absolute.

Nonetheless, the claim that Malians "belonged" to the new state was more than an assertion of independence. It went hand in hand with attempts to direct their labor toward building the new nation. Migrants evoked suspicion for their lack of commitment to national construction; at best, they were held at arm's length, and at worst they were vilified or dismissed by the US-RDA and by the military regime that would succeed it.[51] In other words, if for the French government they were familiar "strangers," for the US-RDA they were well-known adversaries. Men and women who left Mali – or who had departed earlier, from Soudan – represented two very different political threats to the new regime. Over the years, students and intellectuals, who were fewer in number than economic migrants, would critique the US-RDA from "the Left" with increasing virulence and violence. These attacks stung not only because the state had more often than not sent them abroad in the first place, but also because it needed them to return with their skills. Their students in Paris had long been a thorn in the side of West African governments, and that aggravation grew worse over time. By the spring of 1968, responding to political crisis at home rather than in Paris, Mali's ambassador would insist that the party's leadership "must grasp the fact that Paris, being only a few hours from Mali, has unfortunately become a political suburb of Bamako."[52] Once abroad, young intellectuals were hard to control, and the Party's responses ranged from cutting off their scholarships to keeping

---

[51] It was not until after the 1991 democratic transition that migrants came to be regarded by the Malian state as both full "citizens" of Mali and a valuable set of allies in the country's economic growth; Gary-Tounkara (2008).

[52] The party's delegate would propose that no further students be sent until those already present had left, thereby dissolving the Malian students' association, the *Association des étudiants et stagiaires maliens en France* (AESMF), which was partly funded by the FEANF; *P-V de la réunion extraordinaire tenue à l'ambassade*, April 8, 1968, confidential, no. 11/AMP-SC, BPNCMLN 150. The party would of course have preferred to see its own (J)US-RDA succeed in Paris. The issue went back to at least 1962; P-V, BPN, May 16, 1962, BPNCMLN 77.

them in the country if they returned during school vacations (as did those studying in the USSR).[53]

On the other end of the political spectrum, party cadres placed merchants and economic migrants, whom they branded as reactionary and self-interested in ways that were sometimes contradictory. For instance, a 1962 party conference in Kayes, the cradle of emigration, noted with satisfaction that taxes had been promptly paid, party cards purchased, and livestock declared. But in the same speech, and virtually the same breath, emigrants and their families came in for intense criticism:

> The youth continue to leave the country, no matter the risk ... Those comrades who leave represent labor lost for the construction of schools, dispensaries, roads, etc. They are absent when they should be building the nation ... Those who would justify their absence by pointing to the money they send home to their relatives must know that those remittances serve only the families to whom they are addressed, and that if all Malians left, the country would be empty and the money alone would not be enough to make [it] as modern as those to which they go ...[54]

The speech condensed the contradictions of the US-RDA's attitude toward migration: Who, after all, was paying the taxes and buying the cards? But such discourse is also striking for its very stability. These terms of debate would change little, even in later years, when some expatriates sought to facilitate the very local tasks the Party had accused them of rejecting; these ranged from boosting production by deploying tractors to providing cleaner water via bore wells.

The US-RDA's interest in migration, and its attitudes toward migrants, had a prehistory that in political terms was as deep as those wells. From the moment the party began to command legislative power in the Territorial Assembly, before independence, it had worked to curtail migration to the Cote d'Ivoire by closing that territory's employers' bureau in Bamako.[55] By 1962, ending the "exodus," as it was invariably called, had become a virtual obsession of the BPN. And what was a territorial issue in the

---

[53] P-V, BPN, March 6, 1962, May 16, 1962, Aug. 21, 1962, BPNCMLN 77; on 1965, BPNCMLN 83.

[54] US-RDA, sous-section de Kayes, Conférence des cadres, *Rapport de Politique Générale*, May 12-13, 1962, BPN98d372. Modibo Keita told the BPN that 42 million CFA had been sent to Kayes from abroad in the first trimester of 1962; May 2, 1962, BPNCMLN 77.

[55] Gary-Tounkara (2008), 199–201. Recall that until the summer of 1960, the existence of the Mali Federation meant that migration to Senegal did not represent the expatriation of labor. For a brief period after the break-up, the political climate favored travel to Abidjan rather than to Dakar. After the re-establishment of Senegalese–Malian relations, which warmed in mid-1963, departures for Dakar (or for France via Dakar) became more frequent.

context of the AOF and its dissolution became an international issue within the subregion, as well as beyond it, at independence. As the country created its own currency and sought to control its economy, the stakes were growing higher and higher. In the eyes of the US-RDA and those experts charged with elaborating the new government's five-year economic plan, doing so meant first and foremost stopping the rural exodus and restricting migrants' movements. The problem of emigration was a constant theme in meetings of the BPN, where Madeira Keita insisted that there were three streams of exodus: the traders, those who sought gold and diamonds (possibly in Guinea and Liberia, but most often in the two Congos), and those who went to France as laborers, taking the place of Algerians. Although the latter stream troubled the BPN the most, Keita argued for "putting the brakes on" all three.[56]

People left Mali for other African destinations, first and foremost, and only some of them traveled on to Europe. Migrants who made it to Bobo-Dioulasso or Abidjan readily obtained papers in the French consulate or embassy in order to travel on to France, Congo-Brazzaville, or elsewhere.[57] Other African countries were not always happy to receive them, and the Ivoirian government threatened to round them up and send them to public works sites.[58] This put the US-RDA in a difficult situation. If the Soudanese expelled (*"réfoulés"*) from Senegal at the time of the Mali Federation's collapse were living symbols of a foundational event in the country's history, the expulsion of economic migrants from the Cote d'Ivoire and Congo-Kinshasa (known at that time as Léopoldville) was rather more awkward. Those migrants did not want to go "home," and the government was unsure what to do with them. According to rumors circulating in Brazzaville in 1964, some who had been sent home from the Cote d'Ivoire three years earlier had been put in prison and forced to work collective fields. As a result, when Congo-Kinshasa expelled thousands of Malians in 1964, they feared returning to Mali. In an attempt to escape the notice of the Malian embassy and its erratic chief, Alioune Diakité, they deserted the temporary lodging set up for them by the

---

[56] P-V, BPN, April 17, 1962, BPNCMLN77.

[57] The Ivoirian government expressed its opposition to Malian emigration via Cote d'Ivoire to France; see Minister of the Interior (France), *Note Circulaire*, May 4, 1962; Minister of the Interior, Côte d'Ivoire to Délégué, Côte d'Ivoire, SCTIP, Dec. 3, 1962, CAC 19940023, Art. 20. On Haute Volta, B. Laussac, Consul de France à Bobo-Dioulasso to M. l'Ambassadeur de France en H.-V. à Ouaga, Nov. 25, 1963, MAE 2541.

[58] P-V, BPN, June 26, 1962, BPNCMLN 77.

Brazzaville government.[59] Instead they found refuge in very crowded conditions with the local Malian community, which included members of the most prestigious Soninké families.[60] Some 1,000 of them only agreed to repatriation after an extensive effort of persuasion by members of a US-RDA mission.[61]

Although Modibo Keita sought to rally support for the displaced, and the government mounted subscription drives on their behalf,[62] the expulsions also gave the BPN a window into the wealth that migrants from what had become Mali sometimes enjoyed abroad. Although some young Malian men had only just arrived in Congo-Kinshasa before being pushed out, the Soudanese community in the two Congos dated from the late nineteenth century. Over that time some of its members had accumulated a great deal of wealth in commerce and, to a lesser extent, in the diamond trade.[63] Some had lost everything in Congo-Kinshasa, whereas others had sent at least part of their wealth out of the country. Many originally sought to cross the river back to Kinshasa as soon as possible, or in any case not to be sent back to Mali. Only the extreme instability of the situation in Congo-Kinshasa, where both criminals and soldiers had attacked West African migrants, turned the tide in favor of repatriation. The wealthy hedged their bets and hung on in Brazzaville after illicitly buying Senegalese passports.[64] The passport had become a weapon of choice in the multidimensional struggle over sovereignty – in its broadest sense of being subject to government – that the US-RDA, Mali's migrants, and other states waged. The head of Mali's emergency mission to Brazzaville deplored the purchasing of Senegalese passports, but – given that most of

---

[59] Diakité deserves a footnote of his own. An unstable element of Mali's diplomatic corps, he provoked constant complaints by his aggressive behavior toward his own countrymen, especially those he thought of as opponents of the regime. Rumored to be in the pay of foreign intelligence, he would later demonstrate his loyalty to the US-RDA and Modibo Keita by shooting off his own finger in a bar in Bamako's Grand Hotel. He was behind some of the US-RDA's most unpopular tactics of policing, surveillance, and repression, and he was imprisoned after the coup of 1968. His career came to an end several years after his release, when he "fell" from a hotel window in Conakry. Campmas (1976), 401–02, 436–37, 478; Imperato (1975), 248.
[60] E.g., that of Mahmadou Lamine and Kadi Drame; Manchuelle (1997).
[61] *Rapport de Mission de Mohamed Sylla à Brazzaville pour la rapatriement des ressortissants Maliens expulsés du Congo-Léopoldville*, n.d. (Dec. 14, 1964), BPNCMLN 278.
[62] See letters collected in BPN181d623.
[63] On Sahelians in the Congos, see Manchuelle (1997), 194–96 and infra; Whitehouse (2012). Amin insists that relatively few "Senegalese" – many of whom were actually Malians, Guineans, or Nigerian Hausa – actually traded in diamonds; (1969), 163–65. He may have underestimated their presence; Bredeloup (2007).
[64] *Rapport de Mission de Mohamed Sylla . . .*, BPNCMLN 278.

those who had Malian passports in Brazzaville had either got them there or in embassies in Accra and Abidjan – he also urged the government at home to make it harder for his fellow citizens abroad to obtain travel papers from the country's embassies. The idea of denying passports to potential migrants was not a new one; this is partly what made the French practice of providing such papers so maddening to the new regime.[65] The Brazzaville episode also exposed the mutual suspicion and even hostility that prevailed between migrants and expatriates, on the one hand, and the US-RDA government, on the other.

Before the Congolese expulsions, Mali's frustrated BPN had already turned to coercive means to control the country's emigrants. In July 1962, just days before the controversial introduction of the Malian franc, the Malian government asked the French ambassador in Bamako whether it would be possible to repatriate forcibly all of the Malians in France. Two primary targets presented themselves: the "recruiters" based in the Parisian region who convinced others to emigrate, and who should be the first to be expelled; and French shipping companies whose agents persuaded Malians to depart from the ports of Dakar and Abidjan.[66] The request was a bold one, in keeping with the rough and tumble diplomacy of the period. The French rejected it out of hand. Although the Ministry of Foreign Affairs had expressed concern at the increasing numbers of migrants, it instructed its ambassador in Bamako, Fernand Wibaux, to reply that the responsibility for controlling departures lay with the African states and not with the French government or French enterprises such as the shipping companies.[67] Be that as it may, the idea of any kind of mass expulsions – on either side – can hardly have been appealing to France at the time, as the government sought to protect the interests of its own emigrant community in new African states, the newest of which was Algeria.

The US-RDA leadership would not be deterred. In February or March 1963, even as the new convention on circulation between France and Mali was being signed, Malian diplomats in Conakry and Dakar actually boarded the ocean liner *Brazza*, which was headed for France; they

---

[65] P-V, BPN, June 26, 1962, BPNCMLN 77.
[66] GOM, MAE, Division Politique to Amb. France, Bamako [Note Verbal], July 4, 1962, #678/AE.DP, with reference to *Note verbal* of June 14, 1962, #1970, MAE 2541. See also P-V, BPN, June 26, 1962, BPNCMLN 77.
[67] MAE to AMBAFR BKO, July 31, 1962, #04042; *Note pour la Direction des Affaires Administratives et Sociales, Conventions Administratives et Sociales*, July 24, 1962, #340/DAM, MAE 2541.

intended to "prevent the departure of their nationals who figured among the emigrants."[68] If the accord being negotiated with Paris would remain somewhat lax, Malian policy would be more muscular. In a move that ironically echoed the collapse of the Mali Federation – when the Soudanese leadership was expelled from Dakar on a sealed train to the border – Malian diplomats asked their Senegalese counterparts to send thirty-six of these aspiring immigrants back to Bamako on the train and under escort.[69] The gesture was symbolic, but the nation badly needed labor at home. A government delegation sent to France to study the situation of migrants there expressed the wish that the flow of unskilled labor be transformed into a *"migration de formation,"* suggesting rather disingenuously that the labor force lacked training rather than lucrative employment in Mali.[70] The US-RDA continued to be highly critical of the political orientation of the migrants – Modibo Keita castigated them as "stateless" (*apatrides*) – even as it adopted an aggressive posture toward France that precluded easy cooperation between the two governments. Thus, although they signed an accord on immigration that was essentially identical to those France would later sign with Mauritania and Senegal, the interests of elements of the Malian administration continued to diverge in many ways from both those of its interlocutor and those of its neighbors.

Senegal and Mauritania together claimed half the population of "African workers" in France – or half the passports, in any case. Unlike Mali, both were deeply invested in maintaining close and amicable relationships with the former imperial power. Mauritania in particular relied on France to counter Moroccan challenges to its sovereignty, which the North African and Arab states in general did not recognize as legitimate (they thought the state a colonial creation). Yet *Mauritanie Nouvelle*, the government newspaper, reported on the poor conditions in which African laborers in France lived, and it used language remarkably similar to Madeira Keita's in calling for African states to "put the brakes on the exodus."[71] Shortly after *Mauritanie Nouvelle*'s article appeared, the French and Mauritanian governments signed a new accord on labor migration that applied to citizens of both states; they now needed

---

[68] *Les Travailleurs d'Afrique Noire en France*, May 1963, CAC 19940023, Art. 20.
[69] Lucien Paye, AMBAFR BKO, March 9, 1963, #418, MAE 2541.
[70] INPS, 1963. See P-V, BPN, June 12, 1962, BPNCMLN77.
[71] Diop M. Mokhtar, "Faut-il freiner l'emigration massive des travailleurs africains à l'étranger?," *Mauritanie Nouvelle*, June 12, 1963.

passports, health certificates, labor contracts, and repatriation deposits.[72] The bar to migration was higher, but still low. If the accords were the same as those adopted in Mali and Senegal, the stakes were different. Unlike Mali, Mauritania's real source of income lay in a mining industry that had contracted in late 1962, resulting in the dismissal of "hundreds" of workers from construction sites on the railroad and at Nouadhibou (then known as Port-Etienne).[73] In 1963, major new investments were afoot. Mauritania might not have needed to hang on to all of its own labor, but it did need to be able to attract expatriate specialists in order to realize new mining operations. But the balance to be maintained was as diplomatic as it was economic, because the stakes were much lower than the number of migrants would suggest. Many of the "Mauritanians" arriving in France in the year before the accord was signed neither drained labor from nor sent money to Mauritania, for the simple reason that they were not Mauritanians. They were Malians or Senegalese who had purchased Mauritanian identity cards. As many as two-thirds of the "Mauritanians" who entered France in 1962 and the first months of 1963 did so with fake documents they had purchased from the personnel at the country's embassy in Dakar.[74]

As for Senegal, France had already shaped its postcolonial sovereignty once – at the breakup of the Mali Federation – and President Senghor's personal power depended on French support. This point was once again driven home by his narrow political defeat of Prime Minister Mamadou Dia in a constitutional crisis in 1962. But maintaining close ties with France did not mean letting people move around as they wished. In the immediate wake of independence, Senegal sought to bring migrants home, but according to a study published by Souleymane Diarra in 1968, the number of Senegalese workers in France quickly rebounded, as new arrivals replaced returning migrants.[75] In 1965, Senghor's government began to demand exit papers from Senegalese nationals who sought to leave its territory.[76] The new demand was one element in a general crackdown against civil servants and police officers involved in producing false papers

---

[72] "Signature d'une convention entre la République Islamique de Mauritanie et la France," *Mauritanie Nouvelle*, July 24, 1963.
[73] Diarra (1968), 901.
[74] Note, no source [R.G.?], secret, July 15, 1963, CAC 19940023, Art. 20. Note that this report is dated the same day as the Franco-Mauritanian accord was signed. Compare Tel. départ, DAM, Direction des Conventions Administratives et des Affaires Consulaires, to Amb. Fr. Bamako, Nouakchott, Dakar, June 29, 1963, MAE 2541.
[75] Diarra (1968), 902.
[76] SDECE, *Note*, Jan. 26, 1965, CAC 19940023, Art. 20.

for aspiring migrants. For a brief moment, the gloves were off: Senegal arrested several of its own civil servants, deported a broker in false papers to Guinea, and replaced the director of its National Police.[77] The country's best known former migrant, a one-time student whose poems famously expressed the bitterness of exile, spoke out against "a dangerous [phenomenon of] immigration that can only end in unemployment, misery and illness."[78]

Two struggles were coming into the open, one between competing states eager to recognize migrants as "theirs" – and for a variety of reasons to hinder their movement – another between states and the migrants themselves. A much-reduced former empire sought to preserve its status in the world and to balance competing economic interests, even as it tried to control its borders and to discriminate among migrants. A trio of newly independent states pursued divergent objectives, ranging from Mali's self-consciously "revolutionary" regime, which worked to break its colonial ties, to Senegal's conservative nationalism, which sought to preserve them. Many migrants were just as ambivalent about the new states as their governments were about them; the students among them were even more harshly critical, and certainly more vocal. By the mid-1960s, in the wake of the accords, documents on citizenship, nationality, employment, and health structured the system of migration. Many West African migrants short-circuited that system through forgery, falsification, and the simple sharing of papers.[79] In the early 1960s, Malians became Senegalese by crossing the border, where relatives would get them Senegalese identity cards. If Senegalese passports became hard to obtain, one could purchase Gambian passports. Once used to enter France (frequently via the Canaries and Spain) the passports were sent back to Senegal, often to be used again at the Dakar-Yoff airport.[80] Cheaper still were Voltaïque

---

[77] Ambassade de France, Dakar, *Notes de Renseignements*, Aug. 31, 1964, #2147/SCTIP/SL; Sept. 17, 1964, #2294/SCTIP/SL; Oct. 3, 1964, #2441/SCTIP/SL; Dec. 22, 1964; SDECE, *Note*, Jan. 26, 1965, CAC 19940023, Art. 20.

[78] Senghor quoted in *Note: Les Migrations de travailleurs originaires d'Afrique noire*, March 14, 1967, SN/RG/INF./8'S./no. 304, CAC 19940023, Art. 20.

[79] Although recognizing the sophistication of the traffic in false papers, Diarra attributes migrants' participation to ignorance and naiveté. This argument has not aged well; (1968), 923.

[80] In Dakar, such papers went for 15,000 CFA per use. Pref., Dir SCTIP to Dir. R.G. de la Sûreté Nationale, April 11, 1968, #386, CAC 0019850087, Art. 9; Min. d'état chargé de la D.N., SDECE, *Fiche: Filières d'entrée clandestine ...*, Oct. 9, 1969, FPU 2832; Min. Interieur, Direction de la Sûreté Nationale to Chef de la 5ème Division des R.G., Bordereau d'envoi of report by Préfecture de Police, June 19, 1969; and SCTIP, "Sisyphe", Dec. 4, 1969, #1.930, CAC 19940023, Art. 20.

identity cards,[81] and Nigerien papers were also on the market. All manner of false papers circulated. Failed students could acquire diplomas they had never earned,[82] and aspiring migrants could readily obtain false work contracts from Citroën in Dakar. The French were aware of at least two apparently distinct circuits of exchange of work contracts and identity cards (one ran between a Frenchman and a Senegalese based in Dakar, another between Senegalese and Gambians in Dakar and France).[83] The Senegalese government reported to the French embassy that it would expel one of the men supplying the false contracts, but embassies themselves were often the focal points of a brisk trade in identity cards: Mali recalled its most aggressive consular apparatchik from Paris when Bamako discovered he had been circulating fraudulent cards to his countrymen.[84]

As the locus of the struggle to control African migration shifted to the border posts themselves, migrants and immigration officers developed a new set of mutual expectations. Thus, for example, in 1969, French police turned back two young men coming in from London with identity cards from the Cote d'Ivoire and Upper Volta, at which point, "they asked naively to be sent back, not to London, but to le Touquet, 'a place where it's easy to get across the border.'"[85] The officers took their plea as evidence that a new route was opening in the north, which was in turn another symptom of a metastasizing set of migrant networks. As French border restrictions tightened and, simultaneously, air travel became the norm, African "tourists" began to appear coming from rather chic spots such as Milan, as well as Prague and the Canary Islands. After 1974, policies were tougher, but the system was not necessarily tighter. A decade after the Senegalese expulsion, it must have been embarrassing for France's Minister of Justice to warn his country's diplomats in Dakar not to accept certificates of French nationality generated in certain provincial towns in France where they had been "handed out nonchalantly – at the very least – by the judge."[86] The system was compromised inside and out, and

---

[81] At 5,000 CFA; l'Officer du police, chef du poste de police de l'air du nord to M. le Commissaire divisionnaire, chef du service regional des R.G., March 25, 1969, #190, CAC 0019940023.
[82] See the case recounted in BPN13 5d527.
[83] Ambassade de France, *Note de Renseignements*, Aug. 18, 1964, #2009/SCTIP/SL; Ambassade de France, *Note de Renseignements*, Aug. 31, 1964, #2147/SCTIP/SL, CAC 0019940023, Art. 20.
[84] MAE (France) to Amb. Fr. Bamako, Nov. 27, 1967, #0410, MAE 2536.
[85] Direction Centrale des R.G., Paris, Feb. 4, 1969, CAC 19940023, Art. 20.
[86] M. le Garde des Sceaux, Min. Justice to CGF à Dakar, March 18, 1976, CAC 19960311.

some immigration officers were simply refusing to accept ostensibly valid cards. The problems that plagued Rougier's 1925 proposal to establish a regime of identity papers across the AOF remained.

Passports were not the answer. In a mild irony, as states began to insist on them to secure their writ and to anchor migrants' identities, and as bureaucrats and politicians debated the extent to which West Africans were "foreigners," migrants themselves sought to become *other* foreigners, more foreign foreigners. This raises another question: If one was already the emblematic West African migrant – a young man from Kayes, the Senegal River valley, or Casamance, perhaps speaking little French – what made one less foreign in France than, say, a Gambian? What did France "recognize" in itself in the form of such a stereotypical migrant? And what did Mali, Mauritania, or Senegal recognize? There is no ready answer. The French state literally failed to come to terms with West African migration, as its civil servants struggled to define the status of their former fellow nationals, now citizens of new states. At the same time, in response to pressure from immigrants and activists, but also from within its own bureaucracy, it extended a form of government as (often brutal) care.[87] Meanwhile, new African states sought to translate their recently acquired sovereignty over territories to control over people, people who had learned very well how to avoid the impositions of an intrusive state. This messy, many-sided tussle between states and people on the move obscures a process every bit as important as the production of strangers and citizens: the extension of particular forms of government and the emergence of opposition to them.

LIVING

In 1962, the year before the new accords were signed, representatives of the Ministries of the Interior and of Development (*Coopération*) had insisted that in the absence of some kind of migration regime nothing could be done to manage the living standards of African migrants.[88] By the spring and summer of 1963, a consensus to that effect had emerged among the French ministries and agencies involved.[89] But even as such

---

[87] On the simultaneous extension of care-giving and policing, see Ticktin (2011). This combination was neither novel nor paradoxical; Wilder (2005), 341 n65.

[88] Dir. de la Cooperation Culturelle et Technique, Min. Cooperation à M. le Préfet de la Seine, Feb. 15, 1962, #06197/DCT/GS, CAC 19770346, Art. 10.

[89] See, e.g., SAM, *Note pour M. le Premier Ministre*, Sept. 13, 1963, #361758, CAC 19770346, Art. 10.

a rudimentary regime came haltingly into practice, French civil servants, particularly in the Social Service for Immigrant Assistance, were already asking aloud whether it was not in the interest of the migrants themselves that some more formal juridical situation be established, something stricter than the duo of the *contrôle* (medical examination) and the contract. In the eyes of the director of the service, three central problems encountered by African workers in the area of Paris lent themselves to government intervention: lodging, health, and employment. Racial discrimination did not, of course, figure in this trinity, but the Director implicitly pointed to the continued colonial nature of African migrants' exceptional status when she asked, "Wouldn't a less liberal regime ultimately be better for those concerned?" The Ministry of the Interior could only agree as it pursued the creation of a "special system," one that would at a minimum address the needs of migrants in at least two of those three key areas of French social policy, namely health and housing.[90]

The problems were real. The very housing shortage that helped to create the market for unskilled labor meant that there was little adequate lodging available for West Africans and other migrant workers in France. As a result, West African workers and less-fortunate students often lived in unhealthy and insalubrious conditions, including in the hostels (*foyers*) that the administration and nongovernmental organizations would soon establish for them. Particularly in the early years, many slept in subterranean shelters, such as the basements of Algerian cafes. In such conditions, and in the cold and damp that often prevail in Paris and northern France, the tuberculosis bacillus that many of them carried with them flared up. In 1969, the R.G. reported that one in five Parisian tuberculosis patients was African; coming at the same problem from the opposite perspective, a doctor practicing in Montreuil, just outside Paris, reported that one in ten of the numerous African migrants living there had the disease.[91] The fact that many Africans suffered from tuberculosis became a recurring argument for restricting the admission of their compatriots into France.[92]

---

[90] Réunion du Jan. 7, 1965 du Comité National du Service social de la main d'oeuvre étrangère, CAC 0019810201, Art 5. It would take several more years, and a sharp economic downturn, for employment to rival the predominance of health and housing in the politics of immigration.

[91] Direction Centrale des R.G., *Immigrés Africains en France*, July 15, 1969, see also Direction Centrale des R.G., Jan. 30, 1969, CAC 0019940023, Art. 20; Brumpt et al. (1965); Dr. Somia (1965), 129.

[92] For instance, in reports dated some six years apart, the R.G. and the National Police cited the (documented) prevalence of tuberculosis and the (alleged) prevalence of venereal

Well-Known Strangers 147

That tuberculosis provided an argument for restricting migration is hardly novel; public health concerns have long been at the core of immigration control. Striking in this particular instance is the rapidity with which medical attention to the rise of tuberculosis seemed to be translated into the calibrated imposition of new controls. On the 26th of March 1963, France's National Academy of Medicine held a meeting on the health of African workers, a discussion in which tuberculosis figured prominently. On the 27th of March, the very next day, Jacques Foccart sent a note directly to President de Gaulle reporting on the meeting and recommending that the government impose on African workers a new system of immigration control grounded in medical inspections.[93] The two pillars of this system would be documented medical records (a medical passport or *carnet sanitaire*) and an employment contract. Mali had signed precisely such a convention a fortnight earlier, and Mauritania and Senegal would follow suit in the months to come. As we have seen, the new system was not very effective, but even after doctors and legislators questioned it in years to come, Foccart would defend it, arguing that the struggle against this "scourge" had to be balanced against the imperative of maintaining good relations with African states. What was needed, from his point of view, was not a *"carte de police"* but a *"carnet sanitaire."*[94]

---

diseases among African workers, along with "delinquency," as compelling reasons to restrict African migration. In the eyes of these security agents, the continued uncontrolled entry of West Africans in France threatened to "introduce in France ... contagious diseases particular to the populations of Black Africa"; *Les Travailleurs d'Afrique Noire en France*, May 1963, CAC 19940023, Art. 20. Although it is hard not to see the latter phrase as a racialist euphemism, Jacques Foccart believed it encompassed leprosy, tuberculosis, and syphilis; Foccart, SGCAAM, *Contrôle sanitaire des travailleurs africains en France*, Note à l'attention de M. le Président de la République, Président de la Communauté, March 27, 1963, FPU2832. This fear endured, becoming a standard argument for governing immigrants; see Direction Centrale des R.G., *Immigrés Africains en France*, July 15, 1969, CAC 0019940023, Art. 20. The link between tuberculosis and migration from Algeria was well established, as many former migrants returned from France with the disease; Rosenberg (2012), 686–87.

[93] Foccart, SGCAAM, *Contrôle sanitaire* ..., March 27, 1963, FPU 2832. The medical meeting is also cited in *Les Travailleurs d'Afrique Noire en France*, May 1963, CAC 19940023, Art. 20. See also Diarra (1968), 990–95; Brumpt et al. (1965); Somia (1965).

[94] Foccart correspondance with Etienne Bernard, Pres., Comité National de Défense contre la tuberculose, Jan. 9 and 15, 1968, and Foccart's handwritten marginalia on the former, FPU 2832. His office would agree that those who refused treatment for tuberculosis should be deported, but consistently sought the application of existing conventions over the imposition of new ones; MS notes in a hand other than Foccart's on S. G. du Gouvernement to Foccart, Jan. 8, 1968, convocation to interministeriel meeting, Secretariat Générale du Gouvernement, ordre du jour for Jan. 12, 1968, dated Jan. 8, 1968, secret. Foccart maintained this position the following year; Foccart, SGCAAM to Y. Bourges, Sec. d'Etat auprès du MAE, n.d. (Sept. 1969), FPU 2832.

Foccart was not known for being a soft touch. His attention to the importance of African workers' health, and to the broader public health issues surrounding it, speaks directly both to his *realpolitik* and to the ways in which he, France's point man on African affairs for the next three decades, conceived of the brief of government.

The thorny and contentious issue of housing posed even more starkly the question of what government is and does, or what it should be and do. As recent and frugal immigrants, West Africans often occupied tawdry and in some cases illegally rented rooms in hotels owned by Algerians, in the storage areas of Algerian cafes, and in disused or abandoned buildings. As the West African presence in France was highly localized and considered temporary, the shared lodging that they occupied did not capture the attention of a broader public until the bitterly cold winter of 1963, which followed immediately on a peak in the number of people arriving from West Africa.[95] As their suffering in freezing temperatures gradually became known, a "movement of solidarity of the French population developed spontaneously[,] pushed by an humanitarian instinct."[96] If ordinary citizens offered gifts of coats and blankets to their newly arrived neighbors, argued sociologist Jean-Pierre N'Diaye, neither the government nor France's powerful labor unions appeared to take much notice of the deplorable conditions in which this apparently disposable labor force existed. "Here the contradiction between the barbarism of an entire economic and political system, based on man's exploitation of man [sic], and the liberal and 'humanist' cultural tradition reaches the point of rupture," he commented acidly.[97] Whether we recognize the same contradiction as N'Diaye or see humanitarianism as complementary to the system he indicted, the grinding crisis of housing would slowly generate new forms of politics.

After the weather turned warm and the spring migration accords were signed, it would take another seven years, the convergence of African and French workers' activism and the accidental asphyxiations of several men for the living conditions of West African workers to become a scandal again. By that time the "social ... [and] moral cost" of migration had engendered a growing bureaucratic sentiment that "having disciplined Algerian migration, the time seems to have come to discipline Black

---

[95] These monthly averages more than doubled between 1962 and 1963, while remaining relatively small in absolute terms; MAE 2541.
[96] N'Diaye (1970), 12.
[97] N'Diaye (1970), 12–13.

immigration."[98] "Disciplining," however, had a distinct history, one more subtle than such a policeman's phrase would suggest. The process of disciplining – of making subject to power, or of extending sovereignty over migrants – was intertwined with the problem of lodging, the social logic of its amelioration, the precise forms that amelioration took, and the suspicion and resistance those in turn engendered. Taken together, those issues would dominate migrants' political struggles throughout the 1970s.

That decade had begun on a somber note, one that awakened the French public to the drama of immigrants' housing. At New Year's, 1970, five Malian workers were found asphyxiated in their lodging in Aubervilliers, where they had attempted to warm themselves by burning charcoal indoors. The story made headlines.[99] On the day the men were buried, a Portuguese family of four was found dead from the same cause; they had lain undiscovered throughout the holiday fortnight.[100] The miserable conditions in which immigrant workers lived had become a public scandal, pushed by the tactic of rent strikes and by the public tragedy of needless deaths. "4 spigots for 700 renters," ran one press clipping.[101] "Only one African worker in five is able to find decent housing," read another.[102] No one would have argued that West Africans were decently housed in 1970. They often found themselves crammed into disused spaces, some without heating, many without water or windows. Basements, storage spaces, and disused factories accommodated dozens of men in bunkbeds, which they often shared in shifts. Even in a period in which *bidonvilles* were well established in France – and virtually unknown in the Sahel – the conditions in which these migrants lived were extreme. As late as 1969, some in the government would suggest that the types of workers' hostels that had been established for Algerian workers under colonial rule should have been adequate for the West Africans who followed them, as they were single workers remaining in France temporarily. Indeed that was the solution the government pursued. If the juridical status of Algerian

---

[98] *Etude sur l'immigration des travailleurs africains en France*, May 30, 1969, unsigned, agency unclear, this copy marked "Note en copie à M. le Bellec, chargé de mission, secrétariat générale à la Présidence de la République," CAC 19940023, Art. 20. This appears to be a memo drawn on in Guy le Bellec, *Note à l'attention de M. le S. G. [Foccart, sur] les travailleurs africains en France*, May 31, 1969, FPU 2832.
[99] Gastaut (2000), 52–3.
[100] N'Diaye (1970), 13.
[101] Press clipping, "Le Logement des travailleurs africains," journal not indicated, June 24, 1969, CAC 19940023, Art. 20.
[102] Clipping of article by J.-P. Dumont, journal not indicated, Oct. 25, 1969, CAC 19940023, Art. 20.

workers' hostels had excluded West African workers, then new hostels would be built, to be run by private associations. So went the plan, even if the mechanics were more complicated.

The social logic of improving workers' housing, and along with it their collective health, was a somewhat contorted one ripe with potential for the pursuit of self-interest. Quasi-governmental associations played a crucial role in it. Funding for hostels for West Africans would come indirectly from the *Caisse nationale des allocations familiales*, a social welfare fund into which, as migrants, they paid, but to which they did not have access. Although in principle their families "at home" had the right to allocations adjusted to the cost of living in that country, migrants paid the same amount into the *Caisse* as did citizens. The difference between what they contributed and what they could in theory receive was substantial. That difference was in turn paid into the coffers of a distinct organization, the *Fonds d'Action Sociale* (FAS).[103] The FAS, too, was an inheritance from the Algerian migrant workers' regime, having been created in 1958 in order to "fund ... social welfare programs that exclusively served 'French Muslims from Algeria,'" thereby addressing some of the Algerians' grievances while keeping money out of the hands of the FLN. By 1959, more than half of its funding went to housing programs for Algerian workers.[104] In 1964, two years after Algeria's independence, FAS's brief expanded to include immigrants of any origin, West Africans among them.[105] By the late 1960s, FAS directed its funds for housing through distinct associations that were not government agencies and which were intended to be nonprofit. They also, according to a 1901 law, had to be run by French citizens.[106] And that was the clincher.

---

[103] Lyons (2009), 71–2; Manchuelle (1987), 530–31.
[104] Lyons (2009), 67, 72. The FAS also funded the publication of *Cahiers nord-africaines*, which later became *Hommes et Migrations*; Lyons (2009), 79. In 1965 the renamed journal published a special issue entitled "Approche des problèmes de la migration noire en France" that included texts by Delavignette, Brumpt, and Somia, cited herein.
[105] Lyons (2009), 85; N'Diaye (1970), 30.
[106] This was one of the great complaints of African activists, notably Sally Ndongo and the Union générale des travailleurs sénégalais en France; UGTSF (1970), 23–24, 78. It limited their capacity to organize legally to defend their collective interests and induced them to ally themselves with citizens. The law was changed under the Socialist government in 1981; Manchuelle (1987), 550; "Du nouveau pour les associations d'immigrés," *Bulletin du Comité Français des Amis du Mali* 2 (1982). This in turn allowed immigrants' associations to obtain legal standing and to seek formal partnerships with organizations interested in fostering development in the Sahel with the ultimate aim of encouraging migrants to return; Daum (1998); Dedieu (2012), 117–18.

FAS money was workers' money, the vast majority of it coming from their own paycheck contributions. A fraction of it was earmarked for workers' families abroad, and another portion – the difference between the cost of living in France and at "home" – was to be devoted to the benefit of the workers themselves. According to a tract the Communist League distributed to West African workers in the foyers, FAS's directors were "giving out with one hand what they received with the other." To whom did they give it? Private French-led "shell associations" ("*associations bidons*") that would build housing to rent to workers at prices deemed high.[107] Who led such associations? French citizens, most of whom had served in the colonial administration.[108] Who managed the foyers day to day? Ex-colonial soldiers, whether French, or occasionally, West African.[109] Whether it was the complex financial arrangements behind the FAS or simply the fact that African migrants refused to pay high rents for inadequate spaces, the question of housing drove African political mobilization beginning in the late 1960s, increasingly attracted the attention and support of French intellectuals and Leftists, and is seen as setting a precedent for the *sans-papiers* movements of the 1990s.[110]

My goal here is not to offer a history of the movement, or even of the moment.[111] But focusing on one example helps us to understand how the problem of housing generated particular forms of politics, and why it is that West African workers carried out more rent strikes than work stoppages.[112] The strike against the FAS-funded association known as ASSOTRAF and its foyers (those at 43 rue Pinel in Saint Denis and in a disused factory on 119 Ave. Lenine in Pierrefitte) offers a good snapshot of the overlapping networks of managers, establishments, migrants, and activists.[113] In those foyers, hundreds of African tenants paid 70–80

---

[107] Préfecture de Police, copy of Communist League tract distributed at foyers in the Parisian *bainlieux*, Dec. 16, 1969, CAC 19940023, Art. 20. See also N'Dongo (1975), 72–3.

[108] N'Diaye (1970), 30.

[109] Spire (2005), 210–11; Min. Interieur, DSN to Chef de la 5ème Division des R.G., Bordereau d'envoi de report by Préfecture de Police, June 19, 1969, CAC 19940023, Art. 20. At least one such African veteran in Marseille was considered well disposed towards the PCF; Min. Interieur, DGSN, DRG, Feb. 12, 1965, CAC 19960311, Art. 7.

[110] On the latter point, Guèye (2006); Ticktin (2011), ch. 1.

[111] For those, see the secondary sources cited herein, from Manchuelle (1987, ch. 10) and Quiminal (1991: 96–108) to Guèye (2006) and Dedieu (2012).

[112] One work stoppage took place in Rouen in 1967, before the wave of rent strikes; N'Dongo (1976), 71.

[113] On this strike, in addition to the archival documents cited below, see N'Dongo (1975).

francs a month to sleep in cold dirty rooms with as many as twenty-six beds, intense humidity, and minimal sanitation; in Pierrefitte the sole common room – which they had once used for literacy classes – had been turned into another dormitory. ASSOTRAF was a nonprofit association, in keeping with its mandate. Yet, according to a tract circulated by the Communist League, the association's by-laws assured that its president, Guy Larcher, who was a friend of Senghor's and a "former *colon*, deputy [and] senator representing Senegal," and his secretary-general could receive indirect remuneration in the form of "allocations."[114] However, he got his pay, by 1969, Larcher might have wondered if it was worth it. Some of his tenants on the rue Pinel were charged with threatening to kill him, and he was under orders from the municipality of Saint Denis to undertake renovations that had long been left unfinished there.[115] In Pierrefitte, too, a rent strike was gathering steam. Boubacar Bathily, a French citizen of Senegalese origin, was jailed and two Malians deported in connection with the renters' movement, which lasted from 1969 until 1971 and shifted from Saint Denis to Pierrefitte.[116] The renters' demands were multiple: repairs and renovations to the building, its sanitary facilities, and its ventilation; the establishment of a common room for meetings; the right to receive visits and to organize; and the dismissal of the manager. In both cases, the tenants won better housing,[117] but their victory was a modest one, at best. If migrants emerged from the strikes better organized and generally better housed, some had been deported, the "shell associations" endured, and many within the French civil service urged abandoning laissez-faire policies toward African migrants for something much more aggressive. In this case, too, more "care" meant more surveillance and more policing.

Migrants' associations would henceforth be in the middle of a broad struggle over sovereignty and self-determination between migrants and governments, French and African alike. The case of Garba Traore, a Malian, further reveals what was at stake in that struggle. A former career soldier in the colonial military, Traore ran some of the rare foyers that do

---

[114] Préfecture de Police, copy of tract, Dec. 16, 1969, CAC 19940023, Art. 20; on Larcher generally, who is identified as "Larché," see Manchuelle (1987), 529.
[115] Préfecture de Police, PMA, Dec. 5, 1969, CAC 19940023/30.
[116] Press clipping, "Deux expulsions et une arrestation de travailleurs africains," journal not indicated; Direction Centrale des R.G., *Immigrés africains en France*, July 15, 1969, CAC 19940023, Art. 20.
[117] N'Dongo (1976), 73.

Well-Known Strangers   153

not appear to have been funnels for FAS funds.[118] The fact that they were not run by "shell" associations did not make conditions in his foyers any less miserable, and only a few months after the beginning of the rent strike on the rue Penil, his foyer on the rue Gabriel Péri in Ivry experienced a strike of its own.[119] The strike went on for some time, and Traore had great trouble resolving it. In contrast to the ASSOTRAF case, in which the government sanctioned strike leaders, in this case it was Traore himself who wound up looking at jailtime and a hefty fine. He had already been in the dock twice before – once for assault, once for fraud – and by 1969 the police were considering deporting him.[120] Less well connected and less politically adroit than Larcher, Traore was vulnerable. But the strike on rue Péri, and even its outcome, might matter less than the scenario it reveals. Traore was more than a manager. From the point of view of the police, he was a *passeur*, or a trafficker in papers and people.[121] From that of activists, he was a "*marchand de sommeil*," literally a "sleep merchant."[122] From that of the residents of his foyers, he had earned both those sobriquets, but he was also, and perhaps above all, a *diatigi*, the kind of often-malevolent "host" Malian migrants had encountered in the Gold Coast and the Congo, for example, since the interwar years.[123] The latter phenomenon was not novel to West Africans, only new in the Seine-Saint Denis.

---

[118] Traore's associate Abdou Doumbia had sought funding from the FAS, but was rebuffed; Moussa Camara, Pres. ATMF, to Prime Minister, France, Sept. 29, 1970 (sic date); Min. du Travail, de l'Emploi et de la Population, Direction de la Population et des Migrations to Moussa Camara, Dec. 14, 1970, #00324; Abdou Doumbia, Sec. Administratif, ATMF, p/o Moussa Camara, Pres., to M. le Maître des Requêtes au Conseil d'état, Directeur de la Population et des Migrations, April 5, 1971. #6/AD. FPU 2827.

[119] Some sources suggest that Traore established these foyers himself, effectively "owning" them (or holding a long-term lease). Others indicate that he was merely a manager, representing other interests. In either case, Traore was the primary target of the strikes. Min. Interieur, DSN to Chef de la 5ème Division des R.G., Bordereau d'envoi of report by Préfecture de Police, June 19, 1969; and press clipping, "Grève des loyers au 'foyer africain' d'Ivry," journal not indicated, June 28, 1969, CAC 19940023, Art. 20.

[120] N'Dongo (1975), 83–4; Min. Interieur, DSN to Chef de la 5ème Division des R.G., June 19, 1969, CAC 19940023, Art. 20.

[121] Min. Interieur, DSN to Chef de la 5ème Division des R.G., June 19, 1969, CAC 19940023, Art. 20.

[122] N'Dongo (1975), 83.

[123] The term "diatigi" is a Mandekan term that bears some explanation. One's host is called a "*diatigi*"; he or she (*diatigimuso*) is held to be responsible for looking after visitors, and if necessary serving as an interlocutor with locals in a foreign place. This is, of course, generally a positive relationship, and long-term guests very often employ the family name (*jamu*) of their *diatigi*. However, in the context of long-distance labor migration in

154 From Empires to NGOs in the West African Sahel

Whereas the FAS-funded "shell" associations offered opportunities for those like Larcher who both held French citizenship and could claim to "know" Africans, African-run associations offered another set of political possibilities that figures such as Traore could exploit. Those possibilities were diverse. Such associations ostensibly protected workers' interests, but in practice they made it possible for governments, French or African, to surveil their citizens abroad. For ill-intentioned *diatigiw*, too, they offered a way to counter protest movements that might have emerged within their communities. The French police identifed Traore as a leading figure first in the *Association des travailleurs maliens en France* (ATMF) – an organization from which he would eventually split, as it maintained a pro-Keita orientation in the wake of the coup – and later in the *Regroupement des travailleurs maliens en France* (RTMF), which Mali's military government fostered in the early 1970s.[124] During the strike against ASSOTRAF foyers in Saint Denis, a number of Traore's allies in the ATMF, including Abdou Doumbia and Diango Cissoko, wrote to the deputy mayors of Montreuil and Saint Denis urging them not to support the strike, which they blamed on "trouble-makers," particularly Sally N'Dongo, a prominent, vocal, and self-promoting Senegalese advocate for migrants' rights who had been on the scene for more than a decade.[125] Their pleas went nowhere, partly because these were Communist municipalities in Paris' "Red Belt." In

particular, the newly arrived are vulnerable to exploitation by those of their community who have been in place longer. In cocoa and coffee-producing territories in West Africa, cynical first-comers had become *diatigiw*. They hosted new arrivals from their own countries of origin, but at a high price. They found work for them, but sold their labor to local landlords. They fed and supported them, but expected a hefty return on their investments. In the potentially more difficult – or at least more regulated – environment of the hostels of 1960s Paris, it is difficult to distinguish between *diatigiw* and other operators and opportunists who had gotten in on the act of sheltering African workers for profit; see, e.g., INPS, 1963. Tighter controls created a market niche for *passeurs*, specialists in procuring papers who claimed to assure entry into France for their clients. On *diatigiw* and migration in Africa, see Gary-Tounkara (2003, 2008), Whitehouse (2012: 45, 50) and Dougnon (2011), which uses the equivalent Dogon term *hogon*. For a fictional portrayal of traffickers and *diatigiw*, see Doukouré (1978).

[124] For the former, Min. Interieur, DSN to Chef de la 5ème Division des R.G., June 19, 1969, CAC 19940023, Art. 20; and *Note: les Autorités gouvernementales maliennes animent en France une association* ... origin not indicated, Nov. 3, 1975; for the latter, handwritten list of "presidents d'honneur" of the RTMF in RTMF to Min (Interieur?), n.d., attached to Préfecture, Seine Saint-Denis, Direction de l'Administration Générale to M. le Min. de l'Interieur, D.G. de la police nationale, sous-direction des étrangers et de la circulation transfrontière, Feb. 22, 1977, #004758, and *Note*, origin not indicated, Dec. 11, 1973, CAC 19960134, Art. 17.

[125] Abdou Doumbia, Secretary Administratif, ATMF to Deputé Maire de la Commune de Saint-Denis, Aug. 23, 1971, #24/AD; Diango Cissoko, S.G. ATMF to Deputé Mairie de la Commune de Montreuil, Aug. 30, 1971, #25/AD; Doumbia to Min. Interieur, July 21,

response to Doumbia, Montreuil's municipal leadership expressed support for the tenants' strike and suspicion of the ATMF's motivations.[126]

National governments adopted quite the opposite tack. In the years to come, both African and French governments would attempt to set workers' associations against each other and to inoculate themselves against the emergence of political opposition in the foyers.[127] They did not entirely succeed, but throughout the 1970s, migrants' associations would jostle each other, competing for a mandate that would allow them to claim that they represented people from Mali, Senegal, or Mauritania – each of which had its own groups, based loosely on nationality – and to wrest representation from French-led associations such as ASSOTRAF or the *Association pour la formation technique de base des Africains et Malgaches residant en France* (AFTAM).[128] Loyalties shifted quickly, sometimes reversing entirely.

By 1976, relations between the Malian community and its embassy in Paris, and especially between the RTMF and the government of Moussa Traore, had deteriorated to such a point that Abdou Doumbia – a longtime ally of Garba Traore and a Svengali-like figure within the divided community of expatriate Malians – wrote the Malian head of state to castigate him for failing to defend their interests or even their dignity

---

1971. See also ATMF, "Ultime Appel aux Maliens," n.d.; all in FPU 2827. Cissoko would go on to hold various positions of authority within the Malian government under the Second and Third Republics. In 2012-13, he served as interim Prime Minister under acting President Dioncounda Traore. On N'Dongo, an early protégé and later fierce critic of Senghor, see Dedieu (2012), 33–38. For criticisms of Senghor, see, e.g., UGTSF (1970), ch. 7. Note that in the French system, deputy mayors tend to the day-to-day running of municipalities, as mayors often simultaneously hold other, more elevated positions in government.

[126] Manoel, Maire-Adjoint, Ville de St-Denis to Abdou Doumbia, Sec., ATMF, Aug. 31, 1971, MM/NJ 2365, FPU 2827. On the "Red Belt," see Stovall (2001).

[127] After 1968, Mali's junta made several attempts to exert political control over Malian migrants and their associations, without great success; see, e.g., Préfecture de Police, *Un Congrès extraordinaire des travailleurs maliens doit se tenir à Montreuil les 30 et 31 aout*, Aug. 27, 1969, FPU 2832. In 1972, Moussa Traore delegated his feared right-hand man Tiécoro Bagayoko to the task; FPU 2832, FPU 2827, CAC 19960134, Art. 17. On Bagayoko, see Ch. 6. Senegal made a similar attempt to create a unique association, led by people sympathetic to Senghor's government; Préfet de Police, Cabinet, to S.G. pour la Communauté et les AAM, MAE, Min. Interieur, et al., Jan. 11, 1971, #Ass17729 [sic] CAB/SD, FPU 2827.

[128] See, e.g., "Travailleurs de Montreuil" to French Minister of the Interior, Jan. 11, 1972, CAC 19960134, Art. 17; on AFTAM, N'Diaye (1970), 113, 118–19; on Senegalese and Malian associations generally, Dedieu (2012), ch. 1. A list of African associations, which its creators noted was out of date and perhaps inaccurate, is attached to Min. Etat/ Min. Interieur/ Dir. de la Réglementation et du Contentieux, Nov. 15, 1976, CAC 19960134, Art. 17.

abroad.[129] At the same time, Doumbia was attempting to build closer relations with high-level civil servants in the French Ministry of the Interior, who he hoped would help him to procure newly necessary residency permits for some of his clients.[130] Senegalese associations had been wrestling with each other and their home government for years, particularly after Senghor had consolidated his power in the constitutional crisis of 1962. An *Amicale des Travailleurs Sénégalais de la Région Parisienne* (ATSRP) had worked from (but not with) the embassy before evolving into the *Union Générale des Travailleurs Sénégalais en France* (UGTSF), which the prolific and often redundant N'Dongo would go on to use as a vehicle to attack Senghor.[131] All the African-run associations sought to stave off AFTAM, a quasi-official, state-supported association created in 1962, which had begun operating foyers two years later.[132] When African Leftists organized a meeting on the housing problem on March 8, 1963 (coincidentally the day France and Mali signed their accord), N'Dongo, representing the ATSRP, stood up to accuse French-run associations, implicitly – and then explicitly – AFTAM, of using their benevolent activites to camouflage the trafficking of papers and the exploitation of migrants.[133] At least some African associations did the same. During the rent strikes, foyer managers like Traore, who was also an honorary president of the RTMF, confiscated the identity cards of striking tenants.[134] Little surprise, then, that associations marked by subterfuge, competition, and suspicion, would never coalesce into a movement.[135]

---

[129] Abdou Doumbia, Sec.-Gén., RTMF, to M. Moussa Traore, Président du CMLN and Chef du Gouvernement de République du Mali, et al., Dec. 1, 1976; Doumbia to MAE, Mali, et al., Jan. 31, 1977; BPNCMLN D326.

[130] Hervé de Charette [Directeur de cabinet de Paul Dijoud au secrétariat d'État chargé de l'Immigration] to M. Aurillac, Directeur du Cabinet, Min. Interieur, March 15, 1976; Abdou Doumbia, RTMF, to Claude Goudet, D.G. de la Réglementation, Min. Interieur, July 24, 1979; CAC 19960311, Art. 7.

[131] N'Diaye (1970), 115; Dedieu (2012), 32-33, 35-36. Dedieu argues for N'Dongo's redundancy and cut-and-paste mode of production as a rhetorical strategy; (2012), 40–41.

[132] Diarra (1968), 1000–001. AFTAM also provided TB screening and language and literacy lessons, as contemporary African immigrant-oriented NGOs in Paris and New York City continue to do.

[133] N'Diaye (1970), 115, 118-19; N'Diaye, et al., (1963), 30–31. The meeting was organized by the Bureau d'études des réalités africaines (BERA), which had been created by N'Diaye and other African students in November 1962 and which briefly published a serial, *Réalités Africaines*.

[134] Police de l'Air et des Frontières (PAF), Dec. 4, 1974, CAC 19960135, Art. 17.

[135] Dedieu (2012), 62.

Well-Known Strangers 157

A movement would, nonetheless, emerge. The rent strikes had broken out before any formal associations became involved, and they were directed partly at them. The tactic of the rent strike would quickly become firmly fixed in the political arsenal of the immigrants.[136] This had not happened overnight. In 1968 and 1969, African and French members of radical left-wing organizations, particularly Maoists, had attempted to politicize African workers and to support, or perhaps to capitalize on, the emergent renters' movement, which had not yet become a popular one. French police were perhaps overeager to attribute the emergent movement to the after-effects of May 1968, but in doing so they underestimated both the depth of migrants' grievances and the dynamism of political life "at home" in West Africa itself.[137] They did, however, touch on an important and long-running problem: when long-time allies of African anticolonialism such as Michel Leiris, André Gide, and Jean-Paul Sartre adopted the cause of African migrants and their rights, they spoke out in their favor and often in their place. In years to come Michel Foucault and Jean Genet would add their own voices to this discordant chorus.[138] By 1974, politicians had joined the intellectuals, and a movement of resistance against expulsions from a SOUNDIATA-run foyer in the 14th arrondissement attracted support from a broad swath of the French left, including then-leader of the Socialist Party and future President François Mitterrand. On visiting the foyer – from which the tenants' group sought to be rehoused *en masse* – Mitterrand remarked to the press that he had lived in better conditions as a prisoner of war in Germany.[139] Whatever metaphor one chose, the immigrants' cause had arrived, not a moment too soon. Six months later, the government would declare "the end" of immigration.[140]

---

[136] On the distinct forms of collective action used by the *sans papiers* movement of the 1990s, in which Africans were a minority, see Siméant (1998).
[137] E.g., Préfet de Police to Min. Interieur, Aug. 22, 1969, #69.1587, FPU 2832.
[138] N'Diaye (1970), 28–29; Quiminal (1991), 105; N'Dongo (1976), 75–76. See, e.g., Michel Leiris, "Un témoignage: chez les maliens d'Ivry sur Seine," *le Monde*, Jan. 13, 1970.
[139] *Situation du Foyer de la 'Soundiata,'* document without identification (Préfet de Police?), Jan. 24, 1974, FPU 2827.
[140] Notably, from January 1975, a residency permit (*titre de séjour*) would be required of citizens of all sub-Saharan African countries. The requirement would be gradually but firmly applied to citizens of the Sahelian countries in spite of their previously exceptional status; Min. Interieur to M. le Préfet de la Seine St-Denis, April 15, 1975; *Conditions d'immgration des ressortissants des états d'Afrique au sud du Sahara*, March 4, 1975, CAC 19960134, Art. 17. Expulsions would soon begin, but a second and paradoxical effect of "the end" of immigration was that the West African population in France set down deeper roots as more women in particular came and settled.

If tuberculosis had focused the attention of French authorities on African migrants, housing became the cause that migrants themselves would rally around, and it fostered important political alliances with French leftists, progressives, and unions. Insofar as unhealthy housing catalyzed illness, the two issues are themselves causally related. But they are also intertwined, as dual expressions of a particular form of power – or idea of government – that characterized the postwar and postimperial French state. That state, particularly in its system of social welfare, continued to "govern different people differently"; ironically, Bathily, one of the "Senegalese" leaders of the anti-ASSOTRAF movement, was ejected from the foyer on rue Pinel because he was a French national.[141] Thus, for more than a decade after the empire's most drastic contraction, the messy categories that had characterized it continued to structure possibilities for both exploitation and political mobilization of migrants. As the phenomenon of immigration became an electoral rather than an administrative issue from 1974, the ultimately effective pressure to consider West Africans as foreigners would not come solely from beyond the borders of the recently formed Hexagon.[142] Nor did it come from migrants alone. Rather it emerged partly from *within* the French bureaucracy and citizenry itself and only after years of insistent demands from African states, particularly Mali. Sahelians became foreigners due to a confluence of interests that were not their own, but also as an unintended effect of migrants' activism, which rendered them newly visible and perhaps, in Sayad's terms, unrecognizable.

CONCLUSION

Let's return to Robert Delavignette, stepping off a bus in Paris in 1965. If the migrants he met did not "give the impression" of being strangers to French society, they were, as Pap Ndiaye noted, politically invisible, at least for a time. They often profited from their invisibility to cross newly national boundaries, but that same quality made life in France enormously difficult, partly provoking the struggles in workers' hostels. If West

---

[141] Press clipping, "les Travailleurs africains protestent contre les conditions d'hébergement en France," journal not indicated, Aug. 6, 1969, CAC 19940023, Art. 20.

[142] See Gastaut (2000); Laurens (2008). Laurens emphasizes internal administrative pressure to set new controls on immigration dating from the 1960s, an interpretation that the evidence presented here would support. He argues that the economic downturn of 1974 gave an ex post facto rationale for a process already underway.

Africans were well-known strangers, they were also someone else's citizens, as newly independent states would come to insist. The new government of Mali – to a much greater extent than that of Mauritania or Senegal – worked to produce and secure the quality of "foreigner" with the idea that it was creating a new nation and a new citizenry. Yet neither the movement of West African workers to France nor the movement of pilgrims and pastoralists along the Sahel were truly "Malian," "Senegalese," "Mauritanian," or "French" migrations. They were patterns of movement that became national (and therefore international) under the "suns of independence" (B., *yérétatilew*).

What then was specifically "French" or "Malian" about them? In the former case, the particular form and the broadly inclusive ambitions of the French Community, as well as the state thinking sustained by civil servants, many of whom had begun their careers in the colonies. In the latter case, the thin thread represented by the US-RDA's practices in the loose weave of migratory patterns, structural inequality, and postimperial policy. Identifying the aleatory and indeterminate juridical status of West Africans in France and in Sudan in the years immediately around independence confronts us with an unanticipated fact: it was Mali rather than France that first sought aggressively to diminish and control migration to France, and it did so before other West African states. By the same token, it was a newly independent Sudan that ultimately pushed France and Britain to create travel documents for "their" pilgrims.

This incomplete history of migration reveals something more than states thinking about themselves, in Sayad's terms, and people thinking about the states that sought to include or exclude them. The intersection of two axes of migration – one across the Sahel, the other to and from France – and two strands of analysis implicitly poses another question often cast into shadow by the suns of independence: in an era of recomposing states, what was the function of government? In Sudan it appeared modest – the extension of sovereignty for sovereignty's sake – but ran deeper than that. In the *hijaz*, a distant new republic in the western Sahel asserted the citizenship of, and its claims over, those who appeared to be in danger of being enslaved. Meanwhile in Khartoum, West Africans seeking to confirm their French nationality hoped to secure some form of belonging that popular sovereignty, in the form of national independence, might otherwise have eroded. In France, West Africans' intolerably indeterminate status, and its effects in the politically charged domains of healthcare and housing, gave way to a particular form of governmental rationality over a new set of subjects.

But newly necessary passports, visas, and other documents did not secure rights;[143] people attempted to do that. Papers simply aided the work of bureaucracies as they attempted to channel migration.

The political calculus of inclusion and exclusion, of facilitating or impeding mobility, had changed dramatically over the course of a few decades, while the technology of control changed rather little. States simply came closer to producing, but not controlling, identity documents with features such as photographs and fingerprints, which Rougier had envisioned in the 1920s, and which until quite recently still figured on national identity cards in the Sahel. Ironically, such aggressive tools of exclusion or inclusion, and the categories of restrictive political membership that they quite concretely represent, both opened an enormous space for subterfuge and provoked immigrants and activists into generating new forms of politics intended to oppose them, or at least mitigate their effects.

In the case of the Sahel in the 1960s, 1970s, and beyond, such politics took diverse forms. By the mid-1970s, Malians in France were creating cooperatives and other community-oriented associations to provide access to education and healthcare to those they had left behind, and they would actively seek foreign partners to help them carry out their projects at home.[144] Other associations, some of them led by French citizens and funded by FAS, advocated not only that migrants return "home," but also that they return to farming. Returned migrants led celebrated experiments in modernized, cooperative agriculture in Senegal and Mali. In doing so, they acted, at least in part, in keeping with French policy.[145] More important, however, they and their peers abroad had begun to reject the paradoxically passive form of citizenship forced on them by the new Sahelian republics – above all, Mali, which distrusted and virtually disowned its diaspora – and confirmed by the French government. Often working independently of them, French and American Leftists generated a newly international activism, each of their organizations characterized by its own admixture of solidarity, anticolonialism, and "miserablism," or a strong association of Africa with suffering and passivity. Such activism would play a key role in transforming a vicious regional drought and a cluster of brutal but distant

---

[143] Cf. Torpey (2000); see McKeown (2008), esp. 17; Lewis (2007).
[144] Daum (1998).
[145] Dedieu (2012), 113–17.

political struggles into profound humanitarian and human rights crises in which national citizenship, albeit important, was no longer the ultimate marker of political belonging. In doing so, it would help set in motion a series of reactions, ricochets, and unintended consequences that would alter the meaning of government in the Sahel and beyond.

PART III

INTRODUCTION TO PART III

SAVING THE SAHEL

What could be more miserable than the drought-stricken Sahel? The bush is dead, a pastoralist told the Nigerien scholar Dioulde Laya in 1974.[1] Some in Mali argue that it's been dead ever since, a death represented by the absence of wildlife. Rainy-season hunters seek scarce rabbits; the novice might hope for the tracks of antelope, but the larger game is gone and the only hoof prints belong to goats.[2] Still, the bush is not dead, only dry, and the highways are hopping.

As the Introduction suggested, anyone sitting on the side of Mali's national highway at any time since the 1990s would have discerned a pattern in the vehicles that passed. Depending on the day of the week, a few old "bens," or trucks, might head for rural markets, so swollen with baggage and passengers that you can only wonder if they are more likely to tip or to burst. The occasional 18-wheeler passes, jerry cans and bedding slung from its belly, always going farther than you are. Every now and then, a bus slides down the road, its wheels so far out of alignment that it seems to move like a camel, the feet on each side moving in sync, one side always ahead of the other (Figure 1). Those buses will stop at roadblocks. Frenetic markets will form around them, bursting like bubbles when the buses move on, after papers are inspected, prayers performed, purchases made. Bush fruit, roasted meat, hard-boiled eggs, peanuts, and soft drinks. Students treat themselves; mothers might buy packets of cookies for children who will wave them like trophies; young people looking for labor demur. Do the people who glide through in white 4 × 4s consume these

[1] Laya (1978).
[2] Author's fieldnotes, August 2011.

FIGURE 1 A bus slides down the road

things? How distant a memory are the bush fruits of the rainy season, or do they know them at all? The savvy chauffeur stops, he loads the roof rack with sacks of charcoal, cheaper than gas and preferred for cooking. Their low price belies their volume: 3,500 CFA can buy a sack that once held 100 kilos of imported rice, now stuffed with the remnants of Mali's forests. That driver might be working for a "project" against deforestation. Or to build latrines for rural schools. Or to support women's cooperatives. Or a thousand other initiatives, each equipped with an acronym, a plaque, and the best of intentions. The person sitting on the side of the road will see the ebb and flow of local markets on the move. The visible signs of vibrant social life. And the white 4 × 4s cutting like sharks through roads they were not meant for. Whatever "government" is on these roads, it is stationary, present at the border crossings between administrative districts, absent for long stretches, immobile. Take your motorbike; gendarmes and customs agents will wave to you as you pass. It's the NGOs that are on the move. They are visible, powerful, and appear to be unstoppable. Their Land Cruisers are festooned with snorkels that allow them to swim through flooded zones without stalling. It might not be clear who is sovereign, but the Land Cruiser is king of the road. Lucky you if you catch a ride.

Saving the Sahel

The road is more than a narrative device or the lazy site of a traveler's observation. The Sahel might be defined by its location, but even that is relative to the desert, itself on the move. Empirically, the Sahel is characterized by mobility: human, pastoral, essential. Seen from the outside, it is bound by poverty, stitched together by foreign aid and interventions, and held in the loose grip of more or less feeble states. This perception is not new. It is, however, inadequate. Closer to the mark is the idea that in countries such as Mali and Niger, "aid functions like a form of governmentality,"[3] manipulated by states and NGOs alike. When did that become true? A key moment in that history – the condition that makes possible the dominance of white 4 x 4s – was the drought and famine of the 1970s and the crises and coalitions they engendered.

Mobility and poverty were never so tightly bound as they were during that drought, even if the very poorest could not go far. Tens of thousands of people, most of them pastoralists, fled the Sahara and its margins, virtually emptying the Adagh.[4] These were not the migrants of Kayes and the Senegal River Valley, who had left for other reasons and who would begin to make their voices heard in France during those same years. Those displaced by the drought moved quietly in search of pasture and relief. Although the drought affected the whole of the Sahel, many of those hit hardest came from northern Mali and Niger. Outside Niamey, hastily built camps swelled with refugees whose plight was soon broadcast to the world, much to the chagrin of a discreet and inward-looking Malian government whose citizens had fled, preferring the aid of neighbors.[5]

The crisis surpassed the capacity of West African states to meet it, and it produced both a wave of international relief efforts and a new collective identity for the Sahel. Anchored in the aftermath of that episode, Chapter 5 moves between young African nation-states, the populations they claimed, and the emerging world of nongovernmental organizations. It analyzes the famine of 1973–74 as a formative moment in international history and in the shaping of the new Sahel. At virtually the same time, ad hoc alliances of anticolonial and human rights activists emerged to contest the power of Mali's government to torture and imprison its opponents, particularly in legendary but hidden Saharan prisons. Chapter 6 argues that, as with the relief efforts, human rights campaigns slowly and subtly

---

[3] Rossi (2007), 145. See also Klute (1999).
[4] Boilley (2003).
[5] DuBois (1974); "Bamako Radio Condemns Niger Article on Refugees," Bamako Domestic Service in French, Oct. 23, 1974, *Foreign Broadcast Information Service*.

altered the nature and meaning of government in the region in ways that were as meaningful as they were unseen.

By the time the drought bit, little more than a decade after independence, the Malian Sahara had already become the theater of a discreet and bitter past. From the late 1950s, local leaders and colonial officers and administrators had worked to keep the Sahara French even as territorial autonomy increased in the south and rebellion raged in Algeria. French politicians went so far as to begin creating a new Saharan economic entity, the OCRS, which was to be carved out of the northern reaches of Soudan, Niger, and Chad, as well as vast southern stretches of Algeria.[6] The OCRS was a hybrid and ungainly creation with two essential characteristics: it was Saharan, and it would remain French. Although this ambitious project was ultimately a dead letter, some Saharans never accepted the fact that the northern reaches of the colony of Soudan became Malian territory. Many Tuareg – Kel Adagh in particular, but others as well – refused to be governed by "Blacks" from the South, whom they considered slaves. In light of what was happening along the pilgrimage routes, the US-RDA leadership saw them through the same distorted lens.[7] In other circumstances, those tensions may have lain dormant, but the US-RDA planned to rule the desert much more actively than the French had ever done: irrigation, agriculture, and the end of slavery were the order of the day.[8] Open rebellion broke out in 1963–64, and the new Malian army, its Saharan allies, and bands of rebels fought an extraordinarily vicious war of ambushes, sneak attacks, and retaliatory strikes that took a heavy toll on both civilians and combatants.[9] The Malian Sahara threatened to become a place without limits or laws, a theater of individual violence and collective punishment. Rumor has it that Captain Diby Sylas Diarra, who commanded the counter-insurgency, had a special oven in Kidal in which he literally cooked prisoners to death before (in some versions of the story) consuming them.[10] Those rumors are not worth much – they represent a pun on Diarra's given name "Diby," which in Bambara is a homonym for

[6] Boilley (1993); Lecocq (2010), 48–52.
[7] Lecocq (2010). Two other studies analyze the entangled histories of slavery and race-as-ancestry in the greater region; Hall (2011b) for the Niger Bend from ca. 1600, and de Moraes Farias (2001) for the deeper past of Songhay–Tuareg relations north and east of Gao, from 1000–1500. As Chapter 3 demonstrated, such questions were especially acute at the time of independence.
[8] Lecocq (2010), ch. 3.
[9] Boilley (2012 [1999]) and Lecocq (2010) offer authoritative studies of the rebellion.
[10] Lecocq (2010), 217. The image of the Saharan fringe as a place of violence and brutality remains a vibrant one in Malian political consciousness. That image has long been

grilled meat – but other atrocities were very real. During the rebellion the army poisoned wells in the Adagh and confined Tuareg nomads to designated safe zones. Its officers declared anyone they encountered outside those zones to be rebels by default, but settling under the eyes of the army exposed Tuareg women to harassment, forced labor, and sexual coercion.[11] That ugly history would later condition responses to the drought, as many Kel Adagh preferred to flee Mali for Niger rather than to rely for relief on a military they distrusted (and which some accused of withholding aid from them).

Under the cloud of general insecurity stirred up by the rebellion in 1964, unidentified gunmen shot dead three well-known political prisoners, including two of the US-RDA's most prominent one-time opponents. These men had been convicted of treason and consigned to the care of the army.[12] The government could offer no coherent explanation of how they had died while under military escort, and in the end it did not need to. All of this happened in relative obscurity, a long way from the cameras and press conferences that had recorded negotiations for independence or that would accompany appeals for emergency drought relief in years to come. Here, the crudest meaning of sovereignty – naked power over life and death – appeared to poke through the cloak of government like a badly broken bone piercing both flesh and fabric. A short decade later, international attention to drought victims and to political prisoners held in the desert would temper such a stark reading. After years of drought and violence, Sahelian governments no longer looked to bright horizons. Instead, they faced sharp limits. Over time, humanitarian relief, which bled into longer-term development aid, and human rights activism would become increasingly powerful forces within the Sahel, steadily contributing to a redefinition of what government was and could be. That long moment began in 1973.

---

grounded in Tuareg rebellions and their suppression – at least as much as in the prison camps – and has been compounded by the rebellion and jihadist takeover of 2012. It remained strong even in times of peace; see, e.g., el hadj Boua Kanté Sissoko, "Fête de l'indépendance dans la cité de la 'Barbarie,'" *l'Aurore*, 763, Sept. 20, 2001.

[11] Lecocq (2010), 209–12; see also Boilley (2003).
[12] See Chapter 6.

5

Governing Famine

Circa 1960, the Sahel boasted a bright future, at least in the vision of the region's planners.[1] Yet by the early 1970s that future was fading fast. Rains had failed for several years, and the huge herds of the 1950s and 1960s were dying for want of pasture. In 1973 and early 1974, drought and famine seemed to foreclose the possibility of an agriculturally productive Sahelian zone, one whose livestock would fuel new national economies and help feed southern neighbors.[2] That particular Sahelian future was no longer ambitious, it was delusional.[3] In the absence of rain, the herds themselves seemed to shrivel. In Niger, the river ran so low that, for the first time in living memory, giraffes could ford it.[4] Farmers watched their fields burn under the sun. Their crops would be scorched, never harvested. The exodus of tens of thousands of pastoralists and nomads, and smaller numbers of farmers, appeared unstoppable and

---

[1] Zolberg (1967); Jones (1976).
[2] Among the best contemporary studies of the drought and famine relief figure Copans (1975, 2 vols.), Derrick (1977), Glantz (1976), and Sheets and Morris (1974). See more recently Bonnecase (2010b; 2011, ch. 5). One of the key questions was what role colonial and postcolonial government policies had played in causing the famine; Franke and Chasin (1980). For an answer framed in the *longue durée*, see Alpha Gado (1993); see also Glenzer (2002).
[3] Giri (1983).
[4] ORTF, "Six millions d'hommes vont mourir," *Magazine 52*, first broadcast 31 May 1973, available on http://www.ina.fr/notice/voir/CAF93029564, last viewed 20 Feb. 2014. By the time this story made it to a conference in Niamey, the giraffes had become chickens; comments of sociologist Macouta Dangui to "Colloquium on the effects of drought ... " held in Niamey, June 1976, consulted as Sahel MfAs 044. On rivers running low, see Derrick (1977), 548.

Governing Famine

irreversible.[5] Many were not expected to survive. Those predictions would prove too dire,[6] but displaced pastoralists who had taken refuge in Niger's cities thought that it would take years to reconstitute their herds.[7] Meanwhile foreign analysts, like emergency room doctors, proposed extreme measures over what seemed to them an inanimate and unfamiliar form, which some saw as an inert body politic, others as its carcass. An international conference in July 1973 proposed "evacuating" the Sahel entirely. To that idea Senegalese President Léopold Sedar Senghor responded sharply, riposting that African civilization would thereby lose one of its defining traits, and "not the least noble, not the least beautiful."[8] Still, journalists wrote obituaries for an entire region that was "slipping out of human use."[9] By their reckoning, the future of the Sahel was not only parched, it was impossible. This was the end of the road.

Yet disaster was opportunity, if not for foreign capital, as some argued,[10] for a new political form that was neither state nor empire. True, foreign powers stumbled over each other to provide the aid that only they could, as military transport planes leapfrogged long stretches of the Sahel to reach isolated regions like that around Timbuktu. American, German, and Soviet aircraft – as well as those from several NATO countries that had never had a presence in the Sahel – moved an enormous amount of grain, much of it American in origin, causing French diplomats to grumble that "our absence is glaring."[11] But the relief effort was more than another Cold War tournament. Although foreign governments rather

---

[5] Kel Adagh Tuareg in particular sought refuge in Niger, Algeria, and later Libya. The experience of widespread exile would pose fundamental social challenges for decades to come; Boilley (2003), Lecocq (2004).
[6] De Waal (2005a [1989]), 25–28.
[7] Laya (1978).
[8] Senghor's speech to the founding conference of the CILSS, quoted in SEAE, Mission Permanente d'Aide et de Coopération auprès de la Rép. de Haute-Volta, *Rapport de Mission: Conférence des chefs d'état des pays sahéliens touchés par la sécheresse, Ouagadougou du 4–12 Sept. 1973*, attached to Jean Thomas, chargé d'affaires Ouagadougou to Michel Jobert, MAE, DAAM, July 19, 1973, #219 DAM, FPU 2820. The conference to which Senghor referred may have been that which created the United Nations Sudano-Sahelian office, which became the UNDP-Drylands Development Centre in 2001; see http://www.undp.org/drylands/history.html, consulted Feb. 22, 2012.
[9] Sterling (1974), 98; see also Held (1974).
[10] Meillassoux (1974).
[11] Louis Dallier, Ambassador of France to Mali, to Foccart, March 13, 1974, #1025/SP; Foccart, *Note à l'attention de M. Journiac*, June 25, 1973, #416/73; A. Richard, *Note à l'attention de M. [Foccart]*, Dec. 14, 1973, FPR 555. France did have several transport planes operating in the region; *l'Aide de la France aux états de la Sahel victimes de la sécheresse* (1973), 9.

than private organizations provided the vast majority of emergency aid, another future beckoned from the space between distant states and displaced populations. Foreign voluntary agencies, which would come to be known as NGOs, began to fill that gap as they adopted an ever greater role in delivering relief.[12] A long moment marked by a state-centered developmentalism began to give way to another, still emerging one in which humanitarian interventions intersected with extra-African governmental policies that would later flourish in the thin soil of neoliberal initiatives.

Yet for the Sahel, 1973–74 was *not* a neoliberal moment, and that traumatic time cannot be reduced to the backstory of another. It was a moment when *longue durée* historical dynamics and cyclical natural phenomena intersected with a particular global conjuncture. No single overarching narrative can embrace all of the processes at work. An economic crisis that afflicted the world at large began in 1974, but the Sahel was parched for water as much as it was for oil. An oil embargo by producers in the Middle East had radically uneven effects in the Sahel. The rulers of Nigeria, the northern part of which is integrated into the Sahelian zone by history, climate, and language, reaped great benefit from it.[13] Across the remainder of the region, drought and famine destabilized young governments, and the high cost of imported fuel and the declining demand for the region's own modest exports worked like a riptide to knock newly national economies off their uncertain feet. In the years to come such forces would draw them inexorably farther away from solid ground. Niger, whose uranium mines could have made it another rare African beneficiary of soaring energy markets, would prove no exception. Rather, the country's president, Hamani Diori, would pay a high political price for its economic good fortune: while attempting to renegotiate mining contracts with the French, he would be ushered offstage by a coup d'état.[14] Any analysis of

---

[12] Bonnecase notes that the term "NGO" appeared in the UN charter but was not in wide use until the 1970s; (2008), 391. In English, the term "voluntary agencies" (or "Volags") was preferred. On the "invasion of the acronyms," of which "NGO" was the avant-garde, see Nugent (2012), Ch. 8.

[13] As Michael Watts observed, perhaps too pessimistically, "Nigeria could ... afford to devote some of its newfound oil wealth to [the] enormous but ultimately futile task" of attempting to support a vast Sahelian population of farmers and herders; Watts (1983), 389. CARE soon began to ask why exactly it was investing in the Nigerian Sahel when the country's economy was apparently booming. Executive Committee meeting, May 23, 1973, CARE 9.

[14] Amb. Fr. Niger to MAE, DAAM, *Synthèses périodiques* #3, Jan. 31 to Feb. 1, 1974; #5, Feb. 28 to March 13, 1974; #6, March 14 to 27, 1974, FPU 783. Chief of Staff Seyni Kountché would stage a coup d'état on the night of April 14–15, 1974.

the Sahel in this period must bear in mind that Diori and other actors who had already left the stage were absent, and other futures were foreclosed. Just as the interludes in Shakespeare's dramas might introduce us to new minor characters who blossom in the absence of the major players, in the "emergency" Sahel a new politics took form while Diori, Modibo Keita, Madeira Keita, and their comrades languished in prison. Nonetheless, in political discourse the last battle was still being fought.

Proud intellectuals blasted hand-wringing outsiders as neocolonial,[15] even as new actors emerged on the scene for whom the history of colonialism meant very little. Entrepreneurial NGOs – some aggressive, others discreet – would work with West African governments to produce a novel political form, the first hints of which would emerge in the context of the emergency. This new form was never stable, and the line that runs between it and the politics of the present is broken and irregular. That said, such agencies recognized the famine as an exceptional moment, and they saw it as one of possibility and invention.

It was also a moment of definition. By its very name, the short-lived Mali Federation had attempted to revive a Sahelian history of grandeur. Little more than a decade later, a more modest and enduring association of Sahelian states emerged from a meeting of government ministers in Ouagadougou. The *Comité permanent inter-Etats de lutte contre la sécheresse dans le Sahel* (CILSS) defined the region not by its past, but by its miserable present, declaring in its first resolution that the Sahel was a "disaster zone" (*"zone sinistrée"*) and in its second that its future was unknowable, demanding above all more scientific and social scientific research.[16] The governments that made up CILSS agreed to work together, with Upper Volta (now Burkina Faso) taking the lead, to focus the world's attention on the vicious drought that was crippling the region.[17] Following a meeting of Sahelian heads of state in September 1973, CILSS dispatched a delegate to seek emergency aid abroad. Voltaique President General Sangoulé Lamizana launched a diplomatic offensive to secure the attention and the assistance of foreign powers, notably through the United Nations.[18] His success contrasted sharply with the cold shoulder U.N.

---

[15] See, e.g., Senghor's response to the French Leftists who signed "*De quoi meurent les Africains?*," a statement discussed below; Copans (1975), n.p.

[16] *Réunion des Ministres sur les problèmes posés par la secheresse, Rapport*, Ouagadougou, March 23–24, 1973 (sic; actual meeting was March 26–27), Hoover 13/7. On the creation of CILSS, see Robinson (1978); Jeanneret (1983); Somerville (1986).

[17] CILSS (1973a, 1973b).

[18] Bonnecase (2011), 253–54.

Secretary General U Thant had given Mali two years earlier when Bamako had asked for food aid.[19] By late 1973, the effects of the drought were visible, even if their scale was still unknown. The scale of investment required would soon become clear. CILSS would seek $1.5 billion in aid and investment, but Diori had wanted to ask for much more.

In 1978, CILSS doubled its original request, but bilateral and multilateral aid committed to the eight CILSS states amounted to only a little over $1 billion, much of it in loans.[20] By then the countries composing the Organization for Economic Cooperation and Development (OECD), led by France and the United States, had created a "Club du Sahel" on which Paris cast a wary eye, believing it could become a stalking horse for U.S. interests in the region.[21] The Club was designed to pull together donor nations and international NGOs in a "flexible, informal" fashion "under the leadership of the CILSS," to promote development and, above all, to make the Sahelian region self-sustaining in food production.[22] These were large-scale, ambitious, governmental programs, and they exceeded the capacity of Sahelian states to absorb them. The Club was at pains to subordinate itself, at least publicly, to CILSS, but that apparent concentration of power masked what Kent Glenzer refers to as a "fragmentation of responsibilities [by which, in the wake of the drought,] the definition of problems, the planning of operations and the distribution of resources passed into the hands of foreign technical agencies and experts."[23] This newly broken ground was fertile soil for international NGOs, which would soon take root and quickly flourish.

ENGAGING THE SAHEL

Within this novel scenario, three types of nongovernmental activity, and not necessarily the most prevalent or the most powerful, deserve particular

---

[19] Seydou Traore, Permanent Representative to the UN (Mali), to Sec. Gen. UN, 23 April 1971 and Sec. Gen. UN to Traore, May 25, 1971, UN S-0198-0006-23.

[20] Funding commitments reported in 1978 date to 1976. Various documents, notably *Club des Amis du Sahel*, n.d.; OECD, Secretariat of the Club du Sahel, *The Club du Sahel: Multidonor collaboration to facilitate the identification and appraisal of development projects within the Sahel* (Working Document), June 13, 1978; and OECD, *Communication de Anne de Lattre à la réunion du CAD et des organisations de financement arabes*, June 19–20, 1978, all in ANF 5AG1410. See also de Lattre (1979); Naudet (1999); and T. Johnson, "6 African Nations End 14-day Talks," *New York Times*, Sept. 13, 1973.

[21] *Note pour le Ministre de la Coopération*, #02773, Dec. 16, 1976, ANF 5AG1410.

[22] *Club des Amis du Sahel*; OECD, *Communication de Anne de Lattre . . .*, ANF 5AG1410. The phrase "*des amis*" seems to have dropped out of usage.

[23] Glenzer (2007), 123. Here a caution might be expressed, as economic planning before 1974 was also often the work of expatriate experts.

scrutiny because they reveal how irregular and unpredictable the move from statist politics to novel forms of nongovernmentality was. The three are hardly representative, but each would come to be embedded in an increasingly dense constellation of relief organizations, development agencies, and social experiments.

The arrival of the American organization known as the Cooperative for American Relief Everywhere (CARE), testified to the emergence of muscular international NGOs as major players on the Sahelian scene. CARE's archives reveal how entrepreneurial and aggressive its agents were as they sought to pry open a political space in which to act. The fact that Nigerien scholar and former NGO worker Boureima Alpha Gado characterized CARE-Mali as a "state within the state" by the 1980s is both a measure of its success in doing so and testimony to the absence of a more precise political language.[24] CARE was never a state, but it was closely bound to the U.S. Agency for International Development (US-AID), and it took on some of the aspects of government.

Other than the fact that they were both American organizations, CARE could hardly have been more different from the American Friends Services Committee, more commonly known as the Quakers or the Friends. The Friends' intervention in the Sahel was anchored by a social experiment in settling displaced nomads in an entirely new village. This project, known as Tin Aicha, attempted to create something new from the torn fabric of Saharan and Sahelian social life in the darkest months of the drought and in the years that followed. As heroic as the Friends' efforts might have been, their own ambivalence about the project was never fully assuaged.

Other organizations, much more politically engaged than the Friends, shared their doubts even as they developed their own emergent and more-or-less durable practice of postcolonial solidarity. As expressed by American organizations such as Africare and Relief for Africans in Need in the Sahel (RAINS) and by French groups such as the *Association Française d'Amitié et de Solidarité avec les Peuples d'Afrique* (AFASPA) or the *Comité d'Information Sahel*, this solidarity represents a third distinct form of engagement. Foreign activists expressed it in the particular, even parochial, idioms seen as most salient in their own national context – race for the Americans, class and *tiers mondisme* for the French[25] – even as they considered it organic. This was *not* charity, even if its proponents were

---

[24] Alpha Gado (1988), 482; see also 486–88.
[25] To take just two examples. Other European relief agencies and missions were numerous on the ground, and there are many other stories to be told.

often strangers to their homologues. Predominantly African-American organizations such as Africare and RAINS sought to fuse the politics of racial solidarity in the United States with an international and diasporic vision.[26] French activists, like those in AFASPA, took a similar path, building on the remnants of an imperial labor movement and privileging a Marxist analysis that left little place for race. This form of intervention as solidarity would become a minor if enduring theme in a new internationalism, one in which African sovereignty and the dynamics of political opposition had to be accorded an expanding role. This solidarity fell into sync with the interests and often the personal history of the pro-Communist Left, but politically astute actors like Diori, whom they might have excoriated, knew how to engage it as well.

CARE

Let us begin with CARE, precisely because it was virtually unique as an NGO. Born in the 1940s of the desire to provide direct, person-to-person assistance between the United States and war-torn Europe, by the 1970s it had no particular vocation or domain of expertise other than its proud, internal self-definition as an "operational programming and managerial agency."[27] Two other characteristics distinguished it from its peer organizations. First, it was bound to the American government. It operated in very direct cooperation with US-AID, belying both its own identification as a "nongovernmental" organization and the U.S. government's rhetorical commitment to a form of free market capitalism, which CARE represented neither at home nor abroad. Instead, CARE was one of the great beneficiaries of the American law known as Public Law (P.L.) 480, which essentially assured American farmers of a market and secured price controls (or floors) by setting up the federal government as the buyer of last resort for unwanted grain and dairy products.[28] To a significant degree, P.L. 480 enabled CARE by giving the "managerial agency" something to

---

[26] On African-American international activism in this period, see Plummer (2012).
[27] Walter (Wally) Cox, country dir., CARE-N to Ray[mond] Rignall, Regional Program Officer, NY, Niger-NY, #728, June 20, 1977, CARE 142. Studies of CARE include Linden (1976), Campbell (1990); see also notably Ferguson (1994).
[28] Winders (2009), 147, 149–50. Ironically, socialist countries reluctant to send food aid because they diagnosed the need for it as a "crisis of capitalism" may have acted in a more strictly free market manner than did the liberal democracies, which intervened in both domestic and African markets. Brun makes a version of that argument; Copans, ed. (1975), 106.

manage. Thus, the vast majority of CARE's funding came from US-AID – more than 80% in 1970; 70% in 1980 – meaning that as US-AID's priorities changed, so did those of its client organization.[29] By 1981, other American NGOs considered CARE and Catholic Relief Services to be "agents of the federal government, [which were] not private, or voluntary, or independent."[30] Indeed, not only did the two organizations coordinate very closely, but Americans who had previously worked in West Africa for CARE often returned as employees of US-AID, which paid better.[31] The second distinguishing characteristic of CARE was its compulsion to straighten out the kinks in aid delivery, kinks which were highly profitable to well-placed entrepreneurs. CARE's early inexperience in the Sahel and its lack of connections there initially led it to enable – and later stumble into conflict with – state elites who were converting aid money into private wealth. Such conversions would become characteristic of Sahelian politics for decades to come, setting up the political elite as a rentier class controlling access to resources generated by long-term development aid and short-term emergency intervention. As the saying goes, the guest does not choose where he spends the night.

Niger

Our story of CARE must start in Niger, where its first Sahelian interventions took place.[32] Part of the reason CARE became deeply rooted in Niger before engaging with other Sahelian countries is circumstantial: the country was seeking partners just as the organization was looking for openings. As drought became famine, CARE was already moving into place. Here a detour into Niger's politics is merited. At first glance, few places look as "neocolonial." In addition to hosting a French military base, the government relied on hundreds of French "*coopérants*," civilian employees

---

[29] McCleary (2009), 25–6, 125; Linden (1976), 26–29. In 1974, CARE had a programming budget of 111 million USD. Nearly 92 million (roughly 83%) came from P.L. 480 funds; *Report to the Board of Directors, CARE programming fiscal year (FY) 1974*, Oct. 23, 1974, CARE 10.
[30] McCleary (2009), 137.
[31] Donald Sanders, *Visit to CARE-Mali*, March 29, 1979, CARE 392.
[32] In 1973, CARE had minor Food-for-Work (FFW) projects in Nigeria, as well as in Liberia and Kenya. India was its major site of intervention, occupying more than half of CARE's programming budget of 96 million USD. By way of comparison, Liberia received 1.2% of that money, half of its allotment being P.L. 480, and Israel received 1.3%, almost all of it from P.L. 480. *Report to the Board of Directors, CARE programming FY 1973*, Oct. 24, 1973, CARE 503.

seconded to Niger on short-term contracts, in order to fill the ranks of the civil service. By contrast, the first Nigerien Treasurer General was named as late as 1973.[33] Along with the *coopérants*, such powerful behind-the-scenes figures as Don-Jean Colombani – one-time governor, later ambassador, and later still, one of several informal intermediaries between Niger and France – had a heavy hand on the central administration, rendering the country "one of the least Africanized in francophone Africa."[34] Indeed, as did his Gabonese counterpart Omar Bongo, President Diori relied on a French chief of staff (*directeur du cabinet*), Nicolas Lecas, from 1959 to 1974.[35]

Still, although such a situation would have been unimaginable in Mali or Guinea, Niger's neocolonial profile can be somewhat deceiving. In the early 1970s, Diori was in his own fashion gingerly pushing out of the French mold. There are two common ways of perceiving this vast landlocked nation largely dominated by the desert: either as the distant dusty hinterland of a region increasingly oriented over the *moyenne durée* toward the sea, or as one of the strategic centers of an Afro–Arab world, at a North and West African crossroads.[36] The latter prevailed at the moment of French conquest and remains more useful here. Roughly a decade after independence, Niger's relations with the rest of the region and the world had begun to take on multiple forms. Niger was establishing relations with Colonel Mu'ammar Qadhafi's Libya, had withheld support for the Biafran secession from neighboring Nigeria (which France and Cote d'Ivoire championed), was profiting from a relationship with Canada that marginalized Quebec's francophone nationalism, and was seeking revision of cooperation agreements with France.[37] Although the former metropole continued effectively to control the uranium industry, that vital sector of the economy was diversifying, and American oilmen were prospecting in the Sahara.[38] In the first months of 1974, Diori's push to renegotiate agreements on uranium mining set him at odds with the French government.

---

[33] Ambassade de France au Niger, *Synthèse périodique* #16, August 16 to 29 1973, FPU 783.
[34] Higgot and Fuglestad (1975), 388. In 1973, Niger had 530 French *coopérants*; *Synthèse périodique* # 1, Jan. 1 to 15, 1973, FPU 783. Among others, note J. Baulin, whose *Conseiller du Président Diori* (1986) represents an important source for Salifou (2010). Baulin worked for Diori until March 1973, when he resigned in order to defend a thesis on the politics of Ivoirian President Félix Houphuët-Boigny.
[35] Idrissa (2001a), 42–3; see also Salifou (2010).
[36] Idrissa (2001b).
[37] Re. Libya, FPU 783; re. cooperation, FPU 1583; re. Canada, Idrissa (2001a), 43.
[38] *Synthèse périodique* #3, Feb. 1 to 15, 1973, and #335/DAM, Nov. 11, 1973, FPU 783.

Production at Arlit, the major point of extraction, had only begun in 1971, and already it was causing Diori two sets of problems. Students condemned his government for having allowed the establishment of what they considered a racially segregated town around the site, one "whose atmosphere hardly differs from that of the racist *cités* of South Africa."[39] Diori could ignore or suppress such criticisms, but the second problem appeared intractable: the mines were bringing into the government's coffers only one-third of the profit that had originally been predicted.[40] Demand remained limited, and even so it was already largely met through contracts that would remain in force through 1978.[41] The timing could not have been worse for a country that needed cash. Still, this scenario suggests that when President Diori called in vain for a Marshall Plan to fight the effects of the drought – as he did repeatedly[42] – he meant what he said when he insisted that he did not seek "charity," but international backing for loans to be repaid with future earnings.[43]

At the same time, Nigerien politics was gradually being brought to a boiling point by ongoing drought, food shortages, crippling hikes in fuel prices, an influx of displaced nomads and Malian refugees, student unrest in the capital, ... the list seemed interminable. Diori's own rhetoric was no help. Before the failed rainy season of 1973, he cast a dark shadow over the year to come when he stated, in a speech marking the anniversary of the creation of the *Parti Progressiste Nigérien* (PPN-RDA), that the challenge that faced the country was "not to live, but [simply] to survive."[44] A few dry months later, while addressing the nation on the eve of *eid al-kabir* (Tabaski), he asked his poorer compatriots to abstain from the ritual sacrifice of a ram: "Those who don't have the means should wait for better days," he argued.[45]

---

[39] Tract distributed in Niamey by Union des Scolaires Nigériens (USN)..., Feb. 14(?), 1973, FPU 1583. See also ADSSD 67J112.
[40] Amb. Fr. N. to Maurice Schuman MAE, DAAM, Jan. 16, 1973, #8/DAM, FPU 1583.
[41] Note à l'attention de M. le S.G.: Niger, Jan. 24, 1974, FPU 1527.
[42] Amb. Fr. Niger to MAE, DAAM, *Synthèses périodiques* # 6, April 4 to 17, 1973; #11, June 4 to 17, 1973; #12, June 18 to July 1, 1973, FPU 783; T. Johnson, "6 African Nations End 14-day Talks," *New York Times*, Sept. 13, 1973.
[43] Paul-Henri Gaschignard, Amb. Fr. Niger to Sec. d'état aux affaires etrangères, Direction de l'Aide au Développement, Sept. 17, 1973, #1992/MP, FPU 2820.
[44] Diori's message to the nation, as printed in *le Niger*, May 21, 1973, cited by Salifou (2010), 226.
[45] *Synthèse périodique* #1, Jan. 1 to 15, 1974, FPU 783. Meanwhile, in the refugee camps outside Niamey, Catholic charities offered rams to Muslims; Brun in Copans (1975), 87–88, 95.

By mid-April 1974, the army was tired of waiting. A junta led by military Chief of Staff Seyni Kountché seized power, imprisoning Diori and disarming the PPN's militia. The coup was bloody, leaving Diori's wife and several others dead. Marginalized by the militia, by the French military presence in Niamey, and by new defense agreements with Libya – and claiming to be scandalized above all by Diori's incoherent response to the drought – the new junta had several strong motives for its action.[46] The thesis that France lay behind the coup is hard to sustain, although it may have served French interests.[47] Immediately beforehand, the rhythm of negotiation over the uranium accords had accelerated sharply. In a meeting in Niamey three weeks before the coup, Diori and Bongo had attempted to mount a common front to demand higher prices from France, a gesture the French ambassador dismissed as unrealistic.[48] Days later, French President Georges Pompidou died unexpectedly (albeit after a long hidden illness), and Diori used the occasion of his funeral to push the uranium question again.[49] Such turmoil at the top might have left a free hand for Jacques Foccart's powerful Africa office, which answered directly to the presidency, to bring Diori down. However, Foccart would later claim to have wanted to stop his fall, not accelerate it.[50] In the end, the French government appears to have merely witnessed a well-planned operation.[51] Its inaction, too, was telling. The coup represented a momentary lapse in France's long-standing engagement in the Sahel.

If that tide seemed particularly low, another current was stirring in the form of the international NGOs. Indeed, even as Niger's government debated uranium prices with the former metropole and entered into a new military accord with Libya in April 1974, it was signing a contract for a multiyear development program with CARE.[52] Kountché's coup would punctuate CARE's intervention in Niger but would not fundamentally alter it. There is more than one reason for this. Not the least of them is the fact that Niger changed its captain, but not its course. Many of Diori's initiatives carried on in his wake, and documents prepared for a PPN party

---

[46] Idrissa (2008), 10; Issa (2008), 133.
[47] Salifou (2010), 248–49.
[48] *Synthèse périodique* #6, March 14 to 27, 1974, FPU783. On this episode and on the uranium trade more broadly, see Hecht (2012), 124-31.
[49] Salifou (2010), 246.
[50] Bat (2012), 238. Baulin confirms this; (1986), 122.
[51] Van Walraven (2013), 838–39.
[52] *Synthèse périodique* #6, March 14 to 27, 1974, FPU783. This would eventually be agreed in an *Activity Implementation Letter*, July 12, 1974, CARE 409.

congress pre-empted by the coup foreshadowed Kountché's resonant phrase, "the Development Society."[53] With such currents swirling, Niger represented uncharted waters for CARE.

"We Should Have Been Here Earlier"

Still, CARE did not come to Niger. Rather, Niger had come to CARE, in the form of an invitation by President Diori, who seized on the possibilities of nongovernmental politics early.[54] In 1972, before the worst effects of the Sahelian drought had truly come to be felt, representatives of the Nigerien government in Washington and New York made contact with CARE, which soon dispatched Peter Reitz to Niamey to scout for possibilities.[55] There the climate for intervention was favorable: President Diori's relations with France were strained, American diplomats encouraged CARE intervention, and US-AID seemed to be searching for partnerships that would allow it to be involved without undertaking its own programs. Reitz quickly concluded, "We should have been here earlier."[56] By mid-1973, CARE was working on a two-year agreement with Niger's government to supply and distribute foodstuffs; the organization would soon have spent nearly half a million dollars in the country.[57] A year later CARE was finalizing an agreement with the Ministry of Development – it is telling in itself that Niger had such a ministry[58] – to launch a two-year project aimed at "subsistence farm people" of the Dallol Bosso valley, near Niamey. The plan made little room for markets and none for herders. It sought instead to assure access to potable water (expressly for people and *not* for livestock), extend irrigation schemes, promote "agricultual diversification," and establish fencing to keep livestock away.[59] The goal was to

---

[53] Idrissa (2001a), 40, 48; Salifou (2010), 247, n67.
[54] *Report to the Board of Directors, CARE programming FY 1974*, Oct. 23, 1974, CARE 10.
[55] Executive Committee meeting, May 23, 1973, CARE 9.
[56] Peter Reitz, *Summary Report: Visit to Niamey*, Nov. 22 to 25, 1972, CARE 142.
[57] *Initiating Programs in Niger – Possible Activities*, CARE, July 2, 1973; possible draft of agreement between CARE and the Government of Niger to "develop and implement a multi-faceted food Distribution and Availability Project of 2 year's duration (July 1, 1973 thru June 30, 1975)"; William R. Dalton, Acting Foreign Disaster Relief Coordinator, Office of Foreign Disaster Relief Coordinator, Bureau for Population and Humanitarian Assistance, *Summary Report: Sahel Region Drought*, Nov. 9, 1973, all in CARE 142.
[58] Bonnecase reports that this Ministry oversaw a "Groupement des Aides Privées." Mali and Upper Volta created similar coordinating committees of NGOs in the 1980s, although these committees apparently straddled the public and the private; Bonnecase (2011), 253, see also 245; Raghavan (1992), 98.
[59] *Activity Implementation Letter*, July 12, 1974, CARE 409.

"create a dependable source of foodstuffs for the central valley," and while pursuing it the organization would offer well over $2 million worth of food in each of the next two years.[60]

These "contributions in kind" opened doors in the Sahel and in the United States. By the summer of 1974, just after the *Atlantic Monthly* published a long and dire article on the Sahel entitled "The Making of a Sub-Saharan Wasteland," CARE could trumpet its efforts in the region with a press release stating that it was at work in Chad, Northern Nigeria, and Niger, where it had contributed millions of dollars of supplies.[61] In 1975, CARE's board of directors noted with satisfaction that "geographically" the Sahel represented the organization's "most important new program region."[62] Having got a Sahelian foothold in Niger, CARE had signed agreements with Chad in March 1974 and with Mali in January 1975.[63] The search for other venues was a necessary one. Shortly after CARE's 1974 press release boasting of the organization's presence in the Sahel, its representative in Niamey was privately reporting to headquarters in New York that "Niger's ability to absorb assistance has been passed."[64] Aid to Chad soon skyrocketed. This aid consisted almost entirely of rural public works projects or food delivery, and would remain important until programming there was suspended entirely in 1980 in the context of that country's civil war, in which both Libya and France were deeply involved.[65] The real question, however, was not whether governments like that of Niger could absorb the aid provided – many doubted that they could[66] – but rather whether CARE could increase their capacity and desire to do so, thereby allowing the organization to continue acting as a funnel for US-AID money. In other words, the dual challenge CARE faced was to make itself indispensable both to Sahelian governments and to

---

[60] *Report to the Board of Directors, CARE programming FY 1974*, Oct. 23, 1974; *Report to the Board of Directors, CARE programming FY 1975*, Oct. 22, 1975, CARE 503.
[61] Sterling (1974) and press release, "CARE opens drive to save African Drought Victims," Aug. 15, 1974, CARE 142.
[62] *Report to the Board of Directors, CARE programming FY 1975*, Oct. 22, 1975, CARE 503.
[63] *Report to the Board of Directors, CARE programming FY 1974*, Oct. 23, 1974; *Report to the Board of Directors, CARE programming FY 1975*, Oct. 22, 1975, CARE 10.
[64] Jack Soldate, CARE/Niger to Leo Pastore, CARE/NY, Nov. 25, 1974, Niger-NY #282, Subject: Activity review, CARE 142. This observation concerning Sahelian governments would become a common but not consensual one; Giri (1983), 290.
[65] *Reports to the Board of Directors, CARE programming for FYs 1974–77*, and *Summary of CARE FY achievements, 1975–80*, CARE 503. On the conflict, Nolutshungu (1996).
[66] John J. McKelvey and "O.S.," *Trip Report*, Oct. 24, 1975, Folder 22, Box 3, sub-series 475D, series 475, RG 1–3, Rockefeller Archive Center.

US-AID. Conjugating the latter task with the former required a kind of infiltration framed in the rhetoric of "smarter" aid. For CARE that term meant relatively modest projects over which it maintained managerial and budgetary control. This approach contrasted with that adopted by "European-based groups," which often funded such small projects directly via payments into host government accounts, and with that favored by Sahelian governments, which preferred "big programs that met [their] needs, not small-bore experiments."[67]

Paradoxically, smaller projects required a bigger footprint. That, in turn, meant stepping on someone's toes. Here a conflict presented itself. Competition between NGOs was not exactly stiff; CARE thought that as few as half a dozen major organizations were operative in Mali and Niger, and that none had "the flexability [sic], depth and potential of CARE."[68] On the other hand, every state worthy of the name has its own "operational programming and managerial agency," its military. Mali had been under military government since 1968, and even as those soldiers began to adopt civilian camouflage in 1974 (see ch. 6), Niger's army staged its own coup. Niamey's new junta sought to exercise greater control over the relief and development activities of its "partners." CARE's donations of food would come to an end, but the organization would maintain its Food-for-Work (FFW) programs, which US-AID particularly favored. In other words, even as the new government pushed back against the visible manifestations of dependence, CARE sought to strike a balance between local political imperatives and institutional interest, while it aimed to integrate itself more profoundly. A few years later, the organization would be much more anxious, as a new AID director in Niamey suggested that his aim to use "food as [a] lever ... to strengthen US influence in Niger" would lead him to engage only in "government to government arrangements," with no role for NGOs in food programming.[69] That, for CARE, would have been the true disaster.

---

[67] Jack Soldate, CARE/Niger to Leo Pastore, CARE/NY, Nov. 25, 1974, Niger-NY #282, CARE 142; quote from Jacques Lauriac to Rignall, Oct. 25 ,1975, Mali-NY #122, CARE 392.

[68] This number would seem to be a serious underestimate. See list of "U.S. voluntary agencies" in *Summary Report: Sahel Region Drought*, CARE 142; CARE-Mali, Pre-Plan Paper, Annual Implementation Plan, Oct. 2, 1975; Donald Sanders, *Visit to CARE-Mali*, March 29, 1979 (quoted), both in CARE 392. Drawing on Brown, Truttin, et al., Bonnecase lists several more active international NGOs; (2011), 250–52. See also, the *AFSC and the Sahel*, June 27, 1974, Loft 7/15, and ACVAFS, MC 655, Boxes 119 and 120.

[69] Frank Bechin to William Langdon, April 2, 1982, Niger-NY #1724, CARE 142.

Mali

In Mali too, the degree of dissonance between CARE's sensitivity to US-AID's policies and its indifference to local politics was striking. There, much as it had elsewhere in the Sahel and across the world, CARE would focus on food production, nutrition, and – to a lesser extent – school construction.[70] On the ground in Bamako, while building schools and developing water resources in the countryside, CARE's local director sought to gain traction by developing nutrition programs. Himself a nutritionist by training, the French-born Jacques Lauriac, director of CARE-Mali, intended early in his tenure to "go in big and even create our own infrastructure" while maintaining a necessary and sizeable management role for CARE in all of its programs.[71] Although his bosses back in New York urged him to trim his sails and to focus on initiatives that the Malian state could eventually take over and manage, Lauriac intended to "assume a key role of counselor, advisor, and programmer in the public health field, specifically in nutrition and related field[s]. Influencing decision making-policies and programs – will be possible and with far reaching consequences [sic]."[72] After false starts with both headquarters and his local interlocutors, late in 1975, Lauriac eventually landed a contract to run a FFW program with US-AID. Although CARE's role was originally limited to that of "consultant-field management" [sic], headquarters "appreciate[d] that the mission will be in a position to exercise an influential voice in matters of program policy and the decision-making process to increase establishment of criteria for project selection."[73] In short, they were in.

Here the CARE logic becomes visible. When Malian officials were "confronted with direct requests for program suggestions and orientation," CARE-Mali complained, they "did not know how to respond and were unable to give ... concrete suggestions for program involvement. [Therefore] CARE has had to push consistently to develop reasonable programs ... This has made it absolutely essential that CARE continually

---

[70] *Report to the Board of Directors, CARE programming FY 1973*, Oct. 24, 1973, CARE 503.
[71] Lauriac to Rignall, Oct. 25, 1975, Mali-NY #122, CARE 392; *Program outlines*, n.d., CARE 142.
[72] Rignall to Lauriac, Aug. 19, 1975, NY-Mali #40, re.: Intended Program Directions; Rignall to Lauriac, Sept. 29, 1975, NY-Mali, #57; Lauriac to Rignall, Nov. 21, 1975, #140; CARE 142.
[73] Rignall, CARE-NY, to Lauriac, CARE-Mali, Dec. 16, 1975, NY-Mali #76; Lauriac to Rignall, Nov. 21, 1975, #140, CARE 142.

inform [Mali's government] of areas where it could be of possible assistance."[74] Simply put, CARE had to market itself. Whatever the causes of the Malians' recalcitrance – soldiers' preferences for orders over initiative or a lack of clarity over what CARE was asking – the result was that CARE representatives were attempting to sell various ministries programs that they had not themselves conceived. This was true in 1975, when the passage above was first written, and it was apparently true under a new country director in 1979, when he cited it in his own Multi-Year Plan for the next decade.[75] By that time, the new director perceived a pattern. Headquarters in New York continued to prefer smaller programs, and CARE-Mali sought to generate initiatives that the government could get behind and eventually take over. But because the government itself preferred "large scale, externally financed development plans [with] extensive direct or indirect budget support components," CARE-Mali had room to maneuver. The organization could work directly with ministries, in any domain it chose, as long as it was willing to do without funding or direct assistance from the government. In concrete terms, that arrangement allowed CARE to generate programs that provided credit to farmers, boosted agricultural production, improved rural water supplies and nutrition, and fed people through FFW programs. Equally real but less visible was CARE's integration "with all levels of Government of Mali administrations [sic]." CARE's emphasis on small programs led it to maintain multiple points of contact with the Malian administration. Here as in Niger, the smaller the project, the bigger the impact in governmental terms.

It is hard to argue with "grassroots" development, but CARE's expansive view of its mission generated conflict with the Malian government in two key sectors: transportation and school construction. On the face of it, both seem anodyne, but transportation had a double edge in Mali. During the famine, the external intervention into the Sahel's collective nightmare had been focused on the major challenge in providing aid, which was how to get food and other forms of aid from Atlantic ports to Sahelian points of distribution. In 1973, the Malian army "functioned remarkably well" in assuring transportation both in the east and along the Dakar–Niger railroad, but getting aid to Mali's sixth region – of which Gao was the principal town and Timbuktu a vital site for distribution – required the establishment of an "air bridge" made up of planes and aircrews on loan

---

[74] CARE-Mali, *Pre-Plan Paper, Annual Implementation Plan*, Oct. 2, 1975, CARE 392.
[75] Tim Aston, Country Dir., Mali, *Mali: Multi-Year Plan 1980–1984, Parts I and II*, Jan. 26, 1979, CARE 392.

from both NATO countries and the Eastern bloc.[76] As emergency relief gave way to recovery and development, the transport sector in Mali became politically charged. Apparently unbeknownst to CARE, some of the most powerful figures in Mali's governing CMLN had privately invested in trucking, which many believe to have funded the infamous "castles of the drought" built by powerful ministers such as Kissima Doukara (Minister of the Interior, of Defense and Security, President of the National Committee for Assistance to Drought Victims) and Karim Dembele (Minister of Transportation). They and their associates ran their own trucking companies, and they may have profited from the emergency purchase of heavy French-made Berliot trucks that were capable of reaching isolated villages even in the rainy season.[77] It is difficult to ascertain how precisely this worked in the context of the drought emergency, but by the late 1970s CARE-Mali was asking headquarters for funds to purchase its own trucks for use in FFW programs. Running its own fleet would allow CARE to make its "contributions-in-kind" more visible.[78] Its interests were clear: efficient delivery of P.L. 480 food aid, whether in the context of a "Mother-Child Health" initiative run with the Ministry of Social Affairs, which relied on commercial trucking, or of a smaller FFW program. Whether through self-righteousness or a lack of guile, CARE, US-AID, and their competitors placed themselves in the awkward position of competing directly with senior government officials on whose good will they relied by trying to cut them out of their own market. CARE thereby set up a conflict – of which the organization seemed unaware, but which it could not win – between the prerogatives of the NGO and those of the state's most powerful agents, between efficient management and what Achille Mbembe, following Béatrice Hibou, would diagnosis as "private indirect government."[79]

School construction, too, was not as straightforward as it seemed. CARE stated its own core interests in ranked order as nutrition,

[76] Dallier, Amb. Fr. Bamako to M. Jobert, MAE, Oct. 23, 1973, #56/DAM, a/s la secheresse au Mali; Min. Interieur, SCTIP to Foccart, SGCAAM, June 15, 1973, FPU 2820; see also Dallier, Amb. Fr. Bamako to M. Jobert, MAE, June 6, 1973, #38/DAM, CADN Bamako 100.
[77] On these purchases, see Dallier, Amb. Fr. Bamako to M. Jobert, MAE, June 6, 1973, #38/DAM, CADN Bamako 100, pg. 12. Dallier mentions no impropriety, but see, e.g., the dossier "le Complot Kassim, Tiécoro," *Sunjata* #0 [sic] (June 5, 1978), 18–22.
[78] Tim Aston, CARE-M to Fred Devine, CARE-NY, Dec. 6, 1978, Mali-NY # 685, CARE 142.
[79] Hibou (1999); Mbembe (2001). Niger also relied partly on commercial transportation, which CARE sought to undermine by having its own trucks; *PL 480 title II FY '81 Operational Plan*, Draft, CARE 142.

agricultural development, education, community improvement, health, and sanitation. In various combinations, these areas of interest were manifest in schools, notably in the form of feeding programs and the construction of classrooms and latrines. As an area of intervention, schools had the advantage of being supported by local associations of parents, "probably [some] of the most active groups involved in community development in Mali," which provided a good deal of the financing for primary education; this was the one sector in which a "cash contribution" from local communities was available.[80] Whether the same dynamic prevailed elsewhere is unclear, but in the 1970s CARE built more than a dozen schools in Chad and was launching a major school construction project in Niger.[81] This was in keeping with its activities elsewhere in the world, notably in Latin America. In Mali it earned CARE its first local media coverage in the form of a newspaper article on a ceremony attended by the American ambassador in which CARE gave the Malian government three schools it had built.[82] Why then, in the months following, did CARE-Mali's school construction programs provoke Malian governors and ministers, earning the organization's pointman a rare dressing down?

CARE was working both sides of the counter, selling school construction to US-AID as part of the latter's "disaster relief operations" before the Malian government had truly bought it.[83] It built its first schools – those the ambassador visited – without winning the support of Sory Ibrahim Sylla, the governor of the region in which they were located. Sylla in turn warned his peers in other regions, as well as the relevant ministers, that CARE was building resource-intensive schools for its own interests, that it was not taking into account the policies of the Malian administration, and that, as the minister conveyed:

[CARE's agents] were "*entrepreneurs*" (contractors [sic]) and that the Malians were not "*grands enfants*" as CARE had apparently attempted to treat them. And whereas that sort of thing might go [sic] in some other countries where [CARE] worked, it would not go here.[84]

[80] CARE-M, *Pre-Plan Paper, Annual Implementation Plan*, Oct. 2, 1975; re. cash contribution, Tim Aston, CARE-M to Bill Schellstede, CARE-NY, Dec. 6, 1978, M-NY #686; Tim Aston CARE-M to Ray Rignall, CARE-NY, Dec. 23, 1977, #549; Donald Sanders, *Visit to CARE-Mali*, March 29, 1979, all in CARE 392.
[81] *Summary of CARE FY achievements, 1975–80*, CARE 503; *Multi-Year Program Fact Sheet [Niger]*, 1975–1979, CARE 407.
[82] Lauriac to Rignall, M-NY, March 16, 1977, #434, CARE 392.
[83] Lauriac to Rignall, Aug. 10, 1976, #292, CARE 142; Randall E. Trudelle, CARE-M to Rignall, CARE-NY, Oct. 21, 1976, M-NY #349, CARE 392.
[84] Memo, July 29 [1977] meeting with Min. Health, CARE 392.

Sylla formally opposed any further school construction by CARE, insisting that under an earlier country director, Lauriac, the organization had marginalized the governor's office, ignored its recommendations, and kept its accounts private, which suggested that "the whole affair was somehow 'dishonest.'"[85] Reconciliation proved impossible, at least in the short term. CARE directed its efforts elsewhere, particularly to First Region, the westernmost. There, in spite of CARE's "less than excellent reputation in the [Malian] corridors of power," and in spite of the fact that Sylla had warned his colleague "against any collaboration with CARE," the governor seemed receptive to allowing CARE to work with local parents' associations in his region.[86] A couple of schools in Bafoulabé were in the offing, and if CARE pushed for it, the country director felt that it could readily have "a twenty to thirty school program in [First] Region alone." That was more than he wanted, and here the interests of the organization become clear.

CARE pursued school construction, which would become its most successful operation in Mali,[87] not, as its country director made clear, to construct schools, but "to improve our standing with the Government of Mali[,] at the same time giving us a legitimate reason for traveling, making field contacts, and, thereby, revealing other viable program possibilities."[88] The government itself did not see rural school construction as a major priority, and even CARE became convinced that local parents' associations could take care of the issue themselves. Yet building schools gave CARE representatives a reason to get out of Bamako – inasmuch as passes were required to travel – and to scout for other activities that could win government support and US-AID funding. In practice, the latter never seemed in doubt, but the former was tough to obtain. The Department of Social Affairs and the Director of National Cooperation were willing to entertain the possibility of working with CARE in spite of various misadventures in the past, but the Ministry of Rural Development, CARE's "ultimate counterpart," remained elusive. The goal then was to use "field exposure" – that is, the publicity and travel that accompanied development activities – to "move in through the middle" of the Malian administration and eventually to make CARE indispensable to some of its basic functions.[89]

---

[85] Memo, dated Aug. 3, 1977, drafted by Chris Conrad, re. Meeting at Governor's office, Aug. 1977, CARE 392. It is of course, quite possible that Governor Sylla wanted a piece of the budget.
[86] Tim Aston CARE-M to Ray Rignall, CARE-NY, Dec. 23, 1977, #549, CARE 392.
[87] Sanders, *Visit to CARE-Mali*, March 29, 1979, CARE 392.
[88] Tim Aston CARE-M to Ray Rignall, CARE-NY, Dec. 23, 1977, #549, CARE 392.
[89] Tim Aston CARE-M to Ray Rignall, CARE-NY, Dec. 23, 1977, #549, CARE 392.

Here it may be helpful to step back from First Region, Mali, and schools. CARE's objective was not to model its goals on those of African governments. It was precisely the opposite. CARE wanted to induce policy changes by Sahelian states by convincing them that they needed what CARE could provide. This was salesmanship as much as it was development or relief, and it set a pattern for years to come. In Niger, CARE stated this very clearly. The organization intended to "ensure survival [and to help] move the rural population beyond the subsistence level," but it also aimed to "supplement the capabilities of the Government of Niger to achieve CARE objectives" and "to work through the service ministries of the Government of Niger so that the changes that are introduced through the project will become institutionalized into the governmental structure."[90] CARE-Mali's goals were much the same. However, attentive to the fact that both governments sought to defend their independence – that as the chairman put it, "these governments are all sovereign, with their own ideas"[91] – CARE's representatives in Niamey knew that they could not "independently design or operate projects."[92] Rather, there as in Bamako, they needed either to persuade local authorities to follow their lead or to convince them that they were in fact leading all along. Ultimately, when it came to projects on nutrition, school construction, and drought relief, management was government. Still, it would have been hard for CARE to look less like a state. With small offices, a tiny staff, and a few vehicles in Bamako and Niamey, CARE was no powerhouse, at least at the time. Instead, it was a subcontractor for US-AID, and its staff sought to hustle up projects locally while navigating between Sahelian ministries and the organization's headquarters in New York. This is the paradox of the NGO: so eager to govern, so unlike a state.

"A PROJECT BEAUTIFUL IN ITS CONCEPTION"

CARE and the American Friends Services Committee (known as the Friends or the Quakers) could hardly have been more different, even if they held some things in common. Both began as minor players in what was becoming the major scene of Sahelian disaster relief, recovery, and

---

[90] Pre-Plan Paper, CARE-Niger, July 1975, CARE 407.
[91] American Council of Voluntary Agencies for Foreign Service (ACVAFS), *Special Meeting on Sahelian Drought*, July 16, 1973, CARE 142.
[92] CARE-Niger, *Pre-Plan Paper*, July 1975, CARE 407.

development.[93] As American organizations, both considered the formerly French Sahel to be unfamiliar territory. Yet CARE's intimacy with US-AID found no echo in the Friends' allergy to it; when a colleague from a sympathetic Christian organization urged the Friends to set aside its "self righteous disdain for using AID funds," his suggestion apparently went nowhere.[94] Where CARE sought openings – "we should have been here earlier" – the Friends debated whether they should be in the Sahel at all. They sought to intervene ethically, and agonized internally over how best to do so.[95] Had they been medical practitioners, CARE would be a surgeon, the Friends, homeopaths. Ironic, then, that the Friends' intervention harmonized with, and indeed may have built on, the Malian government's counter-insurgency plans of ten years earlier.

When the Friends entered the Sahel, they did so softly. They intended to intervene thoughtfully and in keeping with the Friends' mission to diminish or resolve conflict. Although they came on the scene after the drought emergency had abated, the Friends never wanted to be a development agency as such. They sought instead to cultivate peace. Thus, a paradox: they shook hands with a military government in which officers staffed both the ministries and the administration.[96] Ten years earlier, that army had pursued a brutal counter-insurgency campaign against Tuareg rebels. When the Friends arrived, the junta's treatment of political prisoners had made Mali the target of a human rights campaign, one of the first sustained against a sub-Saharan state (ch. 6). By the time that campaign reached its peak in the late 1970s, the Friends' involvement would be coming to an end, as had been planned all along. Still, in contrast with CARE's indifference to the political currents within Niger and, albeit to a lesser extent, Mali, the Friends were attuned to the Malian government's composition, its public declarations, and the initiatives of its local representatives, especially in the early years the *Commandant de Cercle* of Goundam, Captain Kibily Demba Diallo (Figures 2 and 3).

---

[93] E.g., in 1973, when AFSC gave $5,000 in medicines to Mali, CARE devoted $453,869 to relief in Niger; Dalton, *Summary Report: Sahel Region Drought*, Nov. 9, 1973, CARE 142.
[94] Memo to Patricia Hunt from Susan Smith, Re. NY, April 10 1975, dated April 23, 1975, AFSC 42559.
[95] See, e.g, *International Division, Meeting, All Africa Staff, Minutes*, Sept. 11, 1975, AFSC 42540.
[96] In fact, the Friends' scout expressed some confusion over which of his interlocutors were military officers and which were civilians; Povey, *Mali and the West African Drought: Report of a trip*, June 13 to July 28, 1974, Loft 7/15, p. 1. Hereafter, Povey, *Mali*.

FIGURE 2 "Tin Aïcha: Village Pilote," Eva M. and a Tin Aïcha resident; Loft, Box 7/17. Copyright Stanford University.

Most important, and most unlike CARE, the Friends did not seek to sell the Malians a project. Instead, they bought one of theirs. From late 1974, the Friends invested in a turnkey project that had been handed to George

FIGURE 3 Eva M., a man who is likely Kibily Demba Diallo, a resident, and the Tin Aïcha 4 × 4; Loft, Box 7/17. Copyright Stanford University.

Povey, the Friends' scout in the region, by Captain Diallo. The project had originally been conceived by Diallo and Ambeiry ag Rhissa, a local teacher of Tuareg origin;[97] the Friends and their local partners would further elaborate it in the years to come. Captain Diallo planned to settle 100 families of pastoral nomads on the northern shore of Lake Faguibine, a body of water that rises and falls with the seasons, generating marshes, pasturage, and the possibility that the pastoralists might grow crops while they reconstituted their herds. The land was disused, but had a weighty history. Not far away, a French, Barabish, and Kel Intessar column had decimated a raiding party decades earlier; more recently, the colonial administration had encouraged freed slaves of various nomadic groups to farm on the site.[98] Captain Diallo, too, intended to teach the new settlers to farm while the government would provide them health services, education, and marketing opportunities for women's craft production. Another 100 families would join each year. If this experiment in creating a model village of reformed nomads worked, others would follow, thereby

---

[97] By 2013, Ambeiry ag Rhissa had become a leading figure in the Tuareg rebel movement known as the *Mouvement National pour la Libération de l'Azawad* (MNLA).
[98] Hall (2011b), 168–69; Mariko (1993), 199–200; Clarke (2012); see also Marty (1993) and Giuffradi (2005).

sedentarizing the nomads and creating a new future for the Sahel. The first village, "100 sandy km from Goundam," was called Tin Aicha.[99]

The plan, thought Povey, was "beautiful in its conception."[100] Povey had traveled to Mali twice in 1973 to evaluate the possibility for "medical relief" and to deliver medicines on behalf of the Friends.[101] On one of those occasions he had met Captain Diallo,[102] and, the Friends believed, he had left a good impression on members of the Malian government by sharing his photographs of drought victims exclusively with the minister of health, rather than publicizing the calamity as others had done.[103] When the Friends sent Povey back to the Sahel in 1974, the trip was meant to take him to both Mali and Niger. However, after Povey encountered the Tin Aicha possibility, he never made it to Niamey. He seemed to have found a project that fit the Friends' criteria almost perfectly; it was small, both urgent and short-term, and practical. The organization called him back to Philadelphia for consultations.[104] With their blessing, Povey would return to Mali later that year to sign an agreement on the project with the Malian government. Mali would find settlers, provide land, and assure the services of a nurse. The Friends would provide funding, including the salaries of the Malian civil servants involved, and various supplies. Residents – that is, settlers – would cultivate while maintaining a collective herd; later, this would enable them to find the combination of farming and pastoralism that suited them best. This three-year program would cost $100,000 per year, to be borne equally by Mali and the Friends.[105] If the first wave of

---

[99] *Progress report: Project Tin Aicha*, Mali, Feb. through Sept. 1975, AFSC 42557.

[100] Patricia Hunt, Director, Africa/Middle East Program to International Service Division Executive Committee and Members of the Board, re. Possible Program Proposal for Mali, July 10, 1974, Loft 7/15.

[101] *AFSC [sic] and the Sahel*, June 27, 1974, Loft 7/15. The Friends already had relations with Mali, having organized seminars there, invited Malians to participate in its programming abroad, and received Malian visitors in Philadelphia. Povey, *Mali*, 3. Minister of Production Sidi Coulibaly was the most highly placed of the Friends' Malian friends.

[102] Povey, *Mali*, 6.

[103] AFSC (1982), 125. Such others included European journalists, whom the Malian government had harassed and detained. Significant bad blood between the government and foreign journalists, particularly Philippe Decraene of *le Monde*, would contribute to the production of an influential but distorted view of the drought and its effects; Boilley (2012 [1999]), 378–82; on such bad blood, see Amb. Fr. to MAE, Dec. 14, 1973, #66 DAM, CADN Bamako 60. For a critique of press coverage, see Copans (1975), Intro.; for an example, Held (1974).

[104] Patricia Hunt, Director, Africa/Middle East Program, to International Service Division Executive Committee and Members of the Board, re. Possible Program Proposal for Mali, July 10, 1974, Loft 7/15.

[105] AFSC, ISD, *Project for Rehabilitation of Drought Victims in Mali*, July 31, 1974, Loft 7/15; Eva M., AFSC, *Evaluation – Project Tin Aicha, February/September 1975*, Oct. 7,

settlement – 100 families representing some 500 people – succeeded, others would follow. Here the project stumbled. The CMLN had big schemes of its own, what the Friends would later refer to as "a massive and ambitious project designed to help 180,000 refugees."[106] By comparison, Tin Aicha was a tiny project hardly worth the trouble. The government refused to sign the agreement, but Minister of Production Sidi Coulibaly, who had championed the project, apparently persuaded his colleagues to support it as a pilot program for the larger initiative, which never came to pass. The government eventually accepted involvement of the Friends.[107] In any case, resettlement had already begun.

Captain Diallo's "volunteers" for the first wave of settlement at Tin Aicha had lost their herds to the drought. All had sought sanctuary in the camps established for "refugees" (more precisely, "internally displaced persons" or IDPs) outside Goundam and Douékiré.[108] In July 1973, these camps hosted some 1,400 people; by May of 1974, over 8,000 people lived in them. Diallo's concern was that "these nomads were going to live in total inactivity at the state's expense," but the evidence would seem to belie this idea.[109] The rains, were they to come, would begin in June or July. As it happened they did, but by June 1974, most farmers had left the camps to prepare their fields. Herders who had stock or opportunities elsewhere left when they could. Povey reported that 3,000 or so people remained in the camps; they were "the most destitute and hopeless" of the original population.[110] Still, Diallo indicated that the camps were going to be closed, and that land at Tin Aicha would be available to those who wanted it. These were his volunteers.[111]

Nearly half were gone within six months. A few families returned, and others came. Eva M., the Friends' field representative, arrived in February, 1975, and the pace of the project increased. The village was officially inaugurated in June, and at the end of the year the project grew from one

---

1975, Loft 7/16. George Loft and George Povey sought support for the project from the Ford and Rockefeller foundations, apparently without success. Some support came from OXFAM and more from the Dutch government; Loft 7/3 and 7/4. Note that I have chosen to omit Eva M.'s surname.

[106] AFSC (1982), 38.
[107] AFSC (1982), 39.
[108] Many nomads further to the east had sought refuge in Niger, which created real tensions between the two countries; see among others, DuBois (1974), Bugnicourt (1974).
[109] CdC Goundam, Captain Kibily Demba Diallo, *Rapport sur l'execution du projet Tin Aicha*, Nov. 4, 1975, AFSC 42549.
[110] Povey, *Mali*, 6; the quoted phrase appears in AFSC (1982), 36.
[111] AFSC (1982), 54, 56, 58.

village to two, the second being nearby.[112] A well, a cooperative, and a school had been established; with mixed results, the government had assigned a nurse, a teacher, and a "social assistant" to the community. A Qur'anic school teacher had arrived. New families were enrolled and livestock distributed to them (based on family size) until January, 1978. By June, 1979, 1,100 people lived in the two villages that made up the community of Tin Aicha.[113]

The bell jar initiative of founding and sustaining a new community in the Malian Sahel vibrated with a tension between two visions of the villagers' future. One, closer to that of the Malian administration, saw the village's semi-nomadic pastoralists (mostly Kel Intessar Tuareg) becoming sedentary farmers, thereby setting a precedent for the administration to follow elsewhere and realizing one of its long-held desires.[114] One could think of this as a revolutionary vision – Povey certainly did when he asked, "What form of social organization will evolve ... ? [And,] what will be the role of women in this new life?"[115] Surely the Friends' boast that women sat on an elected village council must be seen in that light.[116] The other vision, widely held among the Friends, saw the villagers being equipped with new skills and possibilities allowing them to "choose what life-style they wish to follow [, one] no longer dependent on a system which is ... unadapted or non-viable in post-drought conditions."[117] This new ability to adapt to the radically different conditions of the post-drought Sahel would in turn diminish the "tension and conflict between ethnic groups in the [drought] affected areas."[118] This, somewhat paradoxically, was a conservative vision in which some modified form of

---

[112] Ministre de l'Information, Correspondance de Presse de Goundam [sic], "Tin-Aicha: un an après," n.d. (29 June 1976), Archives de Cercle de Goundam; I thank Dr. Bruce Hall for sharing this document with me. On the establishment of the second village, see AFSC (1982), 62–3.

[113] AFSC (1982), 63.

[114] Lecocq (2010), 155–57; Giuffradi (2005), 814–17.

[115] Povey, *Mali*, 7. Here one might hear echoes of the Keita regime's policies in the North; Lecocq (2010).

[116] Eva M., "Letter from Mali [no. 2]," May 4, 1975, AFSC 42547. Eva M. believed that both the council and female representation on it were unique to Tin Aicha. As we saw in chapter 2, a great effort had been made to create village councils in the 1950s and 1960s; in some drafts of these reforms, women had been considered voters, in others as both voters and potential representatives.

[117] *Progress Report – Project Tin Aicha, Mali, Feb. through Sept. 1975*, Bamako, Oct. 7, 1975, AFSC 42557.

[118] *AFSC [sic] and the Sahel*, June 27, 1974, Loft 7/15. This latter hope did not come to pass, as Bruce Hall has argued persuasively in a book for which contemporary Tin Aicha represents a starting point; Hall (2011b), 5–9.

nomadic pastoralism would remain a real and viable choice for the participants; after all, the project aimed to reconstitute herds. During most of the six years that the Friends were directly involved with the project, the tension between these two visions went unspoken. Even when it was evoked – as, for example, in a letter between two of the Friends most engaged with the project – the language was ambivalent: "the distinction may or may not be important. How do you feel about this?"[119]

That dilemma – to restore or to transform – was one of two. The second was the bell jar itself. Until the end of 1977, the village's Friends-funded dispensary, which served a few hundred people, "received more medicine than all the rest of the *cercle* combined (150,000 people)."[120] Yet the Friends' original idea had not been to make a permanent intervention, but a targeted one for which "responsibility and control for all aspects must be in Malian hands asap [sic]."[121] The Friends had not come to stay, and the slow process of withdrawing from Tin Aicha began in 1978 as scheduled. The government took over the dispensary, and the community lost its ready access to medical supplies. Soon thereafter, a new field representative of the Friends, Stephen Morrissey, arrived and he set out "to integrate Tin Aicha into local governmental structures."[122] At the time, this meant both establishing the community as an official village and creating a section of the new, and sole, political party, the Union Démocratique du Peuple Malian (UDPM), which the CMLN had spawned (ch. 6). The politics of this on the ground must have been complex, but they escape my sources. Still, in 1980, the community would be officially recognized as a village, meaning that its residents no longer paid taxes through the chief of their nomadic fraction. In the eyes of the state, they were no longer nomads, but this way of thinking excluded those who had left with their livestock. A decade later, the Quakers too had pulled up their stakes. Other NGOs, both foreign and domestic, had emerged to pick up where they had left off.[123]

Was this success? The Friends had long been skeptical about the Malian state: attuned to its vagaries, in search of allies within it, and sensitive to the possibility that it was always eavesdropping.[124] They were not entirely

---

[119] Susan Smith to Eva M., Nov. 11, 1975, #P-M 27, AFSC 42551.
[120] AFSC (1982), 83. Doctors Without Borders has recently pursued such projects in southern Mali, using a much larger jar.
[121] Susan Smith to Eva M., Aug. 13, 1975, #P-M 22, AFSC 42551.
[122] AFSC (1982), 66, 130, 132.
[123] Clarke (2012).
[124] Re. the latter, see Hunt to Allains, Nov. 26, 1975, # WA 35, and Susan Smith to Allains, July 29, 1975, #WA 30, AFSC 42544.

Governing Famine

naïve to the complexities of supporting a military government in its attempts to restructure the lives of one nomadic population, the Kel Intessar, with which the army had so recently allied to fight another, the Kel Adagh. Captain Diallo, the Friends' primary interlocutor, was often "obstructive," and in 1975, when a Quaker delegation visited project manager Eva M. in Goundam and Tin Aicha, a sergeant shadowed them.[125] In short, the Friends were acutely aware of the difficulties of reconciling a desire as "Quakers ... to remain unallied ... and receptive to all" with the possibility of "identifying with the oppressors" in West Africa.[126]

In a few short years, the Friends had played an important role in producing both a community and a unit of government. Acutely aware that "independence means something other than unofficial colonialism"[127] – an attitude some of the Friends saw in their peer organizations – they had done everything in their power to coordinate closely with the Malian government and to remain attentive to its prerogatives. Carefully distant from one state, and certainly from US-AID, the Friends were proud to be allied with another. Although they were quite aware that Mali's military government was a difficult partner, they also asserted that Malians must own the project, and were pleased to note, for example, that representatives of both the Ministry of Education and that of Defense had given speeches at the ceremony inaugurating the Tin Aicha project on Eva M.'s arrival in 1975.[128] CARE, the Quakers noted, was not so clever.

POSTCOLONIAL SOLIDARITIES

Like the Quakers, the Paris-based *Association Française d'Amitié et de Solidarité avec les Peuples d'Afrique* (AFASPA) pursued an activism grounded in the language of friendship. Yet AFASPA never practiced a naïve antipolitics. Far from it. The association's political analysis was clear, perhaps too clear. AFASPA's activists knew very well what they thought of West Africa's politics, and they had strong ideas on how to engage. It is easy enough to craft a Goldilocks fable of outside activism in the Sahel in which organizations like CARE are too cynical, the Friends

---

[125] George Loft to AFSC, "Loft/Phila. No. 1," Philadelphia, Oct. 2, 1975, Loft 7/16.
[126] Memo to Patricia Hunt from Susan Smith, Re. NY, April 10 1975, dated April 23, 1975, AFSC 42559; *International Division, Meeting, All Africa Staff, Minutes*, Sept. 11, 1975, AFSC 42540. The Quakers had faced such challenges elsewhere; Feldman (2007).
[127] Memo to Patricia Hunt from Susan Smith, Re. NY, April 10 1975, dated April 23, 1975, AFSC 42559.
[128] Susan Smith to Allains, July 29, 1975, # WA 30, AFSC 42544.

naïve, and AFASPA somewhere in between. More revealing, however, especially given AFASPA's Communist roots, was neither its cynicism nor its "friendliness," but the question of whether its political vision expressed solidarity or what Aimé Césaire, in his 1956 letter of resignation from the French Communist Party, had termed "fraternalism." For Césaire that neologism captured a phenomenon on the Left, "maybe not paternalism ... but something that could be taken for it ... [as a] brother, a big brother, swollen with his superiority and sure of his experience, takes you by the hand ... to lead you on the road on which he knows Reason and Progress can be found."[129] AFASPA was not alone in struggling to balance its commitment to solidarity with its belief in the power of its own political vision. That dilemma was both acute and widely shared at the time of the famine, when Catholic charities were especially active in France and on the ground in the Sahel, and when labor unions and business associations alike contributed to the relief effort.[130] Reaching far beyond the specialized press and even the daily newspapers, French television had broadcast harrowing reports of conditions in Niger and Upper Volta, spurring viewers to action. Beginning in May 1973, letters from ordinary citizens streamed into President Pompidou's offices, asking that their government do more to aid the drought-stricken countries in Africa. Many correspondents stressed their belief that France had a particular obligation to its former colonies, which had contributed mightily to the nation's defense in the two world wars. Others pointed, too, to the presence in France itself of immigrants from impoverished regions of the ex-empire, insisting that they had fled one misery for another. Perhaps, one citizen suggested, the air force, and even the navy, could "bombard the tribes, the villages, the desolated towns with sacks of rice and wheat?"[131]

Such letters demonstrate that postimperial solidarities can hardly be easy ones, but AFASPA's ran deeper than most. Founded by veteran anticolonialists such as Pierre Morlet – a Communist union leader, early political militant in Soudan, and a close associate of Modibo Keita's[132] – and the

---

[129] Cesaire (2010 [1956]), 149. I have slightly altered Chike Jeffers' translation.

[130] See, e.g., the list of active assocations in *l'Aide de la France aux états de la Sahel victimes de la sécheresse* (1973), 20. Catholic associations were particularly active, including running the refugee camps around Niamey. Taithe argues that in the 1970s French Catholic and secular traditions merged in a new humanitarianism represented by Doctors Without Borders and *Médecins du Monde*; (2004).

[131] FPR 555, d. 2.

[132] Morlet had established the Communist study group in Soudan Français along with another Frenchman, Maurice Fayette, in July 1946. Morlet was also a founding member

Marxist geographer and historian Jean Suret-Canale,[133] AFASPA emerged as an organization dedicated to defending the US-RDA leaders imprisoned by the junta in Mali (ch. 6). Coincidentally, AFASPA came into being at nearly the same moment as famine began to strike in the Sahel, and its commentary quickly linked political repression in Mali, emigration to France, and the bundled phenomena of drought, famine, and relief. That set of political concerns would itself soon migrate, or at least drift, to other African issues, including the liberation of the Portuguese colonies, antiapartheid activism, the question of the Western Sahara, and the persecution of intellectuals such as the Camerounian writer Mongo Beti. All, however, were taken as evidence of "neocolonialism." The analysis remained the same, and Mali continued to hover near the center of AFASPA's preoccupations.[134]

As one of its first concrete gestures, in September, 1973, AFASPA contributed a significant amount of medical supplies to Mali's official labor union, l'Union Nationale des Travailleurs du Mali (UNTM). Such activism was immediate, hands-on, and direct. In the opinion of AFASPA it represented the "solidarity" of French workers, particularly those united in the powerful Confédération Générale du Travail (CGT), with their Malian counterparts; in acknowledging the gift, leaders of the UNTM would express the same idea. However, AFASPA's action strained its relations with the French Ministry of Foreign Affairs at the same time as the association was trying to prod the government into devoting more resources to famine relief. While delivering the medicine to Mali with as much publicity as he could muster, Secretary-General Claude Gatignon had declared that French colonial and neocolonial policies had caused the famine afflicting the country.[135]

---

of the Union Soudanaise, having been a member of the Parti Démocratique du Soudan that preceded it. Morlet would eventually be expelled from the AOF by the colonial administration, only to return as a labor negotiator; int., Gabou Diawara, Aug. 16, 2005, Bamako; Danioko (1984), 41, 42, 264; Suret-Canale (1994), 55–56.

[133] Suret-Canale was a doctrinaire figure somewhat marginalized in French academic life. Although his anticolonial stance was strident and long-held, West African intellectuals often did not hold him in high regard. There were at least two reasons for this: his long support for Sekou Touré; and his dismissive attitude toward the work of Cheikh Anta Diop. See Bianchini (2011), including Dieng's afterword.

[134] Guinea, too, held a special status, and its government was spared criticism.

[135] *Bulletin d'Information de l'AFASPA*, 1974 (un-numbered); B. B. Doucouré, "l'AFASPA (association française) fait don de médicaments aux travailleurs maliens," *l'Essor*, 6695, Sept. 20, 1973. The French ambassador remembered the comment bitterly one year later; *Synthèse* 13/74, July 16, 1974, #17/DAM, CADN Bamako 44.

This can hardly have been expected to play well among the French diplomatic corps, but AFASPA's politics was always one of opposition, even when it had direct access to government figures in positions of authority. Following AFASPA's gift of medicines, Gatignon wrote to the French Secretary of State for Cooperation, as well as various senators and legislators, demanding more aid for the Sahel. His letter urged the government to include, in the budget for the year to come, a real response to the request of the Sahelian states as expressed in the Ouagadougou conference at which CILSS was founded.[136] In the National Assembly a few months earlier, the deputy representing Montreuil, Louis Ordu, who was also a member of AFASPA's board, had repeatedly demanded to know how the government intended to confront the Sahelian crisis, "in light of France's particular responsibilities in the affected countries." The offical response was clear: France had offered its aid as early as October 1972, but ultimately it was up to the West African states to "establish a program to counter the effects of the drought and to request the cooperation of foreign governments and international institutions."[137] Still, in both 1973 and 1974, the Secretary of State for African Affairs invited AFASPA's leadership to meetings with his ministry, other relevant state agencies, and fellow nongovernmental organizations at work in the Sahel.[138] Defending the generosity of the French state, and its attention to the ongoing need for aid to the Sahel, in 1973 the Secretary for African Affairs insisted that France was doing what it could, and that it would do more in the year to come.[139] The question then was to whom to send money, and for what. There was no agreement on why, or why the Sahel ailed.

The question had, of course, been raised. *"De quoi meurent les Africains?"* asked an open letter published in *le Monde* on May 22, 1973, and in a more complete version in the *Nouvel Observateur* on the 9th of June.[140] "What are Africans dying of?" asked its signatories, an

---

[136] Gatignon, S.G. AFASPA to Sec. d'Etat à la Coopération, Nov. 5, 1973; Gatignon, S.G. AFASPA to M. le Président [ms. note, "lettre adressée à tous les présidents de groupe, Assemblée Nationale et Senat"], Nov. 6, 1973, ADSSD 67J5.

[137] "Réponses des ministres aux questions écrites, Réponse inséré dans le J.O. du 7 juillet 1973 ...," clipping offered "bien fraternellement" to Gatignon, ADSSD 67J118. Ordu posed his question on May 12, as he had done nine days earlier.

[138] Sec. d'Etat aux Affaires Etrangères to Pres., AFASPA, Nov. 9, 1973, #04298, ADSSD 67J6; Sec. d'Etat aux Affaires Etrangères to Prés., AFASPA, March 11, 1974, #009895 CAB/CT I, ADSSD 67J118.

[139] Sec. d'Etat aux Affaires Etrangères to Gatignon, Sec. Gen., AFASPA, Nov. 12, 1973, #43151, ADSSD 67J6.

[140] The letters were published in reaction to coverage of the Sahel in each journal. *Le Monde* had relied heavily on the agronomist and ecologist René Dumont, whose point of view was not appreciated by many Marxists because he was thought to find African farmers

ephemeral Collective of Africanist Researchers (*Collectif des chercheurs Africanistes*). The Collective provided an unambiguous answer: "policies [*politique*] of development." Such policies were, in their analysis, themselves embedded in the search for profit and the logic of the market. Nominally independent governments simply pursued old colonial policies. The disaster was not only compounded, but ultimately created by the venality and complicity of the French state and the African political elite.[141] Although French unions and some associations of African workers in France rallied around that analysis, it struck skeptics as too neat and formulaic.[142] More importantly, it angered key players in the world of Franco-African politics.

The Collective said bluntly that the first object of its critique had to be the French government and its "so-called cooperation." That object reacted. After the first editorial appeared in *le Monde*, Jacques Foccart's office was abuzz. In the margin of the newspaper clipping, René Journiac, his adjoint, proposed having the French domestic intelligence agency, *les Renseignements Généraux* or "R.G.," determine the political orientation of these "so-called researchers," as if the answer was not already clear.[143] The signatories – including Georges Balandier, Claude Meillassoux, Jean Copans, Catherine Coquery-Vidrovitch, Yves Person, and Jean-Pierre Olivier de Sardan, among others – taught in universities, worked for ORSTOM, or were members of the CNRS. They represented the core of two generations of French Africanists, one that had formed around Balandier and his "engaged sociology," and a second, their students, who were more resolutely Marxist.[144] In one fashion or another, all were civil servants of the state whose policies they decried. Their institutional links did not determine their collective stance, but part of the government hoped they would. A memo from Jacques Foccart's office proposed sending them a warning by cutting back on the funding of those institutions. "We can't let them get away with it ('*il ne faut pas les manquer*'),"

and herders themselves at fault, and because he had published a frank and stinging critique of Africa's young regimes early in their history; see Dumont (1962). Dumont was a pioneer in political ecology. As for *le Nouvel Observateur*, its editors had apparently decided to send their automobile correspondent to cover the story. See Copans (1975), 13, 24, and letters to the *N.O.* by Claude Meillassoux and Guy Nicolas reprinted in the same volume; (1975), 37–39.

[141] "De Quoi ... ?" as reprinted in *Comité* (1974), 257–59.
[142] Held (1974). "Les Travailleurs africains de la région parisienne sont invités par plusieurs associations syndicales et de jeunesse ... " June 25, 1973, 75/PMA, FPU 2827.
[143] MS note by Journiac on clipping of "De quoi meurent ... " *le Monde*, May 22, 1973, FPR 555.
[144] Coquery-Vidrovitch (1999), Dozon (2002).

someone scrawled in a note pinned to the clipping. Apparently they did not; some researchers lost their positions, and others were temporarily blocked from conducting their fieldwork.[145]

The government then undertook a campaign of counter-publicity, insisting that the French state had made great efforts to ease the effects of the famine, the causes of which were natural.[146] In a rare piece of political theater, on a visit to Niger the habitually discreet Jacques Foccart had himself photographed shoveling grain into sacks of rice for distribution to drought victims.[147] If the Marxist argument about structural inequality had been made with vigor and force, it was also a counter-argument to the idea that French cooperation was relieving a natural disaster, rather than one caused by markets and conditioned by inequality. Again, however, our own question is not what caused the famine (or indeed the drought) but what caused its relief. At the time, the question was what form that relief should take. What was the proper role of the state, of international institutions, and of NGOs in saving the Sahel? More than any other, such questions troubled French diplomats and Foccart's deputies. They lay behind the diplomats' efforts to stave off a proposal to delegate a co-ordinating role to the United Nations, which they feared would only advance "anglo-saxon" interests.[148] No less importantly, they motivated Foccart's efforts to reassert the primacy of the state over private associations that had stepped in to fill the gap left by its own perceived inaction.[149] They allow us to see how different conceptions of political power and its object emerged in this moment of crisis. They reveal how different actors sought to offer a new sense of what government is and could be.

Léopold Sedar Senghor, who actually governed, had something to say about that. Let us turn again to the questions the Collective posed: "What are Africans dying of?" and "Who profits from 'independence' and pseudo-'development'?" Their answer was twofold: a politics of

---

[145] Haski (1974), 27.
[146] See, e.g., A. Richard's memo critiquing poor media coverage and understanding of French government efforts; *Famine dans le Sahel*, June 7, 1973, FPR 555.
[147] *le Parisien libéré*, March 1, 1974, clipping in FPU 1527.
[148] SEAE, Mission Permanente d'Aide et de Coopération auprès de la Rép. de H-V, *Rapport de Mission: Conférence des chefs d'état des pays sahéliens touchés par la sécheresse*, Ouagadougou, Sept. 4 to 12, 1973 and M. Lucet, de la part de M. Schonen (OAA, Rome) to MAE, June 21, 1973, #1768/1770, a/s du PNUD et du Sahel; both in FPU 2820.
[149] This is expressed most clearly in Richard's memo *Famine dans le Sahel*, June 7, 1973, FPR 555.

Governing Famine 203

development in which international capital and local rulers colluded. Delivered in a long speech to a party congress, Senghor's reaction was as vigorous as one might expect. Neither agronomists nor meteorologists had supported the intervention of the Collective, he noted. These were instead social scientists and expatriate professors in the Universities of Dakar and Abidjan, "former Negrologists who, howling with the wolves to avoid being eaten, have moved from Negrophilia to Negrophagia (*d'anciens négrologues, qui, hurlant avec les loups pour ne pas être mangés, sont passés de la négrophilie à la négrophagie*)." In Senghor's analysis, the famine was not produced by policies, still less by politics, but by historical forces against which the government had done what it could by lowering taxes on peasants and encouraging the production of grains and other foods over cash crops.[150]

The harsh rhetoric of French intellectuals who targeted Senegal, and Senghor in particular, struck him as a kind of neocolonialism, "a veritable re-conquest, worse – let's dare to say it – a new slave trade (*traite des nègres*)."[151] Senghor attempted to rally his troops by beating the drum of negritude and to defend his flanks by firing on the category of intellectuals whom one might have thought could be his allies: "Let's have the courage to say it to our comrades on the Left – neo-colonialism, even racism, has spread and is eating away at the French Left." This was no dialogue. A "Sahel Information Committee," which emerged from the Collective and was allied with Senegalese workers in France, continued to ask, "Who's feeding on the famine?"[152] However necessary, from their point of view – or "neocolonial" from that of Senghor – nothing could have been more natural than the collective intervention of French Leftist intellectuals into a debate on the policy of their government in its former empire, in the then-Third World, or elsewhere. For American activists, on the other hand, the Sahel was distant and unknown. Yet it is between Harlem and West Africa that the Sahelian drama generated new solidarities.

---

[150] The historical argument had been made early in the drought by Cissoko (1968).
[151] L. S. Senghor, "La Néo-traite des nègres ou la deuxième guerre de l'indépendance," *le Soleil*, 975, July 23, 1973. Two contemporary events compelled this statement: the drought and the reaction of intellectuals to it; and the death in prison of a Senegalese opposition figure, Oumar Blondin Diop, in which the Senegalese state and indeed Senghor himself were thought to be implicated.
[152] In 1974, the Comité Information Sahel published a book entitled *Qui se nourrit de la famine en Afrique?* It includes a statement from the UGTSF; *Comité* (1974), 268–70. On the origins of the Committee, see pp. 255–56.

BETWEEN HARLEM AND THE SAHEL

"The Sahel has to survive. If not, neither will the poor of Mississippi or Harlem," wrote the leaders of RAINS (Relief for Africans in Need in the Sahel), an African-American coalition formed to fight the famine.[153] That argument might have been more true of Montreuil than Mississippi, but behind the geographic particularism lay a broader argument according to which the market economy had impoverished West Africa and African-America alike, while a "subtle form of racism still abroad in the world" limited African nations' room for maneuver.[154] Chaired by Detroit Congressman Charles C. Diggs, Jr. and Columbia University anthropologist and former ambassador to Upper Volta Dr. Elliot Skinner, RAINS was founded in 1973 as a coalition of mostly African-American associations under the broad umbrella of the Inter-religious Foundation for Community Organization (IFCO).[155] The purpose of RAINS was to raise awareness of the crisis in the Sahel and funds for its relief.[156] The well-known photographer Chester Higgins, Jr. helped with the first task when the IFCO sent him on assignment to the Sahel then used his photographs for fund-raising and publicity. Although activities such as Higgins' tour were aimed at generating contributions from individual donors, the strategy of RAINS' leadership was to prod the American government into providing "direct and massive" assistance to its Sahelian counterparts. $50,000 in direct donations was welcome, but RAINS claimed the allocation of $30 million for the "rehabilitation of the Sahel" by the U.S. Congress as a greater victory. A press release from the State Department noted that those funds had been added to the Foreign Assistance Act due partly to pressure from "Black groups" such as Africare and from others such as the Friends.[157] Of course, a significant

---

[153] Undated (1974?) RAINS document, Hoover 13/8. The phrase echoes an idea expressed by Bissau-Guinean revolutionary Amilcar Cabral; Westad (2005), 211. Johnson attests to Cabral's influence amongst African-American activists interested in Africa; (2007), 146.
[154] Skinner, *Suffering in the Sudan-Sahel: a Void to Fill*, n.d. (1974?), IFCO 41/2.
[155] Founded in 1966 to bring minority churches and the United Presbyterian Church together, the IFCO had by the mid-1970s become "the largest minority-controlled foundation in the country"; *Guide to the IFCO Records*, Schomburg Center, NYPL. The IFCO worked to channel funds to community-based organizations, particularly minority congregations with activist agendas; *Guide*; *IFCO's Task Force on African Affairs*, n.d., IFCO 2/7; *Origin of IFCO*, n.d. (1974), IFCO 2/19. On Congressman Diggs, see Minter, Hovey, and Cobb, eds. (2008), 131–33.
[156] IFCO/RAINS policy statement, n.d. (1974), IFCO 41/1.
[157] *Origin of IFCO*, n.d. (1974), IFCO 2/19. Bureau of Public Affairs, Dept. of State, Office of Media Services, "Emergency Disaster Relief for Sahel," press release, Aug. 1973, Hoover 15.

portion of this money would flow through US-AID, and CARE would compete for it.[158] Yet RAINS' policy was to orient its own contributions via CILSS, ensuring that Sahelian governments would have "complete control ... no strings attached."[159] They intended to bolster CILSS by pulling together the combined energies of foreign NGOs under the national governments of the Sahel, thereby reinforcing rather than reducing African sovereignty.[160]

This was a proudly hands-off form of activism, and it took the African Diaspora as its natural frame. A decade after African independence, such politics was being rejuvenated as post-Civil Rights era African-American activists increasingly looked to the continent for allies in a broadening struggle. "It is time for black Americans to go beyond rhetoric, Afros, Dashikis, and African names," activists proclaimed, while RAINS pursued relief in the Sahel and revolution in Southern Africa.[161] This politics was not entirely novel, but it was different, even in its minor expressions from that of the French Left. When AFASPA sought a meeting with the Nigerien ambassador to Paris, they invited him to their offices in the 11th arrondissement. On the other end of the spectrum, the African-American NGO Africare actually had its offices in the Nigerien embassy in Washington, DC, and Hamani Diori served as its chairperson.[162] Founded in 1971, Africare's first project was to provide a public health infrastructure, particularly paramedical training, in the Diffa region of Niger; it was therefore one of the rare NGOs present in the Sahel before

---

[158] By 1974, perceived mismanagement of the U.S. government's relief effort would be the subject of considerable controversy; Sheets and Morris (1974) and "Ex-official [William Morris] blasts U.S. Aid Effort," *International Bulletin* 1, 15, Aug. 9, 1974, press clipping in Hoover 15.

[159] RAINS flyer, n.d. (1974?), Hoover 13/8.

[160] RAINS proposal, Feb. 1974; Ms. notes on "Report from Joy," July 12, 1974; see also clipping "Education for Development and the Sahel," *Action for Development*, Nov. 1974; IFCO 41/3.

[161] *Africare*, eight-page report, n.d. (1973?), Hoover 13/ 2. RAINS' original Sahel focus was meant to be temporary. By 1977, the IFCO would pay closer attention to Southern Africa, supporting the Zimbabwe African National Union (ZANU) in its struggle against White minority rule in Rhodesia as it previously had supported Cabral's *Partido Africano da Independência da Guiné e Cabo Verde* (African Party for the Independence of Guinea [-Bissau] and Cape Verde, or PAIGC). Signaling this shift in emphasis, the final "S" would be dropped from the name RAINS; Minutes of the IFCO task force on African Affairs, Aug. 27, 1977, IFCO 41/5.

[162] From before the organization's inception Diori had been supporting the efforts of the ex-Peace Corps volunteers who would found Africare; Campbell (2011), 3, 5, 14. Future honorary chairmen included President Kenneth Kuanda of Zambia and Voltaique Minister of Development Antoine Dakouré.

the worst effects of the drought. In its early years, Africare worked entirely within the Sahel, with offices in Bamako, Ouagadougou, and Niamey.[163] This was no postimperial circumstance. With roots in the Peace Corps, Africare selfconsciously adopted an African-American profile – its founders were White – and deliberately framed its activities as representing "an African response to an African problem."[164] Such responses were direct, in keeping with the common wisdom of the time. Africare focused on five areas of intervention: "child spacing/maternal and child health; water resource development; nutrition and food production; training of paramedical personnel; consultation for long-range planning." The bundle was both ambitious and focused, aimed particularly at public health initiatives and at "training new leadership rather than on maintaining outside control through foreign assistance and direction."[165]

Yet Africare, too, was working with the American embassy in Niamey, and after 1978, captured US-AID money, which would soon provide 80% of its revenue.[166] This was to be expected. Africare and RAINS had close ties to both Sahelian and American governments because Samuel Adams (of Africare) and Skinner (of RAINS) had served as U.S. ambassadors in the Sahel, respectively to Niger (1968–69) and Upper Volta (1966–69). As Deputy Assistant Secretary of State for Aid, Adams had become one of the highest-ranking African-Americans in the diplomatic corps. The two men knew how government worked on both continents, and Skinner – who had returned to academia following his service – was direct about it: the Sahel consisted of "non-concentrate countries," in which the U.S. role was to be limited. Only intense activism could change that, and it would do more than bring aid to the Sahel. Such activism would also assert African-Americans' full citizenship by demonstrating that "Black people in this

---

[163] Hoover 13/2; Campbell (2011).
[164] "Africare," Hoover 13/2; Campbell (2011).
[165] "Africare," Hoover 13/2, page 2, original emphasis.
[166] "Africare," Hoover 13/2, page 6; *Africare Annual Report, 1976*, Hoover 13/2; McCleary (2009), 192 note 8. The figure of 80% comes from Campbell (2011), 197. See also, Harold Sillcox, CARE-Niger to Peter Reitz, CARE, NY, Nov. 6, 1973; *Pre-Plan Paper, CARE-Niger, July 1975*, CARE 407; and Donald Sanders, *Visit to CARE-Mali*, March 29, 1979, CARE 392. CARE saw itself as being in competition with Africare and at one point contemplated legal action to defend its own name; Board of Directors meeting, Oct. 24, 1973, CARE 9. A decade later, at an NGO conference with government officials in Niamey, CARE was still at pains to distinguish itself from Africare; CARE-Niger, *Discursive Report*, May 1983, CARE 841.

country have the right to insist that their hard-earned tax dollars ... be used to help our people in Africa."[167]

Given their particular histories, could RAINS, or for that matter Africare, be "neocolonial?" The term poorly captures an organization such as Africare aimed at integrating itself into the structures of African government by subordinating its programs to national ministries of health. Both Africare and RAINS sought explicitly to reinforce African governments rather than to work around them. Can the solidarity of Harlem-based African-American activists with Sahelian states and societies be considered "governmental" in any meaningful way? Can that of French Leftists?

CONCLUSION

I argued above that famine relief conditioned a future in which a widening gulf emerged between new states and suffering populations, and that in novel ways international NGOs began to fill that gap. Like wedges, they widened it. Another gap was opening, that between state and "government" in its broadest sense. In a long slow process that began but did not end here, a new phenomenon I dub nongovernmentality began to emerge. It had roots on the Left, where voluntary agencies, trade unionists, and activists in the Diaspora had unwittingly set in motion a course of actions and gestures that would subtly and slowly recondition Sahelian states and redefine what government was. That shift was far too incremental for social scientists, acting in their role as public intellectuals, to recognize, and it would move in a dramatically different direction in decades to come. Yet such a process was only possible because the functions of newly (some argued partially) sovereign states had mapped onto the functions of government emergent from the imperial social welfare states of the mid-twentieth century. States were meant to assure security, health, education, and infrastructure. They also offered varying degrees of protection for their markets, although in the Sahel those markets were often franco-African.

The postcolonial states sought to defend the interests of others with whom they stood in solidarity; each in its own way, Mali, Niger, and their neighbors expressed such principles in the brief romance of the nonaligned movement and in broadcasting pan-African sentiment. That orientation helps explain how and why the government of Hamani Diori in particular

[167] Skinner, *Suffering in the Sudan-Sahel*, IFCO 41/2.

beckoned to external partners, and why they in turn took up its initiatives with enthusiasm. Such appeals to international solidarity might invoke either nostalgia or a world-weary déjà vu in the present, but it is the growing gap between state and government that ought to draw our attention. If we take government to mean the collective attempt to sustain the conditions of life, or to "husband" populations, we might number among those functions schooling, public health, surveillance over the quantity and quality of the food supply, and so on. In the period of study, Sahelian states shared such functions with external actors in ways that were not always visible. Although the political diagnosis of that particular time identified their condition as neocolonial, we might phrase it differently now. In hindsight, one could argue that although the NGOs active in the Sahel were not states, they exercised a peculiar and ever more pervasive form of nongovernmental rationality. Without any real design, balancing between solidarity and self-interest, such organizations laid the groundwork for a future expansion of nonsovereign governmental activity in the Sahel and beyond.

6

Human Rights and Saharan Prisons

The introduction asked whether the domestication of human rights should be counted as one of Africa's triumphs, or if the conquest of Africa is a triumph for human rights. This chapter seeks preliminary answers to these questions among a clutch of Malian political prisoners of the 1970s and the international campaigns of human rights and solidarity generated around them. It scrutinizes two strands of an evolving postcolonial politics: one based in solidarities formed around shared political principles and experiences in Communist study groups, labor unions, and anticolonial parties; the other grounded in the hybrid set of Enlightenment ideals and contemporary tactics known as human rights.[1] It asks what kinds of power lay behind the defense of the powerless in the Sahara and the Sahel.

In the post-Cold War period, human rights became "the dominant moral narrative by which world politics was organized."[2] The decade between the end of the Cold War and the global war that followed September 11, 2001 also marked the "golden years – or at least the boom decade – of nongovernmental politics."[3] West Africa had its place in that parade. As one wave in what appeared to be a rising tide of democratization – marked by the overthrow of Moussa Traore in 1991 and the establishment of the Third Republic the following year– Mali became a darling of the international community and a "good student" of the Bretton Woods institutions. *The New York Times* hailed the country

---

[1] Here I am adopting a narrow view of "human rights" focusing on freedom of speech, freedom to dissent, and conditions of detention as this view prevailed in the 1970s and was the subject of the debates analyzed herein.
[2] McLagan (2007), 304; also Balfour and Cadava (2004), 278.
[3] Feher (2007), 21.

as "an example of what the struggling African continent can become."[4] The country's independent press seemed to thrive, feeding largely on calls for proposals, contracts, and employment opportunities that major funders such as US-AID placed within its pages. Private radio stations mushroomed as well, sometimes with grants from the same AID or from the *Fédération Européenne des Radios Libres,* but thanks also to funding sources that were much less apparent.[5] The transformations taking place in the Sahelian countries, of which Mali provides perhaps the most dramatic example, were not unique to that region of the continent. Political decentralization, the selling off of state enterprises, and the rapid expansion of civil society took place across Africa.[6] In a keen study of Malawi in those and later years, Harri Englund points out that in that southern country, NGO workers translated human rights as freedom, which came to mean personal freedom.[7] As in Mali, the very core of that principle seemed too often to be best expressed cynically if aptly as "freedom to starve."

In the eyes of many Malians, democracy meant disorder, and freedom of speech meant freedom to excoriate the president, his family, and all forms of authority.[8] In the late 1990s, I was stunned by the white-hot and vitriolic political discourse on talk radio. Disk jockeys and callers insulted the president *"père et mère,"* as Malians would say. The insults never truly abated. But in the late 1990s, a minority collection of opposition parties (COPPO) marched in the streets demanding a campaign of civil disobedience to oppose a government it condemned as illegitimate.[9] Teachers and students lost more than one academic year to constant strikes. The students often took to the streets, trashing schools and government buildings in the capitol and in provincial towns alike.[10] They found allies in the unemployed and uneducated youth who were not as lucky but no less angry than they. I remember vividly that when power cuts struck Bamako's Niarela

---

[4] Marc Lacey, "Powell begins Africa tour with praise for developments in Mali," *New York Times* May 24, 2001, pg. A11. See also, along the same lines, "Democracy in Mali," *New York Times* April 29, 1996, pg. A26; Pringle (2005). There is no full history of Mali in this period, but valuable studies include, in addition to those cited below, Sow (2008).

[5] Camara (1998), 63; see also Thierry (2005).

[6] See, e.g., Robins, (2008); Englund (2006); Ferguson (2006). On the challenges such developments pose to "weak" states, see Ferguson and Gupta (2002).

[7] Englund (2006).

[8] More generally, Claude Fay offers the best analysis of the collapse of authority in 1990s Mali, based on research in Bamako and Maasina; Fay (1995).

[9] Sow (2008), 424–28, 431–34.

[10] Fay (1995), 30–32.

neighborhood, young men burned tires in the streets, claiming to light the night. They generated only the smoke and stench of burning rubber, but redefined an act that had so recently formed part of the repertoire of open rebellion as an anodyne effort at service provision and a rebuke of a privatizing power company (in those years *Energie du Mali* was known as "*Energie du Mal*"). The government was struggling to smother the street justice known as "*Article 320*," which condemned suspected thieves to be set alight for 300 CFA in petrol and 20 CFA in matches.[11] I saw a man chased, pummeled, and stoned by a crowd between the mosque and the railroad tracks before a policeman got to him and stood straddling his crumpled figure, pistol drawn to keep the crowd at bay. It was the bravest thing I'd ever seen a policeman do, because at the time, most of those pistols had no cartridges and at best a round in the chamber. If the capital might at times have seemed scarcely governable then, a combustible combination of damning religious arguments and mob violence resurged after 2009, occasionally sending individual government ministers, spokeswomen, and elected representatives into hiding in fear for their lives, and laying the groundwork for further violence during the political crisis that began in 2012.[12]

In this charged political context, free speech and the right to dissent appeared to have been woven – however crudely and certainly not seamlessly – into Malian practices of government. Regardless of who had done the weaving, permitting free speech and unmuzzling the media had become elements of governmental rationality, the value of which seemed to lie precisely in the fact that they translated "out" to international organizations, foreign governments, and the omnipresent donor nations. The fact that such practices translated "in" with less success was the cost of doing business, that is, of governing and "nongoverning," as Mali's entrepreneurs hastily set up NGOs to compete for foreign contracts. The language of human rights was only one of several that they sought to master as they worked to convert foreign funding into local capital. The sharpest critiques of this process, such as those offered by the essayist and ex-Minister of

---

[11] For reasons unknown to me, this same phenomenon is referred to as *bisaaba ani duuru*, or 175 CFA, in Bambara.

[12] In the rainy season of 2009, during a vicious debate over the revision of the country's laws on marriage and the family, public proponents of the law suffered death threats, some of them broadcast over the radio. Less than three years later, a mob beat interim president Dioncounda Traore nearly to death in the presidential palace. One could cite other examples, which contrast strongly with the relative security enjoyed by most residents and visitors throughout this twenty-year period.

Culture Aminata Dramane Traoré, defended human rights in the abstract while pointing out that donor nations and international institutions harped on rights that cost them nothing, such as freedom of speech, while dismissing those that came with a hefty price tag, such as the right to an education, to medical care, or to freedom of movement, including across international borders.[13] Traoré argued that privileging some rights over others devalued political sovereignty and human dignity – in short, that doing so set the "rights" against the "humans" in whom they were said to reside. What's more, citizens of African countries often had little role in determining which rights would be privileged and which questions would be asked.

In the decades since independence, African states and citizens have continued to struggle to reconcile the apparently competing values of international humanitarianism and human rights activism, on the one hand, and African sovereignty on the other. The idea that a zero-sum relationship obtains between the two is not a new one. It dates back to the 1950s, before independence, and became ever more compelling in the 1970s, when human rights emerged as a powerful component of global governance. In the era of African independence, and in the context of the Cold War, the arguments made on both sides were even more cynical than they often are now.[14] The pages that follow consider the moment in which human rights rhetoric became a common element of governmental and non-governmental rationality in light of texts produced in a recent period of intense debate when democratization and free speech entailed reopening old wounds.[15] In doing so, they address the question of how a political language and form of activism that was conceived of as apolitical became antipolitical in practice, eschewing any discussion of power, production, and distribution.[16] A serious history of Africa's present ought to face up to

---

[13] The idea that the latter is a right is far from consensual. Traoré (1999, 2002); see also Englund (2006) and Sissako (2006).
[14] For an influential statement on this problem, see Shivji (1989). For a dictator's version of the argument, see Toure (1978). See also Burke (2010).
[15] Sow's literary study places these texts in context; (2010).
[16] I use the term "antipolitical" here to mean opposed to recognizing or valorizing the motives – as opposed to the mere tactics – of political struggle, rather than opposed to the exercise of power as such. My usage differs from that of James Ferguson, whose classic "anti-politics machine," represented by international development agencies working in Lesotho, expanded the power and the presence of the state while enforcing the "suspension of politics from even the most sensitive political operations"; Ferguson (1994), 256. In post-1991 Mali, as should be clear, the mandate of the state contracted considerably, even if the depoliticization of the manifestly political remained symptomatic. This phenomenon contrasts with that prevalent in Lesotho from 1975 to 1984, the period Ferguson analyzed.

the problem Aminata Dramane Traoré posits: an emergent form of politics, one founded in principle yet allergic to ideology, survived an ideological age to become a global language. Having done so, Traoré argues, it helped to drown out internationally the very genre of open discourse that its champions sought to foster within national boundaries.[17]

Having recognized that problem, ought one not go a step further by attempting to understand how particular forms of politics might have transformed or been transformed by that emerging language? I argue that in the 1970s the principal mode of human rights activism was viral: it worked through an anticolonial political network, but voided it of its politics; it worked to reprogram its host and to produce a new politics of human rights in diminished form. That new politics, having become dominant, went on to reproduce itself.

As represented by Amnesty International, human rights activism did not generate new forms of politics or novel internationalisms without building on old ones, including anticolonial, Leftist, and trade union networks toward which Amnesty's apolitical stance mandated a certain reserve, even rejection.[18] Those networks were in turn the product of struggles within the French empire to integrate trade unions, to win equal pay for equal work, and to expand the domain of African self-government.[19] For this and other reasons, human rights activism in Africa – but not only in Africa – has a postcolonial history that goes beyond the Cold War narrative to which it is readily reduced, and from which Amnesty in particular attempted to salvage it.

1960 is generally taken to be a signal year for African independence, witnessing national sovereignty for the Sahelian states and many others, the collapse of the Congo, and the ever-bloodier repression of the antiapartheid movement in South Africa, as marked by the shooting at Sharpeville. Amnesty International was founded in London the very next year.[20] One of its first investigative missions was to Ghana, a pioneer in self-government, in the wake of Kwame Nkrumah's fall from power. In short, the period

---

[17] Traoré (2002).
[18] Eckel argues that Amnesty's nonideological stance strongly appealed to potential members who sought a "new, postrevolutionary form of civil activism"; (2013), 185, 192 (quote), 200–01. Ironically, AFASPA, a key ally in Amnesty's Mali campaign, represented a hybrid of a pre-1968, PCF-affiliated Leftist politics and an emergent antitotalitarian *tiers mondiste* politics.
[19] On the labor movement in this period, see Cooper (1996), Guèye (2011).
[20] For an understanding of Amnesty's early years, I have relied on Hopgood (2006), Buchanan (2002), and Eckel (2013). For a study of Amnesty's influence within international institutions, see Clark (2001).

when Amnesty acquired "a virtual monopoly as a non-governmental authority speaking the language of universal Human Rights" coincided precisely with the years of African independence.[21] The often-tense relationship between human rights and African sovereignty is neither causal nor merely rhetorical. In the post-independence history of political discourse on the continent they are longtime companions, albeit with their backs often turned to each other.[22] By the late 1970s, they could hardly have been farther apart: military governments dominated African politics just as human rights activism blossomed worldwide.[23] In that moment, political activists and NGOs sought to master the terms and tactics of a new political language. Decades later, we can ask: Which among them succeeded, and at what cost? Answering those questions means stepping back into the Sahel, and into the Sahara, while asking how that zone became the proving ground of a new politics as one postcolonial regime gave way to another.

WHAT WERE THE CAMPS AND WHO WERE THE PRISONERS?

The old politics, represented in Mali by a once-promising government that had become the *ancien régime*, seemed to collapse with hardly a squeak when a group of young soldiers arrested Modibo Keita in November, 1968. Even some of the US-RDA's long-time leaders, pioneers of independence, abandoned the party and its politics without hesitation. Less than a fortnight after the coup, former Vice-President Jean-Marie Koné was condemning Keita's Active Revolution as "an immense political guerilla operation without an immediate socialist objective."[24] The junta imprisoned Modibo Keita, Madeira Keita, and most of the other leaders of the US-RDA, the Chief of Staff of the Malian army, Colonel Sékou Traoré, and militants such as Amadou Seydou Traoré.[25] All were held

---

[21] Hopgood (2006), 54.
[22] For a contrary view of this relationship, see Simpson (2013).
[23] Both the International Covenant on Economic, Social, and Cultural Rights and the International Covenant on Civil and Political Rights came into effect in 1976. Amnesty International won the Nobel Peace Prize the following year. The ranks of international human rights NGOs would swell with the creation of Human Rights First in 1978 and Helsinki Watch in 1979. On the contagious spread of human rights discourse in this period, see Moyn (2010). For competing views setting such discourse in the context of decolonization, see Burke (2010) and Simpson (2013).
[24] Quoted in "Behind the Mali coup," *West Africa* 2688 (Dec. 7, 1968), 1430–31.
[25] Amadou Seydou Traoré was not a leader of the US-RDA. Rather, he ran the *Librairie Populaire* and other state enterprises. Like Madeira Keita, he survived his detention. Through his own historical work, his availability and hospitality toward researchers,

without trial or charges, some for as long as a decade.[26] With the exception of Colonel Traoré, these prisoners would come to be known as "the civilians," and their collective fate contrasted with those of successive waves of prisoners who joined them. Thirty-three soldiers known as "*les militaires*" composed the first of those waves. These US-RDA loyalists, "the revolutionary heart of the army," had hesitated before recognizing the CMLN government, and eventually did so only because they were isolated and vulnerable in their desert garrison in Kidal.[27] In 1969, they were plotting a countercoup meant to restore Keita to power when the CMLN arrested them. Led by Captain Diby Sylas Diarra, this group included Adjudant Guédiouma Samaké and Sergent-Chef Samba Sangaré, both of whom have published memoirs I cite below.[28]

In order to absorb and "re-educate" these prisoners, new camps were established around old garrisons and salt mines in the Sahara. Kidal, Abeibara, Bouressa, In Tadénit (N'Tadjenit), Inakounder, Timbuktu, Nioro, Niono, and Taoudeni composed a penal archipelago, with several of its outposts lying deep in the desert.[29] The most notorious of these, Taoudeni, sits 700 km north of Timbuktu and hundreds of kilometers from the nearest settlement. Through the 1970s, further waves of students, soldiers, trade unionists, and dissidents would join the US-RDA loyalists in detention.[30] Three of these waves stand out. In 1971, a handful of other

and the endeavors of his publishing house, Traoré has very effectively defended Modibo Keita and the US-RDA while damning the military regime. In addition to his own books, some of which are cited herein, he has published the memoirs of Soungalo Samaké and Samba Sangaré.

[26] In 1973, the prisoners at In Tadénit wrote directly to Moussa Traore demanding to be judged; Traoré (2010), 21–22. The fact that they were held without trial continues to trouble ex-prisoners and their descendants, as they were not afforded the opportunity to defend themselves in court. By contrast, after the 1991 coup, Moussa Traore and some of his closest associates were tried on charges of corruption and violence – including murder – in two closely followed trials. However, the charges of murder and assault brought against Moussa Traore and his collaborators were limited to the events of 1991 that led up to the coup. Earlier crimes were not addressed, even if some of the journalists covering the trial referred to Taoudeni (discussed below) as the paradigmatic example of the CMLN's repression; Konaté (1993), 9, 25. Although Traore and others were condemned to death, no one was executed. President Konaré commuted Traore's death sentence to life imprisonment and later pardoned him. Traore lives comfortably at state expense in Bamako.

[27] Sangaré (2001), 14–17.

[28] See also Sow (2010).

[29] G. Samaké (2009 [1998]), 93. It should be noted that some of these places are significant towns, whereas others are isolated desert settlements. Modibo himself was held in garrisons near Bamako, in Kidal, briefly in Kayes, and possibly in Markala. On Kayes, see Traoré (2008), 324.

[30] Traoré offers an extensive list of political prisoners of the military regime, while noting that he has not attempted to establish a complete list of the victims of the regime, "*which even it*

military men, including Captain Yoro Diakité – former leader of the CMLN and the man who signed the decree designating the Saharan salt mine of Taoudeni a "special center for re-education" – was sent there to die. In 1974, a group known as the "intellectuals," which included the novelist Ibrahima Ly, circulated antigovernment tracts in Bamako; their texts earned them arrest, torture, and time in Taoudeni before they were shipped south.[31] In 1978, Moussa Traore imprisoned the most feared members of the CMLN, the so-called "Band of Three" – Minister of Defense, the Interior and Security Kissima Doukara, Minister of Transport Karim Dembele, and Chief of Security Tiécoro Bagayoko, Lieutenants-Colonel all – and their associates, including Minister of Foreign Affairs, Charles Samba Sissoko, and Captain Soungalo Samaké, who would later write *Ma Vie de Soldat*. Many of these men died in detention; others, like Colonel Traoré, did not long survive their release. Controversy still surrounds the death of Modibo Keita in the paratroopers' camp at Djikoroni in 1977; many believe he was poisoned by the CMLN, but his jailer, the same Soungalo Samaké, denies that charge. On the other hand, the fate of Diby Sylas Diarra is well known: he was stomped and whipped to death by a young Tuareg soldier who held him responsible for the immolation of his brother during the rebellion of 1963–64.[32] Grisly as his was, death in exile was nothing new.

can not do"; (2008), 287–302, quote from 287, emphasis in the original. It is not clear that any women were held in the North. There were apparently at least three female political prisoners under the CMLN. Two are unidentified. The third, Mme. Keita Mariam Travélé, Modibo's senior wife, may have been detained for one year in the North before being sent back to the South; Konaré (1993), 357; and int., A. S. Traoré, June 6, 2004. She was among the last of the prisoners to be released; Amnesty International external document, *Prisoners in Mali Suffering from Ill Health*, AFR 37/03/77, n.d. (Nov. 1977), document in author's possession; Traoré (2008), 14. Note the latter source indicates that Mariam Keita was held exclusively in the southern city of Sikasso; this contradicts an earlier interview with Traoré. In the 1970s and afterward, female students opposed the CMLN and the UDPM. At least one of them, Rokia Kouyaté, was assaulted while in detention; Gatigon, Sec-Gen (AFASPA) to Mali's ambassador to Paris, 26 March 1980, ADSSD 67J110. Amnesty International reported that she had been killed; Press release, *Amnesty International Reports Students and Teachers Tortured and Killed in Mali*, AFR 37/01/90, March 25, 1980, document in author's possession.

[31] Ly wrote a classic novel, *Toiles d'araignées* (1997 [1982]) drawn from his prison experiences in Niono, and to a lesser extent, in Taoudeni. The novel focuses on common law prisoners (*cassolamogow*) in the south of the fictional country of Béléya, and it offers a blistering critique of the petty tyrannies and brutal sanctions that characterized military rule. Ly and his comrades apparently spent little time in Taoudeni; Ly (1990), 155–58. Detained at the same time as Ly, released, and arrested again, Victor Sy was sent to Taoudeni for a brief period later in 1974; Centre Djoliba (2002), 297.

[32] G. Samaké (2009 [1998]), 90; Sangaré (2001), 172. On Diarra's background and character, see Traoré (2008), 355–56; Dembélé (2003), 25–28; Lecocq (2010).

Saharan Incarcerations

In the western Sudan, exile had long been privileged as a form of punishment, but colonial rule broadened the scale on which it was practiced.[33] In the mid-nineteenth century, French officials in Senegal sent political prisoners to what they hoped would be permanent exile in Guyana.[34] At the close of the century, prominent figures such as the Guinean empire-builder Samori Touré and the Senegalese mystic Amadu Bamba, leader of the Sufis known as Mourides, suffered exile on an island on the Ogooué River in Gabon. Touré would die there in 1900, and legend has that it Bamba himself washed his body for burial. By 1910, common-law prisoners had begun to return from even more distant jails; for instance, on reaching the end of his sentence in Guyana, a Soudanese man convicted of murder in the Congo sought contact with his family back home.[35] Guyana was a long way away, much farther than the Sahara. Thus, in the first decades of the twentieth century, two things changed in colonial practices of incarceration. As the practice of transferring prisoners across geographic zones as an additional form of punishment became widespread, desert sites began to replace tropical prison camps such as those on the Ogooué or in Guyana. As the colonial military became more confident in its control of the Sahara, the desert began to assume the role it would play after independence as the supreme site of exile.[36] For the history of the Sahel, this is important; the colonial administration simultaneously accentuated and transformed ideas about race that were well established in the intellectual world of the Sahara and the Sahel, and it knit parts of that zone together with regions much farther south.[37] The ideological underpinnings of this transformation may be less significant than its effect: the establishment of a vast

---

[33] During the period of conquest, colonial regimes exiled several African leaders, including Behanzin of Dahomey and the Asantehene Osei Tutu, but the practice of exile is indigenous as well. On British and French practices of exile, see Asiwaju (1979), 54–59.

[34] Louis Faidherbe, Governor Senegal to Minister Colonies, Paris, Feb. 12, 1860. CAOM 1M65.

[35] Mamadou Diakité, no. mle. 36125, camp de Passoura, pénitencier des Roches de Kourou (Guyane Française) to GSF, Aug. 22, 1910, ANM 1F8FA.

[36] The second exile of Amadu Bamba to Mauritania was a case apart, inasmuch as he was assigned to the care of a "friendly" marabout. This was more a question of policy toward African Muslims than elaborating a technique of exile; Robinson (2000), 188–89. On the other hand, the Dahomeyean political dissident Louis Hunkanrin was exiled to Mauritania in the 1930s, and this clearly was an elaborate form of punishment; Suret-Canale (1988b).

[37] Hall (2011b); Lecocq (2010).

territory in which the most extreme forms of political power could be exercised, even if government itself remained scarce.

From the late 1920s, colonial administrators sent men from the prisons of Soudan and Senegal north into the desert. The prisoners traveled shackled together under the surveillance of *gardes-cercle* who would return south with empty manacles after depositing the men at work sites. Many of the detainees died working on the desert tracks (*pistes*), and a few perished of thirst while trying to escape. In 1928, 1929, and 1930, the years for which records are available, the prison at Kidal and construction projects in the Sahara recorded dozens of deaths.[38] A decade later, as the colonial administration sought to make good on an old idea of a trans-Saharan road, Soudan's governor looked once again to "the employment agencies of Africa," the prisons.[39] The chief engineer asked for 120 men, and the governor sought prisoners who had at least two years left to serve and who were healthy enough to work on the road.[40] *Commandants* and wardens volunteered their "hard cases": recidivists, escape artists, and career criminals with long sentences to serve. Although the prisoners were not necessarily expected to die in the desert, at least one *commandant* made it clear that he was indifferent to the fate of his charge, as long as the prisoner did not return to the *cercle* he governed.[41] Few ever did return, meaning that assignment to the desert camps represented a life sentence. The men being sent there were common criminals. One of them, Mamadou Keita, who had been imprisoned for theft on the Dakar-Niger railroad, protested that he had done no more than receive a stolen handkerchief. He died working on the *piste* near In Rha Assela in 1927, leaving only the faintest trace in the archives.[42]

Four decades later, Modibo and Madeira Keita would follow his path to the North, where others would join them. Word of their suffering

---

[38] *Registre d'écrous*, Kidal, ANM 2M309FR, d. 24. Deaths of forced laborers were not unique to the Sahara. The large-scale irrigation project known as the Office du Niger also claimed the lives of many men serving in labor brigades; those men were conscripts, not criminals, and the purpose of the project was not to kill them. Regarding prisoners, Sene argues that their use for road building became common by the late 1930s. Moreover, he demonstrates that mass escapes in Senegal in 1927 led to a reorganization of the prison system in that colony, which may have affected the deployment of prisoners to the Sahara; (2004).

[39] Londres (1929), 223.

[40] Chef du Service des travaux d'aménagements des pistes sahariennes to GSF, Oct. 31, 1938, #190 G; Gouv. p.i. Soudan to various *cercles*, May 28, 1938, #662 APA.3, ANM 1F242FR.

[41] CdC Tougan to Gouv. p.i. Soudan, Nov. 23, 1938, ANM 1F242FR.

[42] *Registre d'écrous*, Kidal, ANM 2M309FR, d. 24.

produced an international movement for their release. What had changed in the meantime? As the hapless recipient of a stolen handkerchief in a distant corner of the empire, Mamadou Keita could be forgotten, whereas high-profile dissidents, intellectuals, and former heads of new nation-states could not. This is an obvious but insufficient answer, for in the 1960s, no such movement had emerged when three prominent opponents of the government were shot dead while in custody of the army.[43] Criticized in the international press, the US-RDA had merely published a defensive communiqué asserting that Mali as a sovereign nation was not obliged to answer to anyone regarding the fate of its detainees.[44] In 1964, that seemed to be enough, but by the 1970s times had changed, and rapidly so. Human rights activism was becoming an increasingly important element of emerging forms of global governance, even as Mali's military government enshrined the exceptional nature of Saharan prisons into law.

Taoudeni

Months after toppling Modibo Keita's US-RDA regime in the coup d'état of November 1968, the CMLN formalized a new role for Taoudeni.[45] Reserved initially for those Keita loyalists within the army who had determined to stage a countercoup, the saltpan would earn a reputation for suffering that would become international. The worst of the prison camps, Taoudeni was a place for dying, not for killing. The forms of assassination practiced there were generally passive, as the principal purpose of the camps was to generate misery. Men were broken down by

---

[43] A popular tribunal convicted Fily Dabo Sissoko, Kassoum Toure, and Hamadoun Dicko of inciting a riot in the capital when the new Malian franc was introduced in 1962. After intense debate within the BPN, death sentences handed down against them were suspended and they were sent to prison in the North; P-V, BPN, Oct. 5, 1962, BPNCMLN 77. They died in obscure circumstances. The government claimed that they were caught in the crossfire while trying to escape during a rebel ambush. Many believe the army murdered them. The memoir of one former officer details the method and place of execution, while claiming that the order came directly from Bamako; Dembélé (2003), 38–43. These were prominent men. Sissoko and Dicko were former deputies in the French National Assembly. On Sissoko, see Sidibe (2007); on Dicko, Pelckmans (2011), *infra*; on both, Gerard (1975). Toure was a prosperous Bamako merchant who was rumored to hold a party card with the low and mystically powerful number seven, having been an early patron of the US-RDA; Campmas (1976), 376.
[44] *Communiqué du BPN de l'US-RDA a/s de la mort des contre-révolutionnaires du 20 juillet 1962*, forwarded by Chargé des Affaires, p.i. to MAE, DAAM, July 29, 1964, #0159; Amb Fr Bamako to MAE, DAAM, July 5, 1964, #144, both in CADN Bamako (hereafter, BKO) 55. On this episode see also Traoré (2010).
[45] The decree is reproduced in Sangaré (2001), 274–76.

humiliation, brutal treatment, forced labor, and the symbolism of chattel slavery represented by salt mining. Former Head of Government Captain Yoro Diakité was stripped naked before his former subordinates, men young enough to be his sons, and made to perform the dance of a young Peuhl girl.[46] In the first years of its existence as a prison camp, the soldiers and officers who were imprisoned at Taoudeni built their own cells by hand. Condemned as *"faso juguw"* or enemies of the nation, each was told that his life was worth nothing. The job of their jailers was to watch them die from overwork, exposure, and malnutrition. Prisoners rounded out their diets with rodents, and struggled to keep their strength as the foul, salty well water wrecked havoc on their digestive tracks. Although many died miserably in dysentery and filth, others met a violent death, beaten with rocks, whips, or the bare hands of their guards. As if to underscore the absolute power over life and death that he held, the first commander of the camp at Taoudeni, Lieutenant Abdoulaye Niantao, insisted on being called the "Moro Naba," after the king of the Mossi who traditionally commanded extreme obedience from his subjects. Until his superiors forbade him to do so, he forced the prisoners to touch their foreheads to the ground and kiss his boots when he passed before them.[47] After the American presidential election of 1976, his ambitions became both international and more modest, and he allowed another of his nicknames to evolve: "Jimmy the Cowboy" now insisted on being called "Jimmy Carter."[48]

The building of the camp was only the first task facing the prisoners. At Taoudeni, the ex-military prisoners were put to work mining salt from the open pans. Because neither the guards nor the prisoners knew how to dig out the salt bars that would eventually enter southern markets, Niantao called on the Bellah miners who worked nearby deposits to instruct the prisoners. Niantao and his subordinates had intended to make the prisoners work without tools, but they quickly learned that this was impossible. Hacking out meter-long slabs of salt from the desert floor required hammers, crowbars, and brute strength, along with certain techniques that the Bellah miners mastered. The prisoners were not accustomed to such work, and in combination with the harsh conditions it killed some of them.

Salt mining was revenge. Beyond the potentially lethal nature of the labor, the mining of salt had great symbolic value for Niantao and for the

---

[46] Dembélé (2003), 77–79. As "Head of Government" under the CMLN, "Un Ancien chef de gouvernement malien meurt en prison," *le Soleil* (Dakar), 982, July 31, 1973.
[47] Dembélé (2003), 58–9.
[48] Sangaré (2001), 92.

Human Rights and Saharan Prisons 221

CMLN. Putting the junta's opponents to work on the mines served to reduce them symbolically to slaves.[49] Such labor was also a reaction to the organization of labor under the Keita regime, which conscripted young men into labor brigades (the *Service Civique Rurale*) and forced both civilians and soldiers to participate in collective farming.[50] Even before the "Active Revolution," elite military units had been reduced to cultivating potatoes in collective fields or putting out brush fires rather than training or doing any of the other things that soldiers do.[51] Many of them felt that such labor was beneath their dignity, and some deeply resented carrying out the kind of slave labor of which the salt bar was the ultimate symbol. After Sangaré, Samaké, and their comrades extracted their first complete bars from the rock-hard surface of the salt pan, Niantao had one of the bars inscribed with a commemorative message he displayed to the prisoners: *"première barre de sel extraite par les traîtres le 1er janvier 1970."*[52] According to Dembélé, he then sent it as a gift to the CMLN.[53]

As the camp at Taoudeni became quietly infamous within Mali, its ongoing salt trade, its legendary past, and the conditions of labor there drew some attention from abroad, but few people in the outside world knew anything about its other contemporary role as a prison camp.[54] Instead, Taoudeni had become an almost mythical place deep in the desert. In 1974, a Briton named Richard Trench sought to follow up on stories that there was a "concentration camp in the middle of the Sahara, a saltpan mined, it was rumored, by political prisoners and slaves."[55] Trench, whose father had been a District Commissioner in Kenya, was far from a

---

[49] Trench (1978), 109, 123. In the past, only two categories of people had mined salt in the Sahara: debtors and slaves. A smattering of publications in the 1960s and 1970s detailed the practice of salt mining there, but avoided discussion of the political context. They were, however, implicitly or explicitly concerned with the question of whether the miners' debt bondage was akin to slavery; see Clauzel (1960); and Meunier (1980); Félix Poussibet "Réflexions sur l'esclavage au Sahara et au sahel Maliens," *Notes Africaines* 162 (1979), 36–42; and Poussibet (1978).

[50] Bogosian (2003); on perceptions of labor and dignity in the Mande world, see Diawara (2003).

[51] See Mann (2003) and Mariko (2001), 119–20.

[52] G. Samaké (2009 [1998]), 43; Dembélé (2003), 61.

[53] Dembélé (2003), 61.

[54] The mines at Taoudeni played a prominent role in Saharan history late in the sixteenth century. In 1585 the mines at Taghaza were abandoned in favor of those at Taoudeni, which had direct trade links with Timbuktu. The Moroccan invasion of the Songhay Empire in 1591 was sparked by Songhay rejections of Saadian claims to the proceeds of the mine. Hunwick (1962, 1999).

[55] Trench (1978), 3.

sympathetic observer; he considered Mali "Africa's answer to Papa Doc's Haiti" and "God's gift to white racialists everywhere."[56] Like many European "Saharans," Trench eventually displayed much greater respect for Moors, Tuareg, and Berbers – the classic colonial "whites" – and became an emotional supporter of the POLISARIO Liberation Front in the Western Sahara.[57] Yet at the beginning of his voyage, as a journalist seeking a story, he was drawn to Taoudeni in spite of rumors that other Europeans had been imprisoned for spying on it.[58] The mine was hidden, he wrote, and "if [it] had anything to hide, I wanted to take it by surprise."[59] Arriving via a camel caravan from the Algerian border, Trench did in fact manage to catch the Malians off-guard. After being detained – and exposed to the deputy commander's pornography collection – Trench caught a glimpse of men gathering camel dung for fuel under the loose surveillance of two soldiers. The "silent, half-dead" eyes he met may have been those of the prisoners, but Trench did not speak to them.[60] He was escorted away, and the miners he talked to later could tell him little about the prisoners, who were kept in a camp some five kilometers away, and whom they saw only when they came near the mine to draw water or collect dung for fuel.[61] If the prisoners were silent, the story was spectacular. Taoudeni soon stood in for all political prisons in the country, representing in common parlance a kind of synecdoche for Saharan prisons.[62] When I naively asked former deputy and member of the CNDR Gabou Diawara, one of the US-RDA stalwarts imprisoned at In Tadénit, if he had been sent to Taoudeni, he scoffed, "You go to Taoudeni to die (*On va à Taoudeni pour mourir*)."[63]

---

[56] Trench (1978), 25, 28–9.
[57] Trench (1978), epilogue.
[58] Trench (1978), 28–29. The origin of this rumor is not clear. However, an Italian trade unionist had been arrested along with Malian colleagues in the early 1970s as they sought to revitalize the Malian labor movement as an autonomous force.
[59] Trench (1978), 29.
[60] Trench (1978), 119–20.
[61] Trench (1978), 123. Trench's report is unique, but he was not the only foreign visitor to Taoudeni in those years. Samba Sangaré reports that while he was being held there at least four tourist convoys approached the saltpans at Taoudeni, because the camp and its well lay on a trans-Saharan route leading to Timbuktu. However, such convoys were visible and audible long before they arrived at the mine. Each time a group approached the mines, guards sent the prisoners back to camp, and if the cars came closer, to their quarters. Occasional prospectors seeking oil and mineral reserves also passed through, and Sangaré was once assigned to accompany such a crew of foreigners while they sought uranium deposits; Sangaré (2001), 223–25, 227–34. Others sought oil and natural gas.
[62] Trench compared it to Kafka's castle, "not so much a place as a state of mind"; (1978), 28.
[63] Int., Gabou Diawara, 16 August 2005, Bamako.

A HUMAN RIGHTS CAMPAIGN

And die they did, over and over again. Yoro Diakité died in at least three different ways in the years between his arrest in 1971 and his death in 1973: credible reports and simple rumors had him shot while trying to escape, struck down by beriberi, and executed outright.[64] Only one of these stories could be true, but it didn't matter. They shared the same endpoint. The deaths in Taoudeni, or rumors about them, led Amnesty International to take on the cause of the Malian political prisoners and to begin lobbying the Malian government to ameliorate the conditions of their detention, to try those who had not been brought before a court, and to release those who were gravely ill.[65] After a period of research and strategizing, Amnesty's Secretary General Martin Ennals traveled to Mali in May 1973 to advocate for the prisoners. On the occasion of the fifth anniversary of the coup d'état that November, he again asked Moussa Traore to release them. By the end of the year, in a rare interview with a foreign journalist, in this case a Pole, the leader of the CMLN responded with discomfort to the question of what had become of the former president and his comrades, who had simply disappeared into detention without trial or judgment. "[Modibo Keita] is doing fine," Traore retorted, "better than I am." Although the interview ran in the government daily *l'Essor*, this particular part of the exchange did not. As the French ambassador noted, Traore "feared straying onto uncertain terrain after recent protests from Amnesty International regarding the fate of the Malian political prisoners."[66]

Pushed by the "Committee to Defend the Democratic Liberties of Mali" (CDLDM) – a group composed of Malian migrants to France and their local allies, which was in contact with the prisoners – Amnesty had begun to acquire increasingly detailed information about the Saharan prisons and those held there in 1970 or 1971.[67] At around the same time, the US-RDA prisoners at In Tadenit smuggled out a letter to the outside world with the

---

[64] Dallier, Amb Fr to MAE, 1 Nov 1972, #747/748; Tel., COMUP Dakar to RFFAB/ARMEES PARIS, 16 June 1973, #036 AMBA T BAMAKO (sic), CADN BKO 63. See also G. Samaké (2009 [1998]), 93–95 ; Sangaré (2001), 194–97.
[65] MAE, *Appel d'Amnesty International pour la libération des prisonniers politiques au Mali*, Nov. 23, 1973, #62 (fragment), CADN BKO 63.
[66] Louis Dallier, Amb Fr Mali to MAE, DAM, Dec. 14, 1973, #66/DAM, CADN BKO 60.
[67] Amnesty International, *Background paper on Mali* 113, Nov. 1974. Document in author's possession. Also, A.I. International Secretariat, memo "To all groups with political prisoners in Mali," June 21, 1974; and attached press release, *Malian Political Prisoner, Seydou Kouyate, is in danger of dying*, Nov. 18, 1973, Amnesty archives, Series II.5 Box I, AFR 37. On the CDLDM, see "Défense des libertés démocratiques," *Bulletin du Comité Français des Amis du Mali* 2 (1982).

help of a Tuareg "brother" who delivered it to Lamine Sow, a union stalwart in Bamako. Sow circulated it, and news of "the letter and its contents" soon aired on Radio Prague.[68] With such good sources, much of Amnesty's information was accurate: Amadou Seydou Traore, who was diagnosed in an Amnesty document as suffering from a liver ailment, told me that that was indeed the case.[69] The CDLDM was in contact with the prisoners, who were otherwise largely cut off from the outside world, and it knew which medications they requested from their families in their rare letters home. Based on those requests, Amnesty knew that many of them were suffering from eye ailments, and feared that some would be allowed to go blind, in spite of the fact that good treatment was available in Bamako's ophthalmological institute, IOTA. US-RDA ideologue and ex-Minister of Planning Seydou Badian Kouyaté and ex-Foreign Minister Ousmane Bâ had been discreetly sent there for care, but they were held there on the upper floors where their doctors were ordered to treat them only at night.[70] Whether they could save the prisoners' vision, nobody knew; several other prisoners had already gone blind.

By the following year, what had begun as a campaign to improve the conditions of detention of some forty prisoners and to ensure that they received a trial had become "a campaign for a general amnesty for all political prisoners in Mali."[71] Amnesty began to beat this drum more and more loudly, bolstered by both a steady if discrete flow of information from within the country and, undoubtedly, by the very drama of the story itself. In 1974, an Amnesty campaign aimed at "francophone West Africa" took Mali as one of its five prominent targets. Gabon, Chad, Cameroon, and the Cote d'Ivoire had also proven deaf to previous Amnesty actions, and the organization's international secretariat had decided to take a different tack vis-à-vis all five of them.[72] Each month, Amnesty chapters

---

[68] Centre Djoliba (2002), 36.
[69] Int., A.S. Traoré, June 4, 2004, Bamako. Although Traoré never knew of the Amnesty campaign before I told him about it, he said that a medical doctor once traveled to the camp and visited the prisoners, apparently some time after Amnesty began to query the CMLN on their fate.
[70] A.I. International Secretariat, memo "To all groups with political prisoners in Mali," June 21, 1974, and *Malian Political Prisoner, Seydou Kouyate* ..., Amnesty archives, Series II.5 Box I, AFR 37.
[71] Amnesty press release, *Amnesty International calls for release of all political prisoners in Mali*, Nov. 13, 1974, and associated background document, Amnesty archives, Series II.5 Box I, AFR 37.
[72] A.I., International Secretariat, June 17, 1974, Re. F/W campaign, Amnesty archives, Series II.5 Box I, AFR 5.

in a designated European country would lead their peers in neighboring countries in a campaign focused on a particular West African government; the next month chapters in another country would take the lead while the target government changed as well. Thus, November would be Mali and France, December Cameroon and Holland, and so on. Rather than focusing strictly on prisoners of conscience, who were few, the Malian campaign would adopt "political prisoners in general." This tactic posed its own problems. First, pairing Mali and France proved to be a bad idea; even if it was made up largely of ex-colonial soldiers, the Malian government proved not at all receptive to being scolded by the former imperial power. Second, compounding the problem of a perceived neocolonialism, the 10,000 postcards that were to be sent to Bamako "could have been more diplomatic [in tone] and would not be used for other countries."[73] Third, Amnesty took on all the prisoners, but it received its information from allies such as the AFASPA and the CDLDM, whose politics provided their raison d'être; they sought the release of the US-RDA prisoners and showed no interest in men like Yoro Diakité who had betrayed them. It is there – and in the distribution of relief through contacts with the families of prisoners – that an apolitical movement met a political one.

AFASPA

With a stark identity and a very sharp form of analysis, AFASPA represented a very different kind of politics from Amnesty, one in which the language of human rights represented a tool to defend a political project, rather than a value in and of itself. Sending letters to Moussa Traore and to the French Minister of Cooperation Pierre Abelin or delivering petitions to the Malian embassy did not represent starkly different tactics from those pursued by Amnesty. However, AFASPA had the kinds of connections that made Amnesty's activism possible.[74] AFASPA's ultimate target was the "neo-colonialism" they believed France under Valéry Giscard d'Estaing represented on the African continent: famine and political repression were symptoms of the same greater evil, and humanitarianism was an alibi for

---

[73] A.I., International Secretariat, October 24, 1974, Re. F/W campaign, Amnesty archives, Series II.5 Box I, AFR 5.
[74] AFASPA sought to publicize the plight of the prisoners in the Sahara and the Sahel beginning in June 1973; a *Comité de défense des prisonniers maliens* had begun to do similar work in 1972. It is not clear if the two associations were entirely distinct, or what connections they might have had with the CDLDM. Préfecture de Police, Note, Nov. 29, 1972; Ministre de l'Interieur, DGPN, DCRG, July 11, 1978, CAC 19960311, art. 7.

the failures of capitalism. Still, its interventions could be pragmatic. The organization's secretary general, Claude Gatignon, wrote repeatedly to French government ministers asking them to take up Modibo Keita's case with the CMLN because he had been a parliamentarian under the Fourth Republic and a minister (*secrétaire d'état*) in the Fifth. Even for an organization as stridently anticolonial as AFASPA, Keita's status as a "former member of the French government" appeared to render French intervention on his behalf altogether "legitimate."[75]

The defense of human rights, particularly Amnesty's version of them, in order to protect the US-RDA prisoners represented a similar tactic on the part of AFASPA's activists. But their liberation was more than a tactical goal. Long and in some cases deep relationships along with shared political visions bound some of the activists to their former comrades. In the first numbers of its *Bulletin*, which would later become *Aujourd'hui l'Afrique*, AFASPA had trumpeted a new solidarity, one that went beyond aid in food and medicine destined for victims of the drought to include victims of political repression. Indeed the liberation of the political prisoners was one of the original causes around which AFASPA attempted to rally activists, and the issue lay behind their very understanding of what postcolonial solidarity meant. In early 1974, even as it mobilized for famine relief, AFASPA launched a "solidarity fund" for the Malian prisoners and their families.[76] The fund would eventually enable freed prisoners such as Kouyaté and Bâ to seek treatment in France, and it provided for medical care for their families as well. When Amnesty chapters in Germany and Holland began to adopt individual Malian political figures as their own "prisoners of conscience," AFASPA enabled the actions they undertook.[77]

Madeira Keita and his family offer perhaps the clearest example. Keita endured an imprisonment as long as any other member of the US-RDA government; he emerged from it physically exhausted but mentally formidable and pursued his political engagement, first clandestinely and later as

---

[75] Gatignon to Président de la République, Feb. 9, 1977. Also, Philippe Sauzay, Chef de Cabinet, Présidence de la République, to Sec.-Gen. (AFASPA), March 21, 1977, #029886; Gatignon to Abelin, Min. Coopération, Sept. 17, 1974; Min. Coopération to Gatignon, Oct. 2, 1974, ADSSD 67J110. Gatignon was a prominent Communist also engaged in Third World causes via the Organization of Solidarity with the People of Asia, Africa, and Latin America (OSPAA).

[76] *Bulletin d'Information de l'AFASPA* (1974).

[77] Correspondence between Pierre Morlet, AFASPA, and Amnesty chapters in Düsseldorf, Tübingen, and Berlin, July 1976, ADSSD 67J110.

one of the "dinosaurs" of the re-emergent US-RDA.[78] A letter he sent from prison in 1973 attests to his faith in his political vision:

> I write to you in perfect health ... I think I owe my condition – which astonishes many – to the good pharmaceutical products that you send to me, to daily exercise, to an appetite that refuses to be disgusted or discouraged by the quality of what is available, and to a cold, lucid courage that sees the situation clearly. The comfort offered by the support and encouragement of my family [as well as] the courage of my wife, my friends, and my faithful comrades re-affirms my unshakeable morale. I thank them all, fraternally.[79]

Censored or not, Madeira Keita was unbreakable. Yet if it seemed that Amnesty and AFASPA could do little for him directly, the French anti-colonialists were able to collaborate with Malian dissidents and Amnesty activists to offer medical treatment to one of his children. They also supported two comrades released before him, Kouyaté and Bâ. While Bâ recuperated in France, Madeira Keita remained imprisoned in the region of Kidal. When the Düsseldorf chapter of Amnesty International adopted his case, under the guidance of the International Secretariat, they knew little about his past or his present condition. Pierre Morlet, one of AFASPA's founders, was soon serving as an intermediary between the German activists and Keita's family, channeling financial assistance to his wife, Madame Keita Nankoria Kourouma, without revealing her address to them. A contribution of 500 DM in July of 1976 must have been a great relief to Kourouma and a great help to her young daughter, who was receiving medical treatment in Paris.[80] By the end of August, mother and daughter were back in Bamako, from whence Kourouma wrote a warm note of thanks to an unnamed "Dear Comrade," likely Morlet.[81] Although Morlet had assured his German counterparts that Kourouma would be told the origin of the gifts she received, neither he nor Bâ knew which chapter of Amnesty had taken on the ex-foreign minister's case, and they did not know to whom to turn for support as he lingered in bad health and a "delicate material situation."[82]

---

[78] Victor Sy uses the term "dinosaurs"; Centre Djoliba (2002), 285.
[79] "Extrait d'une lettre de Madeira Keita," Dec. 20, 1973, ADSSD 67J110.
[80] Gruppe 4, Düsseldorf, Amnesty International to Pierre Morlet, July 29, 1976, ADSSD 67J110. Ironically, the treatment was for the girl's eyes. Madeira Keita's daughter is albino, which explains her vision problems. She is now a prominent lawyer in Bamako. Abrahamane Dicko, "Me Youma Madeira Keita, avocate non-voyante," *les Echoes* (Bamako), Feb. 20, 2009.
[81] "Mme. Madeira" to "Cher Camarade," Sept. 1, 1976, ADSSD 67J110.
[82] Morlet to Amnesty International Gruppe 4, Düsseldorf, Nov. 5, 1976, ADSSD 67J110.

This form of charity was contingent on close relations that it could not foster, given the need for anonymity and security in such cases. Driving the point home, Kourouma wrote that she failed to keep a telephone appointment in Paris as she "did not feel safe."[83] Morlet's long history with the US-RDA (longer, in fact, than Madeira Keita's) enabled him to engage discreetly and effectively with the party's embattled militants. Yet even he was brought up short by the arrival of a younger generation of Malian activists, who announced themselves in two different ways.

First on the scene were the remnants of Mali's far left, including student groups and members of the *Parti Malien du Travail* (formerly the PAI), which had initially welcomed the coup against Keita because he had deviated too greatly from the socialist path. Coming together in the CDLDM, they sought support from the US-RDA's traditional allies on the French Left, the CGT and the PCF (in which leading figures within AFASPA played prominent roles). Yet their political values differed in a key respect from those of an earlier generation: they prized independence above all and showed the same suspicion toward the PCF and the CGT that they accused the French movements of demonstrating toward them. When the CDLDM thanked AFASPA for its willingness not to "get mixed up in" Mali's internal problems, the association's secretary general, Claude Gatignon, was clearly taken aback by the boundaries the Malian dissidents sought to establish: "Can we meet to discuss it at the *Humanité* fair?" he asked.[84] Gatignon's confusion is understandable. The very premise of the association was to follow the "anti-colonial tradition that unites the African and French peoples" by demanding an end to political repression in Africa as in France.[85] In the 1940s and 1950s, the labor movement, and to some extent the US-RDA itself, had been built on a close collaboration not only across the African territories but also between European and African Leftists.[86] A rigidly nationalist and exclusionary politics was not part of that tradition, even if a certain "fraternalism" might have been. The climate of the 1970s was no longer favorable toward an intimate politics of solidarity and trust developed via shared experience, and an emerging practice of human rights activism depended less and less upon it.

---

[83] "Mme. Madeira" to "Cher Camarade," Sept. 1, 1976, ADSSD 67J110.
[84] Gatignon to Sory Ibrahim Keita, CDLDM, August 26, 1974, ADSSD 67J110.
[85] *Bulletin de l'Information de l'AFASPA* (Sept. 1973).
[86] Morlet was not unique. Other European Frenchmen actively involved in the US-RDA include Félix Jouanelle, *commandant* of Ségou through mid-1961, and journalist and broadcaster Pierre Campmas; on the latter see Campmas (1978) and Diallo (2005), 195.

A single sovereignty had long since been parceled out to new nation-states, and Paris was no longer the final object of critique.

The second sign of a new political movement was the arrival on the scene of young intellectuals and their allies who distributed a famous tract entitled "*le Farce électoral*" in Bamako in June 1974. Drawing out the open secret that the CMLN's proposed referendum on a new constitution was nothing more than an attempt to lend window dressing to continued military rule, Ibrahima Ly and his comrades provoked the junta to a much greater degree than they perhaps anticipated. Rounded up, interrogated, and shipped off to Taoudeni, these young Turks were not of the Morlet and Keita generation.[87] Although there can be little doubt that AFASPA was sympathetic to their politics, for Amnesty International their situation seemed almost a textbook case. Indeed it was, and Moussa Traore might have quickly realized that he had created a much bigger drama than a few antigovernment tracts merited. He had this baker's dozen of dissidents brought back from the desert over the objections of Tiécoro Bagayoko; unlike the US-RDA stalwarts, the "*Farce*" crew stood trial, were convicted, and were sentenced to prison.[88] They were held alongside common-law prisoners – Ibrahima Ly was briefly forced to share a cell with a leper – and the Malian government insisted that they were categorically not political prisoners, but simple criminals.[89] In spite of this simulacrum of legality around the repression of political debate, Amnesty quickly latched on to the case, as did the French *Fédération Internationale des Ligues des Droits de l'Homme* (FIDH).[90]

The irony here is bittersweet, as it was not only the Left that was caught in transition. Following the expulsion of Yoro Diakité and Malick Diallo, the CMLN was now visibly torn between two camps, the "hawks" and the "doves." Moussa Traore appeared to be in the latter group, and bringing

---

[87] Note, however, that Ibrahima's elder brother Oumar, who was also arrested, had held an important position in the Keita administration as director of the SOMIEX. Part of their shared opposition to the constitution may have been that it would have excluded Oumar and others who had held positions of authority within the US-RDA government from public service; Campmas (1978), 184. On the arrest of Oumar Ly, see also S. Samaké (2007), 97. In 2013-14, Ibrahim's son Oumar Tata Ly served as Mali's Prime Minister under President Ibrahim Boubacar Keita.

[88] Amb Fr Bko to MAE, April 3, 1975, CADN BKO 63. Note that a 13th person was arrested after the original 12; Mani Diépono is often not counted.

[89] Maïmouna to "Très Chère Amie," Dakar, July 14, 1975; Maïmouna to "Chère Amie," Bamako, July 29, 1974; Pierre Kaldor to "Chers amis" (AFASPA), Jan. 29, 1976, ADSSD 67J110. See also Ly (1997 [1982]), Ch. XX.

[90] FIDH, Communiqué, s.d. (June 1974), ADSSD 67J110.

back the "*Farce*" crew from Taoudeni had brought his differences of opinon with Tiécoro Bagayoko into the open. Better yet, the constitution that the "*Farce*" condemned had affirmed Mali's commitment to the Universal Declaration of Human Rights. When it was approved by 99% of the votes cast, Amnesty's Martin Ennals could not resist pointing out in a letter to President Traore that in light of the constitution's affirmation of the Universal Declaration, the actions committed by the authors of the tract should have no longer been a crime.[91]

That kind of cleverness did not always go down well. If the language of human rights appeared in the new constitution, its presence there was ornamental. In marking the 25th anniversary of the Universal Declaration, Radio Mali had used the occasion to condemn apartheid, Zionism, colonialism, and the Chilean dictatorship of Augusto Pinochet.[92] But human rights at home were something else. The Secretary of the CMLN, Chef de Bataillon Filifing Sissoko, entertained a visit from a French lawyer affiliated with the FIDH who had taken on the "*Farce*" case,[93] but in a sardonic letter brimming with polite hostility, Moussa Traore sent his regrets. "Those whom the Red Cross, the FIDH, and other humanitarian organizations commonly refer to as '*victimes de l'arbitraire*' have been neither abused nor deported [i.e., to places such as Taoudeni]," wrote the President. Rather, "their fate is in the hands of the Malian justice system [and] the judicial process must be allowed to run its course."[94] More and more, the CMLN resented being called to account by the AFASPA, the FIDH, French labor unions, and the international press, notably *Jeune Afrique*. The CMLN saw foreign campaigns for human rights in Mali as "unacceptable interference in their country's internal affairs."[95] Those campaigns put Moussa Traore in a particular bind, as good press abroad would come at the cost of looking weak at

---

[91] *Amnesty International Calls for Release of All Political Prisoners in Mali*, Nov. 13, 1974, Amnesty archives, Series II.5 Box I, AFR 37. The French ambassador's reading was narrower, and it reflected rather neatly the distinction between francophone and Anglophone human rights traditions. Although the constitution assured only limited political rights, the ambassador noted with satisfaction that it guaranteed liberty of conscience within a secular state; Louis Dallier, Amb Fr to MAE, M. Jobert, DAAM, May 10, 1974, #19/DAM, CADN BKO 132.

[92] *Synthèse* 26/73, Dec. 21, 1973, #67/DAM, CADN BKO 43.

[93] *Synthèse* 13/74, July 16, 1974, #17/DAM, CADN BKO 44.

[94] Moussa Traore, President of the CMLN to Thierry Mignon, Paris, Aug. 15, 1974, #227/CMLN, ADSSD 67J110.

[95] Mayzerac, Amb Fr Bko to Jean Sauvagnargues, MAE, DAAM, April 18, 1975, #21/DAM, CADN BKO 63.

home. The stakes were high: there was no way of knowing whether it would be Moussa or his rivals who would follow Yoro Diakité to Taoudeni.

MOUSSA WIELDS THE BLIND MAN'S CANE

What was the effect of such foreign interference? The return to a constitutional regime and the creation of a single political party led by Moussa Traore represented precisely the false liberalization that the "*Farce électoral*" broadsheet had condemned, but the diplomatic cost of dealing harshly with its authors must have seemed more trouble than it was worth. When they did eventually appear before a court on charges of insulting the president, the sentences handed down were considered light: two to four years in prison.[96] The "doves" within the CMLN were growing ever more sensitive to foreign leverage and more cognizant of the need to present a positive image to the outside world.[97] Mali was falling deeper and deeper into debt, and even as the country recovered from the Sahelian famine of 1973–74, its rulers increasingly relied on the stream of foreign aid that continued to arrive. The CMLN desperately sought the renegotiation of the stringent monetary accords established with France in 1967, and it wanted humanitarian and military assistance from both the United States and the USSR.

From the mid-1970s, the rhythm picked up. Elected in 1976, the American head of state Jimmy Carter (Niantao's namesake) hoped to establish a legacy as "the Human Rights president," and he would eventually tie human rights requirements to aid packages. In February 1977, French President Valéry Giscard d'Estaing traveled to Mali to discuss monetary accords and aid. He may have sought the release of both the remaining civilian prisoners and the former soldiers, as his aides had previously assured Gatignon that he would.[98] French membership in Amnesty International was growing very rapidly, up 450% from 1974 to

---

[96] Amb Fr to MAE, Bko, April 3, 1975, coded, CADN BKO 63; cf. Traoré (2008), 291.
[97] See Sennen Andriamirado, "Qui gouverne à Bamako?" *Jeune Afrique* 897 (March 15, 1978), 30–33.
[98] Philippe Sauzay, Chef de Cabinet, Présidence de la Rép, to Sec.-Gen. (AFASPA), March 21, 1977, #029886. Giscard d'Estaing clearly sought improved relations with Mali, and Traore offered diplomatic support on various Saharan issues; see Pres. Giscard d'Estaing to Col. Moussa Traore, Dec. 23, 1977, re. French hostages held by Polisario; Pres. Giscard d'Estaing to Col. Moussa Traore, May 4, 1979, re. debt relief, all in ANF 5AG3 1028.

1978, when the organization could count 300 chapters and 22,000 members in that country alone.[99] The Nobel Peace Prize awarded to Amnesty in 1977 cannot have hurt enrollment. Even if the French ambassador in Bamako warned his government of the futility of attempting to push Mali into entering further into international agreements on the subject, human rights had clearly become an important idiom of African politics.[100] The African Charter on Human and People's Rights was already under discussion, and it would be adopted in 1981. In Bamako, none of this mattered quite as much as relations with the Soviets, whose influence remained considerable. The USSR armed Mali, and it invested heavily in the country's airstrips in order to fight its Cold War battles in southern Africa.[101] Sweeter deals on cotton sales were also on the table and would be signed in 1978.[102] This assistance was partly contingent on releasing the Soviets' US-RDA allies, even though one of their most fervent champions, Madeira Keita, remained imprisoned the longest. It seems likely that Soviet insistence played a greater role than human rights activism in breaking the deadlock within the CMLN over releasing the prisoners, a process which began tentatively in 1975. The French ambassador certainly thought so.[103]

Civilian prisoners such as Gabou Diawara and Seydou Badian Kouyaté began to regain their freedom in a first early wave of liberations in 1975, but more prominent members of Keita's regime, as well as the *militaires*, remained in prison.[104] Over the next two years, the political situation in Mali evolved quickly, and rumors of a general prisoner release began to circulate.[105] Late in 1977 and early in 1978, the survivors of the 1968 group were freed. Most came home, although a few, such as Amadou

---

[99] MAE to M. les Chefs de Missions Diplomatiques et Consulaires, July 7, 1980, #250/ONG, a/s Amnesty International, CADN BKO 132.

[100] Robert Mayzerac to J-F Poncet, MAE, Direction des Nations Unies et des Organisations internationales, March 15, 1979, #321/ NU, a/s le Mali et les droits de l'homme, CADN BKO 132.

[101] See Mayzerac, Amb Fr to MAE, DAM, June 2, 1975, #453-458, CADN BKO 63; see also various documents from 1977-79 in CADN BKO 126, and *Comment on Soviet Activity in Mali*, June 15, 1977, National Security Affairs, Z. Brzezinski materials, Country file, Box 48, Jimmy Carter Presidential Library.

[102] Mazeyrac to MAE, DAAM, March 10, 1978, #369/DAM, CADN BKO 63.

[103] Amb Fr Mali to Diplomatie Paris, June 2, 1975, #453-458, CADN BKO 63.

[104] Int., Gabou Diawara, Bamako, August 16, 2005. *BBC Summary of World Broadcasts*, Second Series, ME 5066/B/5, Nov. 22, 1975, reporting announcement by Radio Mali, Nov. 19, 1975. See also list of liberated detainees, Nov. 18, 1976, CADN BKO 63.

[105] "Mali: Sur la voie de renouveau," *Jeune Afrique* 883 (Dec. 9, 1977).

Seydou Traore, were barred from Bamako and restricted to isolated Sahelian towns.[106] Some, including ex-Chief of Staff Colonel Sékou Traoré, had only enough strength to make it back to their families; a loyal and apolitical man who had probably never been a danger to the regime, he died a few months after returning home.[107] Other ex-prisoners, such as Madeira Keita, would recuperate in Guinea at Sékou Touré's invitation.[108] Years later, when the moment was right, Keita and some of his comrades entered quietly back into the political fray, like crocodiles sliding off rocks.[109]

The release of the civilians was no act of clemency. Moussa Traore's back was against the wall. In May 1977, Radio Mali had announced that "former schoolteacher" Modibo Keita was dead. An anguished dissident abroad took his death as evidence that the remaining prisoners would be killed off, "one by one [as if] over a low flame."[110] The former president's death rocked Bamako, where many believed he had been murdered.[111] His funeral sparked the first large demonstrations against Traore's government, demonstrations that were followed by dozens of arrests.[112] The barracks were also restless. Early in 1978, and just after releasing the last of the US-RDA militants detained since the coup that brought him to power, Traore lashed out at the closest of his former comrades from the CMLN, whom he accused of plotting against him and opposing his

[106] See *Aujourd'hui l'Afrique (Journal de l'AFSPA)* 9 (1977); and int., Amadou Seydou Traoré, Bamako, August 8, 2005.
[107] Int., Adama Sékou Traoré (pseudonym, son of Sékou), Bamako, August 22, 1999. On Traoré, see Mann (2006), ch. 1.
[108] Traoré (2008), 157–63. The politics of the time were turbid, as Touré himself was the object of one of Amnesty's campaigns and had recently killed one of his most prominent rivals, the diplomat Diallo Telli; Lewin (2010), ch. 81; Touré (1978).
[109] Lest this phrase sound pejorative, I should point out that it is a word-play on a Bamana proverb: "No matter how long it remains in the water, a stick will never become a crocodile."
[110] Letter from B. Traore, Dresden, Aug. 12, 1977, to Henri Alleg of *Humanité*, forwarded to "Chers amis" (AFASPA), Aug. 23, 1977, ADSSD 67J6. Alleg was well-known for his public denunciation of the torture he had endured at the hands of French paratroopers in Algeria in 1957; Alleg (2008 [1958]). Mali's torturers are believed to have learned their techniques there.
[111] The cause of Keita's sudden death remains obscure, but it is widely held that he was poisoned by his jailers. For a first-hand account, see S. Samaké (2007). Traore was queried on these occurrences in an "*Interview accordée par le Chef de l'état au correspondant du journal 'Voix d'Afrique,' Juin 1977*"; Kaba (1989), 117–23.
[112] Years earlier, Keita's fall from power had sparked street celebrations; see Sanankoua (1990), 55–56, 178; "Traore asked to use emergency powers when necessary," AFP in English, *Foreign Broadcast Information Service* (hereafter *FBIS*), May 19, 1977; Sow (2008), 389.

political reforms.[113] This "Band of Three" was comprised of Minister of Defense, the Interior, and Security Doukara, Minister of Transport Dembele, and Lieutenant Colonel Bagayoko. Doukara had been Traore's primary rival for years, whereas Bagayoko, for a long time the most feared man in Mali, was characterized in the state-controlled press after his arrest as "personifying terror, injustice, [and] the absence of respect for the human person."[114] He had personally arrested Modibo Keita in 1968, sent the military prisoners to Taoudeni, and packed off students and dissidents to the Sahara.[115] He would be imprisoned alongside Sangaré and Samaké.[116] When he wound up in the salt mines himself, Bagayoko apparently remained loyal to two things: his former boss Moussa Traore, whom he called "*koro*" or older brother, and the Bamakois football club Djoliba F.C.[117] He would die in Taoudeni while his wife Ténimba Bagayoko, herself accused of being a key figure in the alleged coup plot, suffered debilitating torture.[118] The purge was complete. According to Radio Mali, Traore's reprisals had been indiscriminate, like a blind man's cane striking everything in its path. His security services conducted a purge likened to a fine fishing net that neither large nor small fish escaped.[119] Even so, an old politics was

---

[113] For competing analyses of these events, see Sennen Andriamirado, "Qui gouverne à Bamako?" *Jeune Afrique* 897 (March 15, 1978), 30-33, which was foreshadowed by ibid., "Mali: le Moment de choisir est arrivé," *Jeune Afrique* 892 (Feb. 8, 1978), 26-28; and "Mali: Presidential Coup," *Africa Confidential* 19, 7 (March 31, 1978), 3-5. See also "Three Members of Ruling Military Committee Arrested," March 1, 1978; and "Campaign to Form New Political Party Begun," April 8, 1978, both from AFP in English, *FBIS*.

[114] "le Complot Kassim, Tiécoro," 22.

[115] On Bagayoko, see G. Samaké (2009 [1998]), 15, 100; S. Samaké (2007), 166-69; M. M., "Django, le Superman de Bamako," *Jeune Afrique* 897 (March 15, 1978), 32.

[116] *Les militaires* Sangaré and Samaké remained at Taoudeni until completing their sentences in 1979.

[117] On Djoliba F.C., see S. Samaké (2007), 166-69. On Djoliba and '*koro*,' Sangaré (2001), 257-58, 264.

[118] On Bagayoko's death, S. Samaké (2007), 166-69. On his wife, "National Women's Union Officials Arrested in Plot," AFP in English, *FBIS*, April 2, 1978; disability reported by René (sic) Kaldor in a memo "Info. pour l'AFASPA receuillis par Kaldor," Sept. 29, 1979, ADSSD 67J110. On her intended role in the coup, Dembélé (2003), 106.

[119] Sangaré (2001), 246-7. The arrests and purges went on for several weeks, and included S. Samaké. On the arrests, "Three Members of Ruling Military Committee Arrested," March 1, 1978; "More Arrests Made on 'Conspiracy' Charges," March 7, 1978; "Foreign Affairs Minister Arrested for Treason," March 9, 1978; "Arrests of Ranking Officers Involved in Plot Reported," March 13, 1978; and "National Women's Union Officials Arrested in Plot," April 2, 1978, all from AFP in English, *FBIS*. See also, list of "Arrestations depuis le 28 février 1978," 3 April 1978, M 1/1, CADN BKO 63; and "le Complot Kassim, Tiécoro."

beginning to give way to a new one. By mid-1978, with no surviving rivals, the newly promoted Colonel Moussa Traore was in the process of guiding Mali toward what he somewhat paradoxically called "a return to a normal constitutional life [but] not to a civilian regime."[120] This normal life would be lived under a single party, the *Union Démocratique du peuple malien* (UDPM), with him at its head. The Second Republic (1978–1991) was a thin-skinned pseudo-democracy, quick to react to protest but otherwise indifferent to its people. In the years following Modibo Keita's death, Traore would lock up dozens of students, teachers, and activists. Amnesty International adopted some of them as prisoners of conscience, and most had the privilege of standing trial before being sentenced to prison terms comparable to those served by the authors of the "*Farce*" tract of 1974. Many – whether teachers like Victor Sy or students like Rokia Kouyaté – endured torture;[121] student leader Abdoul Karim Camara, known as Cabral, did not survive, but his murder provided the movement with a martyr. As a sign of the times, the text under which Traore's "normal constitutional life" was lived provided amply for human rights.[122]

Years later, contemporary analysts would dub human rights activism a "'politics of the governed' – not a project that aims to govern."[123] The rhetorical move might be a necessary one, but it is like a fast dance step. Can everyone follow? Speaking in defense of people fleeing Vietnam by boat in 1980, Michel Foucault declared that "we are all governed and to that extent in solidarity." Expressed from "a press conference in Geneva ... inaugurating [a] nongovernmental intervention ... in the Gulf of Thailand,"[124] Foucault's solidarity would appear to be a necessarily thin one in comparison with the dense ties of shared principles and experience that bound some in France to the prisoners they were then defending, much less the ties of blood and destiny those prisoners shared with

---

[120] "President Traore Discusses Domestic, International Issues," AFP in French, *FBIS*, Nov. 18, 1978.

[121] For a list, see Sow (2008), 389–90; Traoré (2008), 287–98. On political prisoners in this period, see Gatignon (AFASPA) to Malian Ambassador to France, March 26, 1980, ADSSD 67J110; A.I. "Urgent Action", Index: AFR 37/01/79, Distr: UA. July 25, 1979, and A.I. "Urgent Action", Index: AFR 37/02/79, Distr: UA. Oct. 18, 1979, Amnesty archives, Series II.5 Box I, AFR 37. A series of virtually identical letters written in 1982 by Amnesty activists in support of Mamadou Gologo and Idrissa Diakité can be found in BPNCMLN 277; see also Traoré (2008), 295.

[122] Sow (2008), 358. Sow notes that references to the Universal Declaration of Human Rights appeared in every constitution since that of the République Soudanaise in 1959; 356–59.

[123] Keenan (2007), 67.

[124] Keenan (2007), 67. On this episode, see Taithe (2004), 150.

expatriate dissidents. That said, was Foucault's international solidarity necessarily less real than that which bound certain chapters of Amnesty International to particular prisoners who were strangers to them? These questions remain live ones. Only a cynic would claim that dissidents who attributed their release from prison to the letters of anonymous Amnesty activists while critiquing the neoliberal drift of the Third Republic were settling a debt they did not know they had incurred.[125] Nearly three decades earlier, soldiers had whipped them, shocked them, and battered the naked soles of their feet with sticks before sending them to the salt mines. Only a cynic would ask, were they paying in the currency of sovereignty for a freedom purchased on credit? The act of embracing a human rights rhetoric that placed itself above mere politics might have seemed to offer a way to avoid falling into such a trap. Yet that promise may have been a false one, conditioned on abandoning two political values, sovereignty and solidarity, that animated a new politics in the 1960s and 1970s.

By the 1990s, human rights had become a dominant meme in the discourse of donor nations and the organs of international civil society that exhibited such presence and exercised such power in Third Republic Mali. More than three decades after the US-RDA militants and *les militaires* were freed, and more than twenty years after Traore's own fall from power, internal dissidence and external human rights activism had created a political idiom distinct from the language of strict sovereignty employed by the single-party state before 1991. However, in spite of the efforts of fervent partisans such as the late Demba Diallo – who seized the opportunity presented by Moussa Troare's stint as Chairman of the OAU to establish the *Association Malienne des Droits de l'Homme* in 1988 – that idiom had never quite become an authentic vernacular.[126] A Ministry of Human Rights briefly figured among the dozens of ministries that cluttered the government of the Third Republic after 1991; it did not survive.[127] As a rule, many Malian Islamists, and others as well, rejected human rights arguments out of hand, as not only foreign, but also subordinate to God's law.[128] They had a point. The

---

[125] Victor Sy in Centre Djoliba (2002), 297; Traoré (2008), 155–56.
[126] Bagayogo (1999), 39; Fédération Internationale des ligues des Droits de l'Homme and Association Malienne des Droits de l'Homme (1998–99). The first and final volume of the late Diallo's memoirs does not touch on this episode; Diallo (2005). See also Sow (2008), 393–446.
[127] Dougnon (2011), 87.
[128] On the often-hidden political effects of translating concepts of "Human Rights," see Englund (2006), ch. 2.

phrase "human rights" enters Bambara as "*adamadenw ka sariya*" or "*mogow ka tien*" ("the laws of humanity [lit., ' ... of Adam's children']" or "people's truth"). Neither phrase captured the idea, dear to its champions, that such rights are superior to law, any law, and certainly not to God's law. Derived etymologically from the Arabic "*sharia*," the first phrase in particular is readily contrasted with the laws of God, and Islamists pummeled human rights arguments with this rebuttal. Writing in another register, even the people who might seem to owe the most to human rights activism, ex-prisoners, scarcely use the term in their memoirs.[129] This may be because, for both veterans of what was once "the revolutionary heart of the army" and US-RDA militants such as Amadou Seydou Traoré, skepticism toward the human rights regime is virtually a reflex, one conditioned by local echoes of Cold War politics. The same reflex left them strongly opposed to the neoliberal orientation of the Third Republic.[130] As men who came of age in the moment of independence, they were acutely aware of the frailty of Malian sovereignty and highly sensitive to the symbolic import of selling off state enterprises.[131] Of course, by then those men were elders, but younger generations, too, shared their concerns.

Two loose threads wove through Malian politics – at least until the crisis of 2012 – albeit without circumscribing it.[132] They were intertwined. The first was the need to assert and secure the country's sovereignty and self-determination. The second was the incapacity of successive democratic regimes – the catastrophic failure, in the eyes of many – to provide more than a distant shimmering vision of a brighter future, or indeed any affirmative answer to the question of who or what government was for. It was far from clear that the intellectual-cum-activist tools of human rights practice could seize either thread, much less stitch together an answer to such a fundamental question. Could they do more than offer a patch for a form of government that appeared otherwise dangerously threadbare?

---

[129] A rare and fleeting mention of the concept itself can be found in Sangaré (2001), 249; see also N'Diaye (2010). Unlike the memoirs, Abdoulaye-Sékou Sow's work is a scholarly one. In it he characterizes the arrests of political opponents (including himself) by the CMLN or UDPM as "Human Rights violations"; (2008), 388–91.
[130] Guédiouma Samaké, for example, damns both the putschists who had abandoned the US-RDA's socialist path and the neoliberal road taken by the Third Republic, which he considered the product of "half a revolution"; G. Samaké (2009 [1998]), 107, 109–10.
[131] As Naudet demonstrates, this process was well underway before 1992; (1999), 80.
[132] See, e.g., Bah (2010); Traoré (1999, 2002); Sissako (2006); Kassoum Théra, "Cheikh O. Sissoko: l'après 26 mars a été un échec," *l'Indépendant*, March 27, 2009. On the crisis of 2012, see Lecocq, Mann, et al. (2013).

HUMAN RIGHTS AND MANDE CHARTERS

From the late 1990s, many began to look to the deeper past for fresh answers. In the context of a revived neotraditionalism – latent since at least the 1960s – West African intellectuals "rediscovered" two orally transmitted texts anchored in the thirteenth-century era of the Mali empire, which is taken to represent the heritage of the Mande-speaking peoples.[133] Those texts quickly came to represent a plural, autochthonous, and proudly precolonial tradition of tolerance in the Mande world; they were even held up as proclaiming human rights *avant la lettre*. Confusingly, both are sometimes known as "the Mande Charter," although they may be referred to more precisely as the "Kurukan Fuga" and the lesser-known "Donsolu Kalikan," or "the Hunters' Oath."[134] The Kurukan Fuga took the name of the place at which kings and counselors are said to have mandated a new social order in the wake of Sundiata Keita's defeat of the Susu blacksmith-emperor Soumamarou Kanté in the first half of the thirteenth century. Recently, it has been given the form of a series of distinct articles arranged in the style of a formal juridical document.[135] The Hunters' Oath claims its origins in the same legendary moment, when hunters in their role as the protectors of society laid out their own code of conduct. In its contemporary published form, the Oath maintains the rhetorical style of Mande oral literature, or orature.[136] It is only natural that the styles of the two texts diverge, as each reflects the orientation of its promoter. The contemporary midwife of the Kurukan Fuga was Siriman Kouyaté, who is both a jurist and a descendant of the Kouyaté griot, "Doka the Cat," over whom Sundiata and Soumamarou struggled. Indeed, Kouyaté's family in Kankan is said to possess the *sosobala*, the balaphone seized from Soumamarou at the moment of his defeat, while in the 1990s he sat on that city's court of appeals.[137] The Oath, on the other hand, came to the wider world via Youssouf Tata Cissé, a Malian

---

[133] In what follows, I use the term "text" loosely to refer to both oral and written forms.

[134] On the two texts, see Jolly (2010); Amselle (2001); CELHTO (2008); Diagne (2009); Smith (2010), ch. 12.

[135] See two virtually identical texts: République de Guinée, *Atelier Regional de Concertation entre Communicateurs et Traditionalistes Maninka*, Kankan, March 3 to 12, 1998; and Siriman Kouyaté, *la Charte de Kurukan Fuga: Atelier Regional de Concertation entre Traditionalistes Mandingues et Communicateurs des Radios Rurales*, Radio Rurale de Guinée, Kankan, March 3 to 12, 1998. Unpublished texts in author's possession.

[136] Cissé, Fofana and Sagot-Duvaroux (2003). Note that Cissé, following Kamissoko, dates the Oath to 1222, the year in which, he argues, Sundiata established the empire.

[137] CELTHO (2008); Smith (2010), 753, n4.

ethnographer, who collected it in 1965 – precisely when expatriate experts looked to him to anchor a modernizing sociology[138] – and published it in 1991, and again in 2003. Both texts are products of the circumstances of their production, and more precisely of the moment in which these ideas, which had been part of a curated corpus of orature, were anchored in writing.

The contemporary revival of the Kurukan Fuga has its roots in a pair of workshops held in Upper Guinea, in the Mande heartland, in 1997 and 1998.[139] European NGOs interested in using rural media, particularly radio, had sponsored them in order to promote democracy and human rights. Bringing together "traditionalists, jurists and 'communicators'" from across francophone West Africa, those workshops generated a set of shared adages and precepts. Working from transcripts, Kouyaté would later shape those ideas into a precise, sequentially ordered text. As Eric Jolly argues, this history of recent discovery does not change the fact that the "Kurukan Fuga is as 'true' as other versions or episodes of the Sundiata epic for at least two reasons: those who produced and diffused it had the authority and the legitimacy to do so [that is to say, they were themselves griots]; and its message betrays neither the sense of the corresponding episode in the epic nor the contemporary perspective of Malian and Guinean elites."[140] In fact its champions saw the Kurukan Fuga as a rebuttal to the alleged primacy of such texts as the Magna Carta (1215) or the Declaration of the Rights of Man and of the Citizen (1789), to which they incessantly compared it.[141]

The fact that the Kurukan Fuga emerged from an NGO-funded symposium on good government is hardly incidental to its contemporary significance. The interests of foreign actors had intersected with those of West African neotraditionalists, jurists, and organic intellectuals, even as the latter group offered a powerful rebuttal to the idea that they needed tutoring in governance from Europe. This spirit of unstated opposition among the assembled griots may partly explain why other non-Mandekan

---

[138] Maurice Godelier, "*Proposition pour un programme de développement de l'Institut des Sciences Humaines du Mali (1964–1968)*," Jan. 1965, BPNCMLN 56; see ch. 1.
[139] The Manden, or the Mande heartland (i.e., the legendary core of the former empire), straddles contemporary southwestern Mali and Upper Guinea. Kankan is generally considered the Guinean metropole of the Manden, as Kangaba is for the Republic of Mali.
[140] Jolly (2010), 901.
[141] Jolly (2010), 909; CELTHO (2008). In doing so, they followed a practice already established by the late, influential neotraditionalist Souleyman Kanté, creator of the N'Ko script. Doyen D. T. Niane was more circumspect in his own remarks; CELTHO (2008), 25.

speaking West African intellectuals, such as the Senegalese novelist Boubacar Boris Diop, seized on the Kurukan Fuga as a valorization of the region's intellectual traditions and as a concrete example of its historic integration.[142]

Although the Kurukan Fuga had resurfaced in Guinea, the government of Mali did everything to claim it.[143] Bamako hosted a colloquium in 2007 aimed at standardizing the text and erected a monumental arch near the site where Sundiata's original meeting was said to have been held. In 2009, Mali's Ministry of Culture declared the site part of the country's national patrimony,[144] and UNESCO recognized the Charter itself as part of "the Intangible Cultural Heritage of Humanity."[145] The Kurukan Fuga had arrived, and with it a way out of the zero-sum logic that in earlier decades had seemed to oppose human rights and African sovereignty. Rather than invoking postcolonial failure and the shame of being hectored by outsiders, human rights discourse could now provoke precolonial pride.

Such symbolism is powerful, but it obscures the distance between these texts and the premises of contemporary, "universal" human rights. Both the Kurukan Fuga and the Hunters' Oath argue for a social order. Only the Oath, however, offers a vision that is simultaneously egalitarian and committed to the protection of the vulnerable, the marginalized, and the disenfranchised. In contrast, for instance, the Kurukan Fuga asserts the rights of parents to choose a husband for pubescent daughters irrespective of the girl's age; neither the US-RDA nor for that matter the last colonial administration would have approved. And despite claims that the Kurukan Fuga "abolishes slavery,"[146] it does nothing of the sort. Rather, as do the Qur'an and the sunna, it recognizes the existence of a social category of slaves, "*jon kuru kelen*,"[147] and indicates the appropriate conditions of their servitude in order to limit abuses. "You are the master of the slave, but not of the sack he carries," proclaims Kouyaté's Article 21, expressing a sentiment that resonates with the traditions of the Prophet

---

[142] CELTHO (2008). Smith notes that 8 of 10 contributors to the CELTHO volume were neither Malian nor Guinean but Senegalese; (2010), 753, n7. One might deduce that they would almost certainly have been limited to the French language translation of the original Mandekan.
[143] Smith (2010), ch. 12.
[144] Smith (2010), 756.
[145] See http://www.unesco.org/culture/ich/en/RL/00290; last consulted Jan. 14, 2014.
[146] CELTHO (2008), 121–22.
[147] The phrase appears in the Mandekan text in CELTHO (2008), 43. Its equivalent does not appear in Kouyaté French language text, and many of those who celebrated the Kurukan Fuga would have been unaware of its presence in the original.

Muhammad. Indeed, the text valorizes precisely the social structure that Modibo Keita's government had once hoped to move beyond. It is the Hunters' Oath that unequivocally abolishes slavery with the phrase "*donsolu ko: ko dyònnya shi saara bi*," that is, "the hunters declare that as of today, slavery has been torn out by its roots."[148] Such differences are telling, but they could be – and indeed were – concealed by selective translation or elided altogether. At any rate, the texts were celebrated for their mere existence, not for their content, and slavery was hardly the order of the day. Democracy was.

The Kurukan Fuga, and to a lesser extent the Hunters' Oath, emerged in the context of particular experiments in democratic government, notably the administrative decentralization that NGOs and donor nations promoted in the 1990s. Modibo Keita's First Republic – and even the last colonial administration – had considered decentralization essential, yet failed to achieve it.[149] On picking up this long discarded political project, Malian and foreign analysts alike tended to adopt an historical perspective that privileged reference to the precolonial nineteenth century (and even the thirteenth century) over the actual history of twentieth-century administration. In the same move, they reconfirmed the Manden as the symbolic center of gravity of Malian politics.[150] In that context, the value of a local theory of political power such as the Kurukan Fuga lay in its potential to legitimate – and almost literally to "domesticate" – decentralization, which, in its most recent version, has entailed replacing the lowest rung on the administrative ladder (the *arrondissement*, in which a civil servant governed locally) with a rural commune composed of an elected mayor and councilmen.[151] The Kurukan Fuga offered a tool for thinking through this process of "returning" power to smaller communities and village confederations, a process captured in the phrase "*ka mara la segin so*," which could be loosely translated as "bringing the government closer to

---

[148] More prosaically, "slavery is abolished"; CELTHO (2008), 148–49. See also Cissé and Sagot-Duvaroux (2003). The iconoclastic griot Wa Kamissoko, with whom Cissé collaborated, had previously provoked controversy by arguing that Soumamarou had abolished slavery in the Manden before Sundiata's rise. Kamissoko used a virtually identical phrase to "*dyònnya shi saara bi*"; Cissé and Kamissoko (1988), 203.

[149] On decentralization in the 1990s and since, see C. Fay, Y.F. Koné, and C. Quiminal, eds. (2006); Zobel (1996); Languille (2010). Earlier attempts at decentralization were discussed in ch. 2.

[150] Some analysts went to the other extreme, insisting that only the Tuareg rebellion of the 1990s had succeeded in compelling decentralization; Beridogo (2006), 204. On Mande-centered neotraditionalism and its political effects, see Amselle (2001, 2006).

[151] Amselle (2006), 60–61.

home." From the outside, this might have sounded like democratization, but its partisans often equated decentralization with the exhortation "*ka fanga segin so*," or "to bring *power* home," which merely raised the question "to whom?"

This is no idle question. A considerable gulf separated the forms of government laid out in the Kurukan Fuga – effectively a monarchy, certainly not a republic – from what outside actors (Africans and others alike) thought they saw within it.[152] One would have to look rather hard to find rights secured by the Kurukan Fuga. In the end, it offers a script for governing, not a mode of being governed. Neither is it a script for neoliberal governance, emphasizing instead collective identities and duties. From the outside, the two texts, and their points of divergence, might be seen as testifying to the incomplete domestication of human rights discourse within West Africa, and in deeply historicist terms. Yet they represent neither domestication nor vernacularization, and their value may lie less in their historicity than in the fact that both speak, discordantly, to the linked and ever-pressing questions of what government is and what it is for.

---

[152] Diawara (2011), 435–36.

Conclusion

In the 1990s, much less twenty-odd years later, nothing so abstract as human rights was visible on the road to Douentza. One could see signs of power, in the form of the white 4×4s of international NGOs, and the state was present, if only in traces and at the gendarmes' posts. But much that seemed obvious was not even true.

This is what I learned. In the 1970s, international NGOs had not muscled their way into newly independent African states uninvited. At least some of them were sought out. Once present, they worked to make themselves at home. Shifting from relief to development, CARE's agents burrowed into the administrations of Mali and Niger, seeking to make themselves useful, even necessary, in the wake of the immediate drought emergency. In contrast, even after their own sudden rise to prominence a few years later, human rights organizations remained on the outside looking in. Although they fixed their gazes steadily on a small number of prisoners, they posed an even deeper challenge to the exercise of African sovereignties than did the humanitarians and the development agents. In the long run, both NGOs and human rights campaigns had viral effects, not in the sense of spreading rapidly – although they did – but in the sense of investing other political forms, injecting them with their own particular politics, and reprogramming their hosts. The emergent form of nongovernmentality that they represented was never in and of itself "neoliberal." It did, however, pry open the gap between state and government that crushing debt, structural adjustment, the end of Cold War subsidies, and a host of other factors would combine to widen.

Yet even that story is too simple, for a number of other facts are stubborn. First, the states of Sahelian francophone Africa proved to be more than colonial assemblages; rather, they took on lives of their own. Here I would add an historian's caution to the clear voice of an anthropologist who argues that "We will not [understand how] Africa is governed until we move beyond the myth of the sovereign African nation-state to explore the powerful but almost wholly unaccountable transnational institutions that effectively ... rule large domains of African economy and society."[1] True. But before moving beyond the myth, we have to move through it, recognizing moments when such sovereignties were real and ripe with potential, even if they were narrowly defined and unevenly exercised. They too had effects. But *pace* the premises of modernization theory – and of many nationalists – nation-states were not the sole political bodies to emerge from Europe's waning empires. New networks, alliances, and NGOs did as well. They would quickly come to govern alongside the new states, not over them, but sometimes in their place.

Those political formations did not come from nowhere; many of the most significant of them carried on a tradition of anticolonialist and Communist politics. Already, during the postwar period of imperial reform and in the first years of independence, particular forms of radical anticolonial politics had emerged within the territories of French West Africa. Some were defeated outright, as in Senegal and Niger; others as in Mali, were integrated at least provisionally into what would become single-party states. In the wake of an empire as centralized and tightly bound as the French – or indeed party cultures as intense as that of the postwar PCF or the early US-RDA – ties between activists and intellectuals proved enduring. After 1960, such once-imperial relationships simply became transnational ones. In decades to come, they would continue to evolve.

Those relationships might have mattered little had the Sahel not been struck by such a catastrophic drought, had humanitarian activity in post-1968 France and post-Civil Rights America not evolved as it did, or had a very particular form of human rights activism not begun to gain traction in the North Atlantic nations. But all those things did happen, which leads to a third stubborn fact: the Sahel is both externally oriented – "extraverted" in Jean-François Bayart's terms – and a profoundly historical space.[2] Any analysis of it must conjugate those two characteristics.

A geographic region, a political assemblage, a zone of intervention ... the Sahel is all those things. But like the continent of which it is a part, the

---

[1] Ferguson, (2006), 87; see also Piot, (2010), 8.
[2] Bayart (2000).

Conclusion

Sahel must be taken on its own terms rather than subordinated to familiar narratives and epistemologically powerful yet ultimately parochial forms of knowledge such as those too often offered by the contemporary social sciences.[3] Recognizing the innovation and the importance of new forms of nongovernmentality does not preclude taking West African thought and politics seriously. It relies on it. That in turn means recognizing that in the sovereign states of the Sahel, "to govern" might not mean to manage the conditions of life or to "husband" a population, still less to exert a form of totalizing and internalized power. That compelling interpretation happened to emerge in France at a particularly rich moment in the politics of West African immigrants and their allies, but it was fabricated neither by nor for them. In an imperfect way, it captured elements of their lives there, but not at home and not in Sudan, where struggles for control had been raw and claims of membership intensely disputed. Around the same time as such idioms of "governmentality" emerged, however, nongovernmental organizations began to define the tasks associated with managing the conditions of life as theirs. Some states acknowledged them, too, at least partially. In Niger, Seyni Kountché adopted his predecessor's project by launching the "Development Society," yet neither he nor his Malian counterpart, Moussa Traore, was ever a shepherd exercising "pastoral power." His griots dubbed Traore a lion (B., *waraba*), and the junta's surviving members once wanted to take the vulture as their symbol.[4] Either way, they were devouring the herd, not protecting it. That remained true in Traore's last speech, a warning launched in the face of popular revolt in 1991: "The calf does not know the lion, but his mother does" (B., *misidenin, a te wara don, nka bari ba ... ba y'a don*).[5]

The Lost Republic

After thirty years of neoliberal gnawing and (ever-more adroit) governmental negotiating,[6] the Sahel plunged deeply into crisis in 2012 when Mali fell apart. The causes were multiple, and many extended well beyond the state, its territory, and even the region in which it sits. An internal insurgency became intertwined with networks of criminality and banditry extending across the Sahara and well beyond, and

---

[3] Here I echo Achille Mbembe's critique; (2001).
[4] The latter in reference to the traditional warrior's song "Douga"; Camara (1998), 16.
[5] Kone (1996), 90, 95–6.
[6] On the negotiating, see Bergamischi (2009).

with roots as deep in the capital city as in the distant towns of the Sahara and the historic Sahel. The government collapsed, and the army did too. For long miserable months the black flag of jihad replaced Mali's pan-African tricolor in virtually every town north of the river. An Irish poet had already described it best: things fell apart; the center could not hold; the best lacked all conviction while the worst were full of passionate intensity. Caught short by this drama, African intellectuals struggled to elaborate some kind of analysis of the catastrophe.[7] Meanwhile many outside observers chose to fall back on the most comfortable of clichés rather than engage in the hard work of generating a new critical apparatus to describe the situation that confronted them. None of this served Malians very well. So where were their own intellectuals?

Bar a few signal exceptions,[8] they were remarkably silent, while the country's academics were virtually mute. Structurally adjusted, deeply politicized, and demoralized, the educational system had become, in the eyes of one of its dissidents, the theater of a politics without merit.[9] In years previous, the university frequently ground to a halt in strikes intended to maintain a regime of piecework, in which overburdened lecturers were paid by the graded exam. While they struggled to survive, strikes defending academic freedom or demanding adequate resources for research were nonexistent, but not because those issues themselves did not exist. Instead, collective action defending freedom of speech had become the purview of journalists, rather than intellectuals. Long an anchor of radical politics, the students' union, too, had lost its way. Even as hundreds of thousands of their fellow citizens were displaced, dozens of Mali's students wielded weapons not in defense of the country, but in factional disputes over union leadership and its material perks, which they contested with knives and guns.[10]

Where to turn? An older generation of intellectuals – those who had survived torture and imprisonment under Moussa – had been reduced to

---

[7] E.g., le Mali: le Regard de Boubacar Boris Diop, leSenegalais.net, Feb. 2, 2013, (published online; last consulted March 31, 2013); Samir Amin, Rescuing Mali from Islamist militants, *Pambazuka News* 616, Feb. 14, 2013 (published online; last consulted July 19, 2013).

[8] See notably Manthia Diawara, La France qui gagne est-elle synonyme du Mali qui gagne? Mediapart.fr, Jan. 14, 2013 (published online; last consulted Dec. 5, 2013).

[9] Isaie Dougnon,"In a time of crisis, why are academics so silent?" *University World News* 262, March 9, 2013 (published online; last consulted July 19, 2013).

[10] Author's fieldnotes, Bamako, March and May 2013. To be fair, some of Mali's more honorable officers in the debacle of 2012 had once been student activists.

a sprinkling of survivors, many of them broken. Some elder dissidents could be found in a bar near one river and named after another. There, young lecturers would occasionally stand them a beer. In my old neighborhood, another man who had fought and briefly won the political wars that chased Moussa from office had lost his health and his sight. He'd retired from teaching and trade unionism. He no longer invited delegations of foreign labor activists for Sunday lunch. Unable now to follow his other passion – herding goats along the river in the early evening – he shuffled out a path between mosque and veranda. There he would sit, radio at his side, his eyes no longer strong enough to make out the portraits of Nkrumah and Lenin that hung high on his walls. Were the answers there?

What had been gained and lost in Mali over fifty years became stunningly clear in January 2013, when French forces once more waged war on Malian soil, this time at Bamako's behest. Some of those who had inherited the mantle of dissent asked aloud what it was, in January 2013, that Mali still had left to lose. Honor, sovereignty, self-determination? No doubt each of those values was at stake. In 1960, Mali like its neighbors had proudly proclaimed itself a republic. The obituary of that lost republic is another book. But as I have argued here, after decades of nongovernmentality the question, "What is government?" had become more profound and vital than its counterpart, "Who governs?" The answer to one was not embedded in the other, even as the latter had become ever more immanent, and an answer ever harder to discern.

When I first arrived in Bamako in the mid-1990s, as a young and hapless researcher, the haze was no less thick, even if most of it was my own. My *diatigi* had met me at the airport in a borrowed car; when I flew out a few weeks later, we would end up pushing the same vehicle. But on that night we rode slowly into the city. The road was under construction, and we followed a track that ran alongside it through a world of dust and smoke. Across the disused road, fires and flares burned, separated from us by the construction zone and some kind of ditch. On the other side of that empty space, a line of people walked parallel to our track, their silhouettes flickering between us and the distant flames. I was exhausted and disoriented. My mind leapt to Plato's allegory in which prisoners in a cave, seeing only shadows and particularly those of puppets, take them for what is real. Were my companions and I the prisoners or were we the puppeteers? I could not recall the next narrative twist to the allegory, in which one prisoner is freed, ascends to the surface, and thereafter perceives the shadows differently. I had forgotten that the prisoner who ascends is the philosopher, Plato himself. So in my muddled memory, there we were: the prisoners, the light, the shadows. There was no philosopher, perhaps no puppeteer. But in years to come, on other roads like the one to Douentza, I would wonder: What cast those shadows? And who kept the fires burning?

Works Cited

I. Archives and Archival Collections

ACVAFS, American Council of Voluntary Agencies for Foreign Service, Rutgers University Libraries Special Collections, New Brunswick, NJ
ADSSD, Archives Départementales de la Seine-Saint-Denis, Bobigny
AFSC, American Friends Services Committee, Philadelphia
Agefom, Agence de la France d'Outre-Mer, Press Agency, housed in CAOM
Amnesty International, Amnesty International of the U.S.A., National Office Records, Columbia University Rare Book and Manuscript Library, New York City
ANF, Archives Nationales de France, Paris
ANM, Archives Nationales du Mali, Bamako
ANS, Archives Nationales du Sénégal, Dakar
BPN, Fonds Bureau Politique National (of the US-RDA), housed in ANM
BPNCMLN, Fonds Bureau Politique National (of the US-RDA), Comité Militaire de Libération Nationale (CMLN) and Union Démocratique du Peuple Malien (UDPM), housed in ANM
CAC, Centre des Archives Contemporaines, Fontainebleau
CADN, Centre des Archives Diplomatiques, Nantes
CAOM, Centre des Archives d'Outre-Mer, Aix-en-Provence
CARAN, Centre d'Accueil et de Recherche des Archives Nationales, Paris
CARE, Cooperative for American Relief Everywhere, Manuscripts and Archives Division, The New York Public Library. Astor, Lenox, and Tilden Foundations, New York City
Fonds Meillassoux, Centre d'Etudes des Mondes Africains, Université de Paris-I, Paris
FPR, Papers of Jacques Foccart, Private collection, Archives Nationales de France
FPU, Papers of Jacques Foccart, Public collection, Archives Nationales de France
Hoover, Hoover Institution, Stanford University, Palo Alto, CA
IFCO, Inter-religious Foundation for Community Organization, The New York Public Library, Schomburg Center for Research in Black Culture, Manuscripts, Archives and Rare Books Division, New York City
Jimmy Carter Presidential Library, Atlanta, GA

Loft, George Loft Papers, housed in the Hoover Institution
Lydon Baines Johnson Presidential Library, Austin, TX
MAE, Ministère des Affaires Etrangères, Paris
MIM, Ministère de l'Interieur, Bamako, Mali
Sahel MfAs, Sahel Microfiche Collection, published by University Microfilms International, Ann Arbor, MI
SHAT, Service Historique de l'Armée de Terre, Vincennes, France
SRAD, Service Regional des Archives de Dakar, Senegal
UN, United Nations, Archives and Records Management Section, New York City

II. Periodicals Cited

A. Newspapers

l'Afrique Noire, Dakar
Afrique Nouvelle, Dakar
l'Aurore, Bamako
les Continents, Paris
Coup de Bambou, Conakry
Les Echoes, Bamako
l'Essor, Bamako
l'Essor Hebdo., Bamako
Fraternité, Paris
la Guinée Française, Conakry
l'Indépendant, Bamako
Mauritanie Nouvelle, Nouakchott
Le Monde, Paris
The New York Times, New York City
Le Parisien Libéré, Paris
Phare de Guinée, Conakry
le Soleil, Dakar
Soudan Matin, Bamako
Sunjata, Bamako
Verité, Bamako
Voix de la Guinée, Conakry

B. Online journals

LeSenegalais.net
Mediapart.fr
Pambazuka News
University World News

C. Other contemporary periodicals and serials

Africa Confidential
Aujourd'hui l'Afrique (Bulletin de l'AFASPA)
BBC Summary of World Broadcasts
Bulletin du Comité Français des Amis du Mali
Bulletin d'Information et de Renseignments du GGAOF
Débats de l'Assemblée Nationale (France)
Etudes Guinéennes
Foreign Broadcast Information Service
Jeune Afrique
Journal Officiel de l'Afrique Occidentale Française
Journal Officiel de la République Française (JORF)
Journal Officiel de la République Soudanaise (JORS)
Notes Africaines (Dakar)
West Africa

III. Books, Articles, and Reports

l'Aide de la France aux états de la Sahel victimes de la sécheresse. 1973. Paris: Secrétariat Général du Comité Interministériel pour l'Information.
Adedze, Agbenyega. 2003. In the Pursuit of Knowledge and Power: French scientific research in West Africa, 1938–65. *Comparative Studies of South Asia, Africa and the Middle East* 23, 1–2: 335–44.
Adler, Alfred, and Georges Balandier, eds. 1986. *Afrique Plurielle, Afrique Actuelle: Hommage à Georges Balandier*. Paris: Karthala.
Agier, Michel. 2011. *Managing the Undesireables: Refugee Camps and Humanitarian Government*. Translated by David Fernbach. Malden, MA: Polity.
al-Karansi, Awad al-Sid. 1987. The Establishment of neo-Mahdism in the Western Sudan, 1920–1936. *African Affairs* 86, 344: 385–404
Al-Naqar, 'Umar. 1969a. Takrur: the History of a name. *Journal of African History* 10, 3: 365–74.
   1969b. *West Africa and the Muslim Pilgrimage: An Historical Study with Special Reference to the Nineteenth Century*. Ph.D., School of Oriental and African Studies (University of London).
   1972. *The Pilgrimage Tradition in West Africa: An Historical Study with Special Reference to the Nineteenth Century*. Khartoum: Khartoum University Press.
Alleg, Henri. 2008 [1958]. *la Question*. Paris: Editions Minuit.
Alpha Gado, Boureima. 1993. *Une Histoire des famines au Sahel: étude des grandes crises alimentaires, XIXe-XXe siècles*. Paris: l'Harmattan.
American Friends Service Committee [AFSC]. 1982. *Tin Aicha Nomad Village*. Philadelphia: American Friends Service Committee.
Amin, Samir. 1969. *Le Monde des Affaires Sénégalais*. Paris: Editions de Minuit.
   1973. *Neo-Colonialism in West Africa*. New York: Monthly Review Press.

Amselle, Jean-Loup. 1977. *Les Négociants de la Savane: Histoire et organisation sociale des Kooroko (Mali)*. Paris: Editions Anthropos.
———. 1978. le Mali socialiste, 1960–1968. *Cahiers d'études africaines* 18, 72: 631–34.
———. 1985. Socialisme, capitalisme, et precapitalisme au Mali (1960–1982). In *Contradictions of Accumulation in Africa*, edited by Henry Bernstein and Bonnie K. Campbell, 249–66. Beverly Hills, CA: Sage.
———. 2001. *Branchements: Anthropologie de l'universalité des cultures*. Paris: Flammarion.
———. 2006. Les usages politiques du passé: le N'Ko et la décentralisation administrative au Mali. In *Décentralisation et Pouvoirs en Afrique: En contrepoint, modèles territroriaux français*, edited by C. Fay, Y. F. Koné and C. Quiminal, 39–66. Paris: IRD Editions.
Arendt, Hannah. 1951 [1994]. *Origins of Totalitarianism*. San Diego, CA: Harcourt, Brace.
Asiwaju, A. I. 1979. Control through Coercion: A study of the *indigénat* regime in French West African administration, 1887–1946. *Bulletin de l'IFAN, séries B* 41: 35–75.
Autra, Ray [aka Mamadou Traoré]. 1964. l'Institut National de Recherches et de Documentation de la République de Guinée. *Recherches Africaines* 1–4: 5–35.
Awad, Mohamed. 1966. *Report on Slavery*. New York: United Nations.
Bâ, Amadou Hampâté. 1994. *Oui, Mon Commandant!* Arles: Actes Sud.
Babou, Cheikh Anta. 2005. Contesting Space, Shaping Places: Making room for the Muridiyya in colonial Senegal, 1912–45. *Journal of African History* 46, 3: 405–26.
Bagayogo, Shaka. 1999. *Le Cheminement du Mali vers un Espace Politique Pluriel, Cercle de Réflexion Djoliba*. Bamako: Centre Djoliba.
Bah, Tahirou. 2010. *Mali: Le Procès permanent*. Paris: l'Harmattan.
Balamoan, G. Ayoub. 1976. *Migration Policies in the Anglo-Egyptian Sudan, 1884 to 1956*. Cambridge, MA: Harvard University Center for Population Studies.
———. 1981. *Peoples and Economics in the Sudan, 1884 to 1956: The First Part of a History of Human Tragedies on the Nile (1884 to 1984)*. Rev. and extended ed., edited by J. B. Wyon. Cambridge, MA: Harvard University Center for Population Studies.
Balandier, Georges. 1948a. Erreurs noires. *Présence Africaine* 1, 3: 392–404.
———. 1948b. l'Or de la Guinée Françaises [sic]. *Présence Africaine* 1, 4: 539–48.
———. 1950a. Aspects de l'évolution sociale chez les Fang du Gabon (Afrique Équatoriale Française). *Cahiers Internationaux de Sociologie* 9: 76–106.
———. 1950b. O. Mannoni: Psychologie de la colonisation. *Cahiers Internationaux de Sociologie* 9: 183–86.
———. 1950c. La Participation de l'AEF à la Conférence Internationale des Africanistes de l'Ouest. *Bulletin: Institut d'études centrafricains, nouvelle série* 1, 79–80.
———. 1951. La Situation coloniale: Approche théorique. *Cahiers Internationaux de Sociologie* 11: 44–79.
———. 1952. Contribution à une sociologie de la dépendance. *Cahiers Internationaux de Sociologie* 12: 47–69.

1955a. *Sociologie actuelle de l'Afrique noire: dynamique sociale en Afrique.* Paris: Presses Universitaires de la France.
1955b. *Sociologie des Brazzavilles Noires.* Paris: A. Colin.
ed. 1956. *Le 'Tiers Monde': Sous-développement et développement*, Institut National d'Etudes Démographiques. Travaux et Documents, Cahier No. 27. Paris: Presses Universitaires de France.
1965. Problématique des classes sociales en Afrique noire. *Cahiers Internationaux de Sociologie* 38: 131–42.
1966. *Ambiguous Africa: Cultures in Collision.* Translated by Helen Weaver. New York: Pantheon.
1977. *Histoire d'Autres.* Paris: Stock.
1997. *Conjugaisons.* Paris: Fayard.
2002. La Situation coloniale: Ancien concept, nouvelle réalité. *French Politics, Culture and Society* 20, 2: 4–10.
Balandier, Georges, George Steinmetz, and Gisèle Sapiro. 2010. Tout parcours scientifique comporte des moments autobiographiques. *Actes de la Recherche en Sciences Sociales* 185: 44–61.
Balfour, Ian, and Edouard Cadava. 2004. The Claims of Human Rights: An introduction. *South Atlantic Quarterly* 103, 2–3: 277–96.
Barbour, K. M. 1966. Population Shifts and Changes in Sudan since 1898. *Middle Eastern Studies* 2, 2: 98–122.
Barnett, Michael. 2011. *Empire of Humanity: A History of Humanitarianism.* Ithaca: Cornell University Press.
Barthélémy, Pascale. 2010. *Africaines et Diplômées à l'époque coloniale (1918–1957).* Rennes: Presses Universitaires de Rennes.
Bat, Jean-Pierre. 2012. *Le Syndrome Foccart: La politique française en Afrique, de 1959 à nos jours*, Folio Histoire. Paris: Editions Gallimard.
Baulin, Jacques. 1986. *Conseiller du Président Diori.* Paris: Eurafor-Press.
Bawa Yamba, Christian. 1995. *Permanent Pilgrims: The Role of Pilgrimage in the Lives of West African Muslims in Sudan.* Washington, DC: Smithsonian Institution Press.
Bayart, Jean-François. 2000. Africa in the World: A history of extraversion. *African Affairs* 99, 395: 217–67.
2011. *Les Etudes Postcoloniales: Un Carnaval académique.* Paris: Karthala.
Bechtold, Peter K. 1976. *Politics in the Sudan: Parliamentary and Military Rule in an Emerging African Nation.* New York: Praeger.
Beck, Kurt. 2013. Roadside Comforts: Truck stops on the forty days road in Western Sudan. *Africa* 83, 3: 426–55.
Bergamaschi, Isaline. 2009. Mali: Origins, patterns and limits of donor-driven ownership. In *The Politics of Aid: African Strategies for Dealing with Donors*, edited by Lindsay Whitfield, 217–45. Oxford: Oxford University Press.
Béridogo, Bréhima. 2006. Processus de décentralisation et pluralité de logiques des acteurs du Mali. In *Décentralisation et Pouvoirs en Afrique: En contrepoint, modèles territroriaux français*, edited by C. Fay, Y. F. Koné and C. Quiminal, 199–217. Paris: IRD Editions.
Bernault, Florence. 2001. l'Afrique et la modernité des sciences sociales. *Vingtième Siècle* 70: 127–38.

Bertoncello, Brigitte, and Sylvie Bredeloup. 2004. *Colporteurs Africains à Marseille: Un siècle d'aventures*. Paris: Editons Autrement.

Bianchini, Pascal. 2011. *Suret-Canale: de la Résistance à l'anticolonialisme: entretiens autobiographiques*. Paris: l'Esprit frappeur.

Biobaku, S., and M. al-Hajj. 1966. The Sudanese Mahdiyya and the Niger-Chad region. In *Islam in Tropical Africa*, edited by I. M. Lewis, 425–42. London: International African Institute.

Birks, J. S. 1978. *Across the Savannas to Mecca: The Overland Pilgrimage Route from West Africa*. Totowa, NJ: F. Cass.

Bogosian, Catherine. 2003. The 'Little Farming Soldiers': The Evolution of a labor army in post-colonial Mali. *Mande Studies* 5: 83–100.

Boilley, Pierre. 1993. l'Organisation Commune des Régions Sahariennes (OCRS): Une tentative avortée. In *Nomades et commandants: Administration et sociétés nomades dans l'ancienne A.O.F.*, edited by Edmond Bernus, Pierre Boilley, Jean Clauzel, and Jean-Louis Triaud, 215–39. Paris: Karthala.

——— 1999 [2012]. *Les Touaregs Kel Adagh: dépendances et révoltes: du Soudan francais au Mali contemporain*. Paris: Karthala.

——— 2003. Administrative Confinements and Confinements of Exile: The reclusion of nomads in the Sahara. In *A History of Prison and Confinement in Africa*, edited by Florence Bernault, 221–38. Portsmouth, NH: Heinemann.

Bonnecase, Vincent. 2008. *Pauvreté au Sahel: La construction des savoirs sur les niveaux de vie au Burkina Faso, au Mali et au Niger (1945–1974)*. Ph.D., Paris-I.

——— 2010. Retour sur la famine au Sahel du début des années 1970: la construction d'un savoir de crise. *Politique Africaine* 119: 23–42.

——— 2011. *La Pauvreté au Sahel: du Savoir colonial à la mesure international*. Paris: Karthala.

Bonnet, Jean. 1990. Soundiata. *Hommes et migrations* 1132: 57–59.

Boone, Catherine. 2003. *Political Topographies of the African State: Territorial Authority and Institutional Choice*. New York: Cambridge University Press.

Bourdieu, Pierre. 1993. Esprits d'Etat. *Actes de la Recherche en Sciences Sociales* 96–97: 49–62.

Bredeloup, Sylvie. 2007. *La Diams'pora du fleuve Senegal*. Toulouse: Presses Universitaires du Mirail.

Brenner, Louis. 2000. Amadou Hampâté Bâ: Tijânî francophone. In *La Tijâniyya: Une Confrérie Musulmane à la conquête de l'Afrique*, edited by Jean-Louis Triaud and David Robinson, 289–326. Paris: Karthala.

——— 2001. *Controlling Knowledge: Religion, Power, and Schooling in a West African Muslim Society*. Bloomington: Indiana University Press.

Brot, Michel. 1999. Did the Popular Front have any Significant Impact in Guinée? In *French Colonial Empire and the Popular Front*, edited by Tony Chafer and Amanda Sackur, 188–202. New York: St. Martin's.

Brumpt, L., et al. 1965. Pathologie des noirs transplantés. In Approche des problèmes de la migration noire en France, Special issue of *Hommes et migrations*: 3–58.

Brunschwig, Henri. 1983. *Noirs et blancs dans l'Afrique noire française, ou, Comment le colonisé devient colonisateur, 1870–1914*. Paris: Flammarion.

Buchanan, Tom. 2002. 'The Truth Will Set You Free': The making of Amnesty International. *Journal of Contemporary History* 37, 4: 575–97.
Buell, Raymond Leslie. 1928. *The Native Problem in Africa*. 2 vols. New York: Macmillan.
Bugnicourt, J. 1974. Un peuple privé de son environnement. In *Programme 'Formation pour l'environnement'*. Dakar: IDEP-UNEP-SIDA.
Burbank, Jane, and Frederick Cooper. 2008. Empire, Droits, et Citoyenneté, de 212 à 1946. *Annales: Histoire, Sciences Sociales* 63, 3: 495–531.
Burke, Roland. 2010. *Decolonization and the Evolution of International Human Rights*. Philadelphia: University of Pennsylvania Press.
Burrill, Emily S. (In Press). *States of Marriage: Gender, Justice, and Rights in Colonial Mali*. Athens: Ohio University Press.
Camara, Moussa Makan. 1998. *Questions Brûlantes pour une démocratie naissante*. Dakar: Les Nouvelles Editions Africaines du Sénégal.
Camara, Sikhé. 1973. *La Guinée vers le socialisme*. Conakry: s.p.
Campbell, Penelope 2011. *Africare: Black American Philanthropy in Africa*. New Brunswick, NJ: Transaction.
Campbell, Wallace J. 1990. *The History of CARE: A Personal Account*. New York: Praeger.
Campmas, Pierre. 1976. *L'Union Soudanaise, Section Soudanaise du Rassemblement Démocratique Africain, 1946–1968*. Thèse de 3ème Cycle, Université de Toulouse-le Mirail.
  1978. *L'Union Soudanaise R.D.A.: l'histoire d'un grand parti politique africain*. Collection la Récade. Abidjan: Editions Communication Intercontinentale.
CELHTO [Centre d'études linguistiques et historiques par tradition orale]. 2008. *La Charte du Kurukan Fuga: Aux Sources d'une pensée politique en Afrique*. Paris: l'Harmattan.
Centre Djoliba and Mémorial Modibo Keita. 2002. *Bâtissons la mémoire du Mali démocratique: 26 mars 1991–26 mars 2001, Xe anniversaire*. Bamako: Centre Djoliba and Mémorial Modibo Keïta.
Césaire, Aimé. 2010 [1956]. Letter to Maurice Thorez. Translated by Chike Jeffers, *Social Text* 28, 2: 145–52.
Chafer, Tony. 2002. *The End of Empire in French West Africa: France's Successful Decolonization?* New York: Berg.
Chalfin, Brenda. 2010. *Neoliberal Frontiers: An Ethnography of Sovereignty in West Africa*. Chicago: University of Chicago Press.
Chatterjee, Partha. 1993. *The Nation and Its Fragments: Colonial and Postcolonial Histories*. Princeton, NJ: Princeton University Press.
  2004. *The Politics of the Governed: Reflections on Popular Politics in Most of the World*. New York: Columbia University Press.
CILSS. 1973a. *Report of the Meeting of Experts*. Ouagadougou: CILSS.
  1973b. *Strategy Guidelines for Control of the Drought and Its Consequences*. Ouagadougou: CILSS.
Cissé, Youssouf Tata, and Wa Kamissoko. 1988. *La Grande geste du Mali, des origines à la fondation de l'Empire*. Paris: Karthala/ARSAN.
Cissé, Youssouf Tata, Aboubakar Fofana, and J.-L. Sagot-Duvaroux. 2003. *la Charte du Mandé et autres traditions du Mali*. Paris: Albin Michel.

Cissoko, Sékéné Mody. 1968. Famines et epidemies à Tombouctou et dans la Boucle du Niger du XVI' au XVIII' siècle. *Bulletin de l'IFAN, série B* 30, 3: 806–21.

Clancy-Smith, Julia Ann. 2012. *Mediterraneans: North Africa and Europe in an Age of Migration, c. 1800–1900.* Berkeley: University of California Press.

Clapperton, Hugh. 2005. *Hugh Clapperton into the Interior of Africa: Records of the Second Expedition 1825–1827.* Edited by Jamie Bruce-Lockhart and Paul Lovejoy. Leiden: Brill.

Clarence-Smith, William G. 2006. *Islam and the Abolition of Slavery.* London: C. Hurst.

Clark, Ann Marie. 2001. *Diplomacy of Conscience: Amnesty International and Changing Human Rights Norms.* Princeton, NJ: Princeton University Press.

Clarke, Lindsay. 2012. *Nomads, Quakers, and the Malian State: Sedentarization from Colonial Agrarian Reform to Drought Relief, c. 1940–1960.* Dual MA in International History, LSE/Columbia University.

Clauzel, Jean. 1960. *L'Exploitation des salines de Taoudenni.* Algiers: Institut de Recherche sur le Sahara.

Cohen, William B. 1971. *Rulers of Empire: The French Colonial Service in Africa.* Stanford, CA: Hoover Institution Press.

Comité d'Etudes Historiques et Scientifiques de l'Afrique Occidentale Française. 1939. *Coutumiers juridiques de l'AOF, tome 1: Senegal; tome 2: Soudan Français.* 2 vols. Paris: Larose.

Comité Information Sahel. 1974. *Qui se nourrit de la famine en Afrique? le Dossier politique de la faim au Sahel.* Paris: F. Maspero.

Conklin, Alice. 1997. *A Mission to Civilize: The Republican Idea of Empire in France and West Africa, 1895–1930.* Stanford, CA: Stanford University Press.

2002. The New 'Ethnology' and 'la Situation Coloniale' in interwar France. *French Politics, Culture and Society* 20, 2: 29-46.

Cooper, Barbara MacGowan. 2006. *Evangelical Christians in the Muslim Sahel.* Bloomington: Indiana University Press.

Cooper, Frederick. 1996. *Decolonization and African Society: The Labor Question in French and British Africa.* New York: Cambridge University Press.

2000. Conditions Analogous to Slavery: Imperialism and free labor ideology in Africa. In *Beyond Slavery: Explorations of Race, Labor, and Citizenship in Postemancipation Societies*, edited by Frederick Cooper, Thomas Holt, and Rebecca J. Scott, 107–50. Chapel Hill: University of North Carolina Press.

2002. *Africa since 1940: The Past of the Present.* New York: Cambridge University Press.

2005. *Colonialism in Question: Theory, Knowledge, History.* Berkeley: University of California Press.

2008. Possibility and Constraint: African Independence in historical perspective. *Journal of African History* 49, 2: 167–96.

2009. Alternatives to Empire: France and Africa after World War II. In *The State of Sovereignty: Territories, Laws, Populations*, edited by Douglas Howland and Luise White, 94–123. Bloomington: Indiana University Press.

2014. *Citizenship between Empire and Nation: Remaking France and French Africa, 1945–1960.* Princeton, NJ: Princeton University Press.

Copans, Jean. 1975. *Sécheresses et famines du Sahel*, Dossiers africains. Paris: F. Maspero.
   ed. 2001a. Georges Balandier, lecture et re-lecture, Special issue of *Cahiers Internationaux de Sociologie* 110.
   2001b. La 'Situation Coloniale' de Georges Balandier: Notion conjoncturelle ou modèle sociologique et historique? *Cahiers Internationaux de Sociologie* 110: 31–52.
   2010. *Un demi-siècle d'africanisme africain. Terrains, acteurs et enjeux des sciences sociales en Afrique indépendante*. Paris. Karthala.
Coquery-Vidrovitch, Catherine. 1999. The rise of Francophone African Social Science: From colonial knowledge to knowledge of Africa. In *Out of One, Many Africas: Reconstructing the Study and Meaning of Africa*, edited by William G. Martin and Michael O. West, 39–53. Chicago: University of Illinois Press.
   2001. Nationalité et citoyenneté en Afrique Occidentale Française: Originaires et citoyens dans le Sénégal colonial. *Journal of African History* 42, 2: 285–305.
   2010. Le vote des femmes en AOF, de la seconde guerre mondiale à 1958. In *Les Elections législatives et sénatoriales outre-mer (1848–1981)*, edited by Laurent Jalabert, Bertrand Joly and Jacques Weber, 283–93. Paris: les Indes Savantes.
Cousturier, Lucie. 1920. *Des Inconnus chez moi*. Paris: Editions de la Sirène.
   1925. *Mes Inconnus chez eux*. 2 vols. Paris: Reider.
Crombé, Xavier, and Jean-Hervé Jézéquel, eds. 2007. *Niger 2005: Une catastrophe si naturelle*. Paris: Karthala.
Crowder, Michael. 1967. *Senegal: A Study of French Assimilation Policy*. Rev. ed. London: Methuen.
Daly, M. W. 2007. *Darfur's Sorrow: A History of Destruction and Genocide*. Cambridge, UK: Cambridge University Press.
Danioko, Charles Abdoulaye. 1984. *Contribution à l'étude des partis politiques au Mali de 1945 à 1960*. Thèse de doctorat de troisième cycle, Paris VII.
Daum, Christophe. 1998. *Les Associations de Maliens en France: migrations, développement et citoyenneté*. Paris: Karthala.
De Benoist, Joseph-Roger. 1982. *L'Afrique Occidentale Française de la Conférence de Brazzaville (1944) à l'indépendance (1960)*. Dakar: Nouvelles éditions africaines.
De l'Estoile, Benoît. 2005. Rationalizing Colonial Domination: Anthropology and native policy in French-ruled Africa. In *Empires, Nations, and Natives: Anthropology and State-Making*, edited by Benoît de l'Estoile, Frederico Neiburg and Lygia Sigaud, 30–57. Durham, NC: Duke University Press.
De Lattre, Anne. 1979. *A Conversation with Anne de Lattre: Developing the Sahel*. American Enterprise Institute.
De Moraes Farias, P. F., ed. and transl. 2001. *Arabic Medieval Inscriptions from the Republic of Mali: Epigraphy, Chronicles and Songhay-Tuăreg History*, Fontes historiae Africanae. Oxford: Oxford University Press.
De Suremain, Marie-Albaine. 2004. Faire du terrain en AOF dans les années cinquante. *Ethnologie Française* 34, 4: 651–59.

De Waal, Alexander. 1998. *Famine Crimes: Politics & the Disaster Relief Industry in Africa*. Bloomington: Indiana University Press.

2005a [1989]. *Famine that Kills: Darfur, Sudan, 1984–1985*. Rev. ed. New York: Oxford University Press.

2005b. Who are the Darfurians? Arab and African identities, violence and external engagement. *African Affairs* 104, 415: 181–205.

Decottignies, Roger, and Marc de Biéville. 1963. *Les Nationalités africaines*. Paris: A. Pedone.

Dedieu, Jean-Philippe. 2012. *La Parole Immigrée: Les Migrants africains dans l'espace public en France (1969–1995)*. Paris: Klincksieck.

Delavignette, Robert. 1950. *Freedom and Authority in French West Africa*. London: Published for the International African Institute by the Oxford University Press.

1965. Une receveuse et trois éboueurs. In Approche des problèmes de la migration noire en France, Special issue of *Hommes et Migrations*: 68–72.

Delerm, Robert. 1965. l'Immigration noire en France: perspectives, conséquences. In Approche des problèmes de la migration noire en France, Special issue of *Hommes et Migrations*: 73–81.

Delmet, Christian. 1994. Sur la route du pèlerinage: les Peuls au Soudan. *Cahiers d'Etudes Africaines* 133/135: 473–81.

Dembélé, Assimi S. 2003. *Transferts Définitifs*. Bamako: le Figuier.

Derrick, J. 1977. The Great West African Drought. *African Affairs* LXXVI, 305: 537–86.

Diagne, Souleymane Bachir. 2009. Individual, Community, and Human Rights: A lesson from Kwasi Wiredu's philosophy of personhood. *Transition* 101: 8–15.

Diallo, Abdoulaye. 2008. Sékou Touré et l'indépendance guinéenne: Déconstruction d'un mythe et retour sur l'histoire. *Outre-mers* 96, 358–359: 267–88.

Diallo, Demba. 2005. *Çagoloba! Carnets d'un militant du tiers-monde, 1925–1960*. Bamako: Cauris.

Diarra, Idrissa. 1964. Voies et moyens du socialisme au Mali. *Economie et politique* 123: 97–108.

Diarra, Souleymane. 1968. les Travailleurs africains noirs en France. *Bulletin de l'I.F.A.N. (série B)* 30, 3: 884–1044.

Diarrah, Cheick Oumar. 1986. *Le Mali de Modibo Keita*. Paris: l'Harmattan.

Diawara, Mamadou. 2003. Ce que travailler veut dire dans le monde Mande. In *Le travail en Afrique*, edited by Hélène d'Almeida –Topor and Gerd Spittler, 67–80. Paris: Karthala.

2011. Development and Administrative Norms: The Office du Niger and decentralization in French Sudan and Mali. *Africa* 81, 3: 434–54.

Dimier, Véronique. 2003. Décentraliser l'empire? Du compromis colonial à l'institutionnalisation d'un gouvernement local dans l'Union Française. *Outre-Mers* 90, 338–39: 83–107.

Diop, Majhemout. 1971. *Histoire des classes sociales dans l'Afrique de l'Ouest, Vol. 1: le Mali*. Paris: François Maspero.

Diouf, Mamadou. 1999. Privatisations des économies et des états africains: commentaires d'un historien. *Politique Africaine* 73: 16–23.

2000. Assimilation coloniale et identités religieuses de la civilité des originaires des Quatre Communes (Sénégal). *Canadian Journal of African Studies* 34, 3: 565–87.
Djibo, Bakary. 1992. *Silence! On décolonise … : itineraire politique et syndical d'un militant africain*. Paris: l'Harmattan.
Dougnon, Isaie. 2011. Child Trafficking or Labor Migration? A historical perspective from Mali's Dogon country. *Humanity* 2, 1: 85–105.
Doukouré, Abdoul. 1978. *Le Déboussolé*. Sherbrooke, Québec: Naaman.
Doumbia, Souleymane. 2010. Adhésion à l'ONU: sous le parrainage de la Tunisie et du Ceylon. In *Notre Mali, 1960–2010: Maliba Kera Anw Ta Ye*, edited by AMAP, 78–79. Bamako: AMAP.
Downs, Laura Lee.` 2013. La République garantit l'égalité des citoyen(ne)s. In *Une contre-histoire de la IIIe République*, edited by Marion Fontaine, Christophe Prochasson, and Frédéric Monier, 138–49. Paris: La Découverte.
Dozon, Jean-Pierre. 2002. Georges Balandier dans l'histoire et l'épistémè de l'africanisme français. *Recherches sociologiques* 33, 2: 21–29.
Droz, Bernard. 2008. l'Election législative du 30 Novembre 1958 en Algérie. *Outre-Mers* 96, 1: 29–44.
Du Bois, Victor. 1974. *The Drought in Niger: Part 1: The Physical and Economic Consequences; Part 2: The Logistics of Relief Operations; Part 3: The Flight of the Malian Tuareg; Part 4: The New Refugee Camp at Lazaret*. New York: American Universities Field Staff.
Duffield, Mark. 1981. *Maiurno: Capitalism and Rural Life in Sudan*. London: Ithaca Press.
  1983. Change among West African Settlers in Northern Sudan. *Review of African Political Economy* 26: 45–59.
Dumont, René. 1962. *l'Afrique noire est mal partie*. Paris: Seuil.
Eckel, Jan. 2013. The International League for the Rights of Man, Amnesty International, and the Changing Fate of Human Rights Activism from the 1940s through the 1970s. *Humanity* 4, 2: 183–214.
El Hamel, Chouki. 2002. *La vie intellectuelle Islamique dans le Sahel Ouest Africain (XVI-XIX' siècles): une étude sociale de l'enseignement Islamique en Mauritanie et au Nord du Mali (XVI-XIX' siècles) et traduction annotée de Fath ash-shakur d'al-Bartali al-Walati (mort en 1805)*. Paris: l'Harmattan.
El Shakry, Omnia. 2007. *The Great Social Laboratory: Subjects of Knowledge in Colonial and Postcolonial Egypt*. Stanford, CA: Stanford University Press.
El Sheikh, Fath el Rahman Abdalla. 1975. *Development of Nationality Laws in the Sudan*. LLM Thesis, University of Khartoum.
Ellis, Stephen. 2002. Writing Histories of Contemporary Africa. *Journal of African History* 43, 1: 1–26.
Englund, Harri. 2006. *Prisoners of Freedom: Human Rights and the African Poor*. Berkeley: University of California Press.
Ensor, F. Sidney. 1881. *Incidents on a Journey through Nubia to Darfoor*. London: W. H. Allen.
Ernst, Klaus. 1976. *Tradition and Progress in an African Village: Non-Capitalist Transformation of Rural Communities in Mali*. Translated by Salomea Genin. New York: St. Martin's Press.

Escayrac de Lauture, Pierre Henri Stanislas d'. 1853. *Le Desert et le Soudan.* Paris: J. Dumaine.

1855–1856a. *Mémoire sur le Soudan, géographie naturelle et politique, histoire et ethnographie, moeurs et institutions de l'Empire des Fellatas, du Bornou, du Baguermi, du Waday, du Dar-Four.* Paris: A. Bertrand.

1855–1856b. *Mémoire sur le Soudan, rédigé d'après des renseignements entièrement nouveaux ... troisième cahier: Examen du gouvernement, des institutions militaires, de la religion et des superstitions des peuples du Takrour. Extrait de la bulletin de la Société de Géographie (Janvier et février 1856).* 3 vols. Vol. 3. Paris: Imprimerie de L. Martinet.

Fanon, Frantz. 1959. *l'An V de la Révolution Algérienne: Sociologie d'une révolution.* Paris: François Maspero.

1964. *Pour la Révolution Africaine: Ecrits politiques.* Paris: F. Maspero.

Fassin, Didier. 2011. *Humanitarian Reason: A Moral History of the Present.* Berkeley: University of California Press.

Fay, Claude. 1995. La démocratie au Mali, ou le pouvoir en pâture. *Cahiers d'études africaines* 35, 1: 19–53.

Fay, Claude, Yaouaga Félix Koné, and Catherine Quiminal, eds. 2006. *Décentralisation et Pouvoirs en Afrique: En contrepoint, modèles territroriaux français.* Paris: IRD.

Faysal, Amir. 1963. Ministerial statement of 6 November 1962 by Prime Minister Amir Faysal of Saudi Arabia. *Middle East Journal* 17, 1–2: 161–62.

Fédération Internationale des ligues des Droits de l'Homme and Association Malienne des Droits de l'Homme. 1998–99. Soutenir les défenseurs des droits de l'homme au Mali, Special Issue of *la Lettre bimensuelle de la FIDH* 279.

Feher, Michel. 2007. The Governed in politics. In *Nongovernmental Politics*, edited by Micheal Feher, 12–30. New York: Zone.

Feldman, Ilana. 2007. The Quaker Way: Ethical labor and humanitarian relief. *American Ethnologist* 34, 4: 689–705.

Ferguson, James. 1994. *The Anti-politics Machine: "Development," Depoliticization, and Bureaucratic Power in Lesotho.* Minneapolis: University of Minnesota Press.

2006. *Global Shadows: Africa in the Neoliberal World Order* Durham, NC: Duke University Press.

Ferguson, James, and Akhil Gupta. 2002. Spatializing States: Toward an ethnography of neoliberal governmentality. *American Ethnologist* 29, 4: 981–1002.

Foucault, Michel. 1977. *Discipline and Punish: the Birth of the Prison.* Translated by Alan Sheridan. New York: Pantheon.

2007. *Security, Territory, Population: Lectures at the Collège de France, 1977–78.* edited by Michel Senellart, François Ewald, and Alessandro Fontana; translated by Graham Burchell. Basingstoke, UK: Palgrave Macmillan.

Franke, Richard W. and Barbara H. Chasin. 1980. *Seeds of Famine: Ecological Destruction and the Development Dilemma in the West African Sahel.* Montclair, NJ: Rowman & Allanheld.

Gary-Tounkara, Daouda. 2003. Circulation et reseaux migratoires soudanaismaliens en Afrique de l'Ouest (1932–1974). *Migrations-Société* 15, 90: 67–82.

2008. *Migrants Soudanais/maliens et conscience ivoirienne: les étrangers en Cote d'Ivoire (1903–1980).* Paris: l'Harmattan.

Gastaut, Yvan. 2000. *l'Immigration et l'opinion publique en France sous la Vème République*. Paris: Seuil.
Gérard, Claude. 1975. *Les Pionniers de l'indépendance*. Saint Romain en Gier: Intercontinents.
Giri, Jacques. 1983. *Le Sahel demain: catastrophe ou renaissance?* Paris: Karthala.
Giuffrida, Alessandra. 2005. Metamorphoses des relations de dépendance chez les Kel Antessar du Cercle du Goundam. *Cahiers d'études africaines* 45, 179/80: 805–29.
Glantz, M., ed. 1976. *Politics of Natural Disaster: The Case of the Sahel Drought*. New York: Praeger.
Glenzer, Kent. 2002. La Sécheresse: The social and institutional construction of a development problem in the Malian (Soudanese) Sahel, 1900–1982. *Canadian Journal of African Studies* 36, 1: 1–34.
  2007. 'We Aren't the World': La production institutionnelle du succès partiel. In *Niger 2005: Une catastrophe si naturelle*, edited by Xavier Crombé and Jean-Hervé Jézéquel, 117–44. Paris: Karthala.
Gluckman, Max. 1958. *Analysis of a Social Situation in Modern Zululand*. Manchester, UK: Manchester University Press.
Godelier, Maurice. 2005. la Parenté et l'histoire: Entretien avec Maurice Godelier. *Afrique et histoire* 4, 2: 247–81.
Gosnell, Harold F. 1958. The 1958 Elections in the Sudan. *Middle East Journal* 12, 4: 409–17.
Griaule, Marcel. 1948. l'Action sociologique en Afrique Noire. *Présence Africaine* 1, 3: 388–91.
Grisman, C. S. 1955. West Africans in Eritrea. *Nigerian Field* 20: 41–45.
Gueye, Abdoulaye. 2001. *Les intellectuels africains en France*. Paris: l'Harmattan.
  2006. The Colony Strikes Back: African protest movements in postcolonial France. *Comparative Studies of South Asia, Africa, and the Middle East* 26, 2: 225–42.
Guèye, Omar. 2011. *Sénégal: Histoire du mouvement syndical, la marche vers le Code du travail*. Paris: l'Harmattan.
Guiart, Jean. 1976. A Propos de 'Critiques et politiques de l'anthropologie'. *l'Homme* 16, 1: 151–55.
Hall, Bruce. 2011a. Bellah Histories of Decolonization, Iklan Paths to Freedom: The meanings of race and slavery in the late-colonial Niger Bend (Mali), 1944–1960. *International Journal of African Historical Studies* 44, 1: 61–87.
  2011b. *A History of Race in Muslim West Africa, 1600–1960*. New York: Cambridge University Press.
Hanretta, Sean. 2009. *Islam and Social Change in French West Africa: History of an Emancipatory Community*. New York: Cambridge University Press.
Harrison, Graham. 2010. *Neoliberal Africa: The Impact of Global Social Engineering*. London: Zed.
Harvey, David. 2007. *A Brief History of Neoliberalism*. Rev. ed. New York: Oxford University Press.
Haski, Pierre. 'la Secheresse n'explique pas tout.' *Croissance des Jeunes Nations*, April 1974: 27–30.

Hassan, Salah D. 1999. Inaugural issues: The cultural politics of the early présence Africaine, 1947–55. *Research in African Literatures* 30, 2: 194–221.
Hassoun, Isam Ahmad. 1952. 'Western' migration and settlement in the Gezira. *Sudan Notes and Records* 33: 60–112.
Hawkins, Sean. 2002. *Writing and Colonialism in Northern Ghana: The Encounter Between the LoDagaa and "the World on Paper," 1892–1991*. Toronto: University of Toronto Press.
Hearn, Julie. 2007. African NGOs: The new compradors? *Development and Change* 38, 6: 1095–1110.
Hecht, Gabrielle. 2012. *Being Nuclear: Africans and the Global Uranium Trade*. Cambridge, Mass.: MIT Press.
Held, Jean-Francis. 1974. Visit to an African nightmare. *Atlas World Press Review* 21, 5: 13–15.
Herbst, Jeffrey Ira. 2000. *States and Power in Africa: Comparative Lessons in Authority and Control*. Princeton, NJ: Princeton University Press.
Hibou, Béatrice, ed. 1999. *La Privatisation des états*. Paris: Karthala.
Higgot, Richard, and Finn Fugelstand. 1975. The 1974 coup d'état in Niger: Towards an explanation. *Journal of Modern African Studies* 13, 3: 383–98.
Hino, Shun'ya. 1986. Pilgrimage and Migration of the West African Muslims: a Case study of the Fellata people in the Sudan. *Sudan Sahel Studies* 2: 15–109.
Hmed, Choukri. 2006. Tenir ses hommes: la gestion des étrangers 'isolés' dans les foyers SONACOTRA après la guerre d'Algérie. *Politix* 76: 11–30.
Ho, Engseng. 2006. *The Graves of Tarim: Genealogy and Mobility across the Indian Ocean*. Berkeley: University of California Press.
Hopgood, Stephen. 2006. *Keepers of the Flame: Understanding Amnesty International*. Ithaca, NY: Cornell University Press.
Howland, Douglas, and Luise White, eds. 2009. *The State of Sovereignty: Territories, Laws, Populations*. Bloomington: Indiana University Press.
Hunwick, John O. 1962. Ahmad Baba and the Moroccan invasion of the Sudan (1591). *Journal of the Historical Society of Nigeria* 2, 3: 311–28.
——— ed. and transl. 1999. *Timbuktu and the Songhay Empire: Al-Sa'di's Ta'rikh al-Sudan Down to 1613, and Other Contemporary Documents*. Leiden: Brill.
Idrissa, Kimba. 2001a. La dynamique de la gouvernance: Administration, politique et ethnicité au Niger. In *Le Niger: Etat et démocratie*, 15–83. Paris: l'Harmattan.
——— ed. 2001b. *Le Niger: Etat et démocratie*. Paris: l'Harmattan.
——— ed. 2008. *Armée et politique au Niger*. Dakar: CODESRIA.
Igoe, J., and T. Kelsall, eds. 2005. *Between a Rock and a Hard Place: African NGOs, Donors and the State*. Durham, NC: Carolina Academic Press.
Imperato, Pascal James. 1975. *A Wind in Africa: A Story of Modern Medicine in Mali*. St. Louis, MO: Warren H. Green.
——— and Gavin H. Imperato. 2008. *Historical Dictionary of Mali*. 4th ed. Lanham, MD: Scarecrow Press.
Issa, Mahaman Malam. 2008. le Régime militaire de Seyni Kountché, 1974–1987. In *Armée et politique au Niger*, edited by Kimba Idrissa, 125–62. Dakar: CODESRIA.

Jackson, Stephen. 2005. 'The State Didn't Even Exist': Non-governmentality in Kivu, eastern DR Congo. In *Between a Rock and a Hard Place: African NGOs, Donors and the State*, edited by J. Igoe and T. Kelsall, 165–196. Durham, NC: Carolina Academic Press.

Jeanneret, Charles. 1983. Quelle stratégie pour le Sahel? La difficile harmonisation de la stratégie du CILSS et du Club du Sahel avec les plans de développement nationaux des pays sahéliens. *Canadian Journal of African Studies* 16, 3: 443–77.

Jennings, Michael. 2008. *Surrogates of the State. NGOs, Development, and Ujamaa in Tanzania*. Bloomfield, CT: Kumarian Press.

Jézéquel, Jean-Hervé. 2006. 'Collecting Customary Law': Educated Africans, ethnographic writings, and colonial justice in French West Africa. In *Intermediaries, Interpreters, and Clerks: African Employees in the Making of Colonial Africa*, edited by Benjamin Lawrance, Emily Osborn and Richard L. Roberts, 139–58. Madison: University of Wisconsin Press.

2007. Voices of their Own? African participation in the production of colonial knowledge in French West Africa, 1910–1950. In *Ordering Africa: Anthropology, European Imperialism, and the Politics of Knowledge*, edited by Helen Tilley, 145–72. Manchester, UK: Manchester University Press.

2011. Les professionels Africains de la recherche dans l'etat colonial tardif: le personnel local de l'Institut Français d'Afrique Noire entre 1938 et 1960. *Revue d'Histoire des Sciences Humaines* 24: 35–60.

Johnson, Cedric. 2007. *Revolutionaries to Race Leaders: Black Power and the Making of African-American Politics*. Minneapolis: University of Minnesota Press.

Johnson, G. Wesley. 1971. *The Emergence of Black Politics in Senegal: The Struggle for Power in the Four Communes, 1900–1920*. Stanford, CA: Published for the Hoover Institution on War, Revolution, and Peace by Stanford University Press.

Jolly, Eric. 2010. L'épopée en contexte: Variantes et usages politiques de deux récits épiques (Mali/Guinée). *Annales* 65, 4: 885–912.

Jones, William I. 1976. *Planning and Economic Policy in Socialist Mali and Her Neighbors*. Washington DC: Three Continents Press.

Kaba, Mamadou. 1989 *Nouvelles d'hier... et d'aujourd'hui: le Mali de 1970 à 1980*. Bamako: Jamana.

Keaton, Trica Danielle, T. Denean Sharpley-Whiting, and Tyler Stovall, eds. 2012. *Black France/France Noire: The History and Politics of Blackness*. Durham, NC: Duke University Press.

Keenan, Thomas. 2007. 'Where are Human Rights ... ?' Reading a Communiqué from Iraq. In *Nongovernmental Politics*, edited by Michael Feher, 57–71. New York: Zone.

Kéita, Aoua. 1975. *Femme d'Afrique: la vie d'Aoua Kéita racontée par elle-même*. Paris: Présence africaine.

Keita, Madeira. 1960. Le Parti unique en Afrique. *Présence Africaine* 30: 3–24.

Keita, Modibo S. 1965. *Discours et interventions*. Bamako, Mali: n.p.

Keita, Naffet, ed. 2012. *l'Esclavage au Mali*. Paris: l'Harmattan.

Keita, Sidiki Kobélé. 1978. *Le P.D.G., artisan de l'indépendance nationale en Guinée (1947–1958)*. 2 vols. Vol. 1. Conakry I.N.R.D.G. Bibliothèque nationale.
Klaeger, Gabriel. 2013. Introduction: The perils and possibilities of African roads. *Africa* 83, 3: 359–66.
Klute, Georg. 1999. De la Chefferie administrative à la parasouveraineté régionale. In *Horizons nomades en Afrique sahélienne: Sociétés, développement et démocratie*, edited by André Bourgeot, 167–82. Paris: Karthala.
Konaré, Adam Ba. 1993. *Dictionnaire des femmes célèbres du Mali*. Bamako: Jamana.
Konaté, Hamidou. 1993. *Le Procés Crimes de Sang*. Bamako: Jamana.
Koné, Kassim. 1996. *Bamana Verbal Art: An Ethnographic Study of Proverbs*. Ph.D., Indiana University.
Konings, Piet. 2011. *The Politics of Neoliberal Reforms in Africa: State and Civil Society in Cameroon*. Leiden: African Studies Centre; Bamenda, Cameroon: Langaa.
[Kouyaté], Seydou Badian. 1965. *Les Dirigeants d'Afrique noire face à leur peuple*. Paris: François Maspero.
Lambert, Michael C. 2002. *Longing for Exile: Migration and the Making of a Translocal Community in Senegal, West Africa*. Portsmouth, NH: Heinemann.
Languille, Sonia. 2010. Mali: la politique de décentralisation à l'heure de l'Agenda de Paris pour l'efficacité de l'aide. *Politique africaine* 120: 129–52.
Larkin, Brian, and Brigit Meyer. 2006. Pentecostalism, Islam, and Culture: New religious movements in West Africa. In *Themes in West Africa's History*, edited by Emmanuel Kwaku Akyeampong, 286–312. Athens: Ohio University Press.
Latour, Bruno. 2005. *Reassembling the Social: An Introduction to Actor-Network-Theory*. Oxford: Oxford University Press.
Launay, Robert, and Benjamin F. Soares. 1999. The Formation of an "Islamic Sphere" in French Colonial West Africa. *Economy and Society* 28: 487–519.
Laurens, Sylvian. 2008. '1974' et la fermeture des frontières: Analyse critique d'une décision érigée en *turning-point*. *Politix* 82: 69–94.
Laya, Dioulde. 1978. *La Brousse est morte*. Niamey: IRSH.
Lecocq, Baz. 2004. Unemployed Intellectuals in the Sahara: The Teshumara nationalist movement and the revolutions in Tuareg society. *International Review of Social History* 49: 87–109.
———. 2005. The Bellah Question: Slave emancipation, race, and social categories in late twentieth-century Northern Mali. *Canadian Journal of African Studies* 39, 1: 42–68.
———. 2008. Ranger le chevre et le chou. Paper presented to *Seventh International Conference on Mande Studies [MANSA]*. Lisbon.
———. 2010. *Disputed Desert: Decolonisation, Competing Nationalisms and Tuareg Rebellions in Contemporary Mali*. Leiden: Brill.
———. 2012. The *hajj* from West Africa from a Global Historical Perspective (19th and 20th centuries). *African Diaspora* 5: 187–214.

Lecocq, Baz, Gregory Mann, Bruce Whitehouse, et al. 2013. One Hippopotamus and Eight Blind Analysts: A multivocal analysis of the 2012 political crisis in the divided Republic of Mali. *Review of African Political Economy* 40, 137: 343–57.
Lewin, André. 2009. *Ahmed Sékou Touré (1922–1984), Président de la Guinée.* Vol. 1 (1922-fév. 1955). Paris: l'Harmattan.
——— 2010. *Ahmed Sékou Touré (1922–1984), Président de la Guinée.* Vol. 7 (juin 1977-mars 1984). Paris: l'Harmattan.
Lewis, Mary Dewhurst. 2007. *Boundaries of the Republic: Migrant Rights and the Limits of Universalism in France, 1918–1940.* Stanford, CA: Stanford University Press.
Linden, Eugene. 1976. *The Alms Race: The Impact of American Voluntary Aid Abroad.* New York: Random House.
Lisette, Gabriel. 1983. *le Combat du Rassemblement Démocratique Africain.* Paris: Présence Africaine.
Livre d'Or de la République du Mali. 1963. Paris: l'Afrique nouvelle.
Londres, Albert. 1929. *A Very Naked People.* Translated by Sylvia Stuart. New York: Horace Liveright.
Ly, Ibrahima. 1990. *Paroles pour un continent: la vie et l'œuvre d'Ibrahima Ly.* Paris: l'Harmattan.
——— 1997 [1982]. *Toiles d'araignées.* Arles: Actes Sud.
Lydon, Ghislaine. 2009. *On Trans-Saharan Trails: Islamic Law, Trade Networks, and Cross-Cultural Exchange in Nineteenth-Century Western Africa.* New York: Cambridge University Press.
Lyons, Amelia H. 2009. Social welfare, French Muslims and decolonization in France: the case of the Fonds d'Action Sociale. *Patterns of Prejudice* 43, 1: 65–89.
Macey, David. 2000. *Frantz Fanon: A Life.* London: Granta.
Maffesoli, Michel, and Claude Rivière, eds. 1985. *Une Anthropologie des turbulences: Hommage à Georges Balandier.* Paris: Berg International.
Mamdani, Mahmood. 1996. *Citizen and Subject: Contemporary Africa and the Legacy of Late Colonialism.* Princeton, NJ: Princeton University Press.
——— 2001. Beyond Settler and Native as Political Identities: Overcoming the political legacy of colonialism. *Comparative Studies in Society and History* 43, 4: 651–64.
——— 2007. *Savoirs and Survivors: Darfur, Politics, and the War on Terror.* New York: Pantheon.
Manchuelle, François. 1987. *Background to Black African Emigration to France: The Labor Migrations of the Soninke, 1848–1987.* Ph.D., University of California-Santa Barbara.
——— 1997. *Willing Migrants: Soninke labor diasporas, 1848–1960.* Athens: Ohio University Press.
Manière, Laurent. 2007. *Le Code de l'indigénat en Afrique occidentale française et son application: le cas du Dahomey (1887–1946).* Ph.D., Université Paris-VII.
Mann, Gregory. 2003. Violence, Dignity, and Modibo's New Model Army, 1960–1968. *Mande Studies* 5: 65–82.

2006. *Native Sons: West African Veterans and France in the Twentieth Century.* Durham, NC: Duke University Press.

2013. Anticolonialism and Social Science: Georges Balandier, Madeira Keita, and 'the Colonial Situation' in French Africa. *Comparative Studies in Society and History* 55, 1: 92.

Mann, Gregory, and Baz Lecocq. 2007. Between Empire, *umma*, and Muslim Third World: The French Union and African Pilgrims to Mecca, 1946–1958. *Comparative Studies of South Asia, Africa, and the Middle East* 27, 2: 367–83.

Mannoni, Octave. 1950. *Psychologie de la Colonisation.* Paris: Seuil.

Marie-Andrée de Sacré-Coeur. 1954. l'Activité politique de la femme en Afrique Noire. *Revue Juridique et Politique de l'Union Française* 8, 4: 476–91.

Mariko, Amadou. 2001. *Mémoires d'un Crocodile: du sujet français au citoyen malien.* Edited by Pierre Boilley. Bamako: Editions Donniya.

Mariko, Kélétigui A. 1993. l'Attitude de l'administration face au servage. In *Nomades et Commandants: Administration et sociétés nomades dans l'ancienne A.O.F.*, edited by Edmond Bernus, Pierre Boilley, Jean Clauzel and Jean-Louis Triaud, 193–201. Paris: Karthala.

Marty, André. 1993. La répartition des terres lacustres du Gourma malien. In *Nomades et Commandants: Administration et sociétés nomades dans l'ancienne A.O.F.*, edited by Edmond Bernus, Pierre Boilley, Jean Clauzel and Jean-Louis Triaud, 167–80. Paris: Karthala.

Masquelier, Adeline. 2002. Road Mythographies: Space, mobility, and the historical imagination in postcolonial Niger. *American Ethnologist* 29, 4: 829–56.

Mauxion, Aurelien. 2012. Moving to Stay: Iklan spatial strategies towards socio-economic emancipation in Northern Mali, 1898–1960. *Journal of African History* 53, 2: 195–213.

Mazov, Sergey. 2010. *Distant Front in the Cold War: The USSR in West Africa and the Congo, 1956–1964.* Washington, DC: Woodrow Wilson Center Press; Stanford, CA: Stanford University Press.

Mbacké, Khadim. 2004. *Le Pèlerinage aux lieux saints de l'Islam: Participation Sénégalaise, 1886–1986.* Dakar: Presses Universitaires de Dakar.

Mbembe, Achille. 2001. *On the Postcolony.* Berkeley: University of California Press.

McCleary, Rachel M. 2009. *Global Compassion: Private Voluntary Organizations and U.S. Foreign Policy since 1939.* New York: Oxford University Press.

McKeown, Adam. 2008. *Melancholy Order: Asian Migration and the Globalization of Borders.* New York: Columbia University Press.

McLagan, Meg. 2007. Human Rights, Testimony, and Transnational Publicity. In *Nongovernmental Politics*, edited by Michel Feher, 304–17. New York: Zone.

McLoughlin, Peter F. M. 1962. Economic Development and the Heritage of Slavery in the Sudan Republic. *Africa: Journal of the International African Institute* 32, 4: 355–91.

Meillassoux, Claude. 1968. *Urbanization of an African Community: Voluntary Associations in Bamako.* Seattle: University of Washington Press.

1974. Development or Exploitation: Is the Sahel famine good business? *Review of African Political Economy* 1: 27–33.

1981. *Maidens, Meal, and Money: Capitalism and the Domestic Community.* New York: Cambridge University Press.
Mercier, Paul. 1965. Classes et changements politiques en Afrique Noire. *Cahiers Internationaux de Sociologie* 38: 143–54.
Merle, Isabelle. 2002. Retour sur le régime de l'indigénat: genèse et contradictions des principes répressifs dans l'empire français. *French Politics, Culture and Society* 20, 2: 77–97.
Meunier, Dominique. 1980. Le commerce de sel de Taoudeni. *Journal des Africanistes* 50, 2: 133–44.
Michael, Sarah. 2004. *Undermining Development: The Absence of Power among Local NGOs in Africa.* Oxford: James Currey.
Miers, Suzanne. 2003. *Slavery in the Twentieth Century: The Evolution of a Global Pattern.* Walnut Creek, CA: AltaMira Press.
Minter, William, Gail Hovey, and Charles Jr. Cobb, eds. 2008. *No Easy Victories: African Liberation and American Activists over a Half-Century, 1950–2000.* Trenton, NJ: Africa World Press.
Mitchell, Timothy. 2002. *Rule of Experts: Egypt, Techno-Politics, Modernity.* Berkeley: University of California Press.
Mongia, Radhika Viyas. 2007. Historicizing State Sovereignty: Inequality and the Form of Equivalence. *Comparative Studies in Society and History* 49, 2: 384–411.
Moore, Sally Falk. 1994. *Anthropology and Africa: Changing Perspectives on a Changing Scene.* Charlottesville: University of Virginia Press.
Morgenthau, Ruth Schachter. 1964. *Political Parties in French-Speaking West Africa.* London: Clarendon Press.
Moyn, Samuel. 2010. *The Last Utopia: Human Rights in History.* Cambridge, MA: Harvard University Press.
N'Diaye, Jean-Pierre. 1970. *Négriers modernes: les travailleurs noirs en France.* Paris: Présence Africaine.
N'Diaye, Jean-Pierre, J Bassene, and Denis Germain. 1963. Les Travailleurs noirs en France: Pourquoi les migrations? *Réalités Africaines* 5: 1–120.
N'Diaye, Mamadou Belco. 2010. *Quand le pouvoir délire.* Bamako: EDIM-SA.
N'Dongo, Sally. 1975. *Voyage forcé: Itineraire d'un militant.* Paris: François Maspero.
1976. *Exil, Connais pas...* Paris: Cerf.
Nachtigal, Gustav. 1971. *Sahara and Sudan, Vol. 4: Wadai and Darfur.* Translated by Allan G. B. Fisher, Humphrey J. Fisher, with Rex S. O'Fahey. Berkeley: University of California Press.
Naepels, Michael. 2010. l'Anthropologie face aux temps. *Annales* 65, 4: 873–84.
Naudet, Jean-David. 1999. *Trouver des problèmes aux solutions: Vingt ans d'aide au Sahel.* Paris: Editions de l'OCDE/Club du Sahel.
Ndiaye, Pap. 2008. *La Condition Noire: Essai sur une minorité française.* Paris: Gallimard.
Nolutshungu, Sam C. 1996. *Limits of Anarchy: Intervention and State Formation in Chad.* Charlottesville: University Press of Virginia.
Nugent, Paul. 2012. *Africa since Independence: A Comparative History.* 2nd ed. New York: Palgrave Macmillan.

O'Fahey, R. S. 2008. *The Darfur Sultanate: A History*. New York: Columbia University Press.

Parti Progressiste Nigérien [PPN]. 1961. *l'Independence du Niger et l'unité africaine: Parti Progressiste Nigérien, Section Nigérienne du RDA, Conférences: Aout 1959, Mai 1960, Octobre 1960, Décembre 1960*. Niamey: Service d'Information de la République du Niger.

Pauthier, Céline. 2007. Tous derrière, les femmes devant! Femmes, représentations sociales et mobilisation politique en Guinée (1945–2006). In *Perspectives historiques sur le genre en Afrique*, edited by Odile Goerg, 219–38. Paris: l'Harmattan.

Pelckmans, Lotte. 2011. *Travelling Hierarchies: Roads in and out of Slave Status in a Central Malian Fulbe Network*. Leiden: African Studies Centre.

Pierce, Steven. 2001. Punishment and the Political Body: Flogging and Colonialism in Northern Nigeria. *Interventions* 3, 2: 206–21.

Piot, Charles. 2010. *Nostalgia for the Future: West Africa after the Cold War*. Chicago: University of Chicago Press.

Plummer, Brenda Gayle. 2012. *In Search of Power: African Americans in the Era of Decolonization, 1956–1974*. New York: Cambridge University Press.

Poiret, Christian. 1997. *Familles Africaines en France*. Paris: l'Harmattan.

Pollard, Miranda. 1998. *Reign of Virtue: Mobilizing gender in Vichy France*. Chicago: University of Chicago Press.

Poussibet, Félix. 1978. Notes sur Tâoudannî. *B.I.F.A.N. (B)* 40, 3: 513–55.

Pringle, Robert. 2005. Mali's Unlikely Democracy, *The Wilson Quarterly* 30, 2: 31–39.

Quiminal, Catherine. 1991. *Gens d'ici, gens d'ailleurs: migrations Soninké et transformations villageoises*. Paris: Christian Bourgeois.

Raghavan, N. 1992. Les ONG au Mali. *Politique africaine* 47: 91–100.

Rillon, Ophélie. 2010. Corps rebelles: la mode des jeunes urbains dans les années 1960–1970 au Mali. *Genèses* 81: 64–83.

Roberts, Richard L. 2005. *Litigants and Households: African Disputes and Colonial Courts in the French Soudan, 1895–1912*. Portsmouth, NH: Heinemann.

Robins, Steven L. 2008. *From Revolution to Rights in South Africa: Social Movements, NGOs & Popular Politics After Apartheid*. Rochester, NY: James Currey.

Robinson, David. 1985. *The Holy War of Umar Tal: The Western Sudan in the Mid-Nineteenth Century*. Oxford: Clarendon Press.

2000. *Paths of Accommodation: Muslim societies and French Colonial Authorities in Senegal and Mauritania, 1880–1920*. Athens: Ohio University Press.

Robinson, Pearl. 1978. The Political Context of Regional Development in the West African Sahel. *Journal of Modern African Studies* 16, 4: 579–95.

Rodet, Marie. 2009. *Les Migrantes ignorées du Haut-Sénégal (1900–1946)*. Paris: Karthala.

Roitman, Janet L. 2005. *Fiscal Disobedience: An Anthropology of Economic Regulation in Central Africa*. Princeton, NJ: Princeton University Press.

Rosanvallon, Pierre. 2001. *Le Sacré du citoyen*. Paris: Folio.

Rosenberg, Clifford. 2012. The International Politics of Vaccine Testing in Interwar Algiers. *American Historical Review* 117, 3: 671–97.

Rossi, Bernadetta. 2007. Les paradoxes de l'aide chronique. In *Niger 2005: Une catastrophe si naturelle*, edited by Xavier Crombé and Jean-Hervé Jézéquel, 145–72. Paris: Karthala.
Saada, Emmanuelle. 2002a. La République des indigènes. In *Dictionnaire critique de la République*, edited by Vincent Duclert and Christophe Prochasson, 364–70. Paris: Flammarion.
  ed. 2002b. *Regards croisés*: Transatlantic Perspectives on the Colonial Situation, Special issue of *French Politics, Culture and Society* 20, 2.
Salifou, André. 2010. *Biographie politique de Diori Hamani*. Paris: Karthala.
Sall, Abdoulaye. 1989. *l'Organisation du monde rural du Mali (1910–1988)*. Bamako: Editions-Imprimerie du Mali.
Samaké, Guédiouma. 2009 [1998]. *Le Chemin de l'honneur*. 2nd ed. Bamako: Jamana.
Samaké, Soungalo (Capitaine). 2007. *Ma Vie de soldat*. Bamako: Libraire Traore.
Sanankoua, Bintou. 1990. *La Chute de Modibo Keita*. Paris: Editions Chaka.
Sangaré, Samba. 2001. *Dix ans dans le bagne-mouroir de Taoudenit*. Bamako: la Ruche à livres.
Saul, Mahir, and Patrick Yves Royer. 2001. *West African Challenge to Empire: Culture and History in the Volta-Bani Anti-Colonial War*. Athens: Ohio University Press.
Sayad, Abdelmalek. 2004. *The Suffering of the Immigrant*. Translated by David Macey. Cambridge, UK; Malden, MA: Polity Press.
Schaub, Jean-Frédéric. 2008. l'Histoire Coloniale en question. *Annales: Histoire, Sciences Sociales* 63, 3: 625–46.
Scheele, Judith. 2012. *Smugglers and Saints of the Sahara: Regional Connectivity in the Twentieth Century*. New York: Cambridge University Press.
Schmidt, Elizabeth. 2005. *Mobilizing the Masses: Gender, Ethnicity, and Class in the Nationalist Movement in Guinea, 1939–1958*. Portsmouth, NH: Heinemann.
  2007a. *Cold War and Decolonization in Guinea*. Athens: Ohio University Press.
  2007b. Cold War in Guinea: The Rassemblement Démocratique African and the struggle over Communism, 1950–1958. *Journal of African History* 48, 1: 95–122.
Schumaker, Lynn. 2001. *Africanizing Anthropology: Fieldwork, Networks, and the Making of Cultural Knowledge in Central Africa*. Durham, NC: Duke University Press.
Seeseman, Rüdiger. 2000a. The History of the Tijaniyya and the Issue of *tarbiya* in the History of Darfur. In *Tijâniyya: Une confrérie musulmane à la conquête de l'Afrique*, edited by J.-L. Triaud and David Robinson, 393–437. Paris: Karthala.
  2000b. The Writings of the Sudanese Tijani Shaykh Ibrahim Sidi (1949–1999) with Notes on the Writings of his Grandfather, Shaykh Muhammad Salma (d. 1918) and his Brother, Shaykh Muhammad al-Ghali (b. ca. 1947). *Sudanic Africa* 11: 107–24.
  2011. *The Divine Flood: Ibrahim Niasse and the Roots of a Twentieth-Century Sufi Revival*. Oxford: Oxford University Press.

Sene, Ibra. 2004. Colonisation française et exploitation de la main-d'œuvre carcérale au Sénégal: De l'emploi des détenus des camps pénaux sur les chantiers des travaux routiers, (1927–1940). *French Colonial History* 5: 155–74.

Sheets, Hal, and William Morris. 1974. *Disaster in the Desert: Failures of International Relief in the West African Drought*. Washington, DC: Carnegie Endowment for International Peace.

Shepard, Todd. 2006. *The Invention of Decolonization: The Algerian War and the Remaking of France*. Ithaca, NY: Cornell University Press.

Shereikis, Rebecca. 2001. From Law to Custom: The Shifting Legal Status of Muslim *originaires* in Kayes and Medine, 1903–1913. *Journal of African History* 42, 2: 261–84.

Shivji, Issa. 1989. *The Concept of Human Rights in Africa*. London: CODESRIA.

Sibeud, Emmanuelle. 2007. Du postcolonialisme au questionnement postcolonial: pour un transfert critique. *Revue d'Histoire Moderne et Contémporaine* 54, 4: 142–55.

ed. 2011. Décolonisation et Sciences Humaines, Special issue of *Revue d'Histoire des Sciences Humaines* 24, 1.

Sidibe, Modibo Halassi. 2007. *Fily Dabo Sissoko, un grand sage africain*. Bamako: n.p.

Silberman, Leo. 1958–59. Democracy in the Sudan. *Parliamentary Affairs* 12, 3: 349–76.

Siméant, Johanna. 1998. *La Cause des sans-papiers*. Paris: Presses de Science Po.

Simonis, François. 1993. *Des Français en Afrique – les 'Européens' de la région de Ségou, 1890–1962*. Ph.D., 2 vols. University Paris-VIII.

1995. le Drame de Sakoïba, magistrats et autorités politiques à Ségou (Mali) à la veille de l'indépendance. *Droit et Cultures* 30, 2: 231–41.

ed. 2005. *Le Commandant en tournée: Une administration au contact des populations en Afrique Noire coloniale*. Paris: Seli Arslan.

Simpson, Bradley S. 2013. Self-determination, Human Rights, and the End of Empire in the 1970s. *Humanity* 4, 2: 239–60.

Sissako, Abderrahmane. 2006. *Bamako*. 118 min.: Archipel 33, Chinguitty Films, Mali.

Skinner, Elliot P. 1989. *The Mossi of Burkina Faso: Chiefs, Politicians and Soldiers*. Prospect Heights, IL: Waveland Press.

Smith, Etienne. 2010. *Des arts de faire société: Parentés à plaisanteries et constructions identitaires en Afrique de l'Ouest (Sénégal)*. Ph.D., Institut d'Etudes Politiques de Paris.

Smouts, M.-C. 2007. *Postcolonial Studies dans le débat français*. Paris: Presses de Sciences Po.

Snyder, Frank Gregory. 1965. *One-Party Government in Mali: Transition Toward Control*. New Haven, CT: Yale University Press.

Soares, Benjamin F. 2005a. Islam in Mali in the Neo-liberal Era. *African Affairs* 105, 418: 77–95.

2005b. *Islam and the Prayer Economy: History and Authority in a Malian Town*. Ann Arbor: University of Michigan Press.

Somerville, Carolyn Marie. 1986. *Drought and Aid in the Sahel: A Decade of Development Cooperation*. Boulder, CO: Westview Press.

Somia [Dr.] 1965. Dépistage des candidats à l'embauche des travailleurs de l'Afrique noire dans le département de Seine. In Approche des problèmes de la migration noire en France, Special issue of *Hommes et migrations*: 129.

Sow, Abdoulaye-Sékou. 2008. *L'état démocratique républicain: la problématique de sa construction au Mali*. Brinon-sur-Sauldre (France): Grandvaux.

Sow, Alioune. 2010. Nervous Confessions: Military memoirs and national reconciliation in Mali. *Cahiers d'études africaines* 197. 69–93.

Spear, Thomas. 2003. Neo-traditionalism and the Limits of Invention in British Colonial Africa. *Journal of African History* 44, 1: 3–28.

Spire, Alexis. 2005. *Etrangers à la carte: l'Administration de l'immigration en France (1945–1975)*. Paris: Grasset.

———. 2008. *Accueillir ou reconduire. Enquête sur les guichets de l'immigration*. Paris: Raisons d'agir.

Staudinger, Paul. 1990. *In the Heart of the Hausa States*. Translated by Johanna Moody. 2 vols. Athens, Ohio: Ohio University Center for International Studies.

Sterling, Claire. 1974. Making of a sub-Saharan wasteland. *Atlantic Monthly* May: 98–105.

Stora, Benjamin. 2007. Un besoin d'histoire. In *Postcolonial Studies dans le débat français*, edited by M.-C. Smouts, 293–97. Paris: Presses de Sciences Po.

Stovall, Tyler. 2001. From Red Belt to Black Belt: Race, class, and urban marginality in twentieth-century Paris. *l'Esprit Créateur* 42, 3: 9–23.

Straker, Jay. 2009. *Youth, Nationalism, and the Guinean Revolution*. Bloomington: Indiana University Press.

Suret-Canale, Jean. 1988a. The End of the Chieftaincy in Guinea. In *Essays on African History: From the Slave Trade to Neo-Colonialism*. Translated by Christopher Hurst, 148–78. London: Hurst.

———. 1988b. An Unrecognised Pioneer of the Democratic and National Movement in Africa: Louis Hunkanrin (1887–1964). In *Essays in African History: From the Slave Trade to Neocolonialism*. Translated by Christopher Hurst, 196–219. London: Hurst.

———. 1994. *Les Groupes d'études communistes (G.E.C.) en Afrique Noire*. Paris: l'Harmattan.

Taithe, Bertrand. 2004. Reinventing (French) Universalism: Religion, humanitarianism and the 'French doctors.' *Modern and Contemporary France* 12, 2: 147–58.

Thierry, Perret. 2005. Médias et démocratie au Mali. *Politique Africaine* 97: 18–32.

Thomas, Dominic. 2006. *Black France: Colonialism, Immigration, and Transnationalism*. Bloomington: Indiana.

Thompson, Virginia, and Richard Adloff. 1957. *French West Africa*. Stanford, CA: Stanford University Press.

———. 1981. *Conflict in Chad*. Berkeley, CA: Institute of International Studies.

Ticktin, Mariam. 2011. *Casualties of Care: Immigration and the Politics of Humanitarianism in France*. Berkeley: University of California Press.

Tidjani Alou, Antoinette. 2010. Ancestors from the East, Spirits from the West: Surviving and reconfiguring the exogenous violence of global encounters in the Sahel. *Journal des Africanistes* 80, 1–2: 75–92.
Tilley, Helen. 2011. *Africa as a Living Laboratory: Empire, Development, and the Problem of Scientific Knowledge, 1870–1950*. Chicago: University of Chicago Press.
Timera, Mahamet. 1996. *Les Soninké en France: d'une histoire à l'autre*. Paris: Karthala.
Torpey, John. 2000. *The Invention of the Passport: Surveillance, Citizenship, and the State*. Cambridge UK: Cambridge University Press.
Touré, Abderhamane Baba and Kadari Bamba. 2002. *La Contribution du Parti Malien du Travail (PMT) à l'instauration de la démocratie pluraliste au Mali*. Bamako, Jamana.
Toure, Ahmed Sekou. 1978. *Des Droits des peuples aux droits de l'homme (à S. E. Mr. Valéry Giscard d'Estaing)*. Conakry: N.p.
Traoré, Aminata Dramane. 1999. *l'Etau: l'Afrique dans un monde sans frontières*. Arles: Actes Sud.
———. 2002. *Le Viol de l'imaginaire*. Paris: Fayard.
Traoré, Amadou Seydou. 2008. *Le Salaire des libérateurs du Mali*. Bamako: La Ruche à livres.
———. 2010. *la Mort de Fily Dabo Sissoko et de ses compagnons: Une des pages sombres de notre histoire nationale dont il faut tirer les leçons*. Bamako: la Ruche à livres.
Trench, Richard. 1978. *Forbidden Sands: A Search in the Sahara*. London: J. Murray.
Tshimanga, Charles, Didier Gondola, and Peter J. Bloom, eds. 2009. *Frenchness and the African Diaspora: Identity and Uprising in Contemporary France*. Bloomington: Indiana University Press.
Umar, Muhammad S. 2006. *Islam and Colonialism: Intellectual Responses of Muslims of Northern Nigeria to British Colonial Rule*. Leiden: Brill.
Union générale des travailleurs sénégalais en France [UGTSF]. 1970. *Le livre des travailleurs africains en France*. Paris: F. Maspero.
Union Soudanaise-RDA [U.S.-R.D.A]. 1962. *2' Seminaire de l'Union Soudanaise-R.D.A*. Bamako: n.p.
Van Beusekom, Monica. 2008. Individualism, Community, and Cooperatives in the Development Thinking of the Union Soudanaise-RDA, 1946–1960. *African Studies Review* 51, 2: 1–25.
Van de Walle, Nicolas. 2001. *African Economies and the Politics of Permanent Crisis, 1979–1999*. New York: Cambridge University Press.
Van Walraven, Klaas. 2013. *The Yearning for Relief: A History of the Sawaba Movement in Niger*. Leiden: Brill.
Watts, Michael. 1983. *Silent Violence: Food, Famine, & Peasantry in Northern Nigeria*. Berkeley: University of California Press.
Weil, Patrick. 2002. *Qu'est-ce qu'un Français? Histoire de la nationalité française depuis la Révolution*. Paris: Grasset.

Weil, Patrick, and Stéphane Dufoix, eds. 2005. *L'esclavage, la colonisation, et après* ... : *France, Etats-Unis, Grande-Bretagne*. Paris: Presses universitaires de France.

Westad, Odd Arne. 2005. *The Global Cold War: Third World Interventions and the Making of Our Times*. New York: Cambridge University Press.

Wibaux, Fernand. 1992. Témoignage de Fernand Wibaux, Ambassadeur de France. In *Afrique noire française: l'heure des indépendances*, edited by Charles-Robert Ageron and Marc Michel, 457–62. Paris: CNRS.

Wihtol de Wenden, Catherine. 1994. The French Debate: Legal and political instruments to promote integration. In *European Migration in the Late 20th Century: Historical Patterns, Actual Trends, and Social Implications*, edited by Heinz Fassman and Rainer Münz, 67–80. Laxenburg, Austria: Edward Elgar.

Wilder, Gary. 2005. *The French Imperial Nation-State: Negritude & Colonial Humanism between the Two World Wars*. Chicago: University of Chicago Press.

Willis, Justin. 2007. 'A Model of its Kind': Representation and performance in the Sudan self-government election of 1953. *Journal of Imperial and Commonwealth History* 35, 3: 485–502.

Willis, Justin, and Atta el Battahani. 2010. 'We Changed the Laws': Electoral practice and malpractice in Sudan since 1953. *African Affairs* 109, 435: 191–212.

Winders, Bill. 2009. *The Politics of Food Supply: U.S. Agricultural Policy in the World Economy*. New Haven, CT: Yale.

Winders, James A. 2006. *Paris Africain: Rythms of the African Diaspora*. New York: Palgrave MacMillan.

Wingate, Reginald. 1909. *Memorandum from Lieutenant-General Sir R. Wingate to Sir Eldon Gorst on the Finances, Administration and Condition of the Sudan for 1908*. Cairo: n.p.

Wise, Christopher. 2001. *The Desert Shore: Literatures of the Sahel*. Boulder, CO: Lynne Rienner Publishers.

Works, John A. 1976. *Pilgrims in a Strange Land: Hausa Communities in Chad*. New York: Columbia University Press.

Young, Crawford. 1994. *The African Colonial State in Comparative Perspective*. New Haven, CT: Yale University Press.

Zatzépine, Alexandre. 1975. l'Evolution du droit de la nationalité des républiques francophones d'Afrique et de Madagascar. *Penant: Revue de droit des pays d'Afrique* 84, 748-49: 147–210, 346–80.

Zobel, Clemens. 1996. Les génies du Koma: Identités locales, logiques religieuses et enjeux socio-politiques dans les monts Manding du Mali. *Cahiers d'études africaines* 36, 2: 625–59.

Zolberg, Aristide R. 1966. *Creating Political Order: The Party-States of West Africa*. Chicago: Rand McNally.

1967. The Political Use of Economic Planning in Mali. In *Economic Nationalism in Old and New States*, edited by Harry G. Johnson, 98–123. Chicago: University of Chicago Press.

Index

Abelin, Pierre, 225
Adams, Samuel, 206
AEF (Afrique Equatoriale Française), 30–32, 104n46. *See also* Cameroon, Chad, Congo-Brazzaville, Gabon
AFASPA (Association française d'amitié et de solidarité avec les peuples d'Afrique), 11, 213n18; advocacy for US-RDA prisoners, 225–31; famine relief efforts, 175, 197–200, 205, 226
African Charter on Human and People's Rights, 232
African-American political activism, 176, 203, 204–7. *See also* Africare; RAINS.
Africanization, 62–63, 64–65, 79n164
Africare, 11
AID. *See* US-AID
Algeria, 3, 43, 59, 81, 84, 129, 132, 133n40, 168; Algerian migrants to France, 129, 131, 133n40, 148, 149–50
Alleg, Henri, 233n10
Amenokal, 76, 111, 115. *See also* chieftaincy
Ambeiry ag Rhissa, 192
American Friends Services Committee (AFSC), 175, 189–97, 204
Amicale des travailleurs sénégalais de la région parisienne (ATSRP), 156
Amnesty International, 11, 213–14, 223–25, 227, 229, 231–32, 233n108, 235–36
Association des étudiants et stagiaires maliens en France (AESMF), 136n52

Association des étudiants maliens (AEM), 36
Association des travailleurs maliens en France (ATMF), 154
Association malienne des droits de l'homme, 236
Association pour la formation technique de base des Africains et Malgaches residant en France (AFTAM), 155–56
ASSOTRAF (Association pour l'aide sociale aux travailleurs africains), 151–55, 158
Attaher ag Illi, 76
Autra, Ray, 17n11, 23, 27n49

Ba, Amadou Hampaté, 23, 116
Bâ, Ousmane, 224, 226, 227
Bagayoko, Ténimba, 234
Bagayoko, Tiécoro, 155n127, 216, 229–30, 234
Balandier, Georges, 8, 15, 40–41, 66, 201; in AEF, 30–32; in Guinea, 24–25, 27–30; intellectual influence, 34, 37
Bamba, Amadu, 217
Bawani, Mahamane, 70
Benin. *See* Dahomey
Beti, Mongo, 199
Bongo, Omar, 178, 180
Boni, Nazi, 128
BPN. *See* US-RDA, Bureau Politique National
Brazzaville, conference in (1944), 43, 52. *See also* Congo-Brazzaville
Burkina Faso. *See* Upper Volta

275

Cabral, Amilcar, 204n153
Camara, Abdoul Karim (aka Cabral), 236
Cameroon, 225, 234
Canada, 126, 178
Cardaire, Marcel, 23
CARE (Cooperative for American Relief Everywhere), 11, 175, 176–89, 190–91, 197, 205, 206n66, 243
Carter, Jimmy, 220, 231
Catholic Relief Services, 177
Césaire, Aimé, 198
CGT (Confédération générale du travail), 19, 199, 228
Chad, 58, 64, 101, 224; border with Sudan, 102, 104, 113; CARE and, 182, 187; migrants from in Sudan, 97, 99, 105, 109
Chieftaincy, 9, 21, 28, 33, 62–64, 65–73; union of chiefs, 68–69. *See also amenokal*
Chirac, Jacques, 3, 4
CILSS (Comité inter-états de lutte contre la sécheresse au Sahel), 7n26, 11, 171n8, 173–74, 200, 205
Cissé, Youssouf Tata, 238, 241n148
Cissoko, Diango, 154
Citizenship, 2, 5, 8–10, 56, 91, 120–23, 134, 159–61, 212; African-American, 206–7; as opposed to subject status, 42, 48–49, 51; French, post-independence, 64n95, 150–51, 160; in French Community, 76, 82, 108, 110; in French Union, 21, 43–44, 52–54, 57, 68–69, 126–28; Mali, 74, 135–36, 159–60, 167; Nigeria, 107–8; Sudan, 106–7; Slavery and slave-trading, 113–14, 118
Club du Sahel, 174
CMLN (Comité Militaire de Libération Nationale [Mali]), 186, 194, 196, 215, 216, 219, 220n46, 221, 226, 230; divisions within, 229, 231–32, 233–34
CNDR. *See* US-RDA, Comité, National de Défense de la Révolution
Cold War, 3n7, 5n17, 85, 171, 212, 213, 232, 237, 243; post-Cold War period, 6, 11, 209. *See also* USSR
Collectif des chercheurs africanistes, 201, 203
Colombani, Don-Jean, 178, 180
Comité d'information Sahel, 175, 203
Comité de défense des libertés démocratiques du Mali (CDLDM), 223–25, 228

Comité de défense des prisonniers maliens, 225n74
Community (French), 21, 32–33, 42, 76, 77–82, 105, 108–10, 121, 159. *See also* France, Fifth Republic
Congo-Brazzaville, 32, 132n37, 138–40, 153. *See also* Brazzaville, Conference in (1944)
Congo-Kinshasa (Léopoldville), 84–85, 138–39, 213
Copans, Jean, 201
Coquery-Vidrovitch, Catherine, 201
Cote d'Ivoire: Amnesty International and, 224; migration to, 124, 127, 137, 140
Coulibaly, Ouezzin, 78
Coulibaly, Sidi, 193n101, 194
Coup de Bambou, 19–20
Cousturier, Lucie, 120

Dahomey, 20, 48n28, 69, 83
Darfur, 7, 94n5, 95, 97, 100, 104, 107
de Gaulle, Charles, 43, 52, 81, 84, 147
Decentralization, 63–64, 72–75, 210, 241–42
Delavignette, Robert, 46, 120, 158
Dembele, Karim, 186, 216, 234
Democracy, 11, 209–10, 212, 235, 237, 239; rural democracy, 42, 64–66, 71, 73–76, 241–42. *See also* elections; enfranchisement; women, suffrage
Dia, Mamadou, 81–83, 84, 142
Diakité, Alioune, 138, 139n59
Diakité, Idrissa, 235n121
Diakité, Yoro, 216, 220, 223, 225, 229n31
Diallo, Demba, 236
Diallo, Kibily Demba, 190–197, 192
Diallo, Malick, 229
Diallo, Saifoulaye, 68
Diallo, Telli. *See* Telli, Boubacar Diallo
Diarra, Diby Sylas, 168–69, 215, 216
Diarra, Idrissa, 69, 78, 80, 81, 86
Diarra, Moussa, 76
Diatigiw (hosts), 122, 153–54
Diawara, Gabou, 222, 232
Dicko, Hamadoun, 34n80, 63n89, 77, 219n43; position on 1958 referendum, 80
Diggs, Charles C. (Jr.), 204
Diop, Boubacar Boris, 240
Diop, Cheikh Anta, 199n133
Diop, Majhemout, 80

Index

Diop, Oumar Blondin, 203n151
Diori, Hamani, 4, 172, 176, 178, 179, 180, 205, 207
Diouf, Abdou, 3, 4
Djibo, Bakary, 82n180
Doucouré, Abdoul Wahab, 111, 113n81, 114–16, 118
Doukara, Kissima, 186, 216, 234
Doumbia, Abdou, 153n118, 154–56
Drought, 3–4, 10, 160–61, 165, 202–3, 243–44; "castles of the drought," 186; effects of, 167–69, 170, 172–74, 193n103; Niger and, 179–80; relief efforts, 190, 193–95, 198–200, 226
Dumont, René, 200n140

Egypt, 34, 90, 105, 108
Eisenhower, Dwight D., 112–13
Elections, 56–62, 69, 83; chiefs and, 22n31, 66–67, 76; referendum on constitution of Fifth Republic, 78; in Sudan, 107; village councils, 74–75. *See also* Mothers' vote; Women, suffrage
Enfranchisement, 61–2; of heads of household vs. heads of family, 60; in electing chiefs, 66, 74. *See also* Mothers' vote; Women, suffrage
Ennals, Martin, 223, 230
Eritrea, 102
Etudes Guinéennes, 24–25, 27

Fall, Amadou, 112–13, 117
Famine (1973–74), 3, 10–11, 167, 170–74, 185, 193, 199, 200, 202–3, 207, 225–26, 231
Fanon, Frantz, 1–2, 8, 40n111
Farce electorale de 1974 (tract), 229–31, 235
FAS (Fonds d'Action Sociale), 150–51, 154, 160
Faysal (Prince), 112, 113, 114
Fayette, Maurice, 198n132
FEANF (Fédération des étudiants d'Afrique Noire en France), 37n94
Fédération Internationale des Ligues des Droits de l'Homme (FIDH), 229, 230
FFW (Food-for-Work) programs, 177, 183, 184–86
FLN (Front de Libération Nationale), 1, 6, 84, 150
Foccart, Jacques, 81, 86, 118n108, 146–47, 180, 210, 202

Foucault, Michel, 11, 45n11, 157, 235–36, 245
Foyers (immigrant workers' housing), 146, 148–57
France: as former colonial power, 6, 8, 21, 69, 81, 85, 119, 129, 132n35, 134, 145, 180, 198, 200, 225, 226; conventions signed with African states, 118, 131–33, 135, 140–42, 147; Fifth Republic (1958–), 6, 21, 62, 78, 91, 129; Fourth Republic (1946–58), 21, 53, 57, 121, 126, 226; migration to, 10, 89–92, 120–21, 123, 126, 159, 198–99, 223, 245; nationality, 108–9, 121, 134–35, 144, 159. *See also* Community (French), Citizenship, Union (French)
Friends. *See* American Friends Services Committee (AFSC)

Gabon, 30–32, 217, 224
Gatekeeper state, 7
Gatignon, Claude, 199–200, 226, 228, 231
GEC (Groupes d'études communistes), 17, 198n132, 209
Germany (West), 226, 227
Ghana, 7, 213; migration to, 109n67, 124, 140, 153
Giscard d'Estaing, Valéry, 225, 231
Gologo, Mamadou, 33, 235n121
Governmentality, 2n5, 10, 167, 212. *See also* Nongovernmentality
GPRA (Gouvernement Provisoire de la République Algérienne), 84
Griaule, Marcel, 23, 31n70
Guèye, Lamine, 44, 53n53, 83
Guinea, 6, 8, 15, 33, 34, 38, 84, 86, 138, 178, 233, 238–40; anti-colonial politics in, 16–21, 29–30; chiefs and, 65–66, 69; independence of, 79, 81; social sciences and, 24, 23–28, 33. *See also* Ray Autra, PDG, Sékou Touré
Guyana, 217

Hajj. *See* Pilgrimage
Hettier de Boislambert, Claude, 83
Higgins, Chester (Jr.), 204
Hijra, 10, 110
Historicity, 10, 91, 242
Houphouët-Boigny, Félix, 20, 44, 53–4, 53n53, 78, 83n183

Human rights, 5–8, 10–11, 161, 167, 169, 219, 223–25, 226, 228, 231–33, 235, 243–44; African independence and, 212–14; in Third Republic Mali, 209–12, 236–37, 240, 242. *See* Amnesty International; *see also* African Charter on Human and People's Rights; Universal Declaration of Human Rights
Humanitarianism, humanitarians, 3n7, 5–8, 10–11, 148, 172, 198n130, 212, 225–26, 230, 243–44
Humanitarian aid, 167, 169, 204–5, 231
Hunters' Oath (Donsolu Kalikan) (text), 238, 239–42

Independence, 6, 15, 62, 77–8, 84, 85, 135–36; as 'nobility' vs. 'self-determination,' 79–80, 85
Indigénat, 9, 42, 46; abolition of, 43–4, 53–6; citizenship and, 42–3, 50–51; exemptions from, 48–51, 52–3; practice of, 46–8; reform, 45, 51–3; veterans and, 49, 52–3
Institut des Sciences Humaines (Mali), 40
Institut Français de l'Afrique Noire (IFAN), 22; Bamako, 22n31, 23n33, 32; Brazzaville, 31; Conakry, 22; Niamey, 22n31
Intalla, 76
Inter-religious Foundation for Community Organization (IFCO), 204
Israel, 111

Jeune Afrique, 230
Jouanelle, Félix, 64n95, 228n86
Journiac, René, 201, 238, 241

Kamissoko, Wa, 241n148
Kanté, Soumamarou, 238, 241n148
Katanga. *See* Congo-Kinshasa
Keita, Aoua, 33, 59, 60, 61, 67
Keita, Madeira, 8, 9, 66, 228; as Minister, 1, 27, 33–4, 36–8, 41, 70–73, 74, 77, 80, 82, 85, 111, 114–5, 117, 138; as political activist in Guinea, 16–21, 28–9; as political prisoner, 11, 41, 173, 214, 218, 226–27, 232, 233; as research assistant, 15–16, 22–30
Keita, Mamadou, 218–19
Keita, Mariam Travélé, 216n30

Keita, Modibo, 1, 62, 77, 81, 82, 117, 128, 139, 141; as prisoner, 173, 214, 218, 223, 226, 234; death of, 216, 233
Keita Nankoria Kourouma, 18, 227–28
Keita, Sundiata, 238, 240
Konaré, Alpha Oumar, 215n26
Konaté, Mamadou, 33, 53–54, 70, 128
Koné, Jean-Marie, 33, 73, 214
Kordofan, 7, 95
Koressi, Almamy, 69
Kountché, Seyni, 172n14, 180, 245
Kourouma, Mamadi, 69
Kouyaté, Rokia, 216n30, 235
Kouyaté, Seydou Badian, 33, 36, 224, 226, 227, 232
Kouyaté, Siriman, 238–40
Kurukan Fuga (text), 238–42

Lamizana, Sangoulé, 4, 173
Larcher, Guy, 152–54
Lauriac, Jacques, 184, 188
Lecas, Nicolas, 178
Libya, 178, 180, 182
Lisette, Gabriel, 58
Loi cadre (framework law), 32, 61–4, 68, 69, 105
Louveau, Edmond, 53–4
Lumumba, Patrice, 84
Ly, Ibrahima, 36, 37n94, 216, 229
Ly, Oumar, 229

M., Eva, *191–92*, 194–97
Macoumba, Makane, 62, 70
Mali Empire, 238, 241
Mali Federation, 21, 33, 75, 86, 115, 131n35, 173; break-up of, 15, 77–85, 138, 141
Mali, Republic of, 42, 85, 110, 178, 181n58, 183, 190, 197, 207, 225; Active Revolution (1967–68), 37–38, 76, 214, 221; army 77, 85, 168–69, 185, 190, 196–97, 214–16, 219–21, 237, 246; CARE and, 182, 184–89, 243; convention with France (1963), 131; crisis of 2012–13, 3–4, 42, 211, 237, 245–48; First Republic (1960–68), 1, 6, 8–9, 15, 33, 77; nationality law of 1962, 135–36; radio in, 38n102, 39, 210, 230, 233, 234; Second Republic (1978–1991), 235; street

protests, 34n80, 210–11, 233; Third Republic (1991–), 209, 236–37. *See also* CMLN; Tuareg, Rebellion (1963–64), id. (1990–96)
Malian franc, 6, 38, 85–86
Mande Charter. *See* Kurukan Fuga; Hunter's Oath (Donsolu Kalikan)
Marouchett ag Moussa, 115
Marriage, reform of, 22, 26–7, 240
Marshall Plan (as metaphor), 3, 4, 179
Mauritania, 64, 79n163, 95, 100n28, 118, 121, 123, 141–42, 145, 155, 159, 217n36; convention with France (1963), 131, 141
Mbodge, Mamadou, 78
Meillassoux, Claude, 32n72, 201
Milice. *See* US-RDA, party militia
Mining, 142; gold mining, 28, 29, 138; salt mining, 220–22; uranium mining, 172, 178–80, 222n61
Mitterand, François, 58, 157
Mohamed Ali Ag Attaher Insar, 111, 112, 113n81, 115, 117–8
Monde (le), 193n103, 200, 201
Monod, Théodore, 17
Montout, Iréncé, 19–20
Morlet, Pierre, 198–99, 226–28, 229
Morrissey, Stephen, 196
Mothers' vote, 56–62. *See also* Enfranchisement; Women, suffrage

N'Diaye, Valdiodio, 80
N'Dongo, Sally, 150n106, 154–56
Nationality, 64n95, 91–92, 100–1. *See also* under individual states
Neoliberalism, 5–6, 9, 172, 242, 243
Netherlands, 225, 226
NGOs, 166–67, 172–73, 186, 196, 202, 205, 243–44, 245; Domestic NGOs, 187–88, 210–11; Drought and famine relief and, 180, 183; International NGOs, 174, 177, 198, 200, 207–8, 239, 241. *See also* Amnesty International; Africare; CARE; nongovernmentality; RAINS
Niantao, Abdoulaye, 220–21
Niger, 167, 169, 172, 177–83, 187, 188, 190, 193, 198, 205, 207; as "Development Society," 180–81, 245; CARE and, 177, 180–83, 243; chieftaincy, 64, 65; drought and, 170–71; pilgrims from, 97, 103, 110

Nigeria, 107, 116, 172; as aid recipient, 177, 182; pilgrimage and, 97–98, 103
Nkrumah, Kwame, 213, 247
Nock, Abdoulaye, 70
Nongovernmentality, 2, 3, 11, 167, 173–75, 207–8, 212, 243, 245, 247
Nouvel Observateur (le), 200
Nyerere, Julius, 37, 62, 64

OAU (Organization of African Unity), 236
OCRS (Organisation Commune des Régions Sahariennes), 112, 168. *See also* Sahara, political status at decolonization
OECD (Organization for Economic Co-operation and Development), 174
Office National de l'Immigration (ONI), 129, 134
Oil, exploration and exploitation, 178, 222n61
Olivier de Sardan, Jean-Pierre, 201
Ordu, Louis, 200
Organization of Solidarity with the People of Asia, Africa, and Latin America (OSPAA), 226n75
Ould al-Shaykh, Muhammad Mahmud, 77

PAI (Parti Africain de l'Indépendance), 37n97, 80, 85, 228
Parti de la Fédération Africaine, 81
Parti Malien du Travail. *See* PAI
Passports (and other travel papers), 91, 92, 101, 102–3, 111, 113, 118, 122n7, 139, 143–44, 145, 160
Pastoralism, 8, 67, 94, 165, 167, 170–71, 181, 192–94, 196. *See also* drought; Tin Aicha
PCF (Parti Communiste Français), 20, 61, 198, 228, 244
PDG (Parti Démocratique de Guinée), 17–21, 23, 29n58, 38, 66, 68, 79
Peace Corps, 206
Person, Yves, 201
Phare de Guinée, 29
Pilgrimage, 95, 96n12, 105, 115–7, 119
Pilgrims, 10, 93–4, 99, 100, 101, 105, 117
P.L. 480 (U. S. Public Law 480), 176–77, 186
Pléah, Koniba, 29–30
POLISARIO Liberation Front, 222, 231
Pompidou, Georges, 180, 198
Poujade, Jean, 24
Povey, George, 191–93

PPN-RDA (Parti Progressiste Nigérien-RDA), 179–80
Présence Africaine, 27
PSP (Parti Progressiste Soudanais), 60, 63, 67, 70, 74n145, 76, 85, 111; position on 1958 referendum, 79

Qadhafi, Mu'ammar, 178
Quakers. *See* American Friends Services Committee (AFSC)

Radio. *See* Mali, Republic of, Radio
RAINS (Relief for Africans in Need in the Sahel), 11, 175–76, 204–5, 206–7
RDA (Rassemblement Démocratique Africain), 20, 61, 66, 69, 79. *See also* PDG; PPN-RDA; US-RDA
Refugees, 133, 167, 171, 179, 194
Regroupement des travailleurs maliens en France (RTMF), 154–56
Reitz, Peter, 181
Rent strikes, 151–57
Rougier, Ferdinand, 125, 145, 160

Sahara, 7, 167–68; as zone of detention, 214–15, 217–19, 246; distinct forms of government in, 73, 74, 75–6; political status at decolonization, 81, 112, 113n81; racialization of, 79n164, 117, 222. *See also* OCRS
Sahel, 2, 10–11, 86, 90n3, 91, 210, 214, 217, 243–45, 246; as disaster zone, 3–8, 170–71, 173, 182; as political vs. geographic unit, 7, 167; crisis of 1973–74, 170–74, 190, 193, 195, 202, 204, 208; crisis of 2012–13, 3–4, 245–46. *See also* CILSS; drought; famine
Salt mining. *See* Mining, salt; *see also* Taoudeni
Samaké, Guédiouma, 215, 221, 234, 237n130
Samaké, Soungalo, 215n25, 216, 222n61
Sangaré, Samba, 215, 221, 234
Sano, Mamba, 29
Sartre, Jean-Paul, 31n67, 157
Saudi Arabia, 118; control of pilgrimage, 99, 102, 104, 105, 108; slavery in, 110–14
Sawaba, 29
Senegal, 77–78, 81, 83, 85, 203, 244; convention with France (1964), 131; Four Communes of, 51, 58, 82; migration from, 142–44, 167; migration to, 123, 124, 138
Senghor, Léopold Sedar, 37, 57, 80, 81, 142–43, 152, 155–56, 171, 202
Service des Affaires Musulmanes (SAM), 133
Service Civique Rurale, 221
Sibiry, Paul Traore, 66
Sidi Mohamed ag Zoukka, 115, 118
Sidibe, Mamby, 22n31, 66
Sissoko, Charles Samba, 216
Sissoko, Filifing, 230
Sissoko, Fily Dabo: as deputy, 57–8, 69; as PSP leader, 63n89, 78; death of, 34n80, 219n43
Skinner, Elliot, 204, 206
Slavery and slave trading, 112, 113, 116, 240–41. *See also* Saudi Arabia
Social class (vs. social strata), 37–38, 40, 78
Sociology, 16, 31, 34–36, 39–41, 239
Sokoto, 94, 95, 97–100, 110
Soudan (French), 22n31, 32–33, 42, 53–54, 61, 63–65, 67, 70–77, 78–86, 111–12, 115, 168, 218. *See also* Mali, Federation; Mali, Republic of
SOUNDIATA (association), 133, 157
Sundiata. *See* Keita, Sundiata
Sow, Aissata Coulibaly, 62, 79
Sow, Lamine, 224
Students' political activism, 210, 215, 234, 235, 246. *See also* AESMF; FEANF
Sudan, 4, 8, 9, 90–92, 93–110, 245; census of, 100; colonial administration of, 102; independent government of, 103–6, 115–16, 159; nationality law of 1957, 105–7. *See also* Dar Fur; Kordofan
Suret-Canale, Jean, 199
Sy, Victor, 36, 235
Sylla, Sory Ibrahim, 187–88

Taoudeni, 215–16, 219–23, 229, 234
Telli, Boubacar Diallo, 113n85, 233n108
Tijaniyya, 95, 97n13, 99, 100
Tin Aicha, 175, 191–92, 192–97
Toure, Kassoum, 34n80, 86n194, 219n43
Touré, Samori, 79n165, 217
Touré, Sékou, 17, 21, 27n49, 29n58, 33, 38, 68, 79, 113n85, 233
Traoré, Amadou Seydou, 214, 224, 232–33, 237
Traoré, Aminata Dramane, 212–13

Traore, Dioncounda, 155n125, 211n12
Traore, Dominique, 22n31
Traore, Garba, 152–56
Traore, Moussa, 155, 209, 215n26, 216, 223, 225, 229–31, 233, 235–36, 245, 247
Traoré, Sékou, 214–15, 216, 233
Trench, Richard, 221–22
Tuareg, 222, 224; dissidence of 1950s, 110–12, 115, 117; Kel Adagh, 76, 111, 171n5, 197; Kel Intessar, 111, 192, 195, 197; rebellion (1963–64), 168–69, 190, 216; rebellion (1990–96), 241n150
Tuberculosis, 146–47, 158

U Thant, 174
UDPM (Union Démocratique du Peuple Malien), 76n154, 196, 235
UGTAN (Union Générale des Travailleurs de l'Afrique Noire), 80
UN (United Nations), 84, 85, 113, 117, 171n8, 173–74
UNESCO, 4, 240
Union (French), 43–4, 105, 112, 121
Union Démocratique Ségovienne, 77
Union Générale des Travailleurs Sénégalais en France (UGTSF), 156, 203n152
Union du Mandé, 29–30
Union Nationale des Travailleurs du Mali (UNTM), 199
Union Progressiste Sénégalaise (UPS), 81
United Nations (UN), 84, 85, 113, 117, 171n8, 173–74
Universal Declaration of Human Rights, 230, 236n122

Upper Volta, 65, 78, 83, 138, 173, 181n58, 198, 206
Uranium. *See* Mining, uranium
US (United States), 171, 174, 206, 231
US-AID (United States Agency for International Development), 175, 176–77, 181, 183, 184, 186–89, 190, 205–6, 210
US-RDA (Union Soudanaise-Rassemblement Démocratique Africain), 6, 9, 59, 61–3, 67, 69, 227–28, 244, as governing party, 69, 73, 75, 77, 79, 85, 111, 115, 219; Bureau Politique National (BPN), 33, 62, 70, 112n76; Comité National de Défense de la Révolution (CNDR), 34, 36, 38, 222; coup against, 214, 228; leadership imprisoned, 199, 220, 222, 223–25, 226, 229, 232, 233; party militia (Milice Populaire), 34, 39; policy towards emigrants, 136–37, 139–41, 160; Saharan policy, 73–76, 79n164, 168. *See also* RDA
USSR, 36, 84, 171, 231–32

Veterans, 49, 52–53, 67, 151

Wibaux, Fernand, 63n93, 140
Women: exemption from the *indigénat*, 49–50; political activism, 18, 26, 60, 62, 216n30, 227–28, 234, 235; political status, 75, 195; students in France, 128n121; suffrage, 9, 58–60, 75. *See also* Aoua Keita; Marriage reform; Mothers' vote

Zeyd, 76

BOOKS IN THIS SERIES

1. *City Politics: A Study of Léopoldville, 1962–63*, J. S. La Fontaine
2. *Studies in Rural Capitalism in West Africa*, Polly Hill
3. *Land Policy in Buganda*, Henry W. West
4. *The Nigerian Military: A Sociological Analysis of Authority and Revolt, 1960–67*, Robin Luckham
5. *The Ghanaian Factory Worker: Industrial Man in Africa*, Margaret Peil
6. *Labour in the South African Gold Mines*, Francis Wilson
7. *The Price of Liberty: Personality and Politics in Colonial Nigeria*, Kenneth W. J. Post and George D. Jenkins
8. *Subsistence to Commercial Farming in Present Day Buganda: An Economic and Anthropological Survey*, Audrey I. Richards, Fort Sturrock, and Jean M. Fortt (eds.)
9. *Dependence and Opportunity: Political Change in Ahafo*, John Dunn and A. F. Robertson
10. *African Railwaymen: Solidarity and Opposition in an East African Labour Force*, R. D. Grillo
11. *Islam and Tribal Art in West Africa*, René A. Bravmann
12. *Modern and Traditional Elites in the Politics of Lagos*, P. D. Cole
13. *Asante in the Nineteenth Century: The Structure and Evolution of a Political Order*, Ivor Wilks
14. *Culture, Tradition and Society in the West African Novel*, Emmanuel Obiechina
15. *Saints and Politicians*, Donald B. Cruise O'Brien
16. *The Lions of Dagbon: Political Change in Northern Ghana*, Martin Staniland
17. *Politics of Decolonization: Kenya Europeans and the Land Issue 1960–1965*, Gary B. Wasserman
18. *Muslim Brotherhoods in Nineteenth-Century Africa*, B. G. Martin
19. *Warfare in the Sokoto Caliphate: Historical and Sociological Perspectives*, Joseph P. Smaldone
20. *Liberia and Sierra Leone: An Essay in Comparative Politics*, Christopher Clapham
21. *Adam Kok's Griquas: A Study in the Development of Stratification in South Africa*, Robert Ross
22. *Class, Power and Ideology in Ghana: The Railwaymen of Sekondi*, Richard Jeffries
23. *West African States: Failure and Promise*, John Dunn (ed.)
24. *Afrikaners of the Kalahari: White Minority in a Black State*, Margo Russell and Martin Russell
25. *A Modern History of Tanganyika*, John Iliffe
26. *A History of African Christianity 1950–1975*, Adrian Hastings
27. *Slaves, Peasants and Capitalists in Southern Angola, 1840–1926*, W. G. Clarence-Smith
28. *The Hidden Hippopotamus: Reappraised in African History: The Early Colonial Experience in Western Zambia*, Gwyn Prins
29. *Families Divided: The Impact of Migrant Labour in Lesotho*, Colin Murray
30. *Slavery, Colonialism and Economic Growth in Dahomey, 1640–1960*, Patrick Manning
31. *Kings, Commoners and Concessionaires: The Evolution and Dissolution of the Nineteenth-Century Swazi State*, Philip Bonner
32. *Oral Poetry and Somali Nationalism: The Case of Sayid Mahammad 'Abdille Hasan*, Said S. Samatar

33 *The Political Economy of Pondoland 1860–1930*, William Beinart
34 *Volkskapitalisme: Class, Capital and Ideology in the Development of Afrikaner Nationalism, 1934–1948*, Dan O'Meara
35 *The Settler Economies: Studies in the Economic History of Kenya and Rhodesia 1900–1963*, Paul Mosley
36 *Transformations in Slavery: A History of Slavery in Africa*, Paul E. Lovejoy
37 *Amilcar Cabral: Revolutionary Leadership and People's War*, Patrick Chabal
38 *Essays on the Political Economy of Rural Africa*, Robert H. Bates
39 *Ijeshas and Nigerians: The Incorporation of a Yoruba Kingdom, 1890s–1970s*, J. D. Y. Peel
40 *Black People and the South African War, 1899–1902*, Peter Warwick
41 *A History of Niger 1850–1960*, Finn Fuglestad
42 *Industrialisation and Trade Union Organization in South Africa, 1924–1955*, Stephen Ellis
43 *The Rising of the Red Shawls: A Revolt in Madagascar 1895–1899*, Stephen Ellis
44 *Slavery in Dutch South Africa*, Nigel Worden
45 *Law, Custom and Social Order: The Colonial Experience in Malawi and Zambia*, Martin Chanock
46 *Salt of the Desert Sun: A History of Salt Production and Trade in the Central Sudan*, Paul E. Lovejoy
47 *Marrying Well: Marriage, Status and Social Change among the Educated Elite in Colonial Lagos*, Kristin Mann
48 *Language and Colonial Power: The Appropriation of Swahili in the Former Belgian Congo, 1880–1938*, Johannes Fabian
49 *The Shell Money of the Slave Trade*, Jan Hogendorn and Marion Johnson
50 *Political Domination in Africa*, Patrick Chabal
51 *The Southern Marches of Imperial Ethiopia: Essays in History and Social Anthropology*, Donald Donham and Wendy James
52 *Islam and Urban Labor in Northern Nigeria: The Making of a Muslim Working Class*, Paul M. Lubeck
53 *Horn and Crescent: Cultural Change and Traditional Islam on the East African Coast, 1800–1900*, Randall L. Pouwels
54 *Capital and Labour on the Kimberley Diamond Fields, 1871–1890*, Robert Vicat Turrell
55 *National and Class Conflict in the Horn of Africa*, John Markakis
56 *Democracy and Prebendal Politics in Nigeria: The Rise and Fall of the Second Republic*, Richard A. Joseph
57 *Entrepreneurs and Parasites: The Struggle for Indigenous Capitalism in Zaïre*, Janet MacGaffey
58 *The African Poor: A History*, John Iliffe
59 *Palm Oil and Protest: An Economic History of the Ngwa Region, South-Eastern Nigeria, 1800–1980*, Susan M. Martin
60 *France and Islam in West Africa, 1860–1960*, Christopher Harrison
61 *Transformation and Continuity in Revolutionary Ethiopia*, Christopher Clapham
62 *Prelude to the Mahdiyya: Peasants and Traders in the Shendi Region, 1821–1885*, Anders Bjørkelo
63 *Wa and the Wala: Islam and Polity in Northwestern Ghana*, Ivor Wilks
64 *H. C. Bankole-Bright and Politics in Colonial Sierra Leone, 1919–1958*, Akintola Wyse

65 *Contemporary West African States*, Donald Cruise O'Brien, John Dunn, and Richard Rathbone (eds.)
66 *The Oromo of Ethiopia: A History, 1570–1860*, Mohammed Hassen
67 *Slavery and African Life: Occidental, Oriental, and African Slave Trades*, Patrick Manning
68 *Abraham Esau's War: A Black South African War in the Cape, 1899–1902*, Bill Nasson
69 *The Politics of Harmony: Land Dispute Strategies in Swaziland*, Laurel L. Rose
70 *Zimbabwe's Guerrilla War: Peasant Voices*, Norma J. Kriger
71 *Ethiopia: Power and Protest: Peasant Revolts in the Twentieth Century*, Gebru Tareke
72 *White Supremacy and Black Resistance in Pre-Industrial South Africa: The Making of the Colonial Order in the Eastern Cape, 1770–1865*, Clifton C. Crais
73 *The Elusive Granary: Herder, Farmer, and State in Northern Kenya*, Peter D. Little
74 *The Kanyok of Zaire: An Institutional and Ideological History to 1895*, John C. Yoder
75 *Pragmatism in the Age of Jihad: The Precolonial State of Bundu*, Michael A. Gomez
76 *Slow Death for Slavery: The Course of Abolition in Northern Nigeria, 1897–1936*, Paul E. Lovejoy and Jan S. Hogendorn
77 *West African Slavery and Atlantic Commerce: The Senegal River Valley, 1700–1860*, James F. Searing
78 *A South African Kingdom: The Pursuit of Security in Nineteenth-Century Lesotho*, Elizabeth A. Eldredge
79 *State and Society in Pre-colonial Asante*, T. C. McCaskie
80 *Islamic Society and State Power in Senegal: Disciples and Citizens in Fatick*, Leonardo A. Villalón
81 *Ethnic Pride and Racial Prejudice in Victorian Cape Town: Group Identity and Social Practice*, Vivian Bickford-Smith
82 *The Eritrean Struggle for Independence: Domination, Resistance and Nationalism, 1941–1993*, Ruth Iyob
83 *Corruption and State Politics in Sierra Leone*, William Reno
84 *The Culture of Politics in Modern Kenya*, Angelique Haugerud
85 *Africans: The History of a Continent*, John Iliffe
86 *From Slave Trade to 'Legitimate' Commerce: The Commercial Transition in Nineteenth-Century West Africa*, Robin Law (ed.)
87 *Leisure and Society in Colonial Brazzaville*, Phyllis Martin
88 *Kingship and State: The Buganda Dynasty*, Christopher Wrigley
89 *Decolonization and African Life: The Labour Question in French and British Africa*, Frederick Cooper
90 *Misreading the African Landscape: Society and Ecology in an African Forest Savannah Mosaic*, James Fairhead and Melissa Leach
91 *Peasant Revolution in Ethiopia: The Tigray People's Liberation Front, 1975–1991*, John Young
92 *Senegambia and the Atlantic Slave Trade*, Boubacar Barry
93 *Commerce and Economic Change in West Africa: The Oil Trade in the Nineteenth Century*, Martin Lynn
94 *Slavery and French Colonial Rule in West Africa: Senegal, Guinea and Mali*, Martin A. Klein
95 *East African Doctors: A History of the Modern Profession*, John Iliffe

96 *Middlemen of the Cameroons Rivers: The Duala and Their Hinterland, c.1600–1960*, Ralph Derrick, Ralph A. Austen, and Jonathan Derrick
97 *Masters and Servants on the Cape Eastern Frontier, 1760–1803*, Susan Newton-King
98 *Status and Respectability in the Cape Colony, 1750–1870: A Tragedy of Manners*, Robert Ross
99 *Slaves, Freedmen and Indentured Laborers in Colonial Mauritius*, Richard B. Allen
100 *Transformations in Slavery: A History of Slavery in Africa, 2nd Edition*, Paul E. Lovejoy
101 *The Peasant Cotton Revolution in West Africa: Côte d'Ivoire, 1880–1995*, Thomas J. Bassett
102 *Re-Imagining Rwanda: Conflict, Survival and Disinformation in the Late Twentieth Century*, Johan Pottier
103 *The Politics of Evil: Magic, State Power and the Political Imagination in South Africa*, Clifton Crais
104 *Transforming Mozambique: The Politics of Privatization, 1975–2000*, M. Anne Pitcher
105 *Guerrilla Veterans in Post-war Zimbabwe: Symbolic and Violent Politics, 1980–1987*, Norma J. Kriger
106 *An Economic History of Imperial Madagascar, 1750–1895: The Rise and Fall of an Island Empire*, Gwyn Campbell
107 *Honour in African History*, John Iliffe
108 *Africans: History of a Continent, 2nd Edition*, John Iliffe
109 *Guns, Race, and Power in Colonial South Africa*, William Kelleher Storey
110 *Islam and Social Change in French West Africa: History of an Emancipatory Community*, Sean Hanretta
111 *Defeating Mau Mau, Creating Kenya: Counterinsurgency, Civil War, and Decolonization*, Daniel Branch
112 *Christianity and Genocide in Rwanda*, Timothy Longman
113 *From Africa to Brazil: Culture, Identity, and an African Slave Trade, 1600–1830*, Walter Hawthorne
114 *Africa in the Time of Cholera: A History of Pandemics from 1817 to the Present*, Myron Echenberg
115 *A History of Race in Muslim West Africa, 1600–1960*, Bruce S. Hall
116 *Witchcraft and Colonial Rule in Kenya, 1900–1955*, Katherine Luongo
117 *Transformations in Slavery: A History of Slavery in Africa, 3rd Edition*, Paul E. Lovejoy
118 *The Rise of the Trans-Atlantic Slave Trade in Western Africa, 1300–1589*, Toby Green
119 *Party Politics and Economic Reform in Africa's Democracies*, M. Anne Pitcher
120 *Smugglers and Saints of the Sahara: Regional Connectivity in the Twentieth Century*, Judith Scheele
121 *Slaving and Cross-Cultural Trade in the Atlantic World: Angola and Brazil during the Era of the Slave Trade*, Roquinaldo Ferreira
122 *Ethnic Patriotism and the East African Revival*, Derek Peterson
123 *Black Morocco: A History of Slavery and Islam*, Chouki El Hamel
124 *An African Slaving Port and the Atlantic World: Benguela and Its Hinterland*, Mariana Candido

125 *Making Citizens in Africa: Ethnicity, Gender, and National Identity in Ethiopia*, Lahra Smith
126 *Slavery and Emancipation in Islamic East Africa: From Honor to Respectability*, Elisabeth McMahon
127 *A History of African Motherhood: The Case of Uganda, 700–1900*, Rhiannon Stephens
128 *The Borders of Race in Colonial South Africa: The Kat River Settlement, 1829–1856*, Robert Ross
129 *From Empires to NGOs in the West African Sahel: The Road to Nongovernmentality*, Gregory Mann
130 *Dictators and Democracy in African Development: The Political Economy of Good Governance in Nigeria*, A. Carl LeVan